Best Practice Organisational Excellence

by

Prof. Mohamed Zairi
and
Mr John Whymark

BEST PRACTICE ORGANISATIONAL EXCELLENCE

First impression 2003

Copyright © 2003 ISBN 0-9545879-0-1

Published by

e-TQM College Publishing House

The European Centre for TQM
Bradford University School of Management
Emm Lane
Bradford
BD9 4JL
Tel.+44 (0)1274 234313
Fax. +44 (0) 1274 234311

Dubai Office
e-TQM College
PO Box 500242
Dubai
UAE
Tel. +971 4 391 2110
Fax. +971 4 391 8140

Printed by

Information Press

Southfield Road
Eynsham
Oxford
OX29 1JJ

Jacket design by

Upstart

25 Aireville Crescent
Bradford
BD9 4EU

Contents

List of figures	x
List of tables	xii
Acknowledgements	xiii
Dedication	xiv

Introduction   1
- The meaning of excellence   1
- Notion of sustainability   1
  - *Sustainable performance*   1
- Rationale for a text on organisational excellence   2
- Critical factors for organisational excellence   2
  - *Factor 1. Leadership and top management commitment*   3
  - *Factor 2. People management*   3
  - *Factor 3. Middle management involvement*   4
  - *Factor 4. Training and education*   4
  - *Factor 5. Rewards and recognition*   5
  - *Factor 6. Teamwork*   5
  - *Factor 7. Quality policy and strategy*   5
  - *Factor 8. Communicating for quality*   6
  - *Factor 9. Supplier management*   6
  - *Factor 10. Accredited quality management system*   7
  - *Factor 11. Organising for quality*   7
  - *Factor 12. Managing by processes*   8
  - *Factor 13. Benchmarking*   8
  - *Factor 14. Self-assessment*   9
  - *Factor 15. Cost of quality*   10
  - *Factor 16. Quality control techniques*   10
  - *Factor 17. Measuring customer wants and satisfaction*   10
- References and further reading   12

Chapter 1. The quality improvement continuum: an integrative approach   19
- Continuous improvement: what is it?   19
- Understanding organisations as systems   20
- Deming's contribution to systems thinking   21
  - *Process*   23
  - *Optimisation*   23
- Deming problem solving cycle   25
- Making business process improvement happen: what does it take?   26
- The essentiality of an integrated approach in business process improvement   28
- References   30

Chapter 2. The process of self-assessment   31
- Introduction   31
- Key elements of the self-assessment process   32
  - *Approach*   32
  - *Deployment*   32
  - *Results*   32
- Approaches to self-assessment   33
  - *A matrix chart approach*   33
- Other approaches to self-assessment   37
  - *Introduction*   37
  - *Conditions of excellence*   37
  - *How is the quality fitness review applied?*   40
  - *Rank Xerox Corporation*   43

Appendix 2.1 The 12 conditions of the Westinghouse Electric Corporation total quality review   47

Chapter 3. Self-assessment tools   **50**
Introduction   50
The Deming Prize   51
   Criteria used for assessment of Deming Prize applications   51
The Malcolm Baldrige National Quality Award (MBNQA)   57
   Purpose of MBNQA   58
   Criteria for the assessment of the MBNQA   59
   Scoring system   61
EQA assessment   62
Benefits of self-assessment   65
   Benefits reported by winners of the Deming Prize   65
   Benefits reported from winners of the MBNQA   67
   Benefits reported from winners of the EQA   69
The future of self-assessment   70
References and further reading   72
Appendix 3.1 Benefits of cross-functional management in 102 Deming Prize winners   81

Chapter 4. Leadership: the key driver of business excellence   **82**
Introduction   82
Leadership and management: what is the difference?   82
Leadership in the context of TQM   83
Establishing best practice in leadership   84
   Results of an American study   84
Case studies: winners of prestigious awards   85
   Zytec Corporation   85
   Wallace Co. Inc.   86
   Ritz-Carlton Hotel   86
   Cadillac Motor Car Company   87
   Texas Instruments Defence Systems & Electronics Group (TI-DSEG)   87
   Rank Xerox Ltd   88
Key ingredients for effective quality leadership   89
   Setting the vision and the strategic choice   90
   Communicating the vision, generating corporate commitment   90
   Developing a process-based culture   90
   Recognition of people assets   90
   Performance management   90
   Developing partnerships   90
   External ambassadors   91
   Developing leadership in the organisation   91
References   92
Appendix 4.1 Leadership exercise   93

Chapter 5. Quality policy deployment:
the key driver for performance measurement   **94**
The link between quality policy deployment and performance measurement   94
   An example of a quality deployment process   96
Defining quality policy deployment   99
Examples of quality policy deployment models   99
   Proctor and Gamble   99
   Komatsu Ltd   102
   Hewlett-Packard   103
   Rank Xerox Ltd   103
   Florida Power & Light   105
References   107
Appendix 5.1 Policy and strategy exercise   108

Chapter 6. People management: the key asset — 110
Introduction — 110
Critical factors for people management — 111
Assessment of best HR practices — 112
Benchmarking HRM: a cross-industry analysis — 113
    Elida Gibbs Ltd (EG) — 113
    Central Services Group, Post Office Counters Ltd (CSG) — 116
    Nationwide Building Society — 118
    UK Branch Business at NatWest Bank (UKBB) — 119
    Bird's Eye Walls Ltd (BEW) — 121
Assessment method used — 123
Discussion of practices exhibited — 124
Some conclusions — 124
References — 126
Appendix 6.1 Key HR performance indicators — 127
Appendix 6.2 People management exercise: Mortgage Express — 128

Chapter 7. Resource management: the key sources of "improvement progress" — 130
Information processing and decision making — 130
Marketing management and information processing — 131
Statement of purpose and significance of the study — 131
Significance of the research study — 132
An integrated model of information processing — 132
    Level 1. Top management process — 133
    Level 2. Analytical processes — 133
    Level 3. Operational processes — 133
    Level 4. The supportive processes — 133
    Level 5. Benchmarking for best practice process — 133
Conclusions — 134
Supplier partnerships – a perspective — 134
    Supplier evaluation and selection — 135
    Supplier management — 135
Examples of best practice — 136
    Lucas Automotive — 136
    British Telecommunications Ltd — 137
    Nissan — 139
    Kodak — 140
Ten golden rules of supplier partnerships based on best practice — 143
Financial resources – the vital lifeblood — 144
    Scope of financial management — 145
    Leadership and financial management — 145
    Financial management process — 146
    Review and improvement of financial strategies and practices — 147
    Cost of quality — 148
    Evaluation of investments — 149
    Pay back — 150
    Net present value — 150
    Internal rate of return — 151
    Accounting rate of return — 151
References — 153
Appendix 7.1 Management of resources exercise — 154

Chapter 8. Business process management: the key driver for continuous improvement — 155
Introduction — 155
    What is a process? — 155
    What is business process management? — 155
The importance of accredited quality systems — 156

The importance of quality structure	156
The importance of strategy	157
The importance of process management	158
Elida Faberge Ltd	159
Rank Xerox Corp.	159
British Telecom	160
SmithKline Beecham	160
Building a culture based on process management: examples of best practice	160
The process breakthrough methodology	161
Rank Xerox approach to process improvement and management	162
Process management methodology at Ford Motors	164
Process management at Post Office Counters Ltd	165
Sustaining business process management – some guidelines	166
References	169
Appendix 8.1 Business processes exercise	171

Chapter 9. Managing performance outcomes for business excellence 172

Introduction	172
The GAO performance measurement model	172
The balanced scorecard model	173
An integrated model of total quality-based performance measurement	173
Definition of terms	175
Strategy development and goal deployment	176
Process management and measurement	178
Performance appraisal and management	179
"Break-point" performance assessment	181
Reward and recognition systems	182
Summary	182
Validation of the model	183
Sample selection	183
Analysis of responses	183
Strategy development and goal deployment	185
Process management and measurement	185
Performance management systems	185
Break-point performance assessment	186
Effectiveness of performance measurement	186
Summary	186
References	188

Chapter 10. Managing customer satisfaction 189

Creating a customer-focused culture	189
Customer-supplier relationships	190
Customer satisfaction versus dissatisfaction	190
Achieving customer-focus	191
Measurement of customer satisfaction	191
Customer satisfaction performance measurement models	195
Beyond satisfaction: customer loyalty and retention	196
Some final thoughts on customer-focus	199
References	201

Chapter 11. Managing people satisfaction 202

People – the most valuable asset	202
Process for managing people satisfaction	202
The measures of people satisfaction	204
Best practices adopted for measuring people satisfaction	206
Additional best practices	206
Integration of people satisfaction data	207

Chapter 12. Impact on society — 208
Focusing on community issues — 208
Definition and meaning of corporate social reporting — 209
How to create optimum societal value-added? — 209
Standards of social accountability and reporting — 209
   The CERES Principles — 209
   Other principles and standards — 210
Best practice examples in social responsibility and accountability — 212
   Royal Mail and its focus on the community — 212
   Lever Bros. Ltd — 212
References — 215

Chapter 13. Benchmarking performance for business excellence — 216
Introduction — 216
The Baldrige Index 1996 study — 216
The Bradford study — 219
   Europe — 219
   United Kingdom — 220
Benchmarking performance for business excellence — 221
   Overall business performance — 221
   Benchmarking individual criteria — 221
   Benchmarking against aggregate scores — 221
References — 224
Appendix 13.1 Key successes for winners of the MBNQA — 225
Appendix 13.2 Percentage distribution of scores — 227
   UK Quality Award percentage distribution of scores — 227
   European Quality Award percentage distribution of scores — 230
   Malcolm Baldrige Award distribution of scores — 233
Appendix 13.3 Performance exercise — 235

Chapter 14. Case studies — 236
Rank Xerox — 236
   Market and product range — 236
   Launch of total quality initiatives — 236
   Mission and vision — 236
   Quality policy — 237
   Evolution of the process — 237
   Continuous improvement — 238
   Employee objective setting — 238
   Management of financial resources — 240
   Customer satisfaction – closed loop escalation process — 241
   Overall satisfaction measurement process — 242
   Focus on key measures — 243
Kodak — 245
   Market and products — 245
   Quality deployment — 245
   Ideal supplier characteristics — 245
Nationwide Building Society — 247
   Market and products — 247
   Quality development — 247
   Service satisfaction attributes — 247
Dana Commercial Credit — 250
   Market and product range — 250
   Launch of total quality initiatives — 250
   Mission and vision — 251
   Quality policy — 251
   Evolution of the process — 251
   Continuous improvement — 251
   People satisfaction survey process — 251

Ulster Carpet Mills	253
Market and product range	253
Launch of total quality initiatives	253
Mission and vision	253
Quality policy	253
Evolution of the process	253
Continuous improvement	253
Communication	254
People satisfaction – managing outcomes from surveys	257
Royal Mail	258
Market and product range	258
Launch of total quality initiatives	258
Mission and vision	258
Evolution of the process	259
Continuous improvement	259
Policy deployment	260
Best practice implementation models	261
Best practices for best practice implementation	262
Impact on society – community care	264
Texas Instruments: Defense Systems and Electronics Group	265
Market and product range	265
Launch of total quality initiatives	265
Mission and vision	265
Quality policy	265
Evolution of the process	265
Continuous improvement	266
Managing the strategic process	266
Aligning leadership competencies with business priorities	267
Impact on society – environmental, health and safety management	267
Ritz-Carlton Hotel	269
Market and product range	269
Launch of total quality initiatives	269
Mission and vision	269
Quality policy	269
Evolution of the process	269
Design to Distribution (D2D) (now Celestica)	271
Market and product range	271
Launch of total quality initiatives	271
Mission and vision	271
Quality policy	271
Evolution of the process	272
Process reviews	272
Continuous improvement	274
Success factors	274
TNT	276
Market and product range	276
Launch of total quality initiatives	276
Mission and vision	276
Quality policy	277
Evolution of the process	277
Continuous improvement	278
Key benefits and achievements	278
Next steps and future challenges	279
Custom Research Inc. (CRI)	280
Market and product range	280
Mission and vision	280
Evolution of total quality	280
Continuous improvement	280
Management of data and information	281

Corning Telecommunications Products Division	282
Market and product range	282
Launch of total quality initiatives	282
Evolution of the process	282
Quality policy	283
Mission and vision	283
Continuous improvement	284

Index 285

List of figures

1.1	The concept of business process management	20
1.2	An effective process	22
1.3	The core values, cornerstones and 14 points	24
1.4	Organisation viewed as a system	25
1.5	The PDSA cycle	26
1.6	Intensive use of QA tools in the development process	27
2.1	Self-assessment process	31
2.2	Linkage of approach, deployment and results	33
2.3	Performance approach to self-assessment from MBNQA	35
2.4	An example of the business improvement matrix	40
2.5	Comparison of the MBNQA and Westinghouse Electric Corp. self-assessment criteria	41
2.6	Business excellence criteria	41
2.7	Total quality rating sheet	42
2.8	The total quality fitness review	43
2.9	1994 business excellence model	44
2.10	The process	46
3.1	Baldrige Award criteria framework – dynamic relationships	60
3.2	The European Quality Award model	65
3.3	RADAR logic	67
3.4	The proposed self-assessment model	71
5.1	The quality deployment process	94
5.2	Strategic application of the PDCA cycle	95
5.3	Integrating the voice of the customer with the voice of the process for goal congruence	97
5.4	Integrating process management and performance measurement	97
5.5	Example of quality policy deployment process	98
5.6	A four cycle approach to implementation of strategy	100
5.7	Quality policy deployment	101
5.8	Quality deployment process	102
5.9	Quality policy deployment process at Hewlett-Packard	104
5.10	Quality policy at Rank Xerox	105
7.1	Information processing and integration between other processes	134
7.2	"Golden Circle" at Texas Instruments	146
8.1	Business process management at Elida Faberge	160
8.2	The problem solving process	163
8.3	Quality improvement process	164
8.4	Quality operating system at Ford	166
8.5	Quality improvement process at POCL	167
8.6	BPI at POCL	167
9.1	The GAO performance measurement model	174
9.2	The balanced business scorecard model	174
9.3	Balanced business scorecard example	175
9.4	Performance measurement system model level 1	178
9.5	Performance measurement system model level 2	180
9.6	Performance measurement system model level 3	181
9.7	Performance measurement system model level 4	183
9.8	Performance measurement system model	184
10.1	The Kano model	193
10.2	Many customers do not complain	194
10.3	How many unhappy customers will buy again from the same company?	195
10.4	Rank Xerox closed loop escalation process	196

10.5	Service attributes – best practice approach	197
10.6	How to manage customer loyalty: the customer pyramid model	198
10.7	The value/loyalty matrix	198
10.8	Customer value determinants	199
12.1	Support for community-based activity process	212
12.2	Community action support request sheets	213
12.3	Lever's support for business and employment	214
12.4	Lever's charitable contributions	214
13.1	Benchmarking Company A self-assessment score	222
13.2	Plotting performance gaps	222
13.3	Benchmarking Company A vs BQA self-assessment median	222
13.4	Benchmarking Company A vs EQA self-assessment median	223
13.5	Measuring performance gap through benchmarking	224

UK Quality Award percentage distribution of scores

13.6	Leadership category	227
13.7	Policy and strategy category	227
13.8	Resources category	227
13.9	People management category	228
13.10	Process management category	228
13.11	Customer satisfaction category	228
13.12	People satisfaction category	229
13.13	Impact on society category	229
13.14	Business results category	229

European Quality Award percentage distribution of scores

13.15	Leadership category	230
13.16	Policy and strategy category	230
13.17	Resources category	230
13.18	People management category	231
13.19	Process management category	231
13.20	Customer satisfaction category	231
13.21	People satisfaction category	232
13.22	Impact on society category	232
13.23	Business results category	232

Malcolm Baldrige Award distribution of scores

13.24	1988	233
13.25	1989	233
13.26	1990	233
13.27	1991	234
13.28	1992	234
14.1	Employee objective setting	239
14.2	Management of financial resources	241
14.3	Customer satisfaction continuous improvement	242
14.4	Closed loop process	243
14.5	Overall satisfaction measures	244
14.6	Service attributes	248
14.7	Mission statement of Ulster Carpet Mills	254
14.8	Company values	254
14.9	Communication process at Ulster Carpet Mills	256
14.10	Quality improvement process	262
14.11	How business units feed into the national procedure	263
14.12	Who is involved in the strategic process?	267
14.13	Aligning leadership competencies with business priorities	268
14.14	Chronology of quality	270
14.15	Process review	273

List of tables

1.1	The hierarchy of kaizen linked to the Japanese model	21
2.1	Guidelines for approach and deployment	34
2.2	Guidelines for scoring results	35
2.3	Self-assessment questionnaire – leadership	36
2.4	Self-assessment questionnaire – customer satisfaction	37
2.5	Business improvement matrix – enablers	38
2.6	Business improvement matrix – results	39
2.7	An example of a score sheet	40
2.8	Conditions of excellence for total quality	42
2.9	Desired state, processes – areas to inspect and measures of progress	44
2.10	Business results	45
2.11	The scoring scale	46
3.1	Checklist for the Deming Prize criteria	52
3.2	Deming Application Prize winners	54
3.3	Deming Prize winners of 1992	58
3.4	Selected data on MBNQA applications by category (1983-1993)	60
3.5	2003 Baldrige Award categories, items and point values	61
3.6	Scoring of the approach and deployment areas	63
3.7	Scoring of the results area	64
3.8	Distribution of MBNQA scores 1988-1992: percentage of applicants in range	64
3.9	Criteria for the EQA excellence model	66
3.10	EQA scoring guidelines	68
3.11	Benefits of cross-functional management in 102 Deming Prize winners	81
5.1	How QPD is deployed at Florida Power & Light	106
5.2	Policy and strategy exercise – suggested solution	108
6.1	Aggregated scores	123
7.1	Customer benefits, supplier benefits and mutual benefits	137
7.2	An example of pay back	150
7.3	Non-discounting method of appraisal of projects X and Y	151
7.4	Management of resources exercise – suggested solution	154
8.1	The process breakthrough methodology	161
8.2	The difference between the problem solving and quality improvement processes at Rank Xerox	163
8.3	Purpose of each phase of BPI at POCL	168
8.4	Critical processes and related success factors	171
10.1	Impact of satisfaction on propensity to buy again	192
11.1	Communication feedback mechanisms	203
12.1	Creating societal value-added: a proposed approach	210
12.2	The CERES Principles	211
13.1	Baldrige applicants and S&P 500 common stock comparison, 1990-1995	217
13.2	Baldrige winners and S&P 500 common stock comparison, 1988-1995	217
13.3	Measuring performance gap for Company A self-assessment performance	223
13.4	MBNQA winning companies and their successes	225
13.5	Financial and non-financial measures	235
14.1	Milestones in developing a total quality culture	255
14.2	Deployment of business strategy	260
14.3	Quality evolution	272

Acknowledgements

This book would not have been possible without the help, support and kind co-operation of many individuals and organisations. Perhaps right at the onset, our thanks are due to the many organisations that are quoted in various parts of the manuscript for providing information on their TQ efforts and their exemplar practices. Indeed, the practices that they have integrated with their cultures are ones that can offer true inspiration and useful guidance to other organisations that are aspiring for progress and advancement.

Our thanks are also due to various researchers at The European Centre for TQM who have contributed directly and indirectly to some of the chapters of the book. We would also like to extend our appreciation to all the staff at The European Centre for TQM, our business associates and the TQM fraternity in the UK and around the world. We are also grateful to Mrs Jenny Collett for her efforts in preparing the manuscript for publication.

Dedication

This book is dedicated first and foremost to all men and women who are passionate about quality, continuous improvement, the betterment of humanity and everyone's quality of life. We also wish to dedicate this text to our respective wives, children and families. We do appreciate their forbearance, their patience with us and their unwavering support.

Introduction
The meaning of organisational excellence

The meaning of excellence
As we embark on a new era based on digital means of competitiveness, it is quite appropriate to re-visit the role of total quality management (TQM) in enabling and supporting organisations to face the rigours of a modern business environment. This book is concerned not with aspects related to TQM implementation *per se*, but rather how TQM maturity and sustainability can be established.

Sustainability can perhaps be equated with the principle of excellence, which is now gaining wider acceptance in the business community. The problem of finding a common, acceptable definition of excellence and sustainability is the real purpose behind this book. Tom Peters, for instance, through his seminal work in the aforementioned field, has put together eight attributes considered vitally important for excellence and sustainability (Peters and Waterman, 1982; Peters, 1987; Peters and Austin, 1985). These attributes include:
1. having a bias for action;
2. being close to the customer;
3. allowing autonomy and entrepreneurship;
4. achieving productivity through people;
5. being hands on, value driven;
6. sticking to the knitting;
7. being of simple form, lean staff;
8. having simultaneous loose-tight properties.

Sustainability of excellence and superior performance is a relative concept and as Tom Peters has stated, "there are no excellent companies", only companies striving to attain excellence, through empowerment, benchmarking and continual improvement. While this alone will not guarantee corporate survival, it is the best possible way to achieve it.

Notion of sustainability
The concept of sustainable development has been touted as a new planning agenda. As such, it becomes a fundamental concept which should be an important aspect of all further policy developments. Sustainable development is based on a perceived need to address environmental deterioration and to maintain the vital functions of natural systems for the well being of present and future generations. It is possible to define sustainability as "the ability of an organisation to adapt to change in the business environment to capture contemporary best practice methods and to achieve and maintain superior competitive performance". This concept implies that sustainability is a means for an organisation to maintain its competitiveness. One way, perhaps, to accept the meaning of sustainability is as "a way for an organisation to develop its needs without compromising its future".

Sustainable performance
Sustainability is crucial to company performance. The organisational goal describes where the organisation is headed based upon the business environment and consistent with the corporate vision. Mission statements are used by individual sub-business units (e.g. distribution centres, manufacturing sites, specific operations or modules, etc.) to articulate how they contribute to

the business unit's vision. A mission statement defines the purpose of a business unit. Value statements are time-independent principles that articulate how individuals in the organisation are expected to behave as they pursue the vision and mission. Value statements can make an impact, especially when the values represent changes in behaviour required for the organisation to achieve its vision and deliver its mission. Measuring performance through assessment of the organisation's vision and mission statements is the foundation of a sustainable effective performance measurement system.

In other words, TQM effectiveness and organisational performance can be measured by using a self-assessment framework of quality management, such as the European Quality Award (EFQM), Deming Prize (Japan), and the Malcolm Baldrige National Quality Award (Kunst and Lemmink, 2000). Quality awards have also been established at the national and regional levels for analysing different factors, such as processes, leadership, personnel management and business results, which play a role in the functioning of organisations. The criteria cover a wide range of subjects that are all relevant to quality performance in organisations (Dessler and Farrow, 1990). Awards are indeed strongly based on the foundations of TQM (Bemowski and Sullivan, 1992). Sustainability of TQM in an organisation is determined by the successful implementation of critical success factors (CSFs) as proposed by the award criteria.

Rationale for a text on organisational excellence

The rationale for putting together a text on best practice organisational excellence is supported by the fact that excellence is driven by various critical factors, the presence/absence of which can have a marked effect on organisational performance (Thiagarajan, 1996). These quality factors include top management commitment and involvement, employee empowerment and culture. These factors are known by some writers as the soft aspects of management, while the hard aspects include factors such as improvement tools, techniques and systems (Wilkinson, 1992; Oakland, 1993, 2000).

The key factors which are found to impinge significantly on organisational excellence form the basis of the structure adopted for this text. It is interesting, however, that the main factors considered are those that represent the key criteria of excellence models such as the European Excellence Model or the Malcolm Baldrige National Quality Award Model.

Critical factors for organisational excellence

There are several critical factors that have been tested empirically and identified as key drivers of organisational excellence. It is, therefore, worth considering them individually. The major factors will form the basis of the structure adopted in this text and will be rigorously examined with elaborated cases and examples. Seventeen factors will be considered in the following section, these include:
1. Leadership and commitment.
2. People management.
3. Middle management involvement.
4. Training and education.
5. Reward and recognition.
6. Teamwork.
7. Quality policy and strategy.
8. Communicating for quality.
9. Supplier management.
10. Accredited quality management systems.
11. Organising for quality.

12. Managing by process.
13. Benchmarking.
14. Self-assessment.
15. Cost of quality.
16. Quality control techniques.
17. Measuring customer wants and satisfaction.

Factor 1. Leadership and top management commitment
All quality awards recognize the importance of leadership by placing this item at the top of the list of criteria necessary for successful implementation of quality management.

The European model for excellence (1999) defines leaders as the executive teams, all other managers and those in team leadership positions (Russell, 2000). The quality gurus emphasised the importance of leadership. Deming (1986) calls for managers to institute leadership rather than supervision in the transformation process of the business philosophy. Juran (1993) attributes the failure of the quality initiatives in the West in the 1970s and 1980s to senior managers' lack of personal involvement in quality management. Ishikawa (1985) considers that top managers must assume leadership in quality and quality control. Feigenbaum (1961) considers promoting organisational commitment is achieved as a result of top management commitment (Everett, 2002; Buch and Rivers, 2002). This is based on his principle that quality is everybody's business. Juran (1993) related quality excellence of Japanese companies to the commitment of senior managers to quality. Leiter and Maslach (2002) consider commitment of senior executives as an important factor of TQM and their doubts as the greatest enemy (Kano, 1993). Commitment of top management is also highlighted as a critical factor by several empirical studies (Ramirez and Loney, 1993; Zairi and Yousef, 1995; Ali, 1997; Ahire *et al.*, 1996; Ahire, 1996; Dayton, 2001; Saraph *et al.*, 1989; Flyn *et al.*, 1994; Thiagarajan, 1996; Rao *et al.*, 1999; Zhang *et al.*, 2000; Pun, 2001; Sureshchandar *et al.*, 2001; Lau and Idris, 2001; Li *et al.*, 2001).

The importance of leadership in successful implementation of TQM is also reinforced in the implementation case studies available in the literature (Zairi, 1999a; Whitford and Bird, 1996; Olian and Rynes, 1991; George, 1990; Easton, 1998; McAdam and Kelly, 2002).

Factor 2. People management
Major quality awards consider employee empowerment as a major area of assessment (Zink, 1995). The revised (April 1999) EFQM model of excellence, and indeed the April 2000 revision of the UK Investors in People standard, both place increased emphasis on the consideration of culture and employee motivation in terms of delivering organisational outcomes (Bowden, 2000; Wuagneux, 2002). Kanji and Asher (1993) propose people management, including "teamwork" and "people make quality", as one of the four principles of TQM (also Kanji, 1996, 1998a). Deming (1986) emphasises the importance of empowering employees by giving them the authority and autonomy to do their jobs. Juran (1991) stresses the same idea. Kano (1993) considers employee involvement and commitment to the goals of the TQM process as a condition to its successful implementation (Buch and Rivers, 2002; McAdam and Kelly, 2002).

In their study, Zhang *et al.* (2000) found that employee participation is a critical construct for successful implementation of TQM. Similar findings are reported by Rao *et al.* (1999) and Westlund and Lothgren (2001). Other recent studies identified employee empowerment as a critical factor of TQM implementation (Thiagarajan *et al.*, 2001; Martinez-Lorente *et al.*, 1998; Li *et al.*, 2001; Claver *et al.*, 2001; Davidson *et al.*, 2001; Dale *et al.*, 2001).

Employee empowerment is used as an effective strategy by companies like Toyota and Ford (Ahire *et al.*, 1996). At D2D, the people own processes responsible for the output of the process (Oakland, 2000).

Factor 3. Middle management involvement
Thiagarajan and Zairi (1997a) consider the act of maximising employee involvement in the quality process requires middle managers within the organisation to make major adjustments. The middle management have a particular role to play, since they must not only grasp the principles of TQM, they must go on to explain them to the people for whom they are responsible, and ensure that their commitment is communicated (Oakland, 2000). Only then, says Oakland (2000), will TQM spread effectively throughout the organisation. This emphasises the importance of getting middle managers to "buy-in" and be involved in contributing positively to successful TQM implementation (Crosby, 1989; Ishikawa, 1985).

A survey reported in *Quality Progress* revealed that middle management is the main roadblock to successful TQM implementation. The study recommended that top management should work hard to understand and involve middle managers in designing and promoting TQM. In this regard, Ishikawa (1985) says that middle management can contribute greatly to quality improvement. He calls for top management to provide greater attention to encourage new roles for middle managers. At Nissan UK, supervisors are involved in staff selection, developing and training their staff and motivating and maintaining morale. They are also the channels for all communications to manufacturing staff (Thiagarajan *et al.*, 2001).

Factor 4. Training and education
The Baldrige Award assesses applicant's efforts in providing quality training to its employees. This is also evident in the EQA.

Ishikawa (1985) states that quality begins and ends with training. For Rao *et al.* (1996) training and development are key components of all TQM programmes. Crosby (1979) considers education of the workforce as being the key to developing awareness and understanding of the new quality philosophy. Oakland (2000) adds that quality training must be objectively, systematically and continuously performed.

Education and quality awareness programmes across the whole organisation were emphasised by Feigenbaum (1961), Juran (1974) and Crosby (1979). For Mathews *et al.* (2001a) the training that underpins quality management determines the likely effectiveness of the quality initiatives undertaken. Garvin (1993) attributes failure in TQM programmes and low success rates to the basic fact that TQM requires a commitment to learning.

In fact, Japan's phenomenal productivity success is attributed to the national campaign of training every employer in basic concepts of quality improvement (see Lee and Ebrahimpour, 1985; Juran, 1978; Juran, 1981a, b; Lee and Ebrahimpour, 1985). Zhang *et al.*, (2000) consider investment in education and training vitally important for TQM success. They add, employees should be regarded as valuable, long-term resources worthy of receiving education and training throughout their career (Cebeci and Beskese, 2002). In their findings from a European survey with 450 responses from the UK, Portugal and Finland, Mathews *et al.* (2001b) concluded that top managers and shop floor workers receive training in the areas of "soft" quality tools, quality awareness and customer focus, while middle managers and quality specialists receive most quality-related training. Quality awareness and standards are the areas in which training is most frequently given. Several recent empirical studies revealed that training and education are critical to successful TQM implementation (Thiagarajan and Zairi, 1998; Quazi and Padibjo, 1998; Rao *et al.*, 1999; Zhang *et al.*, 2000; Ali, 1997; Yusof and Aspinwall, 2000; Black and Porter, 1996; Ahire *et al.*, 1996; Flyn *et al.*, 1994; Tamimi and Sebastianelli, 1995; Tamimi, 1998; Pun, 2001; Calisir *et al.*, 2001; and Dayton, 2001).

Factor 5. Rewards and recognition
Crosby (1989) considers recognition as one of the most important steps of the quality improvement process. According to Oakland (2000), TQM is user-driven. Juran (1991) states that recognition can be used as part of the motivation for the cultural change required for TQM implementation. Kemp et al. (1997) consider the recognition procedure as basic to increasing the involvement of all employees in the operation of the business. Many other authors highlight the importance of rewards and recognition in the TQM process (Easton, 1993; Binney, 1992; Townsend and Gebhardt, 1992; Haksever, 1996; Rao et al., 1996, 1999; Li et al., 2001; Dayton, 2001; Martinez-Lorente et al., 1998; Everett, 2002).

A study reported in *Quality Progress* found that best practice units within 86 major corporations used rewards as incentives to advance their TQM process. Results from a US Council of Communication survey concluded that recognition for a job well done is the top motivator of employee performance (Sweatman, 1996 in London and Higgot, 1997). One of the key items that Xerox (USA) considered in developing the road map to achieve quality was introducing a reward system to recognise people who used the quality tools (Rao et al., 1996).

Factor 6. Teamwork
One of the most publicised aspects of the Japanese approach to quality has been the quality circles or kaizen teams (Oakland, 2000; Goh, 2000; Heizer and Render, 1999, 2001). Many companies in the Fortune 1000 adopted quality circles as a way of increasing employee involvement and participation in TQM (Rao et al., 1996).

Reviewing the literature reveals that teamwork is a critical factor in total quality management (Crosby, 1989; Bank, 1992; Kanji and Asher, 1993; Cebeci and Beskese, 2002; McAdam and Kelly, 2002; Everett, 2002). One of the major elements of the human resource focus that has been identified by Mehra et al. (1998) as a critical success factor to the success of TQM programmes is teamwork. This must be a part of any successful programme to improve productivity (Hoffman and Mehra, 1999).

At Rank Xerox Europe, teams from all levels were formed to improve business processes continuously (Rao et al., 1996). Philips recognises that it can only be the best with teamwork, sharing knowledge and communication with each other (Oakland, 2000). In his business excellence model, Kanji (1998a) considers teamwork as a core concept to achieve the principle of people based management. In Oakland's (2000) TQM model teams are considered one of the major components of the model.

Factor 7. Quality policy and strategy
According to Juran and Gryna (1993), strategic quality management is the "process of establishing long-range quality goals and defining the approach to meeting those goals". Quality gurus and writers strongly emphasize the importance of strategic planning process based on total quality (Deming, 1986; Crosby, 1979; Juran, 1974; Zairi, 1994; Oakland, 1993; James, 1996; Ahire et al., 1996; Sinclair and Zairi, 2001; Dayton, 2001; Martinez-Lorente et al., 1998; Sureshchandar et al., 2001; Crepin, 2002; Hitchcock and Willard, 2002).

The Malcolm Baldrige Award (1999) and the European Quality Award (1999) criteria designate a relatively low score to the content of company quality policies in comparison to the practices and results, which arise from policy implementation. This is emphasized by Juran (1991) as he states that most successful TQM organisations ensure that quality goals are incorporated in the overall business plan.

Talking about quality policy and strategy cannot be separated from strategic planning process related to total quality management. Such a process is based on determining the needs and requirements of all stakeholders (including the customer), analysing the competitors' strengths and weaknesses, and identifying the process capabilities (Juran, 1974; Crosby, 1979; Deming, 1986; Oakland, 1993, 2000; Zairi, 1994, 1999b; Haksever, 1996).

Many companies such as Procter and Gamble (Bemowski and Sullivan, 1992), NEC – Japan (Smith, 1994), Rank Xerox (Smith, 1994; Zairi, 1994; Whitford and Bird, 1996), ST Microelectronics (Oakland, 2000) have achieved success in developing, communicating and reviewing strategic plans at all levels in their organisations.

Factor 8. Communicating for quality
According to Kanji and Asher (1993) effective communication is part of the cement that holds together the bricks of the total quality process. It is important in directing employees towards the corporate expectations (Thiagarajan *et al.*, 2001; Dayton, 2001). At British Airways Interior Engineering, the launch of the goals was communicated at a weekly brief to all colleagues. This was followed by a series of workshops run by the general manager to groups of colleagues, until everyone had taken part (Fowles and Edwards, 1999).

Effective communication is important for the success of any quality initiative (Martinez-Lorente *et al.*, 1998; Sureshchandar *et al.*, 2001) and is critical from the beginning of a change effort. Every element of the change must be talked about, presented and discussed across levels of the organisation (Rao *et al.*, 1996; Claver *et al.*, 2001), The key medium for motivating the employees and gaining their commitment to TQM is face-to-face communication and visible management commitment (Oakland, 2000).

A study reported that poor inter-organisational communication was highly rated as an obstacle to a successful implementation programme (Tamimi and Sebastianelli, 1998). Another study revealed that for TQM companies the three most severe obstacles, in rank order based on average severity, were lack of time, poor communication and lack of real employee empowerment (Salegna and Fazel, 2000).

At the Division of Alicante, Telefonica Group in Spain internal communication was defined as an essential tool in moving ahead towards TQM (Claver *et al.*, 2001). At D2D, annual kick off events are held by the managing director where he talks to every employee in small groups on the previous year's performance and strategy in a relaxed atmosphere. At IBM Rochester, posters were important in getting the quality message across to all employees (Zairi, 1999b).

Factor 9. Supplier management
Supplier quality management is an important aspect of TQM since materials and purchased parts are often a major source of quality problems (Zhang *et al.*, 2000). According to Flood (1993) companies should treat their suppliers as long-term business partners. Many authors advocate that companies must establish supply chain partnerships to motivate suppliers to provide materials needed to meet customer expectations (Harrison and St John, 1996; Kumar, 1996; Lambert *et al.*, 1996; Clifton, 2001; Jabnoun, 2000; Thakur, 2002). Wong and Fung, (1999) state that partnerships with suppliers will lead to quality results from the supply chain. According to Kanji and Wong (1999) the creation and enhancement of the customer-supplier partnership is a major quality practice. This is emphasised by Wong and Fung (1999) and David (2002).

The quality gurus believe that suppliers should be viewed as an integral part of the organisation's business operations (Ishikawa, 1985; Deming, 1986; Crosby, 1989). The report of the US General Accounting Office identified the establishment of close supplier relationships by high-scoring Baldrige Award applicants as a key feature, which contributed to improved organisational performance.

A study conducted by Wong (2000) reveals that supplier satisfaction will help increase the level of customer satisfaction. Other recent studies support these findings (Dayton, 2001; Lau and Idris, 2001, Martinez-Lorente *et al.*, 1998; Thiagarajan *et al.*, 2001).

The Philip's Group created a long-term business partnership with its suppliers. They coined the phrase "comakership" to describe the new approach. Comakership simply means working together towards a common goal. Rank Xerox, TI Rayleigh and Locas all adopted a comakership approach with their suppliers to improve quality (Flood, 1993).

Quality-oriented companies no longer have cost as the primary criterion for selecting suppliers and are being more proactive in developing long-term relationships with their suppliers by extending technical support and training to suppliers to improve the process, quality and productivity of their suppliers (Rao *et al.*, 1999; Clifton, 2001).

Factor 10. Accredited quality management system
The ISO 9000 series certification can be defined as the starting point for entering the competition; the ongoing journey towards TQM must deliver the competitive advantage (van der Weile and Brown, 1998) (also see Quazi and Padibjo, 1998; Williams, 1997; Stahan, 2002; Kolka, 2002). Since the publication of the ISO 9000 series of standards in 1987, many companies and organisations use them as an important milestone to mark their quality journeys. Many organisations consider ISO 9000 certification as the first step in the implementation process of TQM (Oakland and Porter, 1994; Shipley, 2002). A documented quality system as part of a TQM strategy can contribute to TQM by managing the organisation's processes in a consistent manner (Zhang *et al.*, 2000). Beattie and Sohal (1999) state that most firms will operate ISO 9000 concurrently with another quality activity, usually TQM (see also Beattie *et al.*, 1999; Quazi and Padibjo, 1998; McAdam and McKeown, 1999; Zhu and Shenerman, 1999; Beskese and Cebeci, 2001).

Kanji (1998b) says that ISO 9000 could be integrated with TQM for the development of a TQM process. The integration of ISO 9000 with TQM generally allows the firm to capture increased profits along the path of quality improvement (Liao *et al.*, 1995 in Huarng *et al.*, 1999). The introduction of ISO 9000 has influenced to a great extent the development of organisational efforts towards quality assurance (Khan and Hafiz, 1999). Oakland (2000) states that to the foundation framework of the customer-supplier chain, processes and the "soft" outcomes of TQM must be added the first hard management necessity – a quality system based on any good international standard.

D2D is among the first in Europe to gain ISO 9000 and pilot the environmental standards BS 7750 (Zairi, 1999b). Nearly all Philips organisations are ISO 9000 certified, thus laying the foundation for continuous improvement or "let's make things better", all the time (Oakland, 2000).

Factor 11. Organising for quality
Juran (1974) sees organisation for quality in terms of structure and people. This requires the determination of activities to be performed, the responsibilities associated with the activities, dividing the work into jobs, determining job responsibilities and authority, inter-job relations and channels of communication. Ishikawa (1985) supports the use of cross-functional management, which can be done through the use of committees. He suggests that in order for organisations to become strong, the vertical levels present must be interwoven through cross-functional control. Juran (1991) emphasizes this suggestion, as the cross-functional nature of TQM requires a suitable infrastructure to support training, project development and teamwork.

Moren-Lozon and Peris (1998) developed an integrated model for strategic management, organisational design and quality management. They classified quality organisation into the quality assurance organisation (characterised conformity) and the TQM organisation (characterised by internal and external customer satisfaction, continuous improvement and employee involvement) indicating low formalisation and centralisation of organisational structure (Jabnoun, 2000).

Oakland (2000) states that authority must be given to those charged with following TQM through with actions that they consider necessary to achieve the goals. The commitment will be questioned continually and will be weakened, perhaps destroyed, by failure to delegate authoritatively. Oakland and Porter (1994) consider that one of the responsibilities of senior management at the early stage of initiating the TQM programme is the set up of a quality organisational structure. Such structure is needed to create a framework, which will enable quality improvement to develop and flourish (also Easton, 1993; Bendell et al., 1993). They consider the quality organisational structure as a key element in ensuring successful implementation of TQM.

Factor 12. Managing by processes
To achieve customer satisfaction, Oakland (1993, 2000) emphasises the importance of managing the internal-supplier relationship as the first step to support the process management. Through a process of translating the customer-supplier chain at all levels, better focus can be achieved and ultimately all work carried out will be of value (Zairi, 2000; McAdam and Kelly, 2002).

A key part of any total quality strategy is the management of processes (Porter and Parker, 1993). According to Ahire et al. (1996) all activities of an organisation must be planned and executed to improve processes that lead to manufacturing quality products. However, quality must be incorporated into these activities with a clear customer focus (Feigenbaum, 2002).

Process refers to some unique combinations of machines, tools, methods, materials and people engaged in production (Juran and Gryna, 1993). One important matter in process management is to ensure that process capability can meet production requirements (Zhang et al., 2000).

The importance of customer focus is also evident from the fact that it is assigned the highest weight among the Malcolm Baldrige Award criteria and the European Quality Award.

D2D trained everyone in process management and improvement, and demonstrated how they are part of a supplier-process-customer chain. Almost 3,500 people received this process training, allowing the processes in D2D to be owned by the people responsible for the output of the process (Oakland, 2000).

Many quality organisations learned the importance of applying clearly defined customer-focus approaches to manage processes rather than the conventional functional approach of management. ICL and Shell Chemicals UK are such companies (Sinclair, 1994). Based on the experience of Shorts Brothers, McAdam (1996) states that process management (process-based approach) improves customer satisfaction and overcomes the problems associated with management through a functional-based approach.

Factor 13. Benchmarking
Many authors see benchmarking as a vital tool in the development of TQM (Sinclair and Zairi, 2000, 2001). According to Oakland (2000) benchmarking measures an organisation's operation, product and service against those of its competitors. It will establish targets, priorities and operations leading to competitive advantage. For Dow et al. (1999) benchmarking can be seen as a "hard" quality practice providing some systematic analysis of the achievement of quality goals. Benchmarking has also been demonstrated to be a catalyst for the success of a number of other organisation change interventions, for example business process re-engineering (Thor and Jarrett, 1999), improved operational performance and

general changes in organisational thinking and action (Cassell *et al.*, 2001). Jarrar and Zairi (2000) state that benchmarking or best practice management is increasingly being recognised as a powerful performance improvement effort for processes, business units and for entire corporations. According to the American Productivity and Quality Centre, best practices are those practices that have been shown to produce superior results, selected by a systematic process, and judged as exemplary, good, or successfully demonstrated.

Dervitsiotis (2000) states that it is noticeable that not only consulting firms but also organisations such as the American Productivity and Quality Centre and the European Foundation for Quality Management are seriously engaged in the promotion of and training in benchmarking as a fundamental approach to achieve business excellence (McAdam and Kelly, 2002).

Benchmarking at Xerox evolved as a sophisticated methodology for process improvement. Several companies picked up the methodology and used it to compare themselves against the competition (Whitford and Bird, 1996; Rao *et al.*, 1996). Yellow Pages (YP) is a division of British Telecommunication plc (BT). YP's primary aim is to be the business information bridge between buyers and sellers. YP uses the business excellence model and was among the nine finalists for the 1998 European Quality Award for Business Excellence (Simpson, 2000). Nadkarni (1995) reports that all Baldrige Award winners applied various types of benchmarking to identify the best practices. Motorola conducted benchmarking against 125 companies.

Factor 14. Self-assessment
Zairi (1994) considers self-assessment as an effective technique to measure the culture of quality within the organisation. According to Conti (1999) the objective of self-assessment is to identify weaknesses that are obstructing the achievement of targets and improvement of performance in general. Self-assessment promotes business excellence by involving a regular and systematic review of processes and results. It highlights strengths and improvement opportunities, and drives continuous improvement (Oakland, 2000).

The introduction of various quality awards has provided impetus for the implementation of TQM (Sinclair and Zairi, 2001). Considerable research has been carried out into the format of the EFQM model of business excellence and its use as a tool for self-assessment (Hakes, 1998; van der Weile *et al.*, 1996). The introduction of internationally respected quality awards (Deming Prize, 1951; MBNQA, 1987; and the EQA, 1992) has provided the opportunity for firms to assess, using the models of total quality management (TQM) and business excellence, which underpin these awards, the strengths and areas for improvement of their approaches to business improvement (Wilkes and Dale, 1998; McAdam and Kelly, 2002). Since the award criteria of MBNQA (1999) and the EQA (1999) are generic and well documented, they serve most often as the model for self-assessment (Kueng, 2000).

Zairi (1994) states that self-assessment can help organisations in measuring performance of processes and enablers and their relationship with results. It seems that tools such as the balanced scorecard, EFQM and Baldrige framework are acting as catalysts to the measurement revolution (Stone and Banks, 1997). Self-assessment, using the Hewlett-Packard peer review teams, caused the spread of best practice within the company and the reviews acted as facilitators of cross-fertilization and improvement across the global organisation (Oakland, 2000).

Factor 15. Cost of quality
Quality costs are used by management in its pursuits of quality improvement, customer satisfaction, market share and profit enhancement. It is the economic common denominator, which forms the basic data for TQM. Quality costing is one measurement technique that has often been used to help justify the adoption of quality improvement efforts to senior managers (Sinclair and Zairi, 2001). A number of world class organisations do employ quality costing measures as an indication of internal quality performance (Dale and Plunkett, 1999). Juran is often given credit for coining the concept of quality costs. He proposed that an optimal quality level could be found where the losses due to defects were equal to the cost of quality control.

The cost of poor quality of an organisation is the difference between the actual operating cost and what the operating cost would be if there were no failures in its system and no mistakes by its staff (Bland *et al.*, 1998).

There are several well-documented field based US studies (Carr, 1992, 1995; Carr and Tyson, 1992) which outline the various innovative techniques utilized by such companies as IBM, Xerox, Tennant, Ford, Westinghouse, Pacific Bell and others. These companies employed cost of quality calculation as an integral part of their quality programme. Xerox applied the cost of quality principles to its US sales and marketing group, realizing an outstanding cost of quality savings of $53 million in the first year. The improvements were relatively painless. Line managers, initially skeptical of cost of quality, began to appreciate the value of this tool. Over the subsequent four years Xerox achieved over $200 million savings in quality costs. Xerox made cost of quality an integral part of its leadership, through a quality programme which defines quality as 100 per cent customer satisfaction (Rao *et al.*, 1996).

Factor 16. Quality control techniques
Statistical process control (SPC) is one of the cornerstones of the model for TQM developed by the European Centre for Total Quality Management (Sinclair and Zairi, 2000). Statistical process control is not only a tool kit; it is a strategy for reducing variability, part of never-ending improvement (Oakland, 2000). Although most statistical techniques have been used in the manufacturing environment, they can be used in non-manufacturing industry, for example the service sector (Xie and Goh, 1999).

SPC helps quality-oriented firms to monitor quality variations and to investigate critical areas where improvements are needed (Deming, 1986). The aim of statistical process control and control charts is first to achieve a stable process and then successively to reduce process variation (Stenberg and Deleryd, 1999). Among the techniques that form the core of statistical process control, control charts are perhaps the most important and widely used tools (Chinna *et al.*, 2000). Juran (1974) emphasizes the importance of quality control tools to achieve both low-defect production and to improve quality.

Another statistical quality control tool to focus on customer satisfaction is the six sigma strategy (Munro, 2000; Coronado and Antony, 2002). Harry and Schroeder (2000) in Munro (2000) define the six sigma strategy as "a disciplined method of using extremely rigorous data gathering and statistical analysis to pinpoint sources of errors and ways of eliminating them". In January 2000 Ford Motor Co. publicly announced that it would be the first automaker to use six sigma to focus on customer satisfaction (Munro, 2000).

Factor 17. Measuring customer wants and satisfaction
Customers are an economic asset. They are not on the balance sheet, but they should be (Claes Fornell, 1994 in Kanji and Wallace, 2000).

Deming calls for total transformation of existing management methods to achieve a culture of continuous improvement for continual customer satisfaction. The emphasis on customer satisfaction or customer-driven quality is considered by many gurus and writers as a major success of the quality management effort (Deming, 1986; Crosby, 1989; Oakland and Porter, 1994; Rao *et al.*, 1996; Spring *et al.*, 1998; Oakland, 2000; Kanji, 1998a, b; Zairi, 1999a, b, 2000; Winser and Corney, 2001; Li *et al.*, 2001; Nakata, 2002; Hitchcock and Willard, 2002). For Oliver (1999) a customer is satisfied when he senses that consumption fulfils some need, desire, goal etc. and that this fulfillment is pleasurable. When a customer recognizes quality, it is reflected in customer satisfaction. Customer satisfaction, in turn, can lead to increased revenue.

A strategic concept, customer satisfaction is concerned with such achievements as customer retention and market penetration (Rao *et al.*, 1996; Allred, 2001). Zairi (1994) considers measuring customer satisfaction as a cornerstone of TQM. The criteria of the Malcolm Baldrige Award and the European Quality Award have established the use of customer information as a key issue in the management of quality. The highest percentages of the awards' scores relate to customer focus and satisfaction.

It should be appreciated that continuous monitoring of customer satisfaction is an invaluable source of information for all strategic business analysis and management. Thus it should play a central role in the company's TQM (Eklof and Westlund, 1998). Continuous improvement is a management philosophy and system that organises employees and processes to maximize customer value and satisfaction. This requires listening to customers and trying to satisfy their needs (Eklof and Selivanova, 2000; Winser and Corney, 2001). Nadkarni (1995) reports that the Selection Corporation (Baldrige Award winner) calls on each of its 120 customers to enquire about the level of satisfaction associated with their products and services.

IBM, DuPont, AT&T and Panasonic have stopped creating products with just the buyer in mind and have started considering the end user as well (Thiagarajan and Zairi, 1997b). These cases not only emphasize the importance of measuring customer satisfaction, but also highlight what Deming (1986) recommended – frequent and continued direct interaction with customers to determine the level of satisfaction. Xerox organises a Visitor Quality Day for customers every six weeks. (Nadkarni, 1995; Rao *et al.*, 1996).

The key factors which have already been highlighted are covered comprehensively in the following chapters. Some of them have been integrated under one heading. The examination of each factor will be supported with best practice examples and applications found to be inherent in world class organisations.

References and further reading

Ahire, S.L., Golhar, D.Y. and Waller, M.A. (1996), "Development and validation of TQM implementation constructs", *Decision Sciences*, Vol. 27, pp. 23-56.

Ahire, S.L. (1996), "An empirical investigation of quality management in small firms", *Production and Inventory Management Journal*, 2nd Quarter, pp. 44-50.

Ali, M. (1997), "An empirical study of total quality management in the Middle East: a proposed model for implementation", University of Bradford, unpublished PhD thesis.

Allred, A. (2001), "Creating customer service worth advertising at Browning Arms", *The TQM Magazine*, Vol. 13 No. 1, pp. 6-11.

Bank, J. (1992), *The Essence of Total Quality Management*, Prentice Hall, London.

Beattie, K. and Sohal, A. (1999), "Implementing ISO 9000: a study of its benefits among Australian organisations", *Total Quality Management*, Vol.10 No. 1, pp. 95-106.

Beattie, V., Brandt, R. and Fearnley, S. (1999), "Perceptions of auditor independence: UK evidence", *Journal of International Accounting Auditing & Taxation*, Vol. 8 No. 1, pp. 67-107.

Bemowski, K. (1992), "Carrying on the P&G tradition", *Quality Progress*, Vol. 25 No. 5, pp. 21-5.

Bemowski, K. and Sullivan, R. (1992), "Inside the Baldrige Award guidelines; Category 1: leadership (part 1)", *Quality Progress*, Vol. 25 No. 6, pp. 24-8.

Bendell, T., Boulter, L. and Kelly, J. (1993), *Benchmarking for Competitive Advantage*, Pitman Publishing, London.

Beskese, A. and Cebeci, U. (2001), "Total quality management and ISO 9000 applications in Turkey", *The TQM Magazine*, Vol. 13 No. 1, pp. 69-73.

Binney, G. (1992), *Making Quality Work: Lessons From Europe's Leading Companies*, The Economist Intelligence Unit, London.

Black, S. and Porter, L. (1996), "Identification of critical factors of TQM", *Decision Sciences*, Vol. 27, pp. 1-21.

Bland, F.M., Maynard, J. and Herbert, D.W. (1998), "Quality costing of an administrative process", *The TQM Magazine*, Vol. 10 No. 5, pp. 367-77.

Bowden, P. (2000), "Delivering organisational excellence by employee values management", *Total Quality Management*, Vol. 11 Nos 4/5, 6, pp. 636-40.

Buch, K. and Rivers, D. (2002), "Sustaining a quality initiative", *Strategic Direction*, Vol. 18 No. 4, pp. 15-17.

Calisir, F., Bayraktar, C. and Beskese, B. (2001), "Implementing the ISO 9000 standards in Turkey: a study of large companies' satisfaction with ISO 9000", *Total Quality Management*, Vol. 12 No. 4, pp. 429-38.

Carr, L. and Tyson, T. (1992), "Planning quality/cost expenditures", *Management Accounting*, October, pp. 52-6.

Carr, L. (1992), "Applying cost of quality to a service business", *Sloan Management Review*, Summer, pp. 72-9.

Carr, L. (1995), "How Xerox sustains the cost of quality", *Management Accounting*, August, pp. 26-32.

Cassell, C., Nadin, S. and Older Gray, M. (2001), "The use and effectiveness of benchmarking in SMEs", *Benchmarking: An International Journal*, Vol. 8 No. 3, pp. 212-22.

Cebeci, U. and Beskese, A. (2002) "An approach to the evaluation of quality performance of the companies in Turkey", *Managerial Auditing Journal*, Vol. 17 No. 1/2, pp. 92-100.

Chinna, K.A., Kadir, S.L. and Abdullah, M. (2000), "Box-chart: combining X and S charts", *Total Quality Management*, Vol.11 Nos 4/5 and 6, pp. 857-62.

Claver, E., Gasco, J., Llopis, J. and Gonzalez, R. (2001), "The strategic process of a cultural change to implement total quality management: a case study", *Total Quality Management*, Vol. 12 No. 4, pp. 469-82.

Clifton, N. (2001), "System suppliers: towards 'best practice'?", *Benchmarking: An International Journal*, Vol. 8 No. 3, pp. 172-90.

Conti, T. (1999), "Vision 2000: positioning the new ISO 9000 standards with respect to total quality management models", *Total Quality Management*, Vol. 10 Nos 4/5, pp. 454-64.

Coronado, R.B. and Antony, J. (2002), "Critical success factors for the successful implementation of six sigma projects in organizations", *The TQM Magazine*, Vol. 14 No. 2, pp. 92-9.

Crepin, D. (2002), "From design to action: developing a corporate strategy", *Quality Progress*, Vol. 35 No. 2, pp. 49-56.

Crosby, P. (1979), *Quality is Free: The Art of Making Quality Certain*, Penguin Books, New York.

Crosby, P. (1989), *Let's Talk Quality: 96 Questions That You Always Wanted To Ask Phil Crosby,* McGraw-Hill, New York.

Dale, B. and Plunkett, J. (1999), *Quality Costing*, 3rd ed., Gower, Aldershot.

Dale, B., Y.-Wu, P., Zairi, M., Williams, A. and Van der Wiele, T. (2001), "Total quality management and theory: an exploratory study of contribution", *Total Quality Management,* Vol. 12 No. 4, pp.439-49.

David, J. (2002), Strategic sourcing: benefits, problems and a contextual model, *Management Decision*, Vol. 40 No. 1, pp. 26-34.

Davidson, A., Chelson, L., Stern, L. and Janes, F. (2001), "A new tool for assessing the presence of total quality", *The TQM Magazine*, Vol. 13 No. 1, pp. 12-24.

Dayton, N.A. (2001), "Total quality management critical success factors, a comparison: the UK versus the USA", *Total Quality Management*, Vol. 12 No. 3, pp. 293-8.

Deming, W.E. (1986), *Out of the Crisis,* Cambridge University Press, Boston, MA.

Dervitsiotis, K.N. (2000), "Benchmarking and business paradigm shifts", *Total Quality Management,* Vol. 11 Nos 4/5 and 6, pp. 641-6.

Dessler, G. and Farrow, D. (1990), "Implementing a successful quality improvement programme in a service company: winning the Deming prize", *International Journal of Service Industry Management*, Vol. 1 No. 2.

Dow, D., Samson, D. and Ford, D. (1999), "Exploring the myth: do all quality management practices contribute to superior quality performance", *Production and Operations Management*, Vol. 8 No. 1, pp. 1-27.

Easton, G. (1993), "The 1993 State of US total quality management: a Baldrige examiner's perspective", *California Management Review*, Vol. 35, pp. 32-54.

Easton, G. (1998), *Learning from Case Studies*, 3rd ed., Prentice Hall, Hemel Hempstead.

Eklof, J.A. and Selivanova (2000), "Corporate quality management practice in Russia: with international comparisons", *Total Quality Management*, Vol. 11 No. 4-6, p. S714, 6 pages.

Eklof, J. and Westlund, A. (1998), "Customer satisfaction index and its role in quality management", *Total Quality Management*, Vol. 9 No. 1, pp. 80-5.

Everett, C. (2002), "Penn State's commitment to quality improvement", *Quality Progress*, Vol. 35 No. 1, pp. 44-9.

Feigenbaum, A. (1961), *Total Quality Control*, McGraw-Hill, London.

Feigenbaum, A. (2002), "The power behind consumer buying and productivity", *Quality Progress*, Vol. 35 No. 4, pp. 49-50.

Flood, R.L. (1993), *Beyond TQM*, John Wiley and Sons, New York.

Flyn, B., Schroeder, R. and Sakakibara, S. (1994), "A framework for quality management research and an associated measurement instrument", *Journal of Operations Management,* Vol. 11, pp. 339-66.

Fowles, R. and Edwards, M. (1999), "Creating a shared vision: and exercise in inspiration and communication at British Airways Interiors Engineering", *Total Quality Management*, Vol. 10 No. 4/5, pp. 548-53.

Garvin, D.A. (1983), "Quality on-line", *Harvard Business Review*, Vol. 61 No.5, pp. 65-75.

George, D. (1990), "The routine involvement of senior managers in the quality improvement process", in Oakland, J.S. (Ed.), *Proceedings of the 3rd International Conference on Total Quality Management,* IFS Ltd, Warwick, UK.

Goh, M. (2000), "Quality circles: journey of an Asian public enterprise", *International Journal of Quality and Reliability Management*, Vol. 17 No.7, pp. 623-31.

Hakes, C. (1998), *The Corporate Self-Assessmet: Handbook For Measuring Business Excellence*, 4th ed., Chapman and Hall.

Hakesever, C. (1996), "Total quality management in the small business environment", *Business Horizons*, March-April, pp. 33-40.

Harrison, J. and St John, C. (1996), "Managing and partnering with external stakeholders", *Academy of Management Executive*, Vol. 10, pp. 46-60.

Heizer, J. and Render, B. (1999), *Operations Management*, 5th ed., Prentice Hall, Englewood Cliffs, NJ.

Heizer, J.H. and Render, B. (2001), *Operation Management Essential*, 6th ed., December, Prentice-Hall, Englewood Cliffs, NJ.

Hitchcock, D. and Willard, M. (2002), "Sustainability: enlarging quality's mission", *Quality Progress*, Vol. 35 No. 2, pp. 43-8.

Hoffman, J.M. and Mehra, S. (1999), "Operationalising productivity improvement programmes through total quality management", *International Journal of Quality and Reliability Management,* Vol. 16 No.1, pp. 72-84.

Huarng, F., Horng, C. and Chen, C. (1999), "A study of ISO 9000 process, motivation and performance", *Total Quality Management*, Vol.10 No. 7, pp. 1009-25.

Ishikawa, K. (1985), *What Is Total Quality Control? The Japanese Way*, Prentice-Hall, Englewood Cliffs, NJ.

Jabnoun, N. (2000), "Restructuring for TQM: a review", *The TQM Magazine*, Vol. 12 No. 6, pp. 395-9.

James, P.(1996), *Total Quality Management: An Introductory Text*, Prentice Hall, Englewood Cliffs, NJ.

Jarrar, Y. and Zairi, M. (2000), "Best practice transfer for future competitiveness: a study of best practices", *Total Quality Management*, Vol.11 Nos 4/5 and 6, pp. 734-40.

Juran, J.M. (1974), *Quality Control Handbook*, McGraw-Hill, London.

Juran, J.M. (1978), "Japanese and western quality: a contrast in methods and results", *Management Review*, November, pp. 27-45.

Juran, J.M. (1993), "A renaissance in quality", *Harvard Business Review*, pp. 42-53.

Juran, J.M. and Gryna, F.M. (1993), *Quality Planning and Analysis*, McGraw-Hill, New York, p. 482.

Juran, J.M. (1991), *Juran on Quality by Design*, Free Press, New York.

Juran, J.M. (1981a), "Product quality: a prescription for the West (Part 1)", *Management Review*, Vol. 70 No. 6, pp. 8-14.

Juran, J.M. (1981b), "Product quality: a prescription for the West (Part II)", *Management Review,* Vol. 70 No. 7, pp. 57-61.

Kanji, G.K. (1996) "Implementation and pitfalls of total quality management", *Total Quality Management*, Vol. 7, pp. 331-43.

Kanji, G.K. (1998a), "Measurement of business excellence"*, Total Quality Management,* Vol. 9 No 7, pp. 633-43.

Kanji, G.K. (1998b), "An innovative approach to make ISO 9000 standards more effective", *Total Quality Management*, Vol. 9 No. 1, pp. 67-78.

Kanji, G.K. and Asher, M. (1993)*, Total Quality Management Process-A Systematic Approach, Advances in Total Quality Management Series*, Carfax Publishing Co., Abingdon.

Kanji, G.K. and Wallace, W. (2000), "Business excellence through customer satisfaction", *Total Quality Management*, Vol. 11 No. 7, pp. 979-98.

Kanji, G.K. and Wong, A. (1999), "Business excellence model for supply chain management", *Total Quality Management*, Vol. 10 No. 8, p. 1147, 22 pages.

Kano, N. (1993), "A perspective on quality activities in American firms", *California Management Review*, Vol. 35 No. 3, pp. 12-31.

Kemp, A., Pryor, S. and Dale, B. (1997), "Sustaining TQM: a case study at Aeroquib Iberica", *The TQM Magazine*, Vol. 9 No. 1, pp. 21-8.

Khan, M.K. and Hafiz, N. (1999), "Development of an expert system for implementation of ISO 9000 quality systems", *Total Quality Management*, Vol. 10 No.1, pp. 47-59.

Kolka, J. (2002), "ISO 9000 and 9004: a framework for disaster preparedness", *Quality Progress*, Vol. 35 No. 2, pp. 57-62.

Kueng, P. (2000), "Process performance measurement system: a tool to support process-based organisations", *Total Quality Management*, Vol. 10 No 1, pp. 67-85.

Kumar, N. (1996), "The power of trust in manufacture retailer relationships", *Harvard Business Review*, November-December, pp. 92-106.

Kunst, P. and Lemmink, J. (2000), "Quality management and performance in hospitals: a search for success parameters", *Total Quality Management*, December, Vol. 11 Issue 8, pp. 1123-33.

Lambert, D., Emmelhainz, M. and Gardner, J. (1996), "Developing and implementing supply chain partnerships", *The International Journal of Logistics Management,* Vol. 7 No. 1, pp. 1-17.

Lau, H. and Idris, M. (2001), "The soft foundation of the critical success factors on TQM implementation in Malaysia", *The TQM Magazine*, Vol. 13 No. 1, pp. 51-60.

Lee, S.M. and Ebrahimpour, M. (1985) "An analysis of the Japanese quality control systems: implications for American manufacturing firms", *SAM Advanced Management Journal,* Vol. 50 No. 2, pp. 24-31.

Leiter, M. and Maslach, C. (2002), "Beating burn-out", *Human Resource Management International Digest,* Vol. 10 No. 1, pp. 6-9.

Levin, R. and Rubin, D. (1994), *Statistics for Management*, 6th ed., Prentice Hall, Englewood Cliffs, NJ.

Li, E., Zhao, X. and Lee, T.-S. (2001), "Quality management initiatives in Hong Kong's banking industry: a longitudinal study", *Total Quality Management*, Vol. 12 No. 4, pp. 451-68.

London, C. and Higgot, K. (1997), "An employee reward and recognition process", *The TQM Magazine*, Vol. 9 No. 5, pp. 328-35.

McAdam, R. (1996), "Developing an appropriate quality award for Northern Ireland", *Managing Service Quality*, Vol. 6 No. 2, pp. 22-5.

Mathews, B., Ueno, A., Periera, Z., Silva, G., Kekale, T., Repka, M. (2001b), "Quality training, findings from a European survey", *The TQM Magazine*, Vol. 13 No. 1, pp. 61-8.

Mathews, B., Ueno, A., Kekale, T., Repka, M., Periera, Z. and Silva, G. (2001a), "Quality training: needs and evaluation – findings from a European survey", *Total Quality Management*, Vol. 12 No. 4, pp. 483-90.

Martinez-Lorente, A., Dewhurst, F.and Dale, B. (1998), "Total quality management: origins and evolution of the term", *The TQM Magazine*, Vol. 10 No. 6, pp. 378-86.

McAdam, R. and McKeown, M. (1999), "Life after ISO 9000: an analysis of the impact of ISO 9000 and total quality management on small business in Northern Ireland", *Total Quality Management*, Vol. 10 No. 2, pp. 229-41.

McAdam, R. and Kelly, M. (2002), "A business excellence approach to generic benchmarking in SMEs", *Benchmarking: An International Journal*, Vol. 9 No. 1, pp. 7-27.

Mehra, S., Sirias, D. and Hoffman, J. (1998), "A critical analysis of total quality mangement implementation", *International Journal of Applied Quality Management*, Vol.1 No.1, pp.12-26.

Moren-Lozon, M.D. and Peris, F.J. (1998), "Strategic approach, organisational design and quality management", *International Journal of Quality Science*, Vol.3 No. 4, pp. 328-47.

Munro, R. (2000), "Linking six sigma with QS-9000", *Quality Progress*, May, pp. 47-53.

Nakata, C. (2002), "Activating the marketing concept in a global context: an MNC country managers' perspective", *International Marketing Review*, Vol. 19 No. 1, pp. 39-64.

Nadkarni, R.A. (1995), "A not-so-secret receipe for successful TQM", *Quality Progress*, Vol. 28 No. 11, pp. 91-6.

Oakland, J S. (1993), *Total Quality Management*, Butterworth-Heinemann, Oxford.

Oakland, J. (2000), *Total Quality Management – Text with Cases*, 2nd ed., Butterworth-Heinemann, Oxford.

Oakland, J.S. and Porter, L. (1994), *Cases in Total Quality Management*, Butterworth-Heinemann, Oxford.

Olian, J.D. and Rynes, S.L. (1991), "Making total quality work: aligning organisational processes, performance measures, and stakeholders", *Human Resource Management,* Vol. 30 No. 3, pp. 303-33.

Oliver, R. (1999), "Whence consumer loyalty?", *Journal of Marketing*, Vol. 63, pp. 33-44.

Peters, T. (1987), *Thriving on Chaos – Handbook for a Managment Revolution*, Macmillan, Basingstoke.

Peters, T. and Austin, N. (1985), *A Passion for Excellence – The Leadership Difference*, Collins, London.

Peters, T. and Waterman, R. (1982), *In Search of Excellence: Lessons from America's Best Run Companies*, Harper & Row, Cambridge, MA.

Porter, L.J. and Parker, A.J. (1993), "Total quality management – the critical success factors", *Total Quality Management*, Vol. 4 No. 1, pp. 13-22.

Pun, K.-F. (2001), "Cultural influences on total quality management adoption in Chinese enterprises: an empirical study", *Total Quality Management*, Vol.12 No. 3, pp. 323-42.

Quazi, H.A. and Padibjo, S.R. (1998), "A journey toward total quality management through ISO 9000 certification – a study on small and medium-sized enterprises in Singapore", *International Journal of Quality & Reliability Management*, Vol. 15, pp. 489-508.

Ramirez, C. and Loney, T. (1993), "Baldrige award winners identify the essential activities of a successful quality process", *Quality Digest*, January, pp. 38-40.

Rao, A., Carr, L., Dambolena, I., Kopp, R., Martin, J., Rafii, F. and Schlesinger, P. (1996), *Total Quality Management: A Cross-functional Perspective*, John Wiley and Sons, New York.

Rao, S., Solis, L. and Raghunathan, T. (1999), "A framework for international quality management research: development and validation of a measurement instrument", *Total Quality Management*, Vol. 10 No. 7, pp. 1047-75.

Russell, S. (2000), "ISO-9000: 2000 and the EFQM excellence model: competition or co-operation?, *Total Quality Management*, Vol. 11 Nos 4/5 and 6, pp. 657-65.

Salegna, G. and Fazel, F. (2000), "Obstacles to implementing quality"*, Quality Progress,* July, pp. 53-7.

Saraph, J.V., Benson, P.G. and Schroeder, R.G. (1989), "An instrument for measuring the critical factors of quality management", *Decision Sciences*, Vol. 20 No. 4, pp. 810-29.

Shipley, D. (2002), "Destination: ISO 9000", *Quality Progress*, Vol. 35 No. 3, pp. 32-9.

Simpson, M. (2000), "A practical approach to benchmarking in three service industries", *Total Quality Management*, Vol. 11 Nos 4/5 and 6, pp. 623-30.

Sinclair, D.A.C. (1994), "Total quality- based performance measurement: an empirical study of best practice", unpublished PhD thesis, University of Bradford.

Sinclair, D. and Zairi, M. (2000), "Performance measurement: a critical analysis of the literature with respect to total quality management", *International Journal of Management Review,* Vol. 2 No. 2, pp. 145-68.

Sinclair, D. and Zairi, M. (2001), "An empirical study of key elements of total quality-based performance measurement systems: a case study approach in service industry"*, Total Quality Management*, Vol. 12 No. 4, pp. 535-50.

Smith, S. (1994), *The Quality Revolution*, Management Books 2000 Ltd, Didcot, UK.

Spring, M., McQuater, R., Swift, K., Dale, B. and Booker, J. (1998), "The use of quality tools and techniques in product introduction: an assessment methodology", *The TQM Magazine*, Vol. 10 No. 1, pp. 45-50.

Stahan, J. (2002), "Transition ISO 9000:2000", *Quality Progress*, Vol. 3 No. 3, pp. 27-30.

Stenberg, A. and Deleryd, M. (1999), "Implementation of statistical process control and process capability studies: requirements or free will?", *Total Quality Management,* Vol. 10 Nos 4/5, pp. 439-46.

Stone, C. and Banks, M. (1997), "The use of customer- and employee-based performance measures of *The Times* top 500 companies", *The TQM Magazine*, Vol. 9 No. 2, pp. 152-8.

Sureshchandar, G.S., Chandrasekharan Rajendran and Anantharaman (2001), "A conceptual model for total quality management in service organisations", *Total Quality Management*, Vol.12 No. 3, pp. 343-63.

Tamimi, N. (1998), "A second order factor analysis of critical TQM factors", *International Journal of Quality and Reliability Management*, Vol. 14 No. 1, pp. 71-9.

Tamimi, N. and Sebastianelli, R. (1998), "The barriers to total quality management", *Quality Progress*, June, pp. 57-60.

Thakur (2002), "Nine reasons to switch to a single supplier system", *Quality Progress*, Vol. 35 No. 3, pp. 61-4.

Thiagarajan, T. (1996), "An empirical study of total quality management (TQM) in Malaysia: a proposed framework of generic application", University of Bradford, unpublished PhD thesis.

Thiagarajan, T., Zairi, M. and Dale, B. (2001), "A proposed model of TQM implementation based on an empirical study of Malaysian industry", *International Journal of Quality & Reliability Management*, Vol. 18 No. 3, pp. 289-306.

Thiagarajan, T. and Zairi, M. (1997a), "A review of total quality management in practice: understanding the fundamentals through examples of best practice applications, Part 1", *The TQM Magazine*, Vol. 9 No. 4, pp. 270-86.

Thiagarajan, T. and Zairi, M. (1997b), "A review of total quality management in practice: understanding the fundamentals through examples of best practice applications, Part 2", *The TQM Magazine*, Vol. 9 No. 5, pp. 344-56.

Thiagarajan, T. and Zairi, M. (1998), "An empirical analysis of critical factors of TQM: a proposed tool for self-assessment and benchmarking purposes", *Benchmarking for Quality Management & Technology*, Vol. 5 No. 4, pp. 291-303.

Thor, C. and Jarrett, J. (1999), "Benchmarking and reengineering: alternatives or partners?", *International Journal of Technology Management*, Vol. 17 No. 7-8, pp. 786-96.

Townsend, P.L. and Gebhardt, J.E. (1992), *Quality in Action*, John Wiley & Sons Ltd, New York.

Van der Wiele, T. and Brown, A. (1998), "Venturing down the TQM path for SMEs", *International Small Business Journal*, Vol. 16 No. 2, pp. 50-68.

Van der wiele, A. et al. (1996), "Self-assessment: a study of progress in Europe's leading organizations in quality management practices", *International Journal of Quality and Reliability Management*, Vol. 13 No. 1, pp. 84-104.

Westlund, A. and Lothgren, M. (2001), "The interactions between quality, productivity and economic performance: the case of Swedish pharmacies", *Total Quality Management*, Vol. 12 No. 3, pp. 385-96.

Whitford, B. and Bird, R, (1996), *The Pursuit of Quality*, Prentice Hall, Englewood Cliffs, NJ.

Wilkes, N. and Dale, B.G. (1998), "Attitude to self-assessment and quality awards: a study in small and medium-sized companies", *Total Quality Management*, Vol. 9 No. 8, pp. 731-9.

Williams, N. (1997), "ISO 9000 as a route to TQM in small to medium-sized enterprises: snake or ladder?", *The TQM Magazine*, Vol. 9 No. 1, pp. 8-13.

Wilkinson, A. (1992), "The other side of quality: 'soft' issues and the human resource dimension", *Total Quality Management*, Vol. 3 No. 3, pp. 323-9.

Winser, J. and Corney, W. (2001), "Comparing practices for capturing bank customer feedback: Internet versus traditional banking?", *Benchmarking: An International Journal*, Vol. 8 No. 3, pp. 240-50.

Wong, A. (2000), "Integrating supplier satisfaction with customer satisfaction", *Total Quality Management*, Vol. 11 Nos 4/5 and 6, pp. 427-32.

Wong, A. and Fung, P. (1999), "Total quality management in the construction industry in Hong Kong: a supply chain management perspective", *Total Quality Management*, Vol. 10 No. 2, pp. 199-208.

Wuagneux, D. (2002), "Quality from the inside out", *Quality Progress*, Vol. 35 No. 4, pp. 60-5.

Xie, M. and Goh T.N. (1999), "Statistical techniques for quality", *The TQM Magazine*, Vol. 11 No. 4, pp. 238-41.

Yusof, S. and Aspinwall, E. (2000), "Critical success factors in small and medium enterprises: survey results", *Total Quality Management*, Vol. 11 Nos 4/5 and 6, pp. 448-62.

Zairi, M. (1994), *Measuring Performance for Business Results*, Chapman & Hall, London.

Zairi, M. (1996), *Benchmarking for Best Practice*, Butterworth-Heinemann, Oxford.

Zairi, M. (1999a), "Managing excellence: leadership", *The TQM Magazine*, Vol. 11 No. 4, pp. 215-20.

Zairi, M. (1999b), "Managing excellence: policy and strategy", *The TQM Magazine*, Vol. 11 No. 2, pp. 74-9.

Zairi, M. (2000), "Managing customer satisfaction: a best practice perspective", *The TQM Magazine*, Vol. 12 No. 6, pp. 389-494.

Zairi, M. and Youssef, M.A. (1995), "Benchmarking critical factors for TQM: part I: theory and foundation", *Benchmarking for Quality Management & Technology*, Vol. 2 No. 1, pp. 5-20.

Zhang, Z. (2000), "Developing a model of quality management methods and evaluating their effects on business performance", *Total Quality Management*, Vol. 11 No. 1, pp. 129-37.

Zhang, Z., Waszink, A. and Wijingaard, J. (2000), "An instrument for measuring TQM implementation for Chinese manufacturing companies", *International Journal of Quality and Reliability Management*, Vol. 17 No. 7, pp. 730-55.

Zhu, Z. and Shenerman, L. (1999), "A comparison of quality programmes: total quality management and ISO 9000", *Total Quality Management*, Vol. 10 No.2, pp. 291-7.

Zink, K.J. (1995), "Total quality management and people management" in Kanji, G.K. (Ed.), *Total Quality Management: Proceedings of the First World Congress*, Chapman& Hill, London.

Chapter 1
The quality improvement continuum: an integrative approach

Continuous improvement: what is it?

This wide ranging philosophy has several meanings and can be applied in different contexts. It is very often referred to as the approach adopted to improve the management of key activities and tasks and thereby enhancing productivity and performance. Others describe it as a "philosophy" of continuous learning, creativity and innovation. There are perhaps three fundamental points to bear in mind when referring to continuous improvement (CI):

1. As stated, this approach is a continuous one and as such the gains and improvements achieved are relative ones and not absolute measures.
2. Continuous improvement does not depend on specialists but rather is a corporate approach which very much relies on wider involvement of employees at all levels.
3. Continuous improvement impacts on behavioural aspects and is geared towards changing people's mindsets and cultural settings.

However we wish to define it, the philosophy of continuous improvement or Kaizen as it is known in Japan, has to be linked to the organisational system and its key constituents:

- policy;
- process;
- people;
- performance.

As Figure 1.1 illustrates, the organisational system and its dynamic functioning depend on the inter-play between enabling factors in order to achieve optimum performance. Continuous improvement is the "envelope" which ensures that each of the four Ps described can be optimised and that the integration and synergy levels built are capable of enhancing overall corporate performance.

A sustainable philosophy of continuous improvement cannot be achieved through a "bolting-on" approach to hierarchical structures and functional settings. As Table 1.1 illustrates, based on the Japanese experience, continuous improvement depends on:

- being driven from a top-down perspective with good vision and strategic direction;
- using CI as a means for achieving corporate goals and key objectives;
- bringing about the most appropriate transformational and necessary changes in order to achieve the desired gain;
- building-in enabling systems and processes;
- educating all employees on problem-solving tools and the meaning of continuous improvement;
- linking continuous improvement to employee development and performance assessment;

- locating a bottom-up performance perspective to change behaviour.

It is therefore important to recognise that at the heart of continuous improvement is the word organisational system and the key processes which make it function.

Understanding organisations as systems

The work on understanding organisations as systems is not new and indeed writers such as Ashby (1965), Beer (1981) and Cluckland (1981) are well known in this field. A definition of a system found in Povey (1997) describes the latter as:

> A set of interactive components that transform inputs and has outputs, and is distinguished from its external environment by a boundary.

Povey (1997) suggests the following list of key characteristics found to be common amongst all types of systems:
- A system has inputs.
- A system does something (there are outputs).
- Addition or removal of a component changes the system.
- Inclusion of a component affects the component.
- A system has merged properties (the whole is greater than the sum of the parts).
- A system has a boundary.
- A system has an environment (outside the boundary) that affects it.
- Someone owns the system.

The organisational system is improved through the management of processes and sub-processes as depicted by Figure 1.2.

A key contribution made in the understanding of organisations as systems is by Dr Edward Deming.

Figure 1.1 The concept of business process management

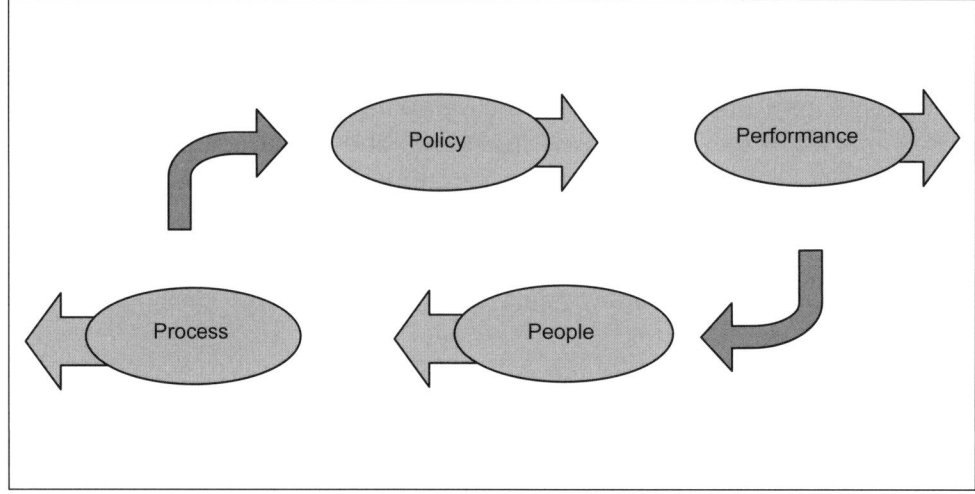

Table 1.1 The hierarchy of kaizen linked to the Japanese model

Management level	Kaizen	Japanese model
Top management	Determined to introduce kaizen as a strategy	TQC
	Provide support and allocate resources	Security/flexibility, job rotation
	Policy for kaizen and cross-functional goals	Cross-functional/matrix design, TQC
	Realise kaizen goals through policy deployment and audits	Detail design of communication system, TQC
	Build systems procedures and structures conducive to kaizen	Detail design of communication system, behavioural approach, TQC
Middle management and staff	Deploy and implement kaizen goals as directed by top management through policy deployment and cross-functional management	TQC, detail design of the communication system
	Use kaizen in functional capabilities	TQC
	Establish, maintain and upgrade standards	No individual bonus, behavioural approach
	Make employees kaizen conscious through intensive training programmes	TQC, union experience, behavioural approach
	Help employees develop skills and tools for problem solving	Ambiguity of roles, union experience, behavioural approach, TQC
Supervisors	Use kaizen in functional roles	TQC
	Formulate plans for kaizen and provide guidance to workers	Unions, detail design of communication system, ratio supervisor:worker
	Improve communication with workers and sustain high morale	Unions, detail design of the communication system
	Support small group activities (TQC) and the individual suggestion scheme	No individual bonus, behavioural approach, TQC
	Introduce discipline in the workshop	TQC, behavioural approach
	Provide kaizen suggestions	TQC, suggestion scheme
Workers	Engage in the kaizen through the suggestion scheme and small group activity	No individual bonus, detail design of the communication system, behavioural approach, TQC, suggestion scheme
	Practise discipline in the workshop	TQC, job rotation, behavioural approach
	Engage in continuous self-development to become better problem solvers	Ambiguity of roles, security/flexibility, behavioural approach
	Enhance skills and job performance expertise with cross-education	Security/flexibility, unions in company, behavioural approach, job rotation

Deming's contribution to systems thinking

Dr Edward Deming is perhaps the key father of the ideas of continuous improvement and organisations functioning as systems. His philosophy, which will be explained in later sections, is very simple:

- Treat workers as partners rather than adversaries.
- Encourage them to use their minds as well as their hands.
- Concentrate on quality production rather than quantity.

Deming has had such an important and significant impact on modern management thinking that following his death on 20 December 1993, *The Times* newspaper wrote the following tribute about him:

> If there was ever a prophet without honour in his town, country, it was Edward Deming (*The Times*, Friday, 24 December 1993).

Figure 1.2 An effective process

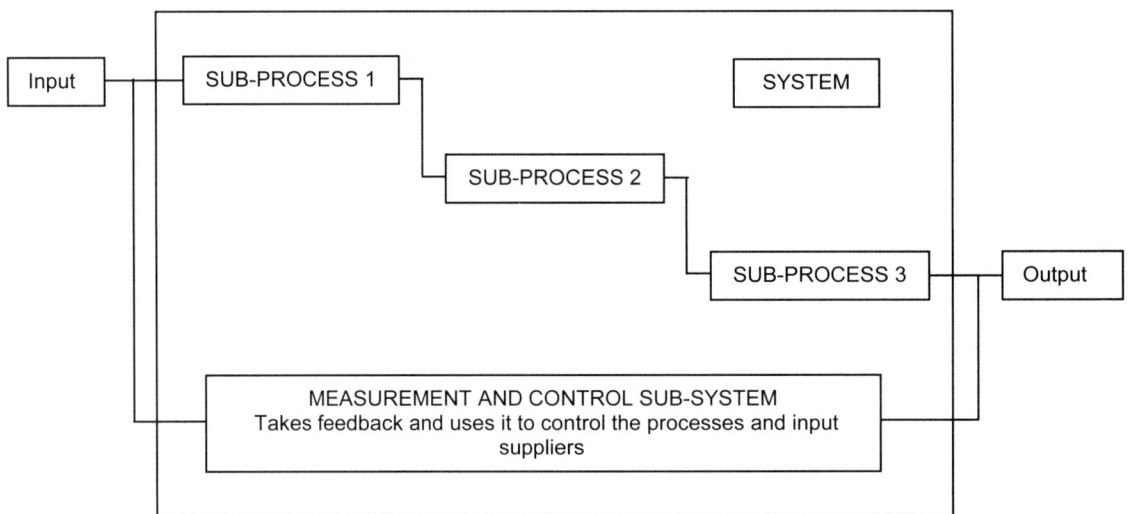

Deming views a business organisation being structured as a system whose sole purpose is to delight the customer. According to Deming, delighting the customer will not come just from a clear understanding of their needs, but rather through continually improving both the system's processes and product. The whole purpose is therefore to optimise the entire system and not some of its components. A system according to Deming (British Deming Association, 1992a) is:

> A network of functions or activities (sub-processes, stages) within an organisation that work together for the aim of the organisation.

In fact systems are only one part of Dr Deming's Four Core Values of Profound Knowledge (Figure 1.3).

> Deming goes on to say (British Deming Association, 1992b):
>
> > A system must possess an aim, and this aim is a value-judgement. Without an aim, there is no system. If you wish, you may call it a process – no matter.

He then says:

> Management of a system is action based on prediction. Rational prediction requires systematic learning and comparison of predictions of short-term and long-term results from possible courses of action.

Deming is reported to have suggested the flow diagram of an organisation as a system, as shown in Figure 1.4. Deming has stated in "The New Economics" (Treite, 1995) that:

> The flow diagram ... was the spark that in 1950 and onward turned Japan around. It displayed to top management and to engineers a system of production. The Japanese had knowledge, great knowledge, but it was in bits and pieces, uncoordinated. This flow diagram directed their

knowledge and efforts into a system of production, geared to the market – namely, prediction of needs of customers.

Essentially, and according to Deming's thinking, the systems view of an organisation means that:
- The organisation has horizontal focus on the customer and the flow of communication and activity is for problem solving and value adding.
- The linkages between various activities are based on corporate goals and synergy levels.
- Work process design is not to keep the individual employees "busy" but rather to fulfil organisational objectives both in the short and long term.

Underlining Dr Deming's thinking is that all endeavours need to focus on process and process optimisation.

Process
In relation to processes, Deming (1986) states that:
> A diagram of any process will divide work into stages. These stages as a whole form a process. The stages are not individual entities, each running at maximum profit – work comes into any stage, changes state, and moves on to the next stage. Any stage has a customer, the next stage. The final stage will send product or service to the ultimate customer.

He also states that: "Every activity, every job is a part of a process".

Optimisation
Optimisation of a system involves elimination of wasteful, undesirable variation. Inability to distinguish between variations caused by the system and those due to the people involved in the system prevents optimisation. Indeed, it may well make things worse (British Deming Association, 1992a).

Deming stresses optimisation of processes and systems in all of his talks. Together with Dr Walter Stewart, they have tried to convey the message that:
- understanding of variation due to common and special causes; and
- improvement of processes

are at the heart of continuous improvement activity.

Unfortunately in many cases senior managers tend to view variation from a "judgemental perspective" and performance is viewed in absolute terms either as good or bad. Deming argues that this approach does nothing to improve processes and is a way of looking for scapegoats and an approach to assign blame.

The use of statistical control tools, and particularly SPC and control charts, is a way of stabilising and optimising processes and removing the focus from individuals and focusing on process and system improvement.

Figure 1.3 The core values, cornerstones and 14 points

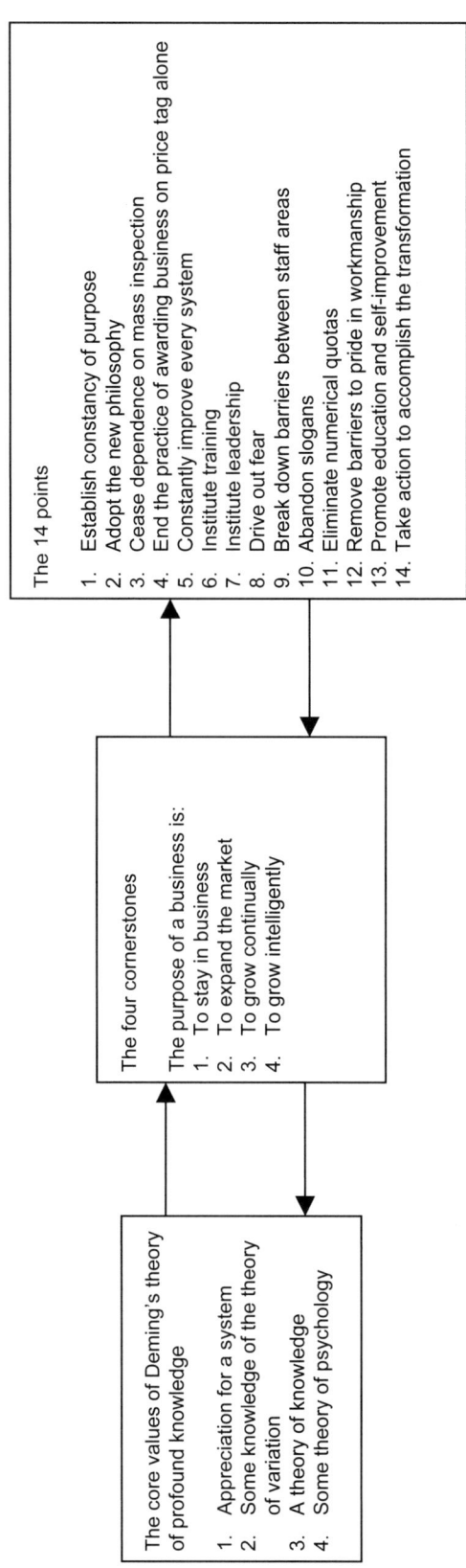

Figure 1.4 Organisation viewed as a system

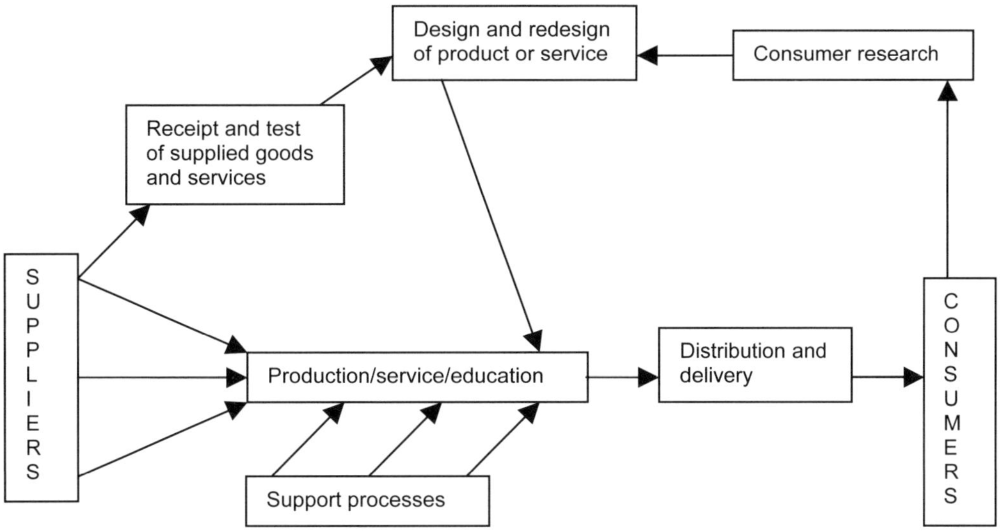

The Deming problem solving cycle

The Deming cycle was first originated by its founder, Walter Stewart. It was the Japanese who renamed it as Deming's cycle back in 1950. The cycle used to be referred to as the P-D-C-A cycle (Plan-Do-Check-Act) and in 1990, Dr Deming renamed it the P-D-S-A (Plan-Do-Study-Act) because: he argued that learning and innovation take place at that stage and, before acting or suggesting how problems could possibly be improved, people need to analyse and understand the problem, gather data and look at possible solutions and alternatives.

As Figure 1.5 illustrates, the whole ethos of the Deming cycle is on innovation and improvement driven by change.

The Deming philosophy, supported by other gurus, is based on the use of statistical tools and techniques, focusing on the process, involving and recognising people and their contributions. These aspects are the key ingredients for effective leadership.

To a question on how much did Dr Stewart's thinking influence him, Dr Deming replied:

> Continually . . . . He provided the means to joy in learning; how to say it; how to think it; how to rank ideas; how to change emphasis. He led me to realise the importance of intrinsic motivation. Give the individual a chance, the way it was years ago. Everything we have has come from positions of economic security, where everybody is free to be responsible to himself. We must learn to think and grow; we must engage in a never-ending cycle of learning (British Deming Association, 1992a).

At the heart of the never-ending cycle of learning comes a set of rules to which managers should subscribe. These are derived from Tribus (1993) and are detailed as follows. Every manager should be competent in elementary statistics:

- process flow charting;
- fishbone diagrams;
- run charts;
- histograms;
- Pareto diagrams;
- scatter diagrams;
- control charts;
- elementary design of experiments.

Figure 1.5 The PDSA cycle

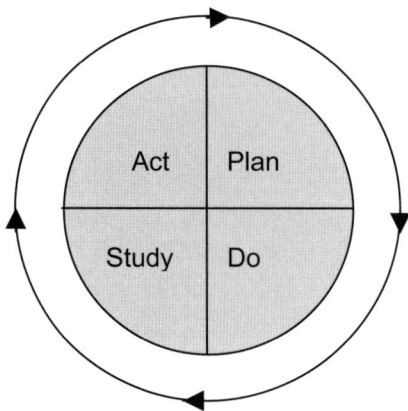

Every manager should learn how to:
- Recognise, define, describe, diagnose and improve the systems for which he or she is responsible.
- Diagnose the variability of a system and decide which variations are due to special causes and thus require special action and which are due to common causes and will therefore require a change in the system's design and operation.
- Lead teams of people from different educational levels in problem identification, data gathering, data analysis and the generation of proposals for solution, implementation and testing.
- Diagnose the behaviour of humans and distinguish those difficulties which are due to the variations in human abilities (15 per cent) and those which are caused by the system (85 per cent) (Juran's rule).

Although in most cases the knowledge and usage of elementary statistical tools are more than adequate, there are many other tools that can be used for a wide variety of purposes. In fact many authors argue that the difference between high performing and low performing organisations is very often due to the extent of reliance on tools and techniques of quality management.

In a recent study comparing the use of quality tools in high quality and low quality organisations (Romel *et al.*, 1996), the authors concluded that the elementary SPC tools are used by all concerned, while other tools tended to be used more in high performing organisations (Figure 1.6). The authors concerned stated that:

> The outstanding quality that helps companies achieve top rates of growth and return is a management leadership task. It entails setting, communicating, and operationalizing ambitions, objectives, redesigning business along the core processes, integrating customers and suppliers, and above all mobilising the workforce. It is not easy to do these things well, but some sophisticated quality tools can help. Managers ignore or abuse them at their peril.

Making business process improvement happen: what does it take?
Perhaps in order to answer this difficult question, one needs to look at the experience of the Japanese and why they managed to build world class competitiveness using the kaizen management philosophy? The three fundamental aspects which kaizen preaches are:

1. customer focus through waste elimination;
2. employee involvement in problem solving; and
3. process orientation using just in time techniques.

There is no "magic wand" or "Japanese miracle" as some would like to believe. It requires shear hard work, good discipline, relentless efforts to create customer satisfaction, teamwork, management by fact and, more importantly, respect for people.

Figure 1.6 Intensive use of QA tools in the development process

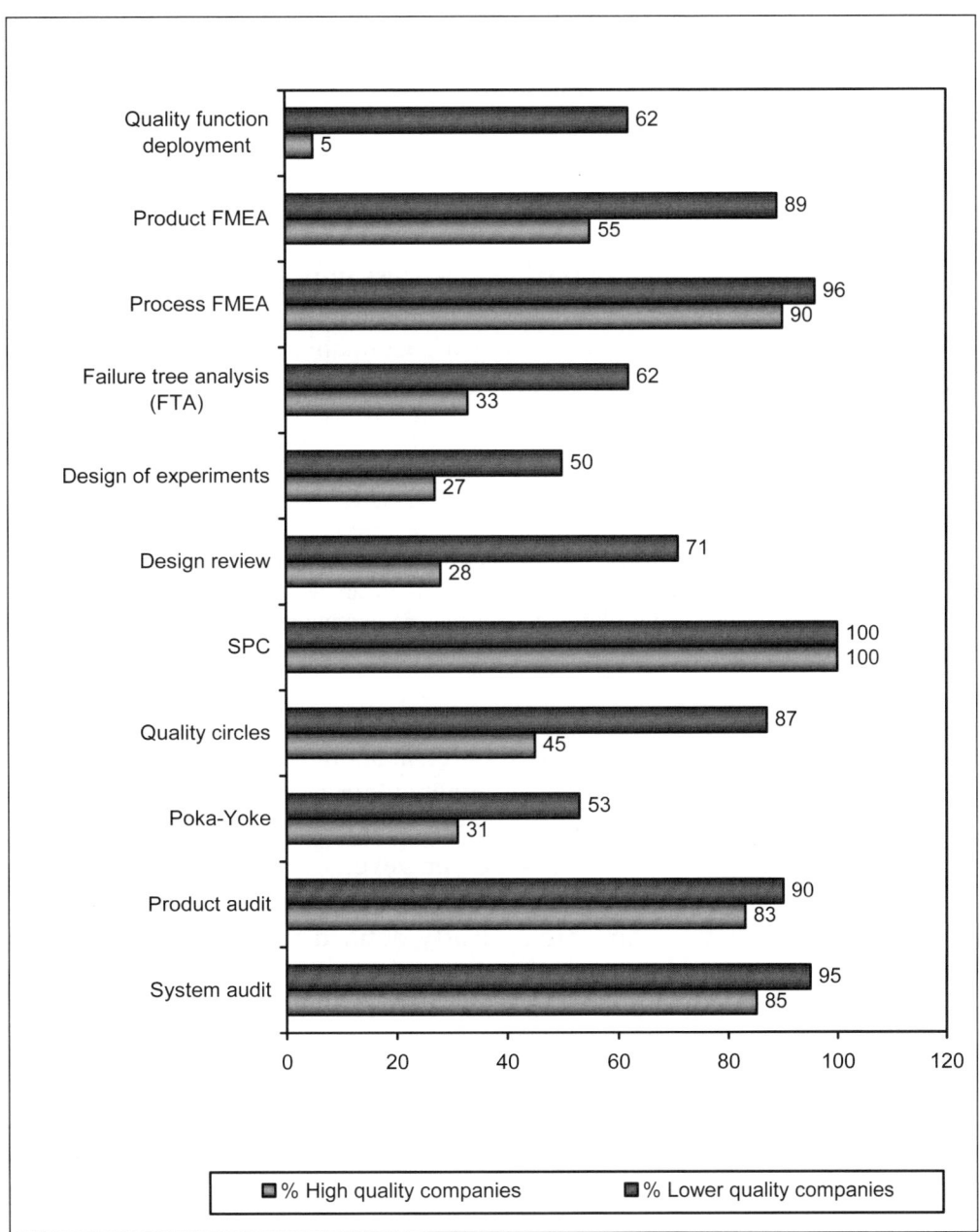

The following list summarises the Japanese management philosophy extremely well (British Deming Association, 1995) and answers very eloquently the previous question on how to create a culture of continuous improvement:
- Leadership from the top.
- Thirst for knowledge and new technology.
- What we all have now is wonderful – but let us, together, find something different and better.
- Things are not black or white, but grey.
- Logic alone is not enough: human nature must be considered.
- Never make "hard decisions", rather create a choice-generation process
- Excessive energy is not burned up in overly egocentric behaviour.
- Less emphasis on the cult of the individual.
- We are in this for the long haul – time itself is not the issue.
- Continuing self-development and self-fulfilment.
- No overt confrontation, but long deliberation for consensus and harmony – and then rapid, effective implementation.
- Co-operation between all groups.

The essentiality of an integrated approach in business process improvement
To support the arguments presented in the previous section, it becomes necessary to examine the issues that can "make or break" as far as creating a sustainable culture of continuous improvement. The key issue of continuous improvement is one of mindset rather than structural and technological changes and enhancements. The various resolutions, which took place in recent years and were based on the latter options, have all been marred with problems. Perhaps at the top of that list is the re-engineering and radical change process revolution. As Hatten and Rosenthal (1999) conclude:

> Some companies unrealistically saw re-engineering as an almost magical silver bullet, capable of solving all their problems in one fell swoop. Most simply failed to appreciate that achieving process-based cost, quality and efficiency gains ultimately depends on continuous effort – i.e. they failed to appreciate that re-engineering, like cost control, is essentially a social process.

The real shift in paradigm that will lead to a process-based culture driven by an ethos of continuous improvement is one which has to be based on changes in management behaviour. A slight shift in the latter will induce a radical change in behaviour at the lower levels and so on. Process improvement comes through conviction and belief in the need for tackling problems and innovating for the customer. It does not however come through the superimposition of technological and structural change on people with opposing views and beliefs. Steering continuous improvement has to come from clearly defined vision/mission and key objectives, their effective deployment and through the regularity of reviews and actions. Without an organic process at the strategic level, a culture of continuous improvement and continuous learning cannot be developed. It will create what might be referred to as "a misfiring principle", a hit and miss approach.

Witcher and Butterworth (1999), in relation to the use of Hoshin Kanri (Hoshin means direction; Kanri means deployment/administration/management), argue that: "TQM provides the means and discipline for self-management at any level of management, not just for the management of an operational process in daily work . . . daily pressures must be managed in such a way as to ensure that they are under control". Hatten and Rosenthal (1999) on the other hand, refer to "organisational slack" thrown away with waste. A practice attributed to the lack of taking a strategic perspective, short-sightedness, short termism and lack of commitment to process improvement and continuous learning.

The argument for an integrated approach is a legitimate one and self-justifiable under the circumstances described in the previous paragraphs. The following points need to be considered:

- Whatever organisations do in the future, it has got to be defined clearly at the strategic level, well articulated and effectively communicated.
- Operational performance in all of its facets will continue to be the most critical aspect of evaluating organisational behaviour. It is, however, futile to review performance in isolation from strategic imperatives and key business objectives. An integration of strategic thinking with organisational performance is thus very critical.
- Continuous improvement is not the outcome of various "bursts" of activity and will not be sustainable if it remains project-focused rather than process-based.
- The key outcome from continuous improvement has to be clear value to the customer, through optimising process performance (i.e. ensuring there is no slack) and eliminating waste.
- The key challenge for instigating a culture of continuous improvement and continuous learning is a "social" one, people-related, rather than a technical one. An evolutionary approach based on paradigm shifts in thinking, believing and doing is a real pre-requisite.

An integrative approach is therefore not a question of choice but rather a necessary evil. Performance and business results have in themselves got to present an integrated picture that is stakeholder orientated. They also have to be based on process orientation, derived from continuous improvement activity, using resources available to the full (slack elimination) and, more importantly, they have to be driven by the social fabric of the organisation, i.e. people who work through belief and conviction. Finally, an integrated approach has to be based on good vision, strong leadership and clear strategic thinking.

References

Ashby, W.R. (1965), *Introduction to Cybernetics*, Chapman & Hall, London.

Beer, S. (1981), *Brains of the Firm*, John Wiley, Chichester, 1981.

British Deming Association (1992a), *A System of Profound Knowledge*, London.

British Deming Association (1992b), *A Perspective on Dr Deming's Theory of Profound Knowledge*, London.

British Deming Association (1995), *The Japanese and Business Transformation*, London.

Cluckland, P. (1981), *Systems Thinking, Systems Practice*, John Wiley, Chichester.

Deming, W.E. (1986), *Out of the Crisis*, Cambridge University Press, USA.

Hatten, K.J. and Rosenthal, S.R. (1999), "Managing the process-centred enterprise", *LongRange Planning*, Vol. 32 No. 3, pp. 293-310.

Povey, B.F. (1997), "Business process improvement", Master of Philosophy Thesis, University of Brighton.

Romel, Günter *et al.* (1996), *Quality Pays*, MacMillan Press Ltd, London.

Tveite, M.D. (1995), *The Deming Philosophy, New Ways to Think About the World*, British Deming Association, London.

Tribus, M. (1993), *The Germ Theory of Management*, British Deming Association, London.

Witcher, B. and Butterworth, R. (1999), "Hoshin Kanri: how Xerox manages", *Long Range Planning*, Vol. 32 No. 3, pp. 323-32.

Chapter 2
The process of self-assessment

Introduction

The process of self-assessment presents a spectrum of alternatives and opportunities from which individual organisations can choose. Although there are clear steps that could be adhered to (Figure 2.1), there is scope for using self-assessment to improve communications, set targets, develop action plans, etc. On the whole, the process of self-assessment is an opportunity for engaging people at all levels and for drawing attention to the potential for improvement and advancement.

Figure 2.1 Self-assessment process

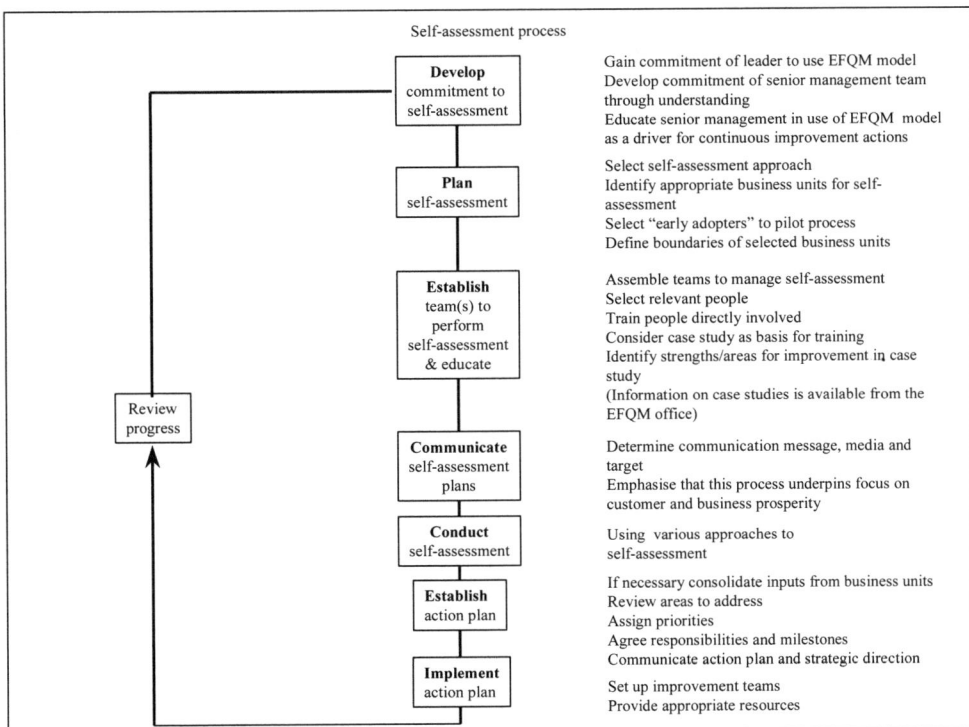

Self-assessment seeks to establish some of the following:
- What is the overall state of business performance?
- What is the balance between enabler criteria and results?
- What are the key areas of strength and which are compatible with world class standards?
- What are the key areas of concern, which need to be optimised and improved for world class standards to ensue?
- What is the baseline performance of our organisation and how do we compare against best-in-class?

- How pervasive is the commitment to TQM and continuous improvement within our organisation?

Whatever the purpose of using self-assessment, the process altogether is very versatile and can be applied flexibly and generically.

Key elements of the self-assessment process

Self-assessment aims to check an organisation's state of progress against a list of excellence criteria. The method used looks at:
- approach;
- deployment; and
- results.

Approach

This area considers how organisations address each criteria and sub-criteria of self-assessment models, in terms of:
- Appropriateness of the methods to the requirements.
- Effectiveness of use of methods and degree to which the approach:
  ○ is systematic, integrated and consistently applied;
  ○ embodies evaluation/improvement cycles; and
  ○ is based on data and information that are objective and reliable.
- Evidence of innovation. This could include significant and effective adaptations of approaches used in other applications or types of businesses.

Deployment

This assesses the extent to which an organisation's approach is applied to all requirements of individual criteria and sub-criteria. The factors used to evaluate deployment include the following:
- Use of the approach in addressing business and item requirements.
- Use of the approach by all appropriate process, units and sections.

Results

This assesses the outcomes of achieving the purposes given in each criteria and sub-criteria. The factors used to evaluate results include:
- current performance levels;
- performance levels relative to appropriate comparisons and/or benchmarks;
- rate, breadth and importance of performance improvements; and
- demonstration of sustained improvement and/or sustained high-level performance.

The linkages between approach, deployment and results are illustrated in Figure 2.2. Each aspect answers the questions on:
- What you do.
- Where you do it.
- How well you do it.

Table 2.1 describes the guidelines for approach and deployment and Table 2.2 illustrates scoring guidelines for the results section.

Figure 2.2 Linkage of approach, deployment and results

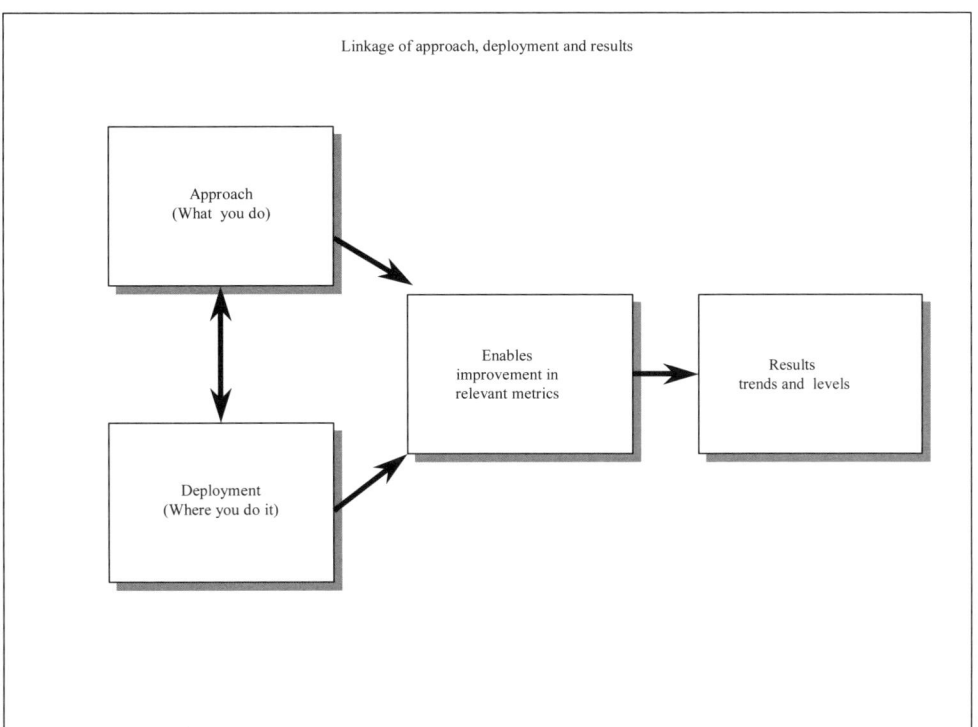

Approaches to self-assessment

There are different types of self-assessment methods with different levels of rigour and complexity associated with them:

- An award simulation approach – requires the preparation of a full document reflecting practices and performances of a business entity in all aspects of management.
- A pro forma approach – less rigorous, single sheet per individual item, using areas of strengths and areas with potential improvement (see example, Figure 2.3, from MBNQA guidelines).
- Workshop approach – to actively involve management teams who would be responsible for gathering the data and presenting the evidence gathered to peers, to achieve consensus and move forward with action plans.
- Questionnaire approach – simple method, as Tables 2.3 and 2.4 demonstrate. An easy way to engage a wider number of people, to create alignment and focus on the most critical areas of the business which need attention.
- Peer involvement approach – to engage employees of a more junior status in formally assessing business units and pulling together a report, similar to the award simulation type of approach.

A matrix chart approach

This is an approach which is based on developing an individual organisation's own profile against a check list of performance levels. This method was developed by British Gas in the UK. The whole approach is referred to as the business improvement matrix. It is used for the following objectives:

- to provide a simple measurement tool which would give a regular snap-shot of performance concerning continuous improvement within a business unit;

- to develop a system which allows a comparison based on nationally recognised criteria which could be used to provide a less introverted view of performance;
- to offer a simple, yet complete, step by step framework to guide managers in the formulation of a plan for the implementation of continuous improvement within each business unit;
- to highlight any "gaps" identified in the planning or implementation process; and
- to encourage all "gaps" to be analysed, understood and the planning of improvements to be modified to ensure a convergent approach towards business improvement.

The business improvement matrix enablers are explained in Table 2.5 and the expected results in Table 2.6. These criteria represent progress on the ladder of excellence.

Table 2.1 Guidelines for approach and deployment

Score %	Approach	Deployment
0	Anecdotal, no systematic approach evident	Anecdotal, undocumented
10	Beginning of a systematic approach is somewhat evident	Isolated units are using quality practices; most are not (key requirements of the item not addressed or not practised by major components)
20	Generally reactive approach to problems. A partially systematic approach is evident to a limited extent. Still reactive to problems	Some units are using quality practices; many are not (key requirements of the item not addressed or not practised by many components)
40	Systematic approach is fully developed Emphasis on prevention. No systematic evaluation or improvement system is in place Some fact-based decision processes are evident. Random improvements may have been made	A few minor gaps in deployment exist (some minor requirements of the item not addressed or not practised by some components). Many work units are in the early stages of development
60	Systematic approach is fully developed. Fact-based improvement system includes at least one evaluation and improvement cycle completed, including some systematic refinement	No major gaps in deployment exist (a few minor requirements of the item not addressed or not practised by a few components). A few work units may still be in the early stages of development
70	Fact-based, integrated improvement system is fully developed. Some systematic evaluation and improvement cycles and refinements are evident	No major gaps in deployment, with many work units in the middle to advanced stages of development (overall requirements of the item are addressed and practised by most components)
80	Fact-based, integrated improvement system is fully developed. Several systematic evaluation and improvement cycles and refinements are evident	No major gaps in deployment, with most work units in the middle to advanced stages of development (overall requirements of the item are addressed and practised by all components)
90	Fact-based, integrated improvement system is fully developed and systematically refined through several evaluation and improvement cycles. Some innovative refinements are evident	No major gaps in deployment, with most work units in the advanced stages of development (overall requirements of the item are addressed and practised by all components)
100	Fact-based, integrated improvement system is fully developed and systematically refined through several evaluation and improvement cycles. Substantial innovative refinements are evident	Approach is fully deployed to all work units with no gaps in deployment. All work units are in the advanced stages of deployment (all requirements of the item are addressed and practised by all components)

Table 2.2 Guidelines for scoring results

Score %	Scoring results
0	No results or poor results in areas reported
10	Data not reported for most areas of importance to the applicant's key business requirements. Limited positive results and trends are evident for the results that are reported
20	Data not reported for many to most areas of importance to the applicant's key business requirements. Some positive results and a few trends are evident for the results that are reported
30	Data not reported for many areas of importance to the applicant's key business requirements. Some positive results and some improvement trends are evident for the results that are reported
40	Data are reported for most key areas of importance to the applicant's key business requirements. Positive trends are reported for many areas of importance to the applicant's key business requirements. No significant adverse trends exist
50	Data are reported for most key areas of importance to the applicant's business requirements, with positive trends in most key areas important to the item and key business factors. Several trends are evaluated against benchmarks or comparisons, with good performance in some areas important to the item and key business factors
60	Data are reported for most key areas of importance to the applicant's business requirements, with no significant adverse trends. Good to very good performance in many key areas important to the item and key business factors. Many trends can be evaluated against benchmarks or comparisons
70	Data are reported for most to all key areas of importance to the applicant's business requirements. Good to excellent improvement trends reported in most key areas, with no adverse trends in key areas important to the item and key business factors. Many trends can be evaluated against benchmarks or comparisons
80	Data are reported for most to all key areas of importance to the applicant's business requirements. Very good to excellent improvement trends reported in most key areas, with no adverse trends in key area important to the item and key business factors. Most trends can be evaluated against benchmarks or comparisons
90	Excellent results and sustained positive trends (no adverse trends) in all key areas important to the item and key business factors. Most trends can be evaluated against benchmarks and comparisons
100	Excellent (world-class) results and strong sustained trends in all areas important to the item and key business factors. Strong evidence of benchmark leadership

Figure 2.3 Performance approach to self-assessment from MBNQA

Table 2.3 Self-assessment questionnaire – leadership

Question	Prompts
Are managers at all levels involved with the total quality effort in your organisation?	Do they take positive steps to: • Communicate with staff? • Act as role models, leading by example? • Make themselves accessible and listen to staff? • Give and receive training? • Demonstrate commitment to total quality?
Are managers/senior managers committed to the development of a consistent culture of quality?	Do they take positive steps to: • Be involved in assessing awareness of total quality? • Be involved in reviewing progress towards total quality? • Include commitment to and achievement to total quality in appraisal and promotion of staff at all levels?
Is there timely recognition of the efforts and successes of individuals and teams?	Are managers/senior managers involved in recognition: • At local, section or group level? • At divisional level? • At the level of the organisation? • Of groups outside the organisation, e.g. suppliers or customers?

An example of a business improvement matrix is shown in Figure 2.4. As far as the scoring is concerned, each box of the matrix is meant to indicate progress of individual business units/organisations, against best-in-class practices:
- Blank boxes – reflect lack of maturity, lack of systematic progress and no action plans being put in place.
- Dark grey boxes – partial implementation and deployment with partial results achieved.
- Light grey boxes – reflect full implementation and full deployment.

Each box in the matrix is scored as follows: blank boxes 0 points; dark grey boxes 0.5 points; and light grey boxes 1 point. The total for each criterion is multiplied by 0.5 to give a value, which is then multiplied by a weighting, as shown in Table 2.7, to give a final score. The weighting factors used for the criteria are based on the EFQM scoring approach.

The discipline of using the business improvement matrix is based on four stages:
1. briefing everyone involved in the assessment exercise;
2. individual rating;
3. consensus meeting – to achieve consensus and provide a more objective view of the entity being assessed; and
4. planning for improvement – discussions taking place during consensus process will form the basis of the development of an action plan.

Table 2.4 Self-assessment questionnaire – customer satisfaction

Question	Prompts
What is the customers' perception of your organisation's products, services and customer relationships?	Areas could include customers' perception of: • Capability of meeting product and service specifications • Reliability of products and services • Delivery performance • Price • Service level performance • Sales and technical support • Product training • Accessibility of key staff • Documentation • Responsiveness and flexibility in meeting customer needs • Complaints handling • Warranty and guarantee provisions • Development of new products and services
Has your organisation got additional measures for customer satisfaction?	Areas could include measurement of: • Repeat business • New or lost business • Defect, error and rejection rates • Delivery performance • Product or service consistency • Product durability and maintainability • Complaints handling • Letters of praise or thanks received • Corrective actions resulting from complaints • Warranty payments • Guarantee provisions made and used • Awards and accolades received • Publicity levels in the media

Other approaches to self-assessment: Westinghouse Electric Corporation

Introduction

Westinghouse Electric Corporation uses a total quality fitness review. This is a customised approach to self-assessment to enable organisations and business units to improve processes and performance. It is based on 12 conditions of excellence. The total quality fitness review contains all the key ingredients of business excellence. Westinghouse Electric Corporation has compared the criteria of their approach against those of the Malcolm Baldrige National Quality Award (MBNQA) and, as Figure 2.5 shows, there is total compatibility between the two systems.

Conditions of excellence

The 12 criteria used for identifying areas for improvement and to assess business performance are illustrated in Figure 2.6. The criteria reflect soft and hard aspects, customer and supplier perspectives and an insight into what is referred to as accountability (results, measurements). Table 2.8 describes each of the 12 criteria.

Best Practice Organisational Excellence

Table 2.5 Business improvement matrix – enablers

Step	Leadership	Policy and strategy	People management	Resources	Processes
10	All managers are proactive in sustaining continuous improvement	Mission and business policy statements cover the whole of the business and everyone understands them	All actions are directed towards realising the full potential of all employees	The organisation's resources are deployed effectively to meet policy and strategy objectives	Key value added processes are understood, formally managed and continuously updated
9	Managers are able to demonstrate their external involvement in the promotion of business improvement as a business philosophy based on their own experience	A process is in place to analyse competitor business strategy and modify unit plans as a result, in order to develop and sustain a competitive advantage	Employees are empowered to run their business processes	A process is in place to identify additional resources which can be used to strengthen competitive advantage	The existence of a formal quality management system can be demonstrated
8	Managers have a consistent approach towards radical continuous improvement across the unit	The policy and strategy processes are benchmarked	The human resource plan for the unit supports the company's policy and strategy for continuous improvement	A system is in place to review and modify the allocation of resources based on changing business needs	Process performance is demonstrably linked to customer requirements
7	The management team is proactive in valuing, recognising and rewarding all employees for continuous improvement	A process is in place to modify policy and strategy as a result of business and operational information	A process is in place to encourage creativity and innovation among employees	A process is in place for identifying, assessing and evaluating new technologies and their impact on the business	A mechanism is in place for developing and using appropriate measures which evaluate processes
6	Managers are visibly involved in the development and support of improvement teams and act as champions	A process is in place to assess the continuing relevance of plans as a result of business and operational information	Improvement teams have been established and supported	Systems are in place to track, monitor and review targeted areas to reduce all other waste including time and rework	The process results are reviewed and fed back into the improvement cycle
5	A process is in place to ensure managers are working with customers and suppliers, and that the effectiveness of this process can be assessed	The unit has policy statements and strategy that cover the nine business improvement matrix headings	Training and development needs are regularly reviewed for all employees and teams. Skill gaps relevant to personal aspirations and business needs are identified	Systems are in place to track, monitor and review targeted areas to reduce material waste	An improvement mechanism for key value added processes has been implemented
4	A process is in place to ensure managers are visibly involved as role models in business improvement within the unit. The effectiveness of the process is reviewed	A process exists and is renewed which promotes a clear understanding of the company's and the unit's mission, CSF and policy statements so that everyone knows and understands them	An effective appraisal system is in place for all employees	A process is in place to manage the dissemination of relevant information to customers, suppliers and employees	An improvement mechanism has been identified and targets for improvement have been set
3	A process is in place to ensure mutual understanding of business issues through two way communication both vertically and horizontally throughout the unit	A process is in place to collect relevant information to enable a review of CSFs and business plans	A process is in place for two way communication of business information within the unit	Partnerships with suppliers are being developed jointly to improve quality, delivery and performance	The effectiveness of existing key value added processes is assessed

(Continued)

2	A process is in place to create and continually increase an open awareness of business issues throughout the unit	A process is in place to collect relevant internal information to enable a review of CSFs and business plans	A public commitment has been given to develop all employees to achieve business goals	A process is in place to identify suppliers for key resources	Key value added processes are identified, flowcharted and/or documented Ownership is established
1	The management team has a process in place to develop their own awareness of the concepts of business improvement	The unit management team has developed a mission statement and CSFs	A process is in place to canvas and track employee opinions	A process is in place to identify what resources are available and how they are being deployed	The main processes within the business are identified

Table 2.6 Business improvement matrix – results

Step	Customer satisfaction	People satisfaction	Impact on society	Business results
10	There is a positive trend in customer satisfaction. Targets are being met. There are some benchmarking targets across the industry	Regular comparison with external companies shows employee satisfaction is comparable with other companies and has improving trends	Views of local society are proactively canvassed. Results are fed back into the company's policies	There are consistent trends of improvement in 50 per cent of key result areas. Some results are clearly linked to approach
9	75 per cent of customer satisfaction targets are being met	Results indicate that employees and their families feel integrated into the work environment	Benchmarking has started for 25 per cent of impact on society targets	All targets are being met and are showing continuous improvement in 25 per cent of trends
8	50 per cent of customer satisfaction targets are being met	Results indicate that people feel valued for their contribution at work	50 per cent of impact on society targets are being met	75 per cent of targets have been achieved. Able to demonstrate relevance of key result areas to business
7	All employees understand targets	Results indicate that people can express their feelings confidently and openly	Results are linked to environmental and social policy. Policy is reviewed	Performance against others in the industry is compared and targets are reviewed
6	The drivers of customer satisfaction have been identified and are used to modify targets	Targets are set in key improvement areas and are published	There is increased public awareness of policies	Improving and adverse trends have been identified, understood and linked to enablers
5	Customer satisfaction levels within the company are compared. Results have a positive trend and some are meeting targets	Trends are established Positive and negative trends are understood. Parameters measured are relevant to employees	There are consistently improving trends in relevant result areas	50 per cent of internal targets have been met
4	The relevance of targets to customer satisfaction can be demonstrated	The effectiveness of two way internal communication is measured	Local perceptions and needs are researched and targets are set for improvement	Trends are compared against the unit's goals and financial objectives
3	Targets are set for improvement	Data is used to plot trends for employee satisfaction	Employees' awareness of relevant result areas is measured	Relevant results are communicated to all employees and key results are published regularly
2	Data is used to plot trends of customer complaints	Key measures of employee satisfaction have been identified	Trends are established and a process is in place to track progress	A system exists for measuring and monitoring key result areas
1	Customer complaints are logged and reacted to on an *ad hoc* basis	Employee grievances are reacted to on an *ad hoc* basis	Result areas have been identified	The unit's key financial objectives have been identified

Best Practice Organisational Excellence

Figure 2.4 An example of the business improvement matrix

Step	Leadership	Policy & strategy	People management	Resources	Processes	Customer satisfaction	People satisfaction	Impact on society	Business results
10									
9									
8									
7									
6									
5									
4									
3									
2									
1									
D. grey	2	1	0.5	1	0	1	1.5	1.5	1.5
L. grey	1	3	2	3	3	4	2	3	3
Sub-total	3	4	2.5	4	3	5	3.5	4.5	4.5
Total (sub-total × 0.5)	1.5	2	1.25	2	1.5	2.5	1.75	2.25	2.25

Table 2.7 An example of a score sheet

Category	Value	EFQM weighting	Score (Value × Weighting)
1. Leadership	1.5	10	15.00
2. Policy and strategy	2	8	16.00
3. People management	1.25	9	11.25
4. Resources	2	9	18.00
5. Processes	1.5	14	21.00
6. Customer satisfaction	2.5	20	50.00
7. People satisfaction	1.75	9	15.75
8. Impact on society	2.25	6	13.50
9. Business results	2.25	15	33.75
Total score			194.25

Each business unit has to validate its own scores and induce positive behaviour for making best practices work. Cross-fertilisation of ideas and external validation takes place through third party visits from senior managers of sister business units and this completes the cycle of the certification process.

How is the total quality fitness review applied?
The review itself is administered through a team of trained managers. Using a series of structured questions, an insight into the effectiveness of each aspect of organisational excellence is arrived at and a score is determined. Appendix 2.1 contains the various prompts for each of the 12 conditions, which can be used to assess standards of performance.

The scoring method is based on a numerical rating system with a maximum score of 100 for each of the 12 conditions. Organisations can assess their current standard and an aggregate score on the total quality rating sheet (Figure 2.7) will reflect where the organisation is in relation to world class standards.

The total quality fitness review process can be directly linked to bottom line results to ensure that improvement plans are working and yielding to effective outcomes. It is also an opportunity for setting performance targets (Figure 2.8).

Figure 2.5 Comparison of the MBNQA and Westinghouse Electric Corporation self-assessment criteria

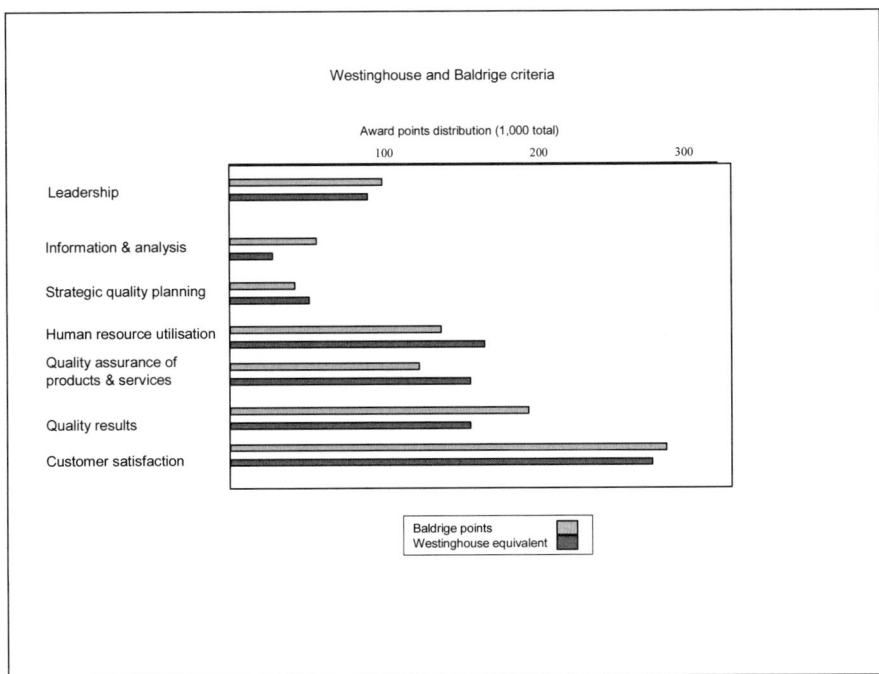

Figure 2.6 Business excellence criteria

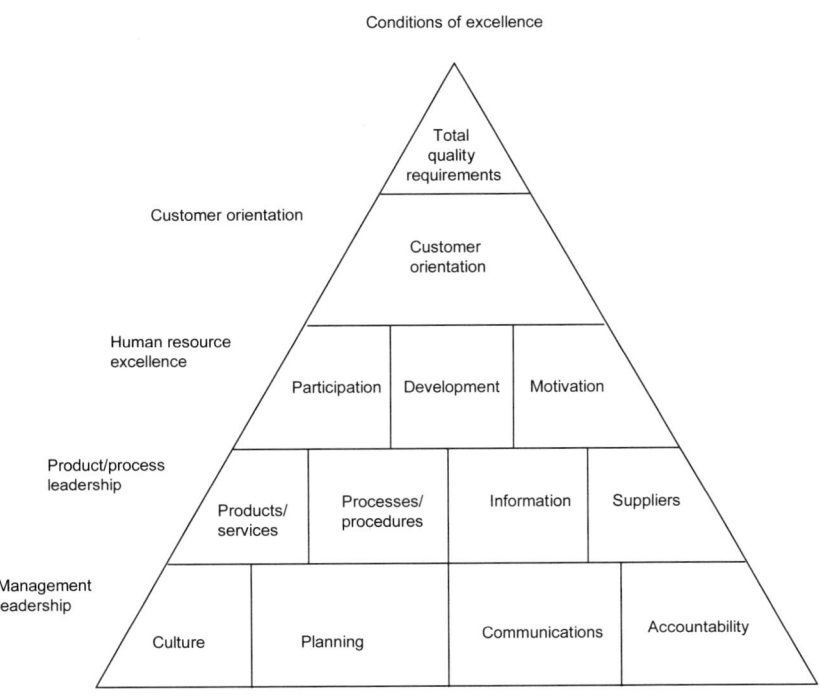

Table 2.8 Conditions of excellence for total quality

Criteria	Description
1. Customer orientation	Satisfying internal and external customers through meeting their requirements and value expectations is the primary task of every employee
2. Participation	All employs participate in establishing and achieving total quality improvement goals
3. Development	People are recognised as key strategic resources. Development opportunities are provided to assure that each employee understands, supports and contributes to achieving total quality
4. Motivation	Employees are motivated to achieve total quality through trust, respect and recognition
5. Products and services	Products and services are appropriately innovative and are reviewed, verified, produced and controlled to meet customer requirements
6. Processes and procedures	Processes and procedures used to create and deliver products and services are developed as an integrated, verified and statistically controlled system using appropriate technology and tools
7. Information	Required information is clear, complete, accurate, timely, useful, accessible and integrated with products, services, processes and procedures
8. Suppliers	Supplied products and services, supplier contributions and supply processes meet all total quality requirements and enhance competitive advantage
9. Culture	Management has established a value system in which individual and group actions reflect "total quality first" and appropriately innovative attitude and direction to meet established world class requirements
10. Planning	Strategic business and financial planning recognises total quality as a primary business objective
11. Communications	Verbal and non-verbal communications are two way, consistent and forceful
12. Accountability	Accountability measures for total quality are established, reported, analysed and used effectively

Figure 2.7 Total quality rating sheet

Total quality rating sheet							
Organisation			Date				
Conditions of excellence	Score						TQFR points
	0	20	40	60	80	100	
1 Customer orientation							
2 Participation							
3 Development							
4 Motivation							
5 Products & services							
6 Processes & procedures							
7 Information							
8 Suppliers							
9 Culture							
10 Planning							
11 Communications							
12 Accountability							

Figure 2.8 The total quality fitness review

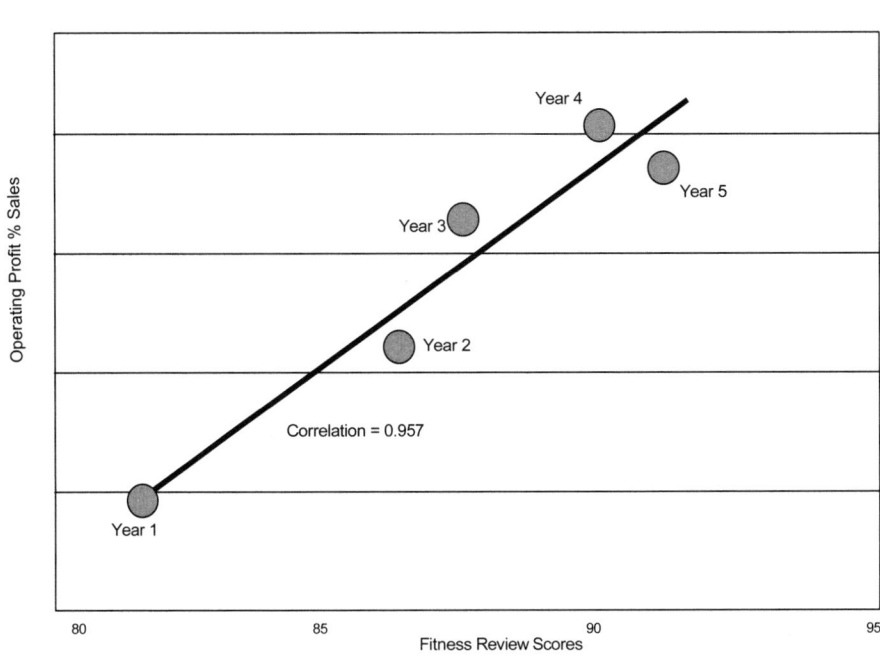

Rank Xerox Corporation
Rank Xerox Corporation uses a customised approach to assess the performance of its business operations world-wide. The business excellence certification (BEC) model has six key elements:
1. Management leadership.
2. Human resources management.
3. Business process management.
4. Customer and market focus.
5. Quality support and tools.
6. Business results.

Figure 2.9 illustrates the business excellence model with the 34 items it covers. Table 2.9 shows the assessment process for elements 1.1 and 1.2 of management leadership in Figure 2.9. The assessment process itself uses a desired state; processes – areas to inspect; and what measures of progress are in place (Table 2.9). The assessment of business results is based on key measures, contributing measures and the key enablers which assist the delivery of individual results. Table 2.10 shows the assessment for elements 6.1 and 6.2 of the business results section in Figure 2.9.

Figure 2.9 1994 business excellence model

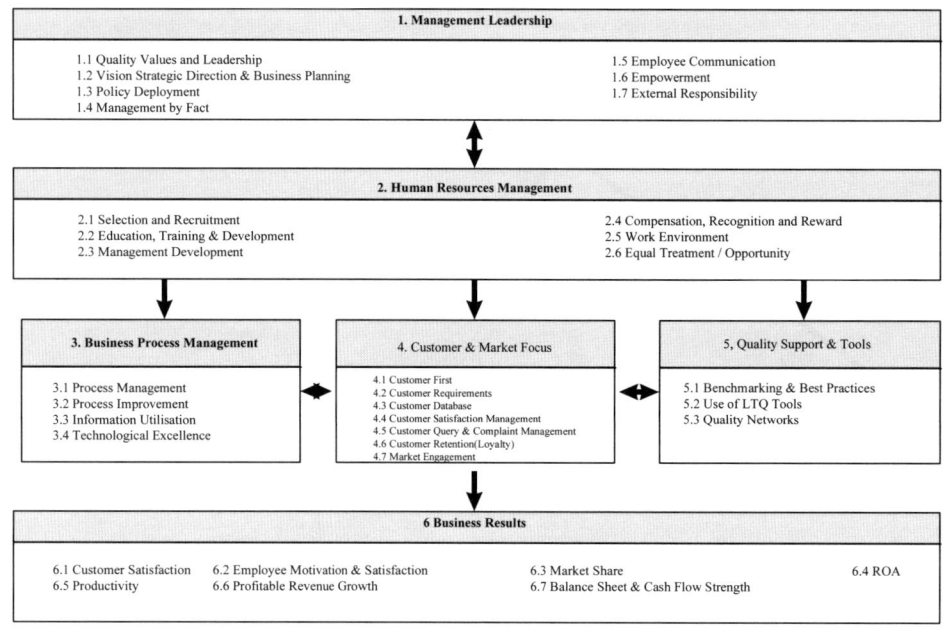

Table 2.9 Desired state, processes – areas to inspect and measures of progress

No.	Element	Desired state	Process – areas to inspect	Measure of progress
1.1	Quality values and leadership	Management lives the Rank Xerox quality policy, continuously promoting and ensuring its application in pursuit of customer value and business results	Management of RX transition Performance against role model behaviour criteria Performance against 23 leadership characteristics and 9 cultural dimensions leadership module implementation External speeches, quality days	Progress towards desired state – plan and actions in place MRP evaluations (trend) ESS results (trend)
1.2	Vision strategic direction and business planning	Management leads the development, deployment and implementation of the vision, the strategic intent, the business plan and the annual operating plan	Maintenance/renewal of the vision Business plan process Contracting process (with business divisions and within the entity Operating plan process	3-5 goals, strategies and annual objectives are established for customer satisfaction, employee motivation and satisfaction, market share and ROA Achievements trend Timeliness: contracts signed on schedule

Table 2.10 Business results

Element and desired state	Key measures	Contributing measures	Key enablers (element/processes[a])
6.1 Customer satisfaction All Rank Xerox customers are very satisfied, repurchase Rank Xerox products and services and recommend Rank Xerox to others as their vendors of choice	On track to 3-5 year goals and achievement of annual objectives: No. 1 position % very satisfied % satisfied % dissatisfied (Loyalty metric to be advised)	Complaint resolution performance (48 hours) Number of complaints Delivery commitments broken Broken call rate Response times tails performance Product performance/features Sales support Loss rate performance Process Problem resolution time performance	Query management process (4.6) Order to collection process Order to install process Product maintenance process Account management process Customer requirements process (4.4)
6.2 Employee motivation and satisfaction Rank Xerox employees are motivated to achieve superior results for their customers	On track to 3-5 year goals and achievement of annual objectives Overall satisfaction index	Work group co-operation Performance evaluation Satisfaction with immediate manager Satisfaction with senior manager Personal development Satisfaction with selection process	(1.1, 1.6) Link with appraisal process (1.3), HRM (2.0) Employee motivation and satisfaction closed-loop management process (1.1) As above (1.1) As above (2.2) As above (2.1)

Note: [a] the element numbers in this column refer to the items in Figure 2.9

Rank Xerox management displays a customer focus, exhibits "role model" behaviour, establishes clear long-term goals and annual objectives, establishes strategic boundaries and provides an empowered environment to achieve world class productivity and business results

The scoring scale uses a similar approach to the EFQM and MBNQA models. It relies on a rating scale of 1-7, and scores are given based on the combined impact of approach, persuasiveness and results (Table 2.11). A rating of 4 is the threshold for a sound system. The business excellence model creates a systematic, world-wide discipline for continuous improvement and breakthrough performance. As Figure 2.10 illustrates the process requires each individual business unit to apply all the elements of BEC on a regular basis, developing action plans for improvement, implementing solutions to problems and monitoring performance gains.

Rank Xerox is discussed in detail as a case study in Chapter 14.

Best Practice Organisational Excellence

Table 2.11 The scoring scale

Rating	Results	Approach	Pervasiveness
1	Anecdotal or generalisation or guess	Anecdotal, no system evident or documented	Anecdotal, isolated, may not be true at all levels
2	Sporadic trends	Sloppy or over bureaucratic	Theory not practice
3	Some positive trends in some of the areas deployed	Beginning of systematic prevention basis	Some core areas of business Management or employees work the problem
4	Positive trends in most major areas Evidence that some results are caused by approach	Sound systematic prevention that includes evaluation/improvement cycles Some evidence of integration into management processes	Some core areas of business Management or employees work the problem
5	Good in major areas Positive trends from some to many support areas Evidence that most results are caused by approach	Sound systematic prevention that includes evaluation/improvement cycles Some evidence of integration into management processes	Core areas of business plus some support areas
6	Good to excellent in major areas Clear evidence that most results are caused by approach	Good integration	From some to many support areas
7	Excellent (world class) results in major areas	Sound, systematic prevention basis refined through evaluation/improvement cycles Excellent integration	Core areas and support areas Full deployment Management, employees and customers work the problem

Figure 2.10 The process

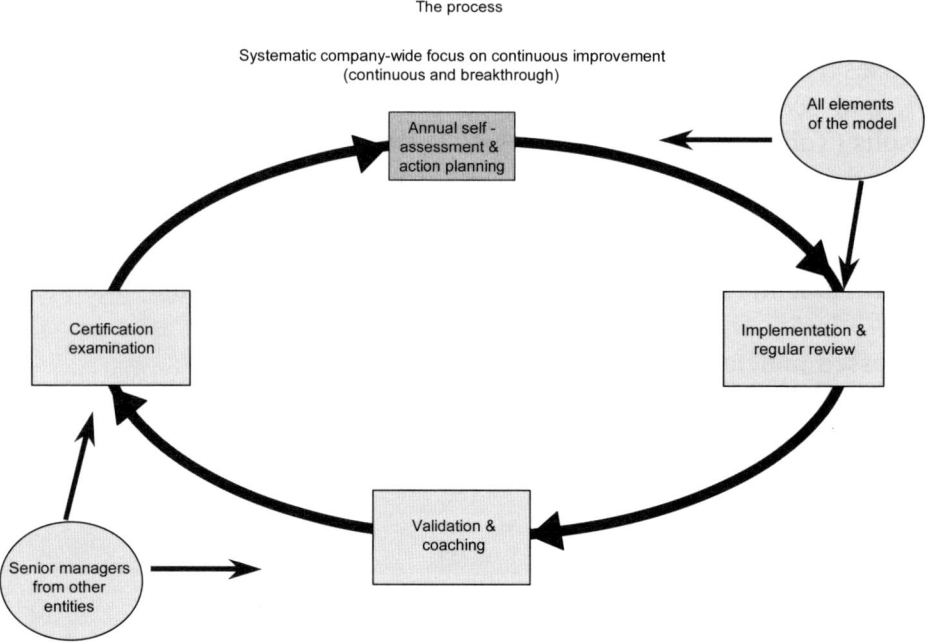

46

Appendix 2.1. Prompts for the 12 conditions of the Westinghouse Electric Corporation total quality fitness review

1. Customer orientation
Satisfying customers through meeting their requirements and value expectation is the primary task of every employee.
   a. Products and services are perceived by customers to be first in total quality.
   b. Meeting customer requirements is the primary objective of all employees.
   c. The organisation's value (as perceived by customers) is compared with competitors' value (as defined by customers) and is used to gain competitive advantage.
   d. Internal customers' (the next person or department in the process) perceptions of performance are measured, evaluated and reported to responsible functions.
   e. The organisation actively seeks ways to make all employees aware of customers and their needs.
   f. Product or service guarantees or warranties are valuable to the customer and create competitive advantage. Data concerning customer views are communicated and used for improvement.
   g. Goals and requirements for the safety and health of customers and the community are known. Procedures for compliance with health and safety standards are known, understood and implemented.

2. Participation
All employees participate in establishing and achieving total quality improvement goals.
   a. Managers are personally and effectively leading the total quality improvement process.
   b. Employee contributions to improvement are actively encouraged by management and implemented when total quality improvement will result.
   c. All functional departments contribute to developing and implementing the total quality improvement process.

3. Development
People are recognised as key strategic resources. Development opportunities are provided to ensure that each employee understands, supports and contributes to achieving total quality.
   a. All employees are developed as key strategic resources.
   b. Development and training needed to support total quality improvement are objectively assessed and documented.
   c. Awareness training is provided to ensure that each employee understands, supports and contributes to achieving total quality.
   d. Each employee receives sufficient training in techniques and job skills to support the total quality improvement process.

4. Motivation
Employees are motivated to achieve total quality through trust, respect and recognition.
   a. Management believes that employees want to do a good job. There is a positive atmosphere of trust and respect between management and employees. Disincentives to change are minimised.
   b. Managers personally, regularly and fairly recognise individuals and groups for measurable contributions to total quality.

5. Products and services
Products and services are appropriately innovative and are reviewed, verified, produced and controlled to meet customer requirements.
   a. Value/cost ratios are known and are globally competitive.
   b. Customer requirements, as well as world class internal product/service standards, are defined.
   c. On-going programmes exist to improve products and services through measurement and analysis of feedback data and incorporation of new technology and methods.
   d. Formal reviews and/or verifications are accomplished to assure that products and services meet all requirements. Products and services are verified before delivery.

6. Processes and procedures
Processes and procedures used to create and deliver products and services are developed as an integrated, verified and controlled system using appropriate technology and tools.
   a. Products, services and the processes and procedures used to create them are jointly designed as an integrated system. Cycle time reduction is a driving force.
   b. The organisation structure supports the processes and procedures as an interactive system.
   c. All processes and procedures are verified before use, thoroughly understood and efficiently managed.

d. Error prevention is emphasised in process and procedure design, and processes are controlled to be error free.
   e. Technology and innovation are planned and effectively utilised in processes and procedures.
   f. Goals and requirements to protect employees from hazards associated with products or services are documented. Procedures for compliance with safety, health and environmental standards are evident.

7. Information

Requirement information is clear, complete, accurate, timely, useful, accessible and integrated with products, services, processes, and procedures.
   a. Information required to support total quality is complete, timely, accurate, useful, secure and clearly and appropriately communicated.
   b. Information quality is recognised as an essential element of total quality. Information systems planning and implementation are done with the involvement of all departments.
   c. External and internal customer requirements are accurately communicated to all departments which must meet them.

8. Suppliers

Supplied products and services, supplier contributions and supply processes meet all total quality requirements and enhance competitive advantage.
   a. Supply requirements are mutually established with all involved internal groups actively participating.
   b. Early and continuous supplier involvement ensures that requirements are mutually established, clearly understood, effectively communicated and consistently met.
   c. Total value is the primary basis for supply decisions.
   d. Purchased products and/or services meet all total quality requirements.
   e. Processes involved in supply activities, from need identification to need satisfaction, are integrated with other processes and plans and are achieving superior operating results.
   f. Total quality of supplied products and services and the effectiveness of the supply processes are measured. Results are communicated to the organisation and suppliers. Performance is continuously improved.

9. Culture

Management has established a value system in which individual and group actions reflect a "total quality first" approach and appropriately innovative attitude and direction to meet established world class requirements.
   a. The organisation is bound together by the belief that total quality is the key to success. "Think total quality – all else will follow" describes the culture. Total quality improvement is seen as a long-term process, not to be compromised by short-term condition.
   b. The right things are being done to encourage and manage change toward world class performance.
   c. Systems used to implement total quality are published, implemented, regularly audited, updated and meet customer requirements. Total quality improvement is supported by procedures, manuals and other documentation which have been implemented by each department.
   d. There is a sense of pride – individual and group.
   e. The organisation structure fosters effective implementation of the total quality improvement process.

10. Planning

Strategic business and financial planning recognise total quality as a primary business objective.
   a. Total quality improvement is seen as a strategic imperative, essential to long-term total business success. Total quality issues important to the business have been identified and are addressed in strategic plans.
   b. Annually revised quality improvement plans are used to detail formal total quality improvement projects with measurable goals for each department.
   c. There is a dynamic organisation plan which ensures that structural changes and people capabilities accommodate changes in the business environment.

11. Communications

Verbal and non-verbal communications are two-way, clear, consistent and forceful.
   a. Total quality policy and requirements are clearly, consistently and forcefully communicated by management and understood by all employees.
   b. Two-way communications occur regularly.
   c. Management actions and non-verbal signals promote total quality improvement and are consistent with verbal communications.

d. The organisation communicates information concerning total quality to others and supports quality improvement activities outside the company.

12. Accountability
Accountability measures for total quality are established, reported, analysed and effectively used.
   a. Performance trends show steady progress towards meeting objectives.
   b. Managers use reports and diagnostic techniques which accurately reflect total quality performance and pinpoint improvement opportunities.
   c. Periodic, detailed, highly visible management progress reviews are used to monitor improvement.
   d. Measures and improvement objectives related to value/price, value/cost and error-free performance are visible and used in each department.
   e. Evaluations of employees' performance include achievement of measurable total quality improvement objectives.

Chapter 3
Self-assessment tools

Introduction

Self-assessment is a new phenomenon in the West where most business organisations seem to be highly interested in measuring the culture of quality. Senior managers have come to recognise that there are powerful tools such as the Malcolm Baldrige National Quality Award (MBNQA) or the European Quality Award (EQA) framework, which can help them assess their strengths and weaknesses in various areas and whether they are deploying their quality efforts in the right way.

Self-assessment helps organisations in many ways, including:
- providing the opportunity to take a broader view on how TQM is impacting on various business operations;
- measuring performance of processes, enablers and their relationship with results;
- measuring in financial and non-financial areas;
- measuring internally and externally, including the community and the environment;
- encouraging objective assessment through third party involvement;
- providing opportunity to benchmark and compare like for like;
- measuring for improvement rather than for hard control;
- creating the desire to do better and perhaps even win awards.

Self-assessment frameworks are therefore not just a means to win awards but, perhaps more importantly, vehicles for embarking on a journey of continuous improvement and the determination to become more competitive. The MBNQA for instance was introduced to promote:
- awareness of quality as an increasingly important element of competitiveness;
- understanding of the requirements for quality excellence; and
- sharing of information on successful quality strategies and the benefits derived from implementation of these strategies.

Although self-assessment is a new practice in the West, this is not the case in Japan. The quality movement in Japan started in 1946 through the birth of the Union of Japanese Scientists and Engineers (JUSE). In 1949, the quality control research group in JUSE was formed to give lectures and provide education on the principles of quality control both in JUSE and the Japanese Standards Association (JSA). In 1950, Dr W.E. Deming was invited by JUSE to give seminars on statistical quality control. In 1951, the Deming Prize was instituted and the Deming Prize Committee was formed. In the same year the first prize was given to:
- Fuji Iron and Steel Co. Ltd;
- Showa Denko KK;
- Tanabe Seyaku Co. Ltd; and
- Yawata Iron and Steel Co. Ltd.

The Deming Prize

The Deming Prize has been around for over four decades. During that time the following awards have been given:
- 53 prizes for individuals' achievements;
- 126 Deming Application Prizes to companies;
- 13 divisions among 12 corporations have won the Deming Prize for Division.

The Deming Prize went through various stages of evolution:
- 1951: the first prizes were given at a ceremony in the Osaka Chamber of Commerce and Industry on 22 September.
- 1957: the Deming Prize for Small Companies was created.
- 1965: the Deming Application Prize for Divisions of Companies was awarded.
- 1970: the Japanese Quality Control Medal was introduced for firms which have won the Deming Prize in the previous five years.
- 1972: a system of honouring a single establishment or place of business was adopted.
- 1974: development of the Deming Prize Award for Individuals.
- 1984: the Deming Prize became international, and overseas companies could apply for it.

Criteria used for assessment of Deming Prize applications

There are ten criteria which are used for assessing Deming Prize applications:
1. Company policy and planning.
2. Organisation and its management.
3. QC education and dissemination.
4. Collection, transmission and utilisation of information on quality.
5. Analysis.
6. Standardisation.
7. Control (Kanri).
8. Quality assurance (QA).
9. Effects.
10. Future plans.

The application document clearly specifies how the assessment is carried out. The manner in which such activities as investigation, research, development, design, purchase, production, inspection, sales etc., which are essential for the proper control of product and service quality and are conducted by each and every segment of the company, is examined and judged. The term "quality control" as used in this guide denotes company-wide quality control (CWQC) based on statistical quality control techniques.

Table 3.1 gives a complete checklist of all the criteria assessed following an application for the Deming Prize; Table 3.2 lists the prize winners from 1951 to 1990.

Table 3.1 Checklist for the Deming Prize criteria

Criteria	Assessment items
1. Policy and objectives	(a) Policy with regard to management quality and quality control (b) Methods in determining policy and objectives (c) Appropriateness and consistency of the contents of objectives (d) Utilisation of statistical methods (e) Deployment, dissemination and permeation of objectives (f) Checking objectives and their implementation (g) Relationships with long range and short term plans
2. Organisation and its operation	(a) A clear cut line of responsibilities (b) Appropriateness of delegation of power (c) Co-operation between divisions (d) Activities of committees (e) Utilisation of the staff (f) Utilisation of QC circle activities (g) Quality control audit
3. Education and its extension	(a) Education plan and actual accomplishment (b) Consciousness about quality and control, understanding of quality control (c) Education concerning statistical concepts and methods and degree of permeation (d) Ability to understand the effects (e) Education for sub-contractors and outside organisations (f) QC circle activities (g) Suggestion system and its implementation
4. Assembling and disseminating information and its utilisation	(a) Assembling outside information (b) Disseminating information between divisions (c) Speed in disseminating information (use of computers) (d) (Statistical) analysis of information and its utilisation
5. Analysis	(a) Selection of important problems and themes (b) Appropriateness of the analytical method (c) Utilisation of statistical methods (d) Tying in with own engineering technology (e) Quality analysis, process analysis (f) Utilisation of results of analysis (g) Positiveness of suggestions for improvement
6. Standardisation	(a) System of standardisation (b) Methods of establishing, revising and withdrawing standards (c) Actual records in establishing, revising and withdrawing standards (d) Contents of standards (e) Utilisation of statistical methods (f) Accumulation of technology (g) Utilisation of statistical methods

(*Continued*)

7. Control (Kanri)	(a)	Control systems for quality and in related areas such as cost, delivery and quantity
	(b)	Control points and control items
	(c)	Utilisation of statistical methods such as control charts and general acceptance of the statistical way of thinking
	(d)	Contributions of QC circle activities
	(e)	Actual conditions of control activities
	(f)	Actual conditions of control state
8. Quality assurance (QA)	(a)	Procedures for new product development – quality deployment (breakdown of quality function) and its analysis, reliability and design review etc.
	(b)	Safety and product liability
	(c)	Process design, control and improvement (Kaizen)
	(d)	Process capabilities
	(e)	Measurement and inspection
	(f)	Control of facilities equipment, subcontracting, purchasing, services etc.
	(g)	Quality assurance system and its audit
	(h)	Utilisation of statistical methods
	(i)	Evaluation and audit of quality
	(j)	Practical conditions of quality assurance
9. Effects	(a)	Measuring effects
	(b)	Visible effects such as quality, serviceability, date of delivery, cost, profit, safety, environment, etc.
	(c)	Invisible effects
	(d)	Computability between prediction of effects and actual records
10. Future plans	(a)	Understanding of the status quo, and concreteness
	(b)	Polices adopted to solve short comings
	(c)	Plans of promotion of TQC for the future
	(d)	Relations with the company's long range plans

The Japanese Quality Control Medal was created to commemorate the world's first International Conference on Quality Control (ICQC) held in 1969 at Tokyo. Its purpose is to up-grade the level of CWQC of the Deming Application Prize recipients. The application for this medal is accepted only when the applicant company has already been awarded the Deming Application Prize (excluding, the Deming Application Prize for Division) more than five years ago.

The examination is carried out on the implementation of CWQC subsequent to the winning of Deming Application Prize. The method of judging is the same as for the Deming Application Prize. When judged qualified, an applicant receives a plaque with a Japan Quality Control Medal from the committee. The winners from 1970 to 1990 are:

- 1970: Toyota Motor Co. Ltd (name of company at the time of the award);
- 1973: Nippon Electric Co. Ltd;
- 1975: Nippon Steel Corporation;
- 1977: Aisin Seiki Co. Ltd;
- 1980: Toyota Auto Body Co. Ltd;
- 1981: Komatsu Ltd;
- 1982: Aisin-Warner Ltd;
- 1985: The Takaoka Industrial Co. Ltd;
- 1990: Aisin Selki Co. Ltd.

Table 3.2 Deming Application Prize winners

Date	Companies			
1951	Fuji Iron & Steel Co Ltd	Showa Denko K.K.	Tanabe Seiyaku Co. Ltd	Yawata Iron & Steel Co. Ltd
1952	Asahi Chemical Co. Ltd Toyo Spinning Co. Ltd	Nippon Electric Co. Ltd Kyushu Cloth Industry Co. Ltd	Shionogi & Co. Ltd	Takeda Chemical Industries Ltd
1953	Kawasaki Steel Corp.	Shin-etsu Chemical Industry Co. Ltd	Sumitomo Metal Mining Co. Ltd	Tokyo Shibaura Electric Co. Ltd
1954	Nippon Soda Co. Ltd	Toyo Bearing Manufacturing Co. Ltd	Toyo Rayon Co. Ltd	
1955	Asahi Glass Co. Ltd	Hitachi Ltd	Honshu Paper Manufacturing Co. Ltd	
1956	Fuji Photo Film Co. Ltd	Konishiroku Photo Industry Co. Ltd	Mitsubishi Electric Corp.	Tohoku Industry Co. Ltd
1957	None			
1958	Kanegafuchi Chemical Industry Co. Ltd Nakayo Communication Equipment Co. Ltd *	Kureha Chemical Industry Co. Ltd	Matsushita Electronics Corp.	Nippon Kokan K.K.
1959	Asahi Special Glass Co. Ltd			
1960	Kurake Spinning Co. Ltd	Nissan Motor Co. Ltd	Towa Industry Co. Ltd*	
1961	Nippondenso Co. Ltd	Teijin Ltd	Nihon Radiator Co. Ltd*	
1962	Sumitomo Electric Industries Ltd			
1963	Nippon Kayaku Co. Ltd			
1964	Komatsu Manufacturing Co. Ltd			
1965	Toyota Motor Co. Ltd			
1966	Kanto Auto Works Ltd	Matsushita Electric Industrial Co. Ltd Electric Components Division@		
1967	Shinko Wire Co. Ltd	Kojima Press Industry Co. Ltd*		
1968	Bridgestone Tyre Co. Ltd	Yanmer Diesel Engine Co. Ltd	Chugoku Kayaku Co. Ltd*	
1969	Shimpo Industry Co. Ltd*			
1970	Toyota Auto Body Co. Ltd			
1971	Hino Motors Ltd			(Continued)

1972	Aisin Seiki Co. Ltd	Saitama Chuzo Kogyo K.K.*		
1973	Sanwa Seiki Manufacturing Co. Ltd	Saitama Kiki Manufacturing Co. Ltd		
1974	Horikiri Spring Manufacturing Co. Ltd Kyodo Surveying Co. Ltd*			
1975	Ricoh Co. Ltd	K.K. Takebe Tekkosho*	Tokai Chemical Industries Ltd*	Riken Forge Co. Ltd
1976	Sankyo Seiki Manufacturing Co. Ltd	Pentel Co. Ltd	Komatsu Zoki Ltd*	Ishikawajima-Harima Heavy Industries Co. Ltd
1977	Aero-Engine & Space Operations@			
1978	Aisin-Warner Ltd	Tokai Rika Co. Ltd	Chuetsu Metal Works Co. Ltd*	
1979	Nippon Electric Kyushu Ltd Hamanakodenso Co. Ltd*	Sekisue Chemical Co. Ltd	Takenaka Komuten Co. Ltd	Tohoku Ricoh Co. Ltd
1980	Kayaba Industry Co. Ltd Kyowa Industrial Co. Ltd*	Komatsu Forklift Co. Ltd	Fuji Xerox Co. Ltd	The Takaoka Industrial Co. Ltd
1981	Aiphone Co. Ltd*	Kyosan Denki Co. Ltd*	Toyko Juki Industrial Co. Ltd Industrial Sewing Machine Division	
1982	Kajima Corp. Yamagata Ltd	Nippon Electric Aisin Chemical Co. Ltd*	Rhythm Watch Co. Ltd Shinwa Industrial Co. Ltd*	Yokogawa Hewlett-Packard
1983	Shimizu Construction Ltd	The Japan Steel Works Ltd	Aisin Keikinzoku Co. Ltd	
1984	Komatsu Zenoah Co. Hokuriku Kogyo Co. Ltd*	The Kansai Electric Power Co. Inc.	Yaskawa Electric Manufacturing Co. Ltd	Anjo Denki Co. Ltd*
1985	Nippon Carbon Co. Ltd Hoyo Seiki Co. Ltd*	Nippon Zeon Co. Ltd Uchino Komuten Co. Ltd	Toyoda Gosei Co. Ltd Texas Instruments Japan Ltd, Bipolar Department@	Toyoda Machine Works Ltd Company Inc.*
1986	Hazama-Gunti Ltd	Toyoda Automatic Loom Works Ltd	Nitto Construction Co. Ltd*	Sanyo Electric Works Ltd*
1987	Aichi Steel Works Ltd	Aisin Chemical Co. Ltd	Daihen Corporation	NECIC Microcomputer Systems Ltd

(*Continued*)

1988	Aisin Keikinzoku Co. Ltd Joban Hawaiian Center@	Asmo Co. Ltd	Fuji Tekko Co. Ltd	Joban Kosan Co. Ltd
1989	Aisin Sinwa Co. Ltd TOTO Ltd	Itoki Kosakusyo Co. Ltd Florida Power & Light Co.#	Macda Corporation Ahresty Corporation*	NEC Tohoku Ltd
1990	Tooyooki Kogyo Co. Ltd*	Aisin Hoyo Co. Ltd	Amada Wasino Co. Ltd	NEC Shizuoka Ltd

Companies awarded the Quality Control Award for Factory by the Deming Committee

1973	Mitsubishi Heavy Industries Co. Ltd		
1974	Kobe Shipyard		
1975	Sekisue Chemical Co. Ltd	Tokyo Plant	Kubota Iron & Machinery Works Ltd Engine Tech-Research Department
1976	Kubota Iron & Machinery Works Ltd		
1977	Sakai Works Japan Aircraft Manufacturing Co. Ltd Atsugi Works		
1979	The Japan Steel Works Ltd Hiroshima Plant		
1980	Kobayashi Kose Co. Ltd Manufacturing Division		
1981	Matsushita Electric Works Ltd. Hikone Factory		
1983	Fuji Electric Co. Ltd, Matsumoto Plant		
1988	Suntory Ltd, Musashino Brewery		
1989	Kobe Steel Ltd, Chofu-Kita Plant	Maeta Concrete Industry Ltd Honsha Plant	
1990	Suntory Ltd Yamanashi Winery		

Notes: * Deming Application Prize for Small Enterprise; @ Deming Application Prize for Division; # Deming Application Prize for Overseas Countries; company names given are the those at the time of awarding

The winners of the Japanese Quality Control Medal in 1991 are discussed below.

NEC Kansai Co. Ltd. This used to be part of New Nippon Electric Co Ltd. Formed in 1983, with a turnover of ¥800 millions it employs 4,050 people and produces VISIs, compound semi-conductors and other electronic parts. Since the introduction of TQM in 1984, NEC Kansai has pioneered many leading edge technologies and made achievements in various areas of quality improvement which led to greatly enhanced business performance.

Nachi-Fujikoshi Corp. A machinery manufacturer with a turnover of ¥13.3 billion, it employs 4,866 workers and mainly designs, manufactures and sells tools, bearings, machine tools, hydraulic machinery and equipment and industrial robots. It uses TQC for managing all its business operations, relies heavily on teamwork and an inter-disciplinary approach to working and has achieved serious benefits from the use of TQM.

Hokushin Industries Inc. This company is a manufacturer of precise function rubber products for information equipment and other related equipment. It has a turnover of ¥278.3 million and employs 641 people. TQM was introduced in 1978 at Hokushin to strengthen the company and improve quality standards. The motto used was "creation and vitality" and, through strong leadership, Hokushin has managed to reduce customer complaints and improve sales.

Winners of the Deming Application Prize for Small Businesses include Sin'ei Industries Co. Ltd, Niigata Toppan Printing Co. Ltd and Aisin Aw Co. Ltd.

Sin'ei Industries Co. Ltd. This company manufactures decorative and functional parts (high-class coating products, highly rust-preventive products, etc.) for automobile bodies. It turns over ¥80 million. TQM was introduced through strong commitment from the top and involving all aspects of the business. A complete culture transformation was achieved where various bottlenecks were removed and QA became a driving force. Quality improvements therefore started to take place at the design stage. The performance was improved considerably. Sin'ei Industries achieved zero delivery deficiency rate and sales and profit targets were often achieved one year ahead of schedule.

Niigata Toppan Printing Co. Ltd. A manufacturer of printed circuit boards, established in 1984, it has a turnover of ¥50 million and it employs 382 people. TQC was introduced in 1986 to strengthen the performance of various business operations. Gradually there was a shift from QA to corporate quality policy and control, which led to great reductions in claims and increased customer satisfaction.

The 1991 Deming Application Prize for Overseas Companies was won by Philips Taiwan Ltd. This company will be examined separately as a case study.

The 1991 Japan Quality Control Medal was awarded to Aisin Aw Co. Ltd, a company established in 1969, specialising in the manufacture of automatic transmissions. Its turnover is currently ¥6,480 million and it employs 4,000 people. TQM was introduced back in 1973 with the motto "Quality First". This led to Aisin winning the Deming Prize in 1977 and the Japanese Quality Control Medal in 1982.

Winners in 1992 are presented in Table 3.3.

The Malcolm Baldrige National Quality Award (MBNQA)
The MBNQA was established by the US Congress back in 1987 to raise awareness about quality and its importance for US business organisations. Malcolm Baldrige, Secretary of Commerce from 1981 until his death in July 1987 in a road accident, championed the whole initiative and, in recognition of his efforts, Congress decided to name the award in his honour. The MBNQA was established to alert senior managers to the need for competing with quality as the key driver and to reward those organisations that excelled in having successful quality

management systems. The award itself therefore was seen as a standard of excellence to help promote quality and, as such, help US businesses achieve high standards of competitiveness.

Table 3.3 Deming Prize winners of 1992

Category	Company name	Industry sector/products	Number employed
Japan Quality Control Medal	Aisin Chemical Co. Ltd	Manufacture of automotive parts	825
	Takenaka Corporation	General construction	11,000
Deming Prize for Individuals	Mr Maswao	Function of counsellor	
Deming Application Prize	Aisin Industry Co. Ltd	Manufacture of automotive parts	3,276
	Iatco Corporation	Manufacture of automotive automatic transmission	2,916
Quality Control Award for Factories	Nissan Motor Co. Ltd	Automotive assembly	4,287
	Toppan Printing Co. Ltd (Electronics Division, Kumoto Plant)	Manufacture of colour filters	242

The National Institute of Standards and Technology (NIST), which is a division of the commerce department, was given the task of administering the award. NIST has always had a role of promoting advanced sciences, safety and competitiveness in US companies. In the task of implementing the new award, NIST is assisted by the American Society for Quality Control (ASQC) which is a non-profit organisation serving more than 80,000 individual members and 700 corporate members in the USA and 62 other countries.

The award has been running successfully for many years now. To date, the following companies have been recognised:
- 1988: Motorola; Commercial Nuclear Fuel Division of Westinghouse Electric Corp.; Globe Metallurgical Inc.;
- 1989: Milliken & Company; Xerox Corp. Business Products and Systems;
- 1990: Cadillac Motor Car Division; IBM Rochester; Federal Express Corp.; Wallace Co. Inc.;
- 1991: Solectron Corp.; Zytec Corp.; Marlow Industries;
- 1992: AT&T Network Systems Group; Texas Instruments Inc.; AT&T Universal Card Services; The Ritz-Carlton Hotel Company; Granite Rock Company.

For the 1993 MBNQA, 76 US companies applied: they represented 32 manufacturing companies, 13 service companies and 31 small businesses. This compares with 90 applications in 1992, when five won the award. Table 3.4 details the breakdown of the number of applications, according to industry sector, from 1988 to 1993.

Purpose of MBNQA
The MBNQA's significance has grown very substantially over the past ten years, as shown by the following facts:
- The MBNQA is now accepted widely as a model for performance excellence. Over 60 countries are now using the criteria for driving the competitiveness of their industry and public sector provision.

- The MBNQA has generated the commitment of the private sector, as well as the US government, in driving quality. The annual government investment is about $5 million and the contribution from the private sector and other states is well over $100 million.
- More than 300 experts from industry, educational institutions, government at all levels and non-profit organisations volunteer to support the assessment and provide guidance.
- The Baldrige winners share their experiences and, to date, executives from the various winning companies have given more than 30,000 presentations.
- Approximately two million copies of the MBNQA criteria have been distributed since the first edition in 1988, and heavy reproduction and electronic access have multiplied that number.

A maximum of only two awards can be won in any particular year, in the following categories:
- Manufacturing.
- Service.
- Small business.
- Education.
- Healthcare.

In 1999 the education and healthcare categories were established and, since then, a total of 47 applications have been submitted in the education category and 42 in the healthcare category. The premise is that any organisation, whether for profit or not, can improve and is capable of becoming excellent. The MBNQA is a generic model and can therefore help schools, universities and hospitals in the same way that it has been helping private sector based organisations.

Criteria for assessment of the MBNQA

The MBNQA assessment framework is developed with a set of criteria that can help improve organisational performance practices, capabilities and results. Furthermore, it is a tool for organisational learning and growth by enabling effective planning and strategic thinking and also by encouraging the adoption of best practice thinking.

The criteria in question are underpinned by a set of guiding principles which can be described as synonymous with excellence. These include:
- Visionary leadership.
- Customer-driven excellence.
- Organisational and personal learning.
- Valuing employees and partners.
- Agility.
- Focus on the future.
- Managing for innovation.
- Managing by fact.
- Social responsibility.
- Focus on results and creating value.
- Systems perspective.

The MBNQA has seven categories which are sub-divided into 19 items, each focusing on areas to address (see Figure 3.1). The criteria and items are listed in Table 3.5.

Table 3.4 Selected data on MBNQA applications by category (1983-1993)

		Manufacturing	Service	Small business	Total
1993	Applications	32	13	31	76
	Site visits				
	Awards				
1992	Applications	31	15	44	90
	Site visits	7	5	5	17
	Awards	2	2	1	5
1991	Applications	38	21	47	106
	Site visits	9	5	5	19
	Awards	2	0	1	3
1990	Applications	45	18	34	97
	Site visits	6	3	3	12
	Awards	2	1	1	4
1989	Applications	23	6	11	40
	Site visits	8	2	0	10
	Awards	2	0	0	2
1988	Applications	45	9	12	66
	Site visits	10	2	1	13
	Awards	2	0	1	3

Figure 3.1 Baldrige Award criteria framework – dynamic relationships

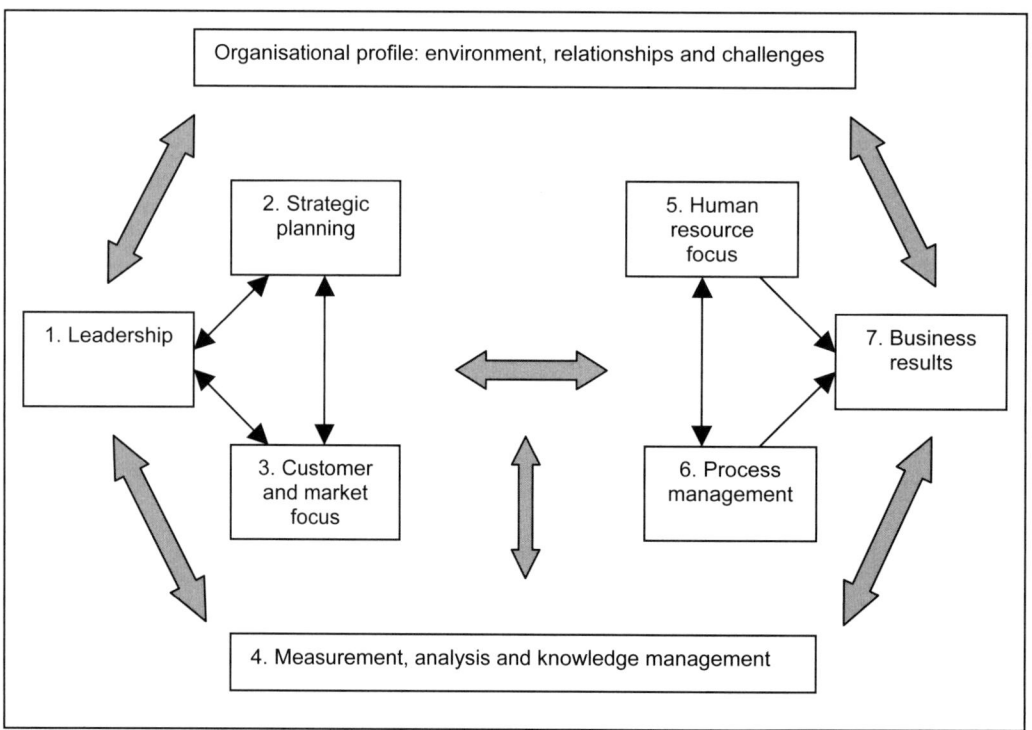

Table 3.5 2003 Baldrige Award categories, items and point values

Category	Item	Item points	Total category points
1. Leadership	1.1 Organisational leadership	70	
	1.2 Social responsibility	50	120
2. Strategic planning	2.1 Strategy development	40	
	2.2 Strategy deployment	45	85
3. Customer and market focus	3.1 Customer and market knowledge	40	
	3.2 Customer relationships and satisfaction	45	85
4. Measurement, analysis and knowledge management	4.1 Measurement and analysis of organisational performance	45	
	4.2 Information and knowledge management	45	90
5. Human resource focus	5.1 Work systems	35	
	5.2 Employee learning and motivation	25	
	5.3 Employee well-being and satisfaction	25	85
6. Process management	6.1 Value creation processes	40	
	6.2 Support processes	45	85
7. Business results	7.1 Customer-focused results	75	
	7.2 Product and service results	75	
	7.3 Financial and market results	75	
	7.4 Human resource results	75	
	7.5 Organisational effectiveness results	75	
	7.6 Governance and social responsibility results	75	450
Total points			1,000

Scoring system

A maximum of 1,000 points can be allocated for each submission. The points given are based on evaluation in the following areas:

- *Approach.* Methods used to deploy the quality effort include:
  - methods, tools, techniques and their appropriateness and effectiveness;
  - how systematic is the approach, how integrated and consistent is it?
  - use of information, facts and objectivity.
- *Deployment.* The implementation of the approach includes:
  - pervasiveness and breadth of application in all processes, activities and tasks;
  - relevance to products and services; and
  - application externally to customers, suppliers.
- *Results.* Outcomes from the whole quality efforts include:
  - performance standards;

- benchmarking;
- rate of performance improvement; and
- breadth and importance of performance improvement.

The scoring guidelines issued by NIST are illustrated are Tables 3.6 and 3.7. Winning scores have varied from year to year. Table 3.8 shows the distribution of written scores from 1988 to 1992.

EQA assessment
The assessment framework of the EQA award (Figure 3.2) is different from the MBNQA. The method is applied differently to the enablers and the results – for enablers, scores given are based on:
- degree of excellence in the approach; and
- degree of deployment in the approach.

For results, scores given are based on:
- degree of excellence of results; and
- scope of results.

This is a big improvement on the MBNQA in that TQM has to be shown to be working, improvements must be visible and easily quantifiable and bottom line results must also be improving.

The criteria for the EQA excellence model are given in Table 3.9. The scoring is based on the RADAR logic (results, approach, deployment, assessment and review) (see Figure 3.3). This logic determines excellence in any organisation by:
- determining that the results it intends to achieve are part of its policy and strategy-making process. Furthermore, these results must reflect present and future needs of stakeholders;
- planning and developing an integrated set of sound approaches to deliver the required results;
- deploying the approaches in a sound way to ensure full implementation;
- assessing and reviewing the approaches and deployment by monitoring and analysing the results achieved and ongoing learning activities;
- identifying, prioritising, planning and implementing improvements wherever needed.

The EQA scoring guidelines are shown in Table 3.10.

Table 3.6 Scoring of the approach and deployment areas

Score %	Approach	Deployment
0	Anecdotal, no systematic approach evident	Anecdotal, undocumented
10	Beginning of a systematic approach is somewhat evident	Isolated units are using quality practices; most are not (key requirements of the item not addressed or not practiced by major components)
20	Generally reactive approach to problems. A partially systematic approach is evident to a limited extent. Still reactive to problems	Some units are using quality practices; many are not (key requirements of the item not addressed or not practised by many components)
30	A systematic approach is evident and still evolving to a limited extent. Still reactive to problems	Some major gaps in deployment still exist (some key requirements of the item not addressed or not practised by some components
40	Systematic approach is fully developed. Emphasis on prevention. No systematic evaluation or improvement system is in place. Some fact-based decision processes are evident. Random improvements may have been made	A few minor gaps in deployment exist some minor requirements of the item not addressed or not practised by some components). Many work units are in the early stages of development
50	Systematic approach is fully developed. Fact-based improvement system includes process evaluation (but no systematic refinements are in place). Random improvements may have been made	No major gaps in deployment exist (a few minor requirements of the item not addressed or not practised by some components). Some work units may still be in the early stages of development
60	Systematic approach is fully developed. Fact-based improvement system includes at least one evaluation and improvement cycle completed, including some systematic refinement	No major gaps in deployment exist (a few minor requirements of the item not addressed or not practised by a few components). A few work units may still be in the early stages of development
70	Fact-based, integrated improvement system is fully developed. Some systematic evaluation and improvement cycles and refinements are evident	No major gaps in deployment, with many work units in the middle to advanced stages of development (overall requirements of the item are addressed and practised by most components)
80	Fact-based, integrated improvement system is fully developed. Several systematic evaluation and improvement cycles and refinements are evident	No major gaps in deployment, with most work units in the middle to advanced stages of development (overall requirements of the item are addressed and practised by all components)
90	Fact-based, integrated improvement system is fully developed and systematically refined through several evaluation and improvement cycles. Some innovative refinements are evident	No major gaps in deployment, with most work units in the advanced stages of development (overall requirements of the item are addressed and practised by all components)
100	Fact-based, integrated improvement system is fully developed and systematically refined through several evaluation and improvement cycles. Substantial innovative refinements are evident	Approach is fully deployed to all work units with no gaps in deployment. All work units are in the advanced stages of deployment (all requirements of the item are addressed and practised by all components)

Table 3.7 Scoring of the results area

Score %	Scoring results
0	No results or poor results in areas reported
10	Data not reported for most areas of importance to the applicant's key business requirements. Limited positive results and trends are evident for the results that are reported
20	Data not reported for many to most areas of importance to the applicant's key business requirements Some positive results and a few trends are evident for the results that are reported
30	Data not reported for many areas of importance to the applicant's key business requirements. Some positive results and some improvement trends are evident for the results that are reported
40	Data are reported for most key areas of importance to the applicant's key business requirements Positive trends are reported for many areas of importance to the applicant's key business requirements. No significant adverse trends exist
50	Data are reported for most key areas of importance to the applicant's business requirements, with positive trends in most key areas important to the item and key business factors. Several trends are evaluated against benchmarks or comparisons, with good performance in some areas important to the item and key business factors
70	Data are reported for most to all key areas of importance to the applicant's business requirements Good to excellent improvement trends reported in most key areas, with no adverse trends in key areas important to the item and key business factors. Many trends can be evaluated against benchmarks or comparisons
80	Data are reported for most to all key areas of importance to the applicant's business requirements Very good to excellent improvement trends reported in most key areas, with no adverse trends in key area important to the item and key business factors. Most trends can be evaluated against benchmarks or comparisons
90	Excellent results and sustained positive trends (no adverse trends) in all key areas important to the item and key business factors. Most trends can be evaluated against benchmarks and comparisons
100	Excellent (world class) results and strong sustained trends in all areas important to the item and key business factors. Strong evidence of benchmark leadership

Table 3.8 Distribution of MBNQA scores 1988-1992: percentage of applicants in range

Score range	1988	1989	1990	1991	1992
0-125	0	0	0	2.8	0
126-250	0	2.5	7.2	13.2	12
251-400	1.6	20.5	18.6	35.8	30
401-600	47.5	37.5	52.6	34.0	40
601-750	34.4	30.0	19.6	14.2	18
751-875	16.4	10.0	2.1	0	0
876-1,000	0	0	0	0	0

Figure 3.2 The European Quality Award model

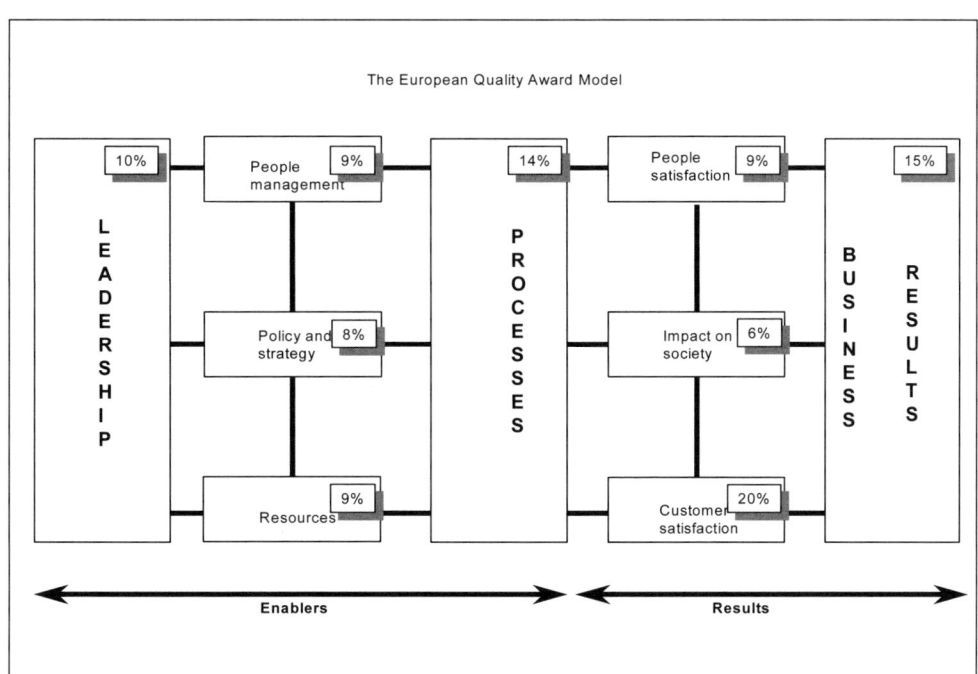

Benefits of self-assessment
Benefits reported by winners of the Deming Prize
Winners of the Deming Prize have been reported to have similar characteristics, as follows (Zairi, 1994a):
- Consistency in managing quality systems.
- Focus on positive quality in terms of innovation, creativity and adding value to the end customer.
- Policy management based on long-term goals rather than yearly financial returns.
- Various methods for managing quality on a daily basis, e.g. seven new tools of TQM and advanced statistical techniques.
- Management methods catering specifically for individual firms, climate, culture and style.

Zairi (1994a) reports for instance on Aisin Aw Co. Ltd, the 1991 Japan Quality Control Medal winner and winner of the Deming Prize in 1977. He states that:
> The company Aisin continued to excel in quality standards and to pioneer new ideas and concepts. In particular, it has made great strides in introducing an integrated approach to new product development (NPD) and research, driven by quality principles.

Aisin achieved the following benefits through self-assessment:
- the realisation of commercially attractive automatic transmission of best quality world-wide;
- production set-up matching the globalisation of Aisin's operation and strategy;
- employees who are highly motivated and full of creativity and vitality;
- a culture of teamwork and inter-functional collaboration, based on the gathering of wisdom, synergy, creativity and the establishment of an R&D network; and
- complete corporate development which is solid and sustainable.

Table 3.9 Criteria for the EQA excellence model

Category	Criteria
1. Leadership	(a) Leaders develop the mission, vision and values and are role models of a culture of excellence
	(b) Leaders are personally involved in ensuring the organisation's management system is developed, implemented and continuously improved
	(c) Leaders are involved with customers, partners and representatives of society
	(d) Leaders motivate, support and recognise the organisation's people
2. Policy and strategy	(a) Policy and strategy are based on the present and future needs and expectations of stakeholders
	(b) Policy and strategy are based on information from performance measurement, research, learning and creativity related activities
	(c) Policy and strategy are developed, reviewed and updated
	(d) Policy and strategy are deployed through a framework of key processes
	(e) Policy and strategy are communicated and implemented
3. People	(a) People resources are planned, managed and improved
	(b) People's knowledge and competences are identified
	(c) People are involved and empowered
	(d) People and the organisation have a dialogue
	(e) People are rewarded, recognised and cared for
4. Partnerships and resources	(a) External partnerships are managed
	(b) Finances are managed
	(c) Buildings, equipment and materials are managed
	(d) Technology is managed
	(e) Information and knowledge are managed
5. Processes	(a) Processes are systematically designed and managed
	(b) Processes are improved, as needed, using innovation in order to fully satisfy and generate increasing value for customers and other stakeholders
	(c) Products and services are designed and developed based on customer needs and expectations
	(d) Products and services are produced, delivered and served
	(e) Customer relationships are managed and enhanced
6. Customer results	(a) Perception measures
	(b) Performance indicators
7. People results	(a) Perception measures
	(b) Performance indicators
8. Society results	(a) Perception measures
	(b) Performance indicators
9. Key performance results	(a) Key performance outcomes
	(b) Key performance indicators

Koura (1993) reports on the benefits resulting from the use of cross-functional management (CFM) within Deming Prize winning organisations. CFM is a concept which was first introduced in the 1960s by Komatsu Ltd. CFM has been applied in different categories covering quality assurance, profit and cost management, production and delivery management, new product development, sales management safety and sanitation management. Appendix 3.1 illustrates the benefits derived from the implementation of CFM in 102 organisations using the Deming Prize (Koura, 1993).

Figure 3.3 RADAR logic

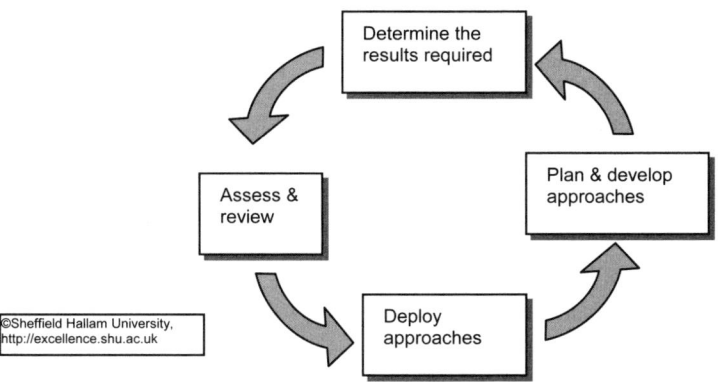

Benefits reported from winners of the MBNQA
Overall, all winners of the MBNQA have reported the achievement of great benefits from self-assessment. Eastman Chemical Co. for instance has established a culture entirely dependent on teamwork, where most employees are members of at least one team and supervisory members of at least two (Deavenport, 1994). Federal Express Corp., winner of MBNQA in 1990, has maintained the quality momentum over the years by strengthening its human resources processes, logistics and customer satisfaction (Pastore, 1995). A study, which looked at 19 winners of the MBNQA between 1988 and 1993 by comparing their quality progress against business performance using a number of commercial indicators (Wisner and Eakins, 1994), concluded that all 19 winners boast significant achievements in the areas of customer service, production costs, product reliability, failure rates and cycle times.

A fictitious exercise reveals that stock shares of MBNQA winners or their parent companies have led to healthy returns since the exercise began in 1991. This exercise was based on the fact that if $1,000 was invested in an MBNQA winning organisation or in the affiliated parent company, the investment would have grown 99 per cent by 1994. As stated by Helton (1995):

> This corresponds favourably to a 41.9% gain on principal if the same dollars had been invested in the Dow Jones Industrials or a 34.1% gain if invested in Standard and Poor's (S&P's) 500 stocks on the award dates.

Table 3.10 EQA scoring guidelines

Score %	Enablers		Results	
	Approach	Deployment	Results	Scope
0	Anecdotal or non value adding	Little effective usage	Anecdotal	Results address few relevant areas and activities
25	Some evidence of soundly-based systems. Subject to occasional review. Some areas of integration into normal operations	Applied to about one-quarter of the potential when considering all relevant areas and activities	Some results show positive trends, some favourable comparisons with own targets	Results address some relevant areas and activities
50	Evidence of soundly-based, systematic approaches and prevention-based systems Subject to regular review with respect to business effectiveness. Integration into normal operations and planning well-established	Applied to about half the potential when considering all relevant areas and activities	Many results show positive trends over at least three years Favourable comparisons with own targets in many areas Some comparisons with external organisations. Some results are caused by approach	Results address many relevant areas and activities
75	Clear evidence of soundly-based systematic approaches and prevention-based systems Clear evidence of refinement and improved business effectiveness through review cycles. Good integration of approach into normal operations and planning	Applied to about three-quarters of the potential when considering all relevant areas and activities	Most results show strongly positive trends over at least three years. Favourable comparisons with own targets in most areas. Favourable comparisons with external organisations in many areas Many results are caused by approach	Results address most relevant areas and activities
100	Clear evidence of soundly-based systematic approach and prevention-based systems. Clear evidence of refinement and improved business effectiveness through review cycles. Approach has become totally integrated into normal working patterns. Could be used as a role model for other organisations	Applied to full potential in all relevant areas and activities	Strongly positive trends in all areas over at least five years. Excellent comparisons with own targets and external organisations in most area. "Best-in-class" in many areas of activity. Results are clearly caused by approach. Positive indication that leading position will be maintained	Results address all relevant areas and facets of the organisation

From the winners of the 1994 MBNQA, the following benefits were reported (Bemowski, 1995):
- AT&T Consumer Communications Services (CCS):
  - with more than 75 million daily interactions with customers, 90 per cent rate the overall quality of AT&T as good or excellent;
  - NPD cycle time was reduced by 50 per cent, from an average of two years, to less than a year.
- GTE Directories:
  - independent studies confirm that GTE directories are preferred in 271 of 274 primary markets;
  - GTE's published error ratio for 1993 was just over 350 errors per one million listings, thus placing the company in best-in-class category.

- Wainwright Industries:
    - since 1992, customer satisfaction moved from 84 per cent to 95 per cent;
    - for some product lines, the production lead time was reduced by 8.75 days to 15 minutes and defect rates were reduced ten fold.
    - on time delivery rate is nearly 100 per cent as opposed to 75 per cent previous to MBNQA. Reduction in product cost is 35 per cent.

Even for those organisations which have won the MBNQA from its inception, the benefits continue to accrue. Rank Xerox for instance, reports that (Frank, 1995):

> Xerox 2000, Leadership Through Quality, supporting the Xerox Management Model with its customers and market central focus, is one of the most important steps taken since achieving the Baldrige Award. Essentially this is a Baldrige Award System in action.

IBM Rochester reports that (Frank, 1995):

> The most dramatic shift in IBM since winning the Baldrige Award has been the present customer view model orientation. We used to run our business and look at processes based upon how we viewed them. We made a fundamental shift, asking our customers how they view us. And now we are looking at our processes through our customers' eyes.

Benefits reported from winners of the EQA

The EFQM produced a report based on a benchmarking study of seven organisations: British Telecom, Kodak, ICL, Lucas Management Systems, Northern Telecom, Royal Mail and TSB (Longbottom, 1995).

Rank Xerox Ltd (Europe) was the first winner of EQA back in 1992. It has over 26,000 employees in 40 European locations. Rank Xerox is a company which is often linked with excellence and quality, and is quoted in most quality textbooks and major management magazines. It recognises the benefits of winning prestigious quality awards such as the EQA (Fournier, 1995):

> The quality-related benefits of an integrated document management strategy go far beyond organisational efficiency and better customer communications. Taking a new look at document management strategy gives companies a tremendous opportunity to consolidate and analyse how they are serving their customers, how they can add value and how they might plan for the future.

Design to Distribution (D2D) was the winner of the 1994 EQA award. D2D is a contract electronics manufacturer and, since winning the award, has signed several major contracts with blue chip companies worth over $200 million (Goodsell, 1995). The deal involves company names such as Pace Micro Technology, Madge Networks, Acorn Computers and On-line Media. In addition, and since winning the EQA, D2D has achieved the following:

- Certification to BS 7750.
- EMAS registration for its printed circuit board production facility.
- Rated best supplier by two of its major customers.

As Goodsell admits:

> The mood at D2D is buoyant and revenue targets are aggressive ($2 billion by the year 2000). We have much to look forward to, and much to do, but we feel we have a sound basis from which to progress and grow.

TNT Express (UK) is one of the largest providers of time-sensitive freight and tailored logistics solutions. It is the UK's market leader in express delivery, providing same day and overnight carriage of urgent documents and parcels. It has won major accolades, including the

1994 UK Quality Award and the 1995 Northern Ireland Quality Award, and it was the 1995 EQA prize winner. As Jones (1995) argues:

> You might not win.... but if you have beaten your previous best you have won a personal battle. That is the whole essence of continuous improvement.

He then goes on to say:

> The European Quality Award is ultimately about using best practice for better business results.

Texas Instruments Europe is famous for integrated circuit technology, the first electronic hand-held calculator, the single-chip microprocessor and microcomputer, the single-chip digital signal processor and the first quantum-effect transistor. TI's main business comes from semiconductors. TI Europe really appreciates the power of self-assessment, as expressed by John Scarisbrick (1995):

> Using the European model for business excellence helps provide and reinforce a common approach to change.... Total Quality (TQ) is not a universal panacea. It is not appropriate in all situations and on all occasions. We look closely at what we call "TQ versus IQ" because large parts of our business are creativity- and innovation-driven and have to strike a balance between harnessing the creative potential of individuals as well as working inside and across our own company boundaries on team efforts. The balance is about doing it better and doing it differently. Doing it better is a continuous improvement model; doing it differently is a process reengineering model. Total quality award winners have thrived in business because they have adapted, not because they have put their faith in just one thing.

Case studies of Rank Xerox, D2D, TNT and Texas Instruments are presented in Chapter 14.

The future of self-assessment

The Deming Prize is nearly 50 years old. Apart from extending the concept, with slight adaptations, there have been no significant changes to the drive for encouraging quality improvement and making quality management deliver performance results. The MBNQA on the other hand is nine years old. There are questions about its future, since the number of applicants for the prize decreased from 106 in 1991 to only 47 in 1995. Some cynics (Ettorre, 1996) have argued that:

> This suggests that, as corporate America's preoccupation with quality has faded, especially in the past two years, the award may have outlived its usefulness.

According to Donald C. Fisher, executive director of Mid-South Quality Productivity Center, (Ettorre, 1996), the real purpose of the MBNQA is not winning the prize but in strategic improvement:

> When you're doing an award, you're trying to dress up an organisation. When you are doing a self-assessment, you're trying to dress down an organisation, to get into the core.

As far as the EQA model is concerned, there is a mood of optimism overall, and the framework has been extended to cover the public sector and education. As Bangemann (1995) says:

> The increasing demand for the self-assessment brochures used for enrolment in the award system (5,000 in 1993 to 15,000 in 1994) is proof enough of the growing quality awareness of European firms.

Tito Conti (1995), one of the key architects of the EQA framework, argues that self-assessment is here to stay. He says:

Self-assessment is an irreplaceable tool for improvement, and is therefore universal in its approach. Awards, on the other hand, are focused on the recognition of excellence and on presenting role models, and rightly so. Research into self-assessment models should be left free and the awards should follow their own logic, until it is convenient to adapt to new developments.

Conti (1995) proposes a new self-assessment model (Figure 3.4) which he says is able to deal with the assessment of "soft categories" such as leadership and people, which currently have no reliable means of being assessed. In addition, the proposed model should measure the effectiveness of such soft criteria. Process measures and business measures should be related according to Conti. He believes that ultimately self-assessment is about business results diagnosis:

> The aim of self-assessment is improvement. It should point out areas of weakness and find their causes. The process should not be limited to assessing enablers, processes and results and to allocating a score. The most important element of the process has to be cross diagnosis which starts from unsatisfactory results, re-examines the processes that cause results, and, if necessary, the system factors, in its search for the root causes of problems.

Figure 3.4 The proposed self-assessment model

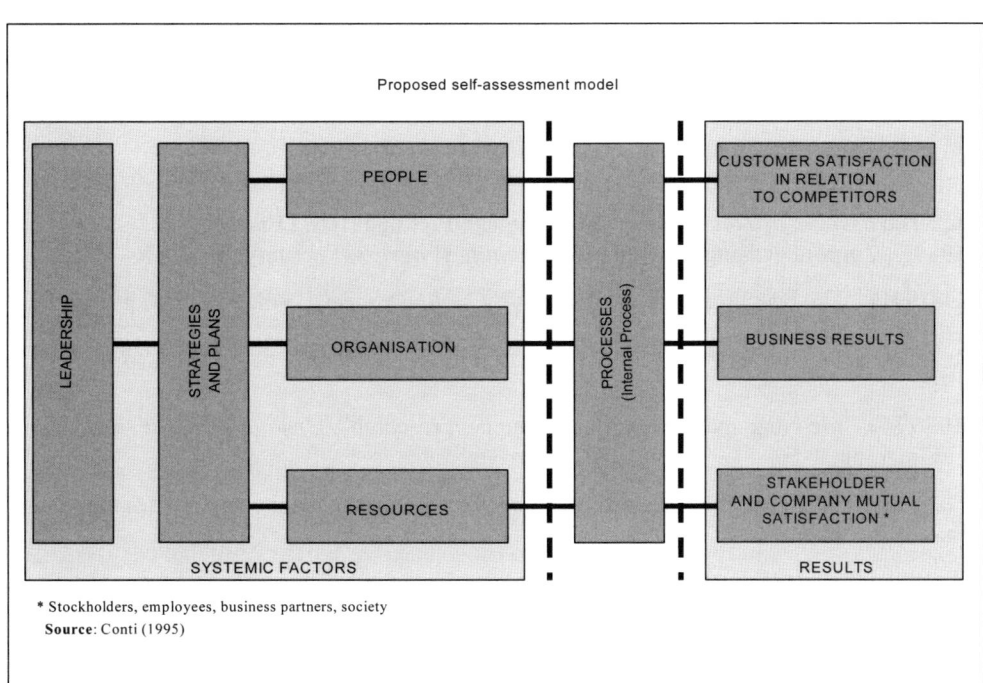

References and further reading

A.T. Kearney (1993), "Total Quality. Time to take off the rose tinted spectacles", *A Survey of a Cross Section of UK Firms,* A.T. Kearney/TQM Magazine Report.

Alexander (1991), "The soft technologies of quality", *Quality Progress,* Vol. 22 No. 1, pp. 24-8.

Allaire, Y. and Firsirotu, M.E. (1984), "Theories of organisational culture", *Organisation Studies,* Vol. 5 No. 3, pp. 193-226.

Alonzo, V. (1995), "Winning strategies. Blind spots", *Incentive,* Vol. 169 No. 1, November, p. 87.

Anonymous (1996), "ISO 9000 - what developments?", *Middle East Quality Review,* Vol. 1 No. 1, pp. 42-5.

Anonymous (1996), "The Mobil survey of ISO 9000 certificates awarded worldwide', *Middle East Quality Review,* Vol. 1 No. 1, pp. 37-41.

Arthur D. Little (1992), "Survey of 500 US manufacturing and service companies" *Key Note Publications Guide to TQM*, Key Note Publications, Hampton, Middlesex.

Ashridge Management College (1993), "Making quality work", research investigation.

Astley, W.G. (1985), "Organisational size and bureaucratic structure", *Organisation Studies,* Vol. 6 No. 3, pp. 201-28.

Atkinson, P.E. (1990), "Creating cultural change", *The TQM Magazine,* February, pp. 13-15.

Atkinson, P.E. and Naden, J. (1989), "Total quality management: eight lessons to learn from Japan", *Management Services,* March, pp. 6-10.

Ballan, E.S. (1982), *How to Design, Analyse and Write Doctoral Research*, University Press of America, New York.

Baker, G. and Starbird, S.A. (1992), "Managing quality in california food processing firms", *Agribusiness,* Vol. 8 No. 2, pp. 155-64.

Bangemann, M. (1995), "Aim for excellence", *American Management Association,* March, pp. 6-8.

Bank, J. (1992), *The Essence of Total Quality Management,* Prentice Hall, London.
Beer, M.C. (1989), "Corporate change and quality", *Quality Progress,* February, pp. 33-5.

Bemowski, K. (1991), "The benchmarking bandwagon", *QualityProgress,* Vol. 24 No. 1, pp. 19-24.

Bemowski, K. (1995), "1994 Baldrige Award recipients share their expertise", *Quality Progress,* Vol. 28 No. 2, pp. 35-40.

Bennett, R. (1986/87), "Meaning and method in management research", *Graduate Management Research,* Vol. 3 No. 3, Winter, pp. 4-56.

Benson, P. *et al.* (991), "The effects of organisational context on quality management", *Management Science,* Vol. 37 No. 9, pp. 1107-24.

Benson, R.S. and Sherman, R.W. (1995), "ISO 9000: a practical step-by-step approach", *QualityProgress,* October, pp. 75-8.

Bergstrom, R.Y. (1995), "Measuring to shape the future through quality", *Production,* Vol. 107 No. 8, August, pp. 50-1.

Best Practice (1997), "Does business excellence work?", *Best Practice,* March, p. 9.

Black, S.A. (1993), "Total quality management: the critical factors", PhD Thesis, University of Bradford.

Bonoma, T.V. (1985), "Research in marketing: opportunities, problems and a process", *Journal of Marketing Research*, Vol. XXII, May.

Bossink, B.A.G., Gieskes, J.F.N. and Pas, T.N.M. (1992), "Diagnosing total quality management – part 1 and 2", *Total Quality Management,* Vol. 3 No. 3, pp. 223-31 and Vol. 4 No. 1, pp. 5-12.

Bossink, B.A.G. *et al.* (1993), "Diagnosing total quality management - part 2", *Total Quality Management,* Vol. 4 No. 1, pp. 5-12.

Bryman, A. (1989), *Research Methods and Organisational Studies,* Unwin Hyman, London.

Camp, R. (1989), "Benchmarking. Part 1: a definition", *Quality Progress,* January, pp. 61-8.

Camp, R. (1989), *Benchmarking: The Search for Industry Best Practices that Lead to Superior Performance*, ASQC Quality Press, Milwaukee, WI.

Carman, J.M. (1993), "continuous quality improvement as a survival strategy: the Southern Pacific experience", *California Management Review,* Vol. 35 No. 3, pp. 118-32.

Case, K.E. and Bigelow, J.S. (1992), "Inside the Baldrige Award Guidelines Category 6: Quality and operational results", *Quality Progress,* November, pp. 47-52.

Chao-Hsien, C. (1988), "The pervasive elements of total quality control", *Industrial Manufacturing,* September-October, pp. 30-2.

Charles, G. (1995), "Inter cultural management associates, ICM: ICM management training in Russia, traps and gaps", *Journal of Management Development*, Vol. 14 No. 5, pp. 15-26.

Chase, R.L. (1990 and 1992), *Winning with Quality,* IFS Publications, Kempston, Bedford.

Choppin, J. (1995), "Total quality management – what isn't it?", *Managing Service Quality,* Vol. 5 No. 1, pp. 47-9.

Churchill, G.A. (1987), *Marketing Research: Methodological Foundations*, Dryden Press, Chicago, IL.

Clarke, P.A. (1972), *Action Research and Organisational Change*, Harper and Row, UK.

Conti, T. (1995), *Improving the Model*, American Management Association, March 1996, pp. 78-80.

Coulson-Thomas, C. (1992), "Quality: where do we go from here?, *International Journal of Quality & Reliability Management*, Vol. 9 No 1, pp. 38-55.

Coyne, B. (1989), "Lotus Cars — effective quality management", *Quality Today,* October, pp. 8-9.

Craig, S.N. (1990), "The case study. a vital yet misunderstood research method for management", *Graduate Management Research,* Vol. 4 No. 4, Spring, pp. 4-26.

Crosby, P. (1979), *Quality is Free: The Art of Making Quality Certain*, Penguin Books, New York.

Crosby, P.B. (1979), *Quality is Free,* McGraw-Hill, New York.

Crosby, P.B. (1967), *Cutting the Cost of Quality: The Defect Prevention Workbook for Managers,* Industrial Education Institute.

Crosby, P.B. (1984), *Quality Without Tears,* McGraw Hill, New York.

Crosby, P.B. (1991), "The Baldrige as a negative", *Quality Progress,* Vol. 24 No. 5, p. 414.

Darvin, D.A. (1988), *Managing Quality,* The Free Press, New York.

Development Dimensions International (1994), *TQM: Forging Ahead or Falling Behind – A Study of Quality Practices,* Development Dimensions International Inc., Bridgeville, PA.

Dean, J.W. and Bowen, D.E. (1994), "Management theory and total quality: improving research and practice through theory development", *Academy of Management Review,* Vol. 9 No. 3, pp. 392-418.

Dean, J.W. and Evans, J.R. (1994), *Total Quality: Management Organisation and Strategy*, West Publishing Co., St Paul, MN.

Deavenport, E.W. (1994), "Winning the Baldrige Award", *Chief Executive,* Issue 95, June, pp. 36-9.

DeLisi, P.S. (1990), "Lessons from the steel axe: culture, technology and organisational change", *Sloan Management Review,* Vol. 32 No. 1, pp. 83-8.

Deming, W.E. (1986), *Out of the Crisis,* Cambridge University Press, Cambridge and MIT Center for Advanced Engineering Study, Cambridge, MA.

Deshpande, R. and Parasuraman, A. (1986), "Linking corporate culture to strategic planning", *Business Horizons,* Vol. 21 No. 3, pp. 28-37.

Devos, L.J.F., Guerrero-Cusumano, J.L. and Selen, W.J. (1995), "ISO 900 in the Low Countries: researching for new heights?", Working Paper, Department of Operations Management, Vesalius College – VUB, Brussels, Belgium.

Downey, H.K. and Ireland, R.D. (1979), "Quantitative versus qualitative: environmental assessment in organisational studies", *Administrative Science Quarterly,* Vol. 24 No. 4, pp. 630-7.

Drucker, P.F. (1990), "The emerging theory of manufacturing", *Harvard BusinessReview*, May-June 1990, pp. 94-102.

Durham University (1992), "The adoption of TQM in Northern England", Durham University Survey.

Easterby-Sinith, M., Thorpe, R. and Lowe, A. (1991), *Management Research: An Introduction*, Sage University Paper Series on Quantitative Applications in the Social Sciences, Thousand Oaks, CA.

Easton, G.S. (1993), "The state of US total quality management: a Baldrige examiner's perspective", *California Management Review,* Vol. 35, pp. 32-54.

(The) Economist, "The cracks in quality", 18 April 1992, pp. 85-6.

Edson, J. and Shannahan, R. (1991), "Managing quality across barriers", *Quality Progress,* February, pp. 45-57.

Eisenthardt, K. (1989), "Building theories from case study research", *Academy of Management Review*, Vol. 14 No. 4, pp. 532-50.

El-Dardiry, M.A. and El-Nahrawy, E.E. (1996), "Benchmarking quality management practices in Egypt and other developed and developing countries", Arab Management Conference, Bradford, UK, 1996.

Ember, L.R. (1995), "Responsible care: chemical makers still counting on it to improve image", *C&EN Washington,* 29 May, pp. 10-17.

Ettorre, B. (1996), *Is The Baldrige Still Meaningful?*, American Management Association, March, pp. 28-31.

Feigenbaum, A.V. (1983), *Total Quality Control,* 3rd ed., (40th anniversary ed., 1990) McGraw-Hill, New York.

Feigenbaum, A.V. (1951), *Quality Control. Principles, Practices and Administration,* McGraw-Hill, New York.

Finniston, F.R.S. (1980), *Engineering Our Future*, HMSO 7794, Chapter 11.

Fournier, B. (1995), "Entering generation X", *European Quality*, European Quality Award Special Report, pp. 18-22.

Frank, C. (1995), "The continuing quest for excellence", *Quality Progress,* December, pp. 67-70.

Freemantle, M. (1996), "Environmental performance improves for many large chemical companies", *C&ENLondon,* 20 May, pp. 30-2.

Gagliardi, P. (1986), "The creation and change of organisational cultures: a conceptual framework", *Organisation Studies,* Vol. 7 No. 2, pp. 117-34.

GAO (1991), *Management Practices: US Companies Improve Performance Through Quality Efforts,* GA0/NSIAD-91-190, General Accounting Office, Washington.

Garvin, D.A. (1988), *Managing Quality*, McGraw-Hill, New York.

Geneen, H.S. (1972), "Fourteen steps to quality", *Quality Progress,* Vol. 5 No. 11, November, pp. 62-6.

Ghobadian, A. and Speller, S. (1994), "Gurus of quality: a framework for comparison", *Total Quality Management Journal*, Vol. 5 No. 3, pp. 53-69.

Glaser, B.G. and Strauss, A.L. (1967), *The Discovery of Grounded Theory: Strategies for Qualitative Research*, Aldine, New York.

Goode, W.J. and Halt, P.K. (1952), *Methods in Social Research*, McGraw-Hill, New York.

Goodsell, D. (1995), "Working hard at winning ways", *European Quality*, European Quality Award Special Report, pp. 24-5.

Gordon, W. and Langmaid, R. (1988), *Qualitative Market Research. A Practitioner's and Buyer's Guide*, Gower, Aldershot.

Greene, R. (1995), *Competent Re-Engineering: Advice, Warnings, and Recipes from Eye Witnesses,* Addison Wesley, Reading, MA.

Groocock, J.M. (1986), *The Chain of Quality,* John Wiley & Sons, Chichester.

Hammer, M. and Champy, J. (1993), *Re-Engineering the Corporation,* Nicholas Brierley, London.

Harris, D.M. and DeSimone, R.L. (1994), *Human Resource Development,* The Dryden Press, Fort Worth, TX.

Helton, B.R. (1995), "The Baldie Play", *Quality Progress,* February, pp. 43-5.

Hendricks, C.F. and Triplett, A. (1989), "TQM: a strategy for '90s management", *Personnel Administrator,* December, pp. 42-8.

Higson, A.W. (1987), "An empirical investigation of the external audit powers", PhD Thesis, University of Bradford.

Hill, S. and Wilkinson, A. (1995), "In search of TQM: employee relations", *Special Issue on TQM,* Vol. 17 No. 3, February.

House, R.J. (1970), "Scientific investigations in management", *Management International Review,* Vol. 4 No. 5, pp. 139-50.

Hunn, M. and Meisel, S. (1991), "Internal communication. Auditing for quality", *Quality Progress,* June, pp. 56-60.

Hutchins, D. (1990), *In Pursuit of Quality,* Pittman, London.

Irani, Z. et al. (1997), "Improving business performance through developing a corporate culture", *The TQM Magazine,* Vol. 9 No. 3, pp. 206-16.

Ishikawa, K. (1985), *What Is Total Quality Control? The Japanese Way?,* Prentice-Hall, Inc., Englewood Cliffs, NJ.

Israeli, A. and Fisher, B. (1991), "Cutting quality costs", *Quality Progress,* January, pp. 46-8.

Jackson, A.E., Safford, R.R. and Swart, W.W. (1995), "A road map to current benchmarking literature", Working Paper, University of Central Florida, Department of Industrial Engineering and Management Sciences, Orlando, FL.

Jones, A. (1995), "Service is our only product", *European Quality*, European Quality Award, Special Report, pp. 62-8.

Juran, J.M. (1951), *Quality Control Handbook*, McGraw-Hill, New York.

Juran, J.M. (1979), "Japanese and Western quality – a contrast", *Quality Assurance*, No. 1, March, pp. 12-17.

Juran, J.M. (1988), *Juran on Planning for Quality,* The Free Press, New York.

Juran, J.M. (1993), "A renaissance in quality", *Harvard Business Review,* July/August, pp. 42-53.

Juran, J.M. and Gryna, F.M. (Eds) (1988), *Juran's Quality Control Handbook,* 4th ed., McGraw-Hill, New York.

Juran, J.M. (1989), *Juran on Leadership for Quality*, The Free Press, New York.

Juran, J.M. (1991), "Strategies for world class quality", *Quality Progress,* Vol. 24 No. 3, pp. 81-5.

Juran, J.M. (1993), "Made in USA: a renaissance in quality", *Harvard Business Review,* Vol. 71 No. 4, pp. 42-50.

Kanji, G., Kristensen, K.K. and Dalhgaard, J.J (1992), "Total quality management as a strategic variable", *Total Quality Management,* Vol. 3 No. 1, pp. 3-8.

Kanji, G.K. (1995), "Quality and statistical concepts", in Kanji, G.K. (Ed.), *Total Quality Management Proceedings,* First World Congress, Chapman & Hall, London.

Kano, N. (1993), "A perspective on quality activities in American firms", *California Management Review,* Vol. 35 No. 3, pp. 12-31.

Kim, K.Y. and Chang, D.R. (1995), "Global quality management: a research focus", *Decision Sciences,* Vol. 26 No. 5, September/October, pp. 561-8.

Kirschner, E.M. (1995), "Production of top 50 chemicals increased substantially in 1994", *C&EN Northeast News Bureau*, 10 April, pp. 16-19.

Kirschner, E.M. (1995), "Small chemical firms' exports to big emerging markets receive boost", *C&EN Northeast News Bureau*, September, pp. 15-19.

Kirschner, E.M. (1996), "Growth of top 50 chemicals slowed in 1995 from very high 1994 rate", *C&EN Northeast News Bureau*, 8 April, pp. 16-20.

Kleiner, B.H. and Corrigan, W.A. (1989), "Understanding organisational change", *Leadership and Organisation Development*, Vol. 10 No. 3, pp. 25-31.

Knight, M. (1988), "Deming – a prophet with new honour", *Production Engineer,* April, pp. 58-9.

Knorr, R.O. (1990), "A corporate self-assessment checklist", *Journal of Business Strategy,* September/October, Vol. 11 No. 5, p. 60.

Komai, H. (1989), *Japanese Management Overseas*, Asian Productivity Organization, Tokyo, Japan.

Koura, K. (1993), "An analysis of the Deming Prize winners: the importance of cross-functional management in improving the corporate health and character", *Proceedings of EOQ 93, World Quality Congress,* June 1993, Helsinki, Finland.

Lawrence, J.J. and Yeh Song, R. (1994), "The influence of Mexican culture on the use of Japanese manufacturing techniques in Mexico", *Management International Review,* Vol. 34 No. 1, pp. 49-66.

Lawton, R.L. (1991), "Creating a customer oriented culture", *Quality Forum,* Vol. 17 No. 1, pp. 5-9.

Layman, P.L (1996), "PVC global outlook brightens as substitution by competitors levels off", *C&ENLondon*, 6 May, pp. 22-5.

Layman, P.L. (1995), "European chemical industry is growing faster", *C&EN*, 23 January, pp. 16-17.

Layman, P.L. (1995), "German chemical industry posts gains for 1994", *C&EN,* 23 January, p. 19.

Layman, P.L. (1995), "Global top 50 chemical producers show rise in profits and sales", *C&ENLondon,* 24 July, pp. 23-4, 27.

Layman, P.L. (1996), "Sustainable development: industry learns to cope, and to tell about it", *C&EN London,* 13 May, pp. 17-19.

Lea, R. and Parker, B. (1989), "The JIT spiral of continuous improvement", *Industrial Management and Data Systems,* No. 4, pp. 10-13.

Leader, C. (1989), "Making total quality management work: lessons from industry", *Aviation Week and Space Technology,* October, pp. 65-9.

Longbottom, D. (1995), "Total quality management in financial services: an empirical study of performance, strategy, and best practice, PhD Dissertation, The European Centre for TQM, Bradford University Management Centre, Bradford, UK.

Lorsch, J. (1986), "Managing culture – the invisible barrier to strategic change", *California Management Review,* Winter, pp. 95-109.

Luther, D.B. (1993), "Advanced TQM: measurements, missteps and progress through key result indicators at Corning", *National Productivity Review,* Winter 1992/1993, pp. 23-36.

Mann, N. (1985), *The Keys to Excellence: The Story of the Deming Philosophy*, Prestwick.

McAdam, R. (1996), "An integrated business improvement methodology to refocus business improvement efforts", *Business Process Re-Engineering & Management Journal,* Vol. 2 No. 1, pp. 63-71.

McClintock, C., Brannon, D. and Maynard-Moody, S. (1979), "Applying the logic of sample surveys to qualitative case studies", *Administrative Science Quarterly,* Vol. 24 No. 4, pp. 612-29.

McKinlay, A. and Starkey, K. (1988), "Competitive strategies and organisational change", *Organisation Studies,* Vol. 9 No. 4, pp. 555-71.

Miller, A. (1996), "Making education our business: lesson and issues", *Education and Training*, Vol. 38 No. 6, pp. 3-9.

Miller, J.G. and Vollmann, T.E. (1985), "The hidden factory", *Harvard Business Review,* September-October, pp. 142-50.

Miller, S. (1995), "Smooth sailing for your quality program", *Quality Progess*, Vol. 28 No. 10, October, pp. 101-3.

Moss Kanter, R. (1983), *The Change Masters,* Simon and Schuster, New York.

Motwani, J.C., Mahmond, E. and Rice, G. (1994), "Quality practices of Indian organisations: an empirical analysis", *International Journal of Quality and Reliability Management,* Vol. 11 No. 1, pp. 38-52.

Nachinias, C. and Nachmias, D. (1981), *Research Methods in the Social Sciences*, Edward Arnold, London.

National Institute of Standards and Technology (1992), *Malcolm Baldrige National Quality Award. 1992 Award Criteria,* National Institute of Standards and Technology, Milwaukee, WI.

Negandhi, A.A. (1983), "Management in the Third World", *Asia Pacific Journal of Management,* September, pp. 15-25.

Oakland, J.S. (1989), *Total Quality Management,* 1st ed., Butterworth-Heinemann, London.

Oakland, J.S. (1993), *Total Quality Management,* 2nd ed., Butterworth-Heinemann, Oxford.

Oakland, J.S. and Beardmore, D. (1995), "Best practice customer service", *Total Quality Management,* Vol. 6 No. 2, pp. 135-48.

Olian, I.D. and Rynes, S.L. (1991), "Making total quality work: aligning organisational processes, performance measures, and stakeholders", *Human Resource Management,* Vol. 30 No. 3, pp. 303-33.

Oliver, J. (1993), "Shocking to the core", *Management Today,* August.

Organizational Excellence (1997), "Self-assessment trends", *Organizational Excellence,* April, p. 18.

Osborne, S. (1996), "The hitch-hiker's guide to innovation: Management innovation and other organisational processes in an inter-agency context", *International Journal of Public Sector Management*, Vol. 9 No. 7, pp. 72-81.

Pastore, R. (1995), "CIO 100 best practices – special delivery", *CIO,* Vol. 8 No. 19, August, pp. 32-42.

Patton, M.Q. (1980), *Qualitative Evaluation Methods,* Sage Publications, Newbury Park, CA.

Patton, M.Q. (1987), *How To Use Qualitative Methods in Evaluation*, Sage Publications, Newbury Park, CA.

Peaff, G. (1995), "Chemical producers post another big earnings gain in second quarter", *C&EN Northeast News Bureau*, 21 August, p. 20.

Peaff, G. (1995), "Sales and profits improve for top 100 chemical producers", *C&EN Northeast News* Bureau, 8 May, pp. 13 -17.

Peaff, G. (1996), "Brazil's allure for chemical industry overshadows rest of Latin America", *C&ENNortheast News Bureau*, 26 February, pp. 15-18.

Peaff, G. (1996), "Chemical company earnings fall moderately in first quarter of 1996", *C&EN Northeast News Bureau,* 20 May, pp. 22-3.

Peaff, G. (1996), "Dow replaces DuPont to lead top 100 US chemical producers", *C&ENNortheast News Bureau,* 6 May, pp. 15-20.

Peaff, G. (1996), "Joint ventures take on greater importance in chemical industry", *C&EN Northeast News Bureau,* 9 September, pp. 15-18.

PERA (1992), *PERA International Survey*, July.

Peters, T. and Austin, N. (1985), *A Passion for Excellence – The Leadership Diffence*, Random House, New York.

Peters, T.J. and Waterman, R. (1982), *In Search of Excellence:Lessons From America's Best-Run Companies*, Harper and Row, New York.

Plunkett, J.J. and Dale, B.G. (1990), "Quality costing", in Dale, B.G. *et al.* (Eds), *Managing Quality*, Philip Allan, Hemel Hempstead.

Porter, L.J. and Parker, A.J. (1992), "Total quality management – the critical success factors", *Total Quality Management Journal,* Vol. 4 No. 1, pp. 13-22.

Porter, L.J. and Rayner, P. (1992), "Quality costing for total quality management", *International Journal for Production Economics*, Vol. 27 No. 1, pp. 69-81.

Quality Progress (1994), "Companies that link quality to reward program report success", *Quality Progress*, Vol. 27 No. 4, pp. 15-18.

Ramirez, C. and Looney, T. (1993), "Baldrige Award winners identify the essentials of a successful quality process", *Quality Digest*, Vol. 14 No. 1, January, pp. 94-114.

Reisch, M.S. (1995), "Rubber consumption is rising, but producers' profits are squeezed", *C&EN Northeast News Bureau*, 14 August, pp. 11-14.

Reisch, M.S. (1996), "As versatility boosts polypropylene growth, producers look to technology", *C&EN Northeast News Bureau*, 15 July, pp. 19-20.

Reisch, M.S. (1996), "Polyester resin producers rush to build more capacity worldwide", *C&EN Northeast News Bureau*, 13 May, pp. 11-13.

Reish, M.S. (1995), "Chemical producers plan only modest increase in capital spending in 1996", *C&EN Northeast News Bureau*, 18 December, p. 13.

Rigby, P.H. (1965), *Conceptual Foundations in Business Research*, John Wiley, New York.

Rothery, B. (1991), *ISO 9000,* Gower, Aldershot.

Sandelands, L. and Drazin, R. (1989), "On the language of organisation theory", *Organisation Studies*, Vol. 20 No. 4, pp. 810-29.

Saraph, J.V., Benson, P.G. and Schroeder, R.G. (1989), "An instrument for measuring the critical factors of quality management", *Decision Sciences*, Vol. 20 No. 4, pp. 810-29.

Scarisbrick, J. (1995), "Transnational excellence", *European Quality,* European Quality Award Special Report, pp. 54-60.

Scholtes, P.R. and Hacquebord, H. (1988), "Beginning the quality transformation, part 1", *QualityProgress*, July, pp. 28-33.

Schonberger, R. (1986), *World Class Manufacturing,* The Free Press, New York.

Schulz, W.G. (1996), "20/20 focus on industry future", *C&EN Washington,* 30 September, pp. 12-14.

Sekaran, V. (1992), *Research Methods forBusiness. A Skill Building Approach*, JohnWiley Publishing, New York.

Sheridan, J.H. (1996), "Lessons from the best", *IW,* 19 February, pp. 13-14.

Sheridan, J.H. (1996), "Manufacturing: the global economic engine", *IW,* 20 May, pp. 17-24.

Silverman, D. (1985), *Qualitative Methodology and Sociology,* Gower, Aldershot.

Simon, J.L. (1969), *Basic Research Methods in Social Science. The Art of Empirical Investigation*, Random House, New York.

Slater, K. (1991), "Performance measurement in the finance function", *Management Accounting,* May, pp. 32-4.

Sproull, N.L. (1988), *Handbook of Research Methods: A Guide for Practitioners and Students in the Social Sciences,* The Scarecrow Press Inc., Metuchen, NJ.

Storck, W. (1995), "The recession of 1996 – a challenge for the chemical industry", *C&EN,* 2 January, p. 15.

Storck, W. (1995), "US companies must deemphasize cost cutting, analyst says", *C&EN,* 6 February, p. 15.

Storck, W.J. (1995), "Earnings increases for chemical producers drive up profitability", *C&EN Northeast News Bureau,* 15 May, pp. 12-15.

Stratton, B. (1991), "The value of implementing quality", *Quality Progress,* Vol. 24 No. 8, p. 5.

Talwar, R. (1993), "Business re-engineering – a strategy driver approach", *Long Range Planning,* Vol. 26 No. 6.

Tayeb, M. (1994), "Japanese managers and British culture: a comparative case study", *International Journal of HRM*, Vol. 5 No. 1, pp. 145-66.

Thayer, A.M. (1995), "Chemical companies extend total quality management boundaries", *C&EN Northeast News,* 27 February, pp. 15-23.

Thayer, A.M. (1995), "Chemical industry R&D spending to increase slightly in 1995", *C&EN Northeast News Bureau,* 16 January, p. 13.

Thayer, A.M. (1996), "Chemical companies take wait-and-see stance toward ISO 14000 Standards", *C&EN Houston,* 1 April, pp. 11-15.

Thayer, A.M. (1996), "Ethylene producers add capacity to buffer cyclical markets, meet demand", *C&EN Houston,* 17 June, pp. 15-17.

Thayer, A.M. (1996), "International health and safety standards rejected", *C&EN,* 30 September, p. 27.

Thiagarajan, T. (1996), "An empirical study of total quality management (TQM) in Malaysia: a proposed framework of generic application", PhD dissertation, Management Centre, Bradford University, UK.

Thiagarajan, T. and Zairi, M. (1997), "Critical factors of TQM implementation: theory, concept and applications through best practice examples", Report No. R97/1, European Centre for TQM, University of Bradford, UK.

Thompson, J.L. (1990), *Strategic Management,* Chapman & Hall, London.

Tinnila, M. (1995), "Strategic perspective to business process redesign", Working Paper, Department of Logistics, Helsinki School of Economics, Finland.

Total Quality Management Institute of Australia (1987), *Invitation to Membership,* Total Quality Management Institute, Sydney.

Tremblay, L.F. (1995), "Chinese chemical market is appealing but the risks are high", *C&EN Hong Kong,* 20 November, pp. 23-31.

Tremblay, J.F. (1996), "Japan Inc. – red or black", *C&EN HongKong,* 30 September, pp. 18-25.

Tremblay, J.F. (1996), "Rapidly deteriorating environments in Asia catch governments unprepared", *C&EN HongKong,* 29 January, pp. 13-15.

Tremblay, J.F. (1996), "South Korean producers risk investing too much too soon in ethylene plants", *C&EN Hong Kong,* 8 July, pp. 18-20.

Tucker, F.G. and Zivan, S.M. (1985), "A Xerox cost centre imitates a profit centre", *Harvard Business Review,* Vol. 65 No. 3, May-June, pp. 168-74.

Tucker, F.G. *et al.* (1987), "How to measure yourself against the best", *Harvard Business Review,* Vol. 65 No. 1, January-February, pp. 8-10.

Vazirl, H.K. (1992), "Using competitive benchmarking to set goals", *QualityProgress,* October, pp. 81-5.

Verespej, M.A. (1996), "Lead, don't manage', *IW,* 4 March, pp. 55-60.

Weston, F.C. (1995), "What do managers really think of the ISO 9000 registration process?", *Quality Progress,* October, pp. 67-73.

Whitehill, A.M. (1991), *Japanese Management – Tradition and Transition,* Routledge, London.

Wilkinson, A., Allen, P. and Snape, E. (1991), "TQM and the management of labour", *Employee Relations,* Vol. 13 No. 1, pp. 24-31.

Wisner, J.D. and Eakins, S.G. (1994), "A competitive assessment of the Baldrige winners", *Total Quality Review,* November/December, Vol. 4 No. 5, p. 15.

Wong, A.L.S. (1992), "The transferability of Japanese management practice: the case of Singapore", PhD Thesis, University of Bradford.

Yarnazaki, M. (1986), "The impact of Japanese culture on management", in Thurow, L.C. (Ed.), *The Management Challenge,* The MIT Press, Cambridge, MA.

Zairi, M. (1992a), *Competitive Benchmarking: An Executive Guide,* Technical Communications (Publishing) Ltd, Letchworth, UK.

Zairi, M. (1992b), *TQM-based Performance Measurement: Practical Guidelines,* Technical Communications (Publishing) Ltd, Letchworth, UK.

Zairi, M. (1994a), "TQM: what is wrong with the terminology?", *The TQM Magazine*, Vol. 6 No. 4, pp. 6-8.

Zairi, M. (1994b), *Measuring Performance for Business Results*, Chapman & Hall, London.

Zairi, M. (1996), "Ishikawa Kaoru (1915-89)", *International Encyclopedia of Business and Management*, Thomson Business Press, UK, pp. 2401-5.

Zairi, M. and Leonard, P. (1994), *Practical Benchmarking: The Complete Guide*, Chapman & Hall, London.

Zairi, M. and Youssef, M.A. (1995), "Benchmarking critical factors for TQM. Part 1: theory and foundation", *Benchmarking for Quality Management & Technology*, Vol. 2 No. 1, p. 520.

Zairi, M., Letza, S. and Oakland, J. (1994), "Does TQM impact on bottom-line results?", *The TQM Magazine*, Vol. 6 No. 1, pp. 38-43.

Appendix 3.1 Benefits of cross-functional management in 102 Deming Prize winners

Category	Step	Results	
Common	General	Strengthen co-operation between divisions	53
		Penetration of conciousness of market in "quality first" and quality assurance concepts	30
		Reorganisation of quality assurance system	25
		Customers display a high level of trust	15
		Improvements in product quality and foundation of quality leadership	15
		Progress made in quality assurance-related standardisation	15
Quality assurance	Design and test production	Reduction of inconvenience to down stream processes due to design	18
	Purchasing & subcontractor production	Reduction of defective items during inspection	22
		Reduction of process defects and defect losses	37
	Production	Reorganisation of process management system	15
	Sales service	Reduction of claims and customer inconvenience	45
		Improvement in rate of customer satisfaction	15
Profit and cost management	Management mind	Improvement in mind of profit and cost management	16
	Improvement activities	Profit and cost improvement activities are more active and thorough	14
New product development	Net sales and inventory	Reduction of inventory and shortage of products	18
	Productivity	Increased productivity	17
	Results	Expansion of new products and improved sales of new products	37
		Increased number of cases of new product development	25
		Increase in net sales, number of products, number of customers	24
	Sales behaviour	Can conduct sales activities emphasising data processing	9
Safety and sanitation management		Zero safety and sanitation accidents	4
		Strengthening of safety and sanitation management system	3

Chapter 4
Leadership: the key driver of business excellence

Introduction

The leadership issue is frequently mentioned as being at the heart of many problems, not just those associated with the implementation of total quality management, but also in guiding organisations with sound strategies for the sustainability of superior competitive performance and long-term prosperity.

Strong leadership can perhaps be more associated with "soft issues" such as providing vision, direction and particularly with the ability of sharing, generating commitment, involving others and creating levels of synergy, consensus, congruence and enlightenment. Strong leadership has to be measured in situational and transformational terms. It is about reacting to adverse situations with wisdom, courage and objectivity, but also it is about vision, risk taking and seeking success and advancement. Style therefore is dynamic and changes according to circumstances (Dimma, 1989):

> The kind of leadership needed in times of crisis or great peril is very different from what is needed in times of stability, peace and prosperity.

Leaders can perhaps be compared to theatre directors, without whose contribution, the play will not happen. Organisational processes are only the arenas, and interpersonal processes represent the actors. Leaders need to identify what the priorities and agendas are for each actor, and they have to bring the various people together so that the act is complete (Zairi, 1991).

Leaders should not focus on themselves but rather be concerned with developing the vision and defining the mission for their organisations (Druker, 1990). Leadership represents the general consensus and the level of readiness and focus there is to achieve the mission. Stayer (1990) compared this with "a flock of geese on the wing". He argues:

> I didn't want an organisational chart with traditional lines and boxes, but a "V" of individuals who knew the common goal, took turns leading, and adjusted their structure to the task at hand. Geese fly in a wedge, for instance, but land in waves. Most important, each individual bird is responsible for its own performance.

Leadership and management: what is the difference?

Kotter (1990) argues that leadership and management are different but complementary processes which are both required to steer organisations towards successful competitiveness. He comments:

> Leadership is different from management, but not for reasons most people think. Leadership isn't mystical and mysterious. It has nothing to do with having "charisma" or other exotic personality traits. It is not the province of a chosen few. Nor is leadership necessarily better than management or a replacement of it. Rather leadership and management are two distinctive and complementary systems of action.

The distinction between leadership and management is perhaps in the fact that the former focuses more on setting the vision and relying on softer skills such as inter-personal skills to communicate the vision and generate commitment and enthusiasm to make it happen. To distinguish between the two, it may perhaps be useful to refer to the following definitions:

> Leadership means vision, cheerleading, enthusiasm, love, trust, verve, passion, obsession, consistency, the use of symbols, paying attention as illustrated by one's calendar, out-and-out drama (and the management thereof), creating heroes at all levels, coaching, effectively wandering around, and numerous other things (Peters and Austin, 1985).

On the other hand, effective management has been compared to the "wagon masters of the Westward movement in the last century" (Ninomya, 1988):

> A wagon master had two jobs. He had to keep the wagons moving toward their destination day after day despite all obstacles. He also had to maintain harmony and a spirit of teamwork among the members of his party and to resolve daily problems before they became divisive. A wagon master's worth was measured by his ability to reach the destination safely and to keep spirits high along the way. He had to do both in order to do either.

Leadership in the context of TQM

Total quality management (TQM) required a special type of leadership in the 1990s. Productivity is defined in terms of human performance through creativity, problem solving, teamwork, value-adding contributions and a dedication and commitment to continuous improvement. Any effective style of leadership in this context will therefore have to have great impact on behaviour modification and changing people's attitudes.

It is no longer valid nor is it sufficient to rely on structural change or sound investment strategies on capital equipment and pioneering technologies. In the 1990s the challenge lies with leaders' ability to transform in a radical way cultures, attitudes, methods of working and so on. Performance of leaders in a modern context does not just hinge around one or two specific tasks. A recent study of 900 leaders has identified four areas where leaders should focus their energies (Bennis and Nanus, 1985):

1. attention through vision;
2. meaning through communication;
3. trust through positioning; and
4. the development of self through positive self-regard.

Perhaps in the context of TQM what is expected of leaders is more of the doing, being more in touch, more aware and being much more concerned with developing means rather than just concerned with ends. Leaders in the context of TQM are more focused on corporate performance rather than just their "now". Leadership in the context of TQM is not about power, authority and control, it is more about empowerment, recognition, coaching and developing others.

Leadership nowadays is considered as a must for survival. It comes from the level of inspiration, commitment generated and corporate determination to perform. The power of modern leadership is in achieving congruence and getting wider ownership of the ultimate task of satisfying customers and building strong competitiveness. Warren Bennis, an author on leadership, is reported to have commented that:

> whips and chains are no longer an alternative. Leaders must learn to change the nature of power and how it is employed (Huey, 1994).

The challenge for leaders in the context of introducing change and modern management philosophies such as TQM is best described in the following quote (Huey, 1994):

As the power of position continues to erode, corporate leaders are going to resemble not so much captains of ships as candidates running for office. They will face two fundamental tasks: first, develop and articulate exactly what the company is trying to accomplish, and second, to create an environment in which employees can figure out what needs to be done and then do it well.

And:

Executives who rose in the traditional systems often have trouble with both. The quantitative skills that got them to the heights don't help them communicate. And if their intelligence, energy, ambition, and self-confidence are perceived as arrogance, it cuts them off from information, which makes the challenge of empowering the work force even more vexing.

Establishing best practice in leadership
Results of an American study

This study was conducted by Easton (1993) as part of a research grant from the Graduate School of Business, University of Chicago. The work assessed 22 organisations representing a mixture of large and small companies and operating in both manufacturing and service sectors. The sample analysed organisations which submitted applications for the Malcolm Baldrige National Quality Award (MBNQA). Although the assessment of each individual company was considered to be subjective (using the MBNQA assessment criteria), the author has had vast experience as an examiner for the MBNQA Award for a number of years.

The assessment conducted during the study focused on the seven criteria covered by the MBNQA:
1. Leadership.
2. Information and analysis.
3. Strategic quality planning.
4. Human resource development and management.
5. Management of process quality.
6. Quality and operational results.
7. Customer focus and satisfaction.

For the purpose of this discussion, and in the context of this chapter, only the first category will be considered. The major findings from the Easton (1993) study have been grouped in terms of strengths and areas for improvement.

Key strengths identified:
- Senior management commitment to quality is unwavering and they spend a substantial amount of their time reminding people of the importance of customers and improving quality. In addition, they put in a lot of effort in educating people, speaking in public, face-to-face contacts with customers, employees and so on.
- Senior management people have developed a vision and set of values to develop a quality culture in their organisations reflected by an obsession with the customer, continuous improvement, teamwork, problem solving, respect for people, focusing on the process and so on.
- The vision is achieving goal congruence in the form of customer understanding and focus and appreciating the importance of internal customers as well.
- Quality is managed through a proper structure such as having a quality council, steering groups, and being active in managing quality improvement teams, the development of suggestions schemes and reward and recognition systems.

Areas for improvement:
- Senior managers' primary focus is on short-term strategic goals which tend to be financial in nature and they lack appreciation of quality measures and improvement measures.
- Senior managers do not take a process-based approach in their decision making and there is poor utilisation of hard facts and information.
- Senior managers have very limited and poor understanding of TQM and its potential. Except for signing declarations, they devote very little time to making it work within their organisations and have little or no knowledge in defining roles for their subordinates for managing quality.
- Senior managers take a "results-oriented approach" rather than a "process-based approach". They set targets in isolation from the process and expect people to perform and deliver the expected results.
- There is poor utilisation of data relating to customers, suppliers and employees. As a result, managers have very poor understanding of causes of problems and what causes variability in their organisations.
- Although a structure for quality might be present, senior managers tend to treat quality as a separate activity from the essentials of running a business and therefore it is given a low priority in comparison with activities which can lead to tangible results in the short term.
- Senior management people take an "internal focus" rather than streamlining all their operations to meet external customer needs. This notion of "we know best what the customer wants" means that quality improvements and measurement from the perspective of the end customer do not really take place.

Case studies: winners of prestigious awards

This section covers various case studies of companies that have won prestigious awards such as the MBNQA and the European Quality Award. In particular the various cases will highlight how leadership is defined, what kind of activities and initiatives are sponsored by senior managers and the level of activity at which they are involved. In other words the purpose of this analysis is really to determine the role of senior managers in TQM implementation.

Zytec Corporation
Zytec Co. was an MBNQA winner in 1991. It designs and manufactures electronic power supplies, and also repairs them as well as CRT monitors. It has a large industrial customer base both in the USA and overseas and is considered to be one of the largest multiple output switching power supply producers in the USA. The company was formed in 1984 and has been using quality principles since its inception.

Leadership at Zytec:
- Zytec's mission is based on three key words: quality, service and value.

    Zytec is a company that competes on value, it provides technical excellence in its products and believes in the importance of execution.

    We believe in a simple form and a lean staff, the importance of people as individuals, and the development of productive employees through training and capital investment.

    We focus on what we know best, thereby making a fair profit on current operations to meet our obligations and perpetuate our continued growth.

- To implement the above vision, Zytec's top management team relied on Deming's 14 points for the management of quality.
- Senior management created a structure for the management of quality and "The Deming Steering Committee" members acted as advisors to various Deming implementation teams whose task was to carry out major improvements to key processes.
- The senior management team developed and communicated the quality statement.
- The senior management team developed an approach for goal development, deployment and review based on best practice. This is referred to as the management by planning (MBP) process, it relies on employee involvement and feed back and drives Zytec towards achieving its short, medium and long-term goals.
- The MBP process is considered to be the best tool for communicating the quality mission, goals and objectives throughout the company.
- Senior managers are very active in promoting awareness of quality through training, seminars and open sharing of Zytec's key learnings. They are also active in talking to customers and suppliers and in major benchmarking initiatives.

Wallace Co., Inc.
This company was founded in 1942 and is family owned. It is a major industrial distributor to the US chemical market but also deals with overseas orders. The major market includes refining, chemical and petrochemical industries. It deals with maintenance and repair operations and engineering and construction projects.

Wallace became committed to quality because it has developed strong partnerships with its major customers who have very high standards of quality and who demand adherence to stringent levels of quality in every sense. Wallace won the MBNQA in 1990.

Leadership at Wallace:
- Wallace has established the Quality Management Steering Committee (QMSC) which is represented by all the senior management team.
- There is a whole structure for managing quality which involves every manager and every employee. This structure is based on teamwork and includes, for example, quality improvement process teams, inter-departmental teams and so on.
- All senior managers have received training on TQM and its working.
- Communication on quality takes place through various vehicles such as visits, meetings, newsletters, posters and exhibitions. The major vehicle for communicating the quality message is, however, the mission statement.
- The mission statement is supported by 16 quality strategic objectives (QSOs). These are meant to drive the entire quality process.

Ritz-Carlton Hotel Company
This is a management company which develops and operates luxury hotels. It employs around 12,000 people and has subsidiary products including restaurants and banquets. Quality was introduced in the Ritz in order to set "Gold Standards" through having distinctive facilities and provide highly personalised services and delivering the best quality food and beverages. The Ritz-Carlton Hotel Company won the MBNQA in 1992.

Leadership at the Ritz-Carlton:
- The senior management team doubles up as the senior quality committee. They personally devise their quality strategy for the whole company.

- Senior management people are actively involved in quality assurance and optimising quality standards.
- The president and CEO communicate the quality vision throughout the organisation.
- Quality at the Ritz-Carlton is implemented through the "Gold Standards". The Gold Standards include:
  - *The credo*: a guide for employees, highlighting that personalised customer satisfaction is the number one priority and also defining the critical characteristics of every product and service.
  - *The three steps of service*: defining activities and decisions related to customer interface.
  - *The Ritz-Carlton basics*: problem-solving process.
  - *A motto*: this is to emphasise commitment to serve customers in a warm and genuine manner.

A case study of Ritz-Carlton is given in Chapter 14.

Cadillac Motor Car Company

Cadillac was founded in 1902 and is a division of General Motors (GM). It competes at the luxury end of the car market and manufactures various models of vehicles. Although quality was always an important aspect of managing operations within Cadillac, the real breakthrough came in the mid-1980s through the introduction of simultaneous engineering (SE), parallel oriented, process-based approach and a culture of work relying on teamwork and problem solving for continuous improvement. Cadillac won the MBNQA in 1990.

Leadership at Cadillac:
- Senior managers are responsible for developing and communicating the vision, values and ways for achieving intended business results.
- Senior managers have been instrumental in the change of work culture to a team-based one and the emphasis on the customer.
- In addition to the overall responsibility of implementing the business planning process (mission > strategic objectives > business objectives > goals > action plans) the top management team initiated the development of the mission:

    > The mission of the Cadillac Motor Car Company is to engineer, produce and market the World's finest automobiles, known for uncompromised levels of distinctiveness, comfort, convenience and refined performance. Through its people, who are its strength, Cadillac will continuously improve the quality of its products and services to meet or exceed customer expectations and succeed as a profitable business.

- Senior managers review the annual business planning cycle and help set targets for the following years. These targets are then communicated throughout the organisation and various group levels are empowered to develop their own specific goals to support the overall corporate targets.

Texas Instruments Defence Systems & Electronics Group (TI-DSEG)

This company is a manufacturer of precision-guided weapons and other advanced defence technology. It is a subsidiary of Texas Instruments Inc. Of its annual sales revenue, 95 per cent comes from precision-guided weapons, airborne radar systems, infrared vision equipment, electro-optic systems and electronic warfare systems. TI-DSEG is highly committed to TQM and believes that its quality goals and business goals are one and the same. The commitment to achieve the highest of quality standards can be demonstrated by TI's determination to achieve Six Sigma quality standards (a defect rate of 3.4 per million) by 1995 and to reduce new product development (NDP) time by 25 per cent each year. TI-DESG won the MBNQA in 1992.

Leadership at TI-DESG:
- Senior management communicates the company's quality values and is very active in promoting and supporting TQM implementation, through attending meetings, talking to employees, answering written letters, using management by walk around (MBWA).
- TI evaluates the quality commitment of all its managers through their annual performance reviews.
- TI has created a proper structure of developing quality based on teamwork, quality improvement teams and other team structures.
- TI is very active in promoting quality externally and is a member of research groups on quality issues, benchmarking associations, and is actively helping the transfer of knowledge within the business community of which it is a part.

A case study of TI-DESG is presented in Chapter 14.

National Roads & Motorists' Association (NRMA)
The Australian association was founded in 1920 and offers services to all its members on a national basis in the motoring field. It is one of the largest motoring organisations in the world with over two million members and is Australia's largest general insurer. NRMA was the winner of the Australian Quality Award (AQA) in 1992.

Quality within NRMA has evolved over the years. Its commitment to establishing a culture of never ending improvement is expressed in the mission statement:

> To provide road service and a range of quality services for members, at the lowest possible cost consistent with sound financial management.
>
> To promote the interests of motorists in good roads, safety and consumer protection.

Leadership at NRMA:
- The organisational structure supports the implementation of TQM.
- Each senior manager has direct line responsibility for continuous improvement in a specific area. The role encompasses many activities including innovation, problem solving, monitoring progress, empowering teams to perform, reward and recognising efforts.
- The CEO is instrumental in the communication of company vision and creating a climate aware of the need to improve quality continuously.
- The deployment of quality takes place through the translation of corporate targets into individual unit plans, goals, reviews and action plan development at various levels.

Rank Xerox Limited
Rank Xerox Ltd is part of Rank Xerox Corporation. It is one of Europe's leading high technology companies. Its customer base represents commercial, industrial and public sector based organisations. They deliver anything from small office copiers, workstations, laser printers, electronic printing systems and colour copiers. The company is represented by 19 operating units.

The implementation of quality at Rank Xerox Ltd started back in 1984, gradually moving away from focusing on the product and service, to an obsession with improving processes and delivering value added to the customer base. Now quality drives the business of Rank Xerox and the culture is one of true quality based on thousands of teams working in different areas and using various tools for carrying out the necessary improvements. Rank Xerox Ltd was the first winner of the European Quality Award (EQA) in 1992.

Leadership at Rank Xerox:

- Members of the senior management team are central to TQM implementation. They developed Rank Xerox's quality policy:

    Rank Xerox is a quality company. Quality is the basic business principle for Rank Xerox.

    Quality means providing our external and internal customers with innovative products and services that fully satisfy their requirements.

    Quality improvement is the job of every employee.

- The quality strategy by which the above quality policy is implemented has evolved from being a goal to a strategy and is now a process relevant to all levels within the organisation. This is referred to as leadership through quality.
- Senior managers lead all training initiatives and on a continuous basis assess the requirements of all employees for continuously improving quality.
- Senior managers are expected to lead by example by using tools and techniques of TQM and taking a process perspective to solve various problems.
- The communication of the quality message takes place through the formal deployment process (policy deployment process). The deployment of goals and the generation of commitment take place through weekly, monthly, quarterly and yearly meetings.
- Rank Xerox uses quality improvement process (improvement) and a six step problem solving process (PSP) to promote a culture of quality. Review of the culture development takes place through appraisal of individual performances, review of quality progress by looking at results and self-assessment.
- Senior managers ensure that quality implementation is adequately resourced through networks, senior appointments and funding.
- Senior managers actively encourage the involvement of customers and suppliers in the quality effort.
- Senior managers promote quality outside Rank Xerox within professional associations, local community, attendance at conferences and seminars, and by writing books and articles.

Rank Xerox is discussed as a case study in Chapter 14.

Key ingredients for effective quality leadership

The discussion in this chapter, whether from the review of the literature or the case studies, indicates that leadership requirements for the 1990s are to a large extent different from what one has been accustomed to in the past. There are areas in which traditionally leaders tended not to be involved but are now required to be so. In addition and in terms of style, leaders in the context of TQM, for instance, are expected to have more of a "hands on" role and, in addition to their brilliance at financial and strategic skills, be good communicators and efficient at inter-personal contacts.

Based on the analysis of the case studies and Easton's (1993) review, the following are perhaps areas where leaders need to focus the core of their activities. These areas could be the pre-determinants of their effectiveness and can be used as a measure of their performance.

Setting the vision and the strategic choice
Leaders in any organisation will be expected to develop the vision of their organisation, reflecting aspirations for the short term, medium term and long term. A healthy mix will ensure that performance delivers in different ways and at different periods of time.

Communicating the vision, generating corporate commitment
Leaders can only be considered to be effective once they have shared their vision with all employees. Many ideas which result in excellent blueprints fail because they remain as "theory" and do not get shared and communicated effectively. The communication of the vision has to be based on a sound framework which reaches everyone in the organisation and which encourages discussion, feed back and involvement. This is very critical since TQM's workings are more or less from a bottom-up approach and, unless there is corporate ownership, no performance will ensue.

Developing a process-based culture
Part of a leader's role in a modern business context is to change the culture of the organisation. One of the essential requirements of TQM is to focus more on the process and less on the individual. It is to organise work so that there is an inter-connectedness between the various roles and appreciation of everyone's efforts, since that which is delivered to the end customer is a team-based effort. Processes represent the capability of the organisation to meet customer requirements both in the short term and long term. The capability to deliver is not dependent on any specific function and has to rely on all the various contributions. Traditional structural approaches do not support the process-based view. Leaders in the context of TQM will, therefore, have to have a team-based structure which cuts across all the functions and boundaries and which will appreciate all the various contributions.

Recognition of people assets
One of the premises of TQM is that people are the most important asset for achieving high standards of competitive performance. This recognition has to be supported by:
- investment in training and employee development;
- involvement, participation in decision making;
- setting goals and targets;
- participation in team projects;
- creativity and innovation encouragement; and
- reward and recognition.

Performance management
Leaders in a modern business context have to realise that performance is not solely measured in terms of financial results (short term) but efforts have to be measured in terms of strengthening the processes, building capability for future demands and ensuring that there is a high level of consistency and confidence in satisfying customer requirements time and time again (long term).

Performance reviews therefore have to take place at various levels and at different intervals in time. This will reflect wider ownership and will indicate that the notion of control is focused on the process, rather than the individual.

Developing partnerships
It is widely recognised that modern competitiveness has to rely on building strong partnerships with customers and suppliers. Effective leadership will be based on creating a

climate of win-win, through perhaps working with fewer suppliers but on a strategic approach, which will help deliver benefits for each party. Issues of capability, resources, commitment to continuous improvement and technical know-how will be taken into consideration when choosing partners. Similarly, leaders can be very instrumental in generating customer commitment when agreeing on long-term working relationships. Regular visits, joint projects, additional services, joint exploration of technological know-how and so on are opportunities which could be exploited effectively for developing partnerships.

External ambassadors
Leaders have a very important role in promoting their organisations, through PR, seminars, conferences, professional associations, local academic institutions and within the wider community. Networking is absolutely essential in modern competitiveness. Through networking, benchmarking activities can take place, to compare practices, methods and performance, to learn new ways and inject them into organisations concerned and, more importantly, networking ensures continuity, perseverance and avoids complacency.

Leaders have also got a role to play within the community by ensuring that there is social responsibility, a caring attitude and development of the community concerned through the creation of jobs and prosperity.

Developing leadership in the organisation
Effective leadership in a modern business context means taking time and effort to develop others and being humble, kind and generous with comments, advice, information, tips and so on. The following Chinese proverb perhaps expresses this last point clearly:

Of the best leader, when he is gone, they will say: "We did it ourselves".

References

Bennis, W. and Nanus, B. (1985), *Leaders: The Strategies for Taking Charge*, Harper & Row, New York, NY.

Dimma, W.A (1989), "On leadership", *Business Quarterly*, Winter, pp. 17-20.

Druker, P.F. (1990), *Managing the Non-profit Organisation*, Butterworth-Heinemann Ltd, Oxford, UK.

Easton, G.S. (1993), "The 1993 state of US total quality management: a Baldrige examiners' perspective", *California Management Review*, Spring, pp. 32-54.

Huey, J. (1994), "The new post-heroic leadership", *Fortune*, February, pp. 18-22.

Kotter, J.P. (1990), "What leaders really do", *Harvard Business Review*, May-June, pp. 103-11.

Kouzes, J. and Posner, B. (1993), *Credibility: How Leaders Gain and Lose It*, Jossey-Bass, San Fransico, CA.

Ninomya, J.S. (1988), "Wagon masters and lesser managers", *Harvard Business Review*, March-April, pp. 84-90.

Peters, T. and Austin, N. (1985), "MBW (managing by walking around)", *California Management Review*, Vol. XXVIII No. 1, Fall, pp. 9-34.

Stayer, R. (1990), "How I learned to let my workers lead", *Harvard Business Review*, November-December, pp. 66-83.

Zairi, M. (1991), *Total Quality Management for Engineers*, Woodhead Publishing Ltd, Cambridge, UK.

Appendix 4.1: Leadership exercise
Leadership is seen as a key organisational success criterion. As Bob Greenleaf the former CEO at AT&T said:
In my experience every time I have examined a world class operation there is a visible leader at the helm who believes in and puts into practice the fundamentals of servant leadership.

Given such a statement you are required to:
1. Identify the top 19 attributes that characterise superior leaders.
2. Indicate how leadership impacts on business results to make an organisation a "world class" operation.

Suggested solution
The top 19 attributes could be (taken from Kouzes and Posner, 1993):
1. Honest: 87 per cent.
2. Competent: 74 per cent.
3. Forward looking: 67 per cent.
4. Inspiring: 61 per cent.
5. Intelligent: 46 per cent.
6. Fair minded: 42 per cent.
7. Broad-minded: 38 per cent.
8. Courageous: 35 per cent.
9. Straightforward: 33 per cent.
10. Imaginative: 31 per cent.
11. Dependable: 29 per cent.
12. Supportive: 26 per cent.
13. Caring: 23 per cent.
14. Co-operative: 20 per cent.
15. Mature: 18 per cent.
16. Determined: 14 per cent.
17. Self-controlled: 13 per cent.
18. Loyal: 10 per cent.
19. Independent: 8 per cent.

The linkage between leadership and business results could be described as follows:
- Mission/values – strategic direction and operational focus – team and individual goals – increased people satisfaction – reduced staff turnover, increased sales, improved efficiency – improved business results.
- Rewards and recognition – increased people satisfaction – reduced staff turnover, potential sales, improved efficiency – improved business results.
- Customer/supplier relationships – reduced wastage, cost of quality and administration costs – improved process efficiency – improved results.
- Quality improvement – cost of quality reduced – improved process efficiency – improved results.
- External focus – corporate citizenship – enhanced image in business and local community, awareness of new techniques and research in academic institutions – customer perception/satisfaction improved – increased sales – improved business results.

Chapter 5
Quality policy deployment: the key driver for performance measurement

The link between quality policy deployment and performance measurement
Quality policy deployment (QPD) is the necessary trigger for processes to perform well and for goals to be achieved. It is the mechanism by which the quality effort is cascaded down throughout the organisation. QPD is a top-down approach and as such tends to be the responsibility of senior managers. Process improvement and measurement is a horizontal effort and quality deployment is a vertical (top-down) approach. As Figure 5.1 illustrates, quality improvement is a continuous effort and as such is not finite. However, quality effects have to be measured and quantified against set targets (Yoji, 1990).

Figure 5.1 The quality deployment process

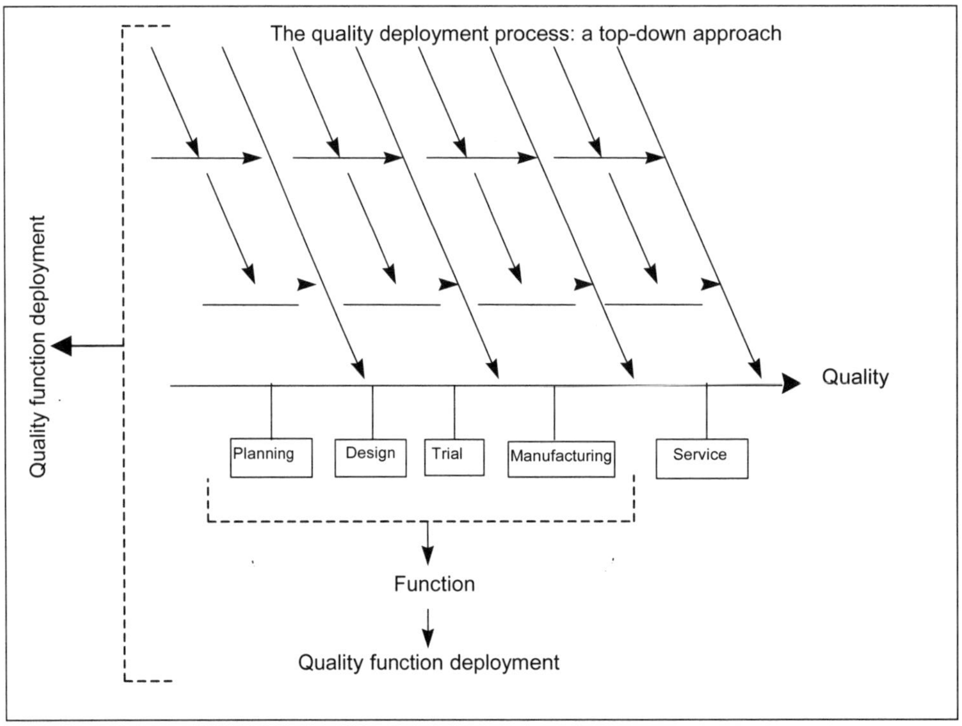

Quality policy deployment is not merely a good communication process, it is a dynamic process where performance measurement is an integral part and where goals are translated into actions throughout the various activities. Quality function deployment is the horizontal process which ensures that performance will ensue from the goal communication effort.

The Deming cycle of Plan-Do-Check-Act (PDCA) can be applied in the context of QPD (i.e. strategical continuous improvement). As Figure 5.2 illustrates (American Supplier Institute, 1989) the PDCA can drive the strategy and ensure that goals are achieved, that adjustments are made as and when necessary and that learning takes place continuously.

Figure 5.2 Strategic application of the PDCA cycle

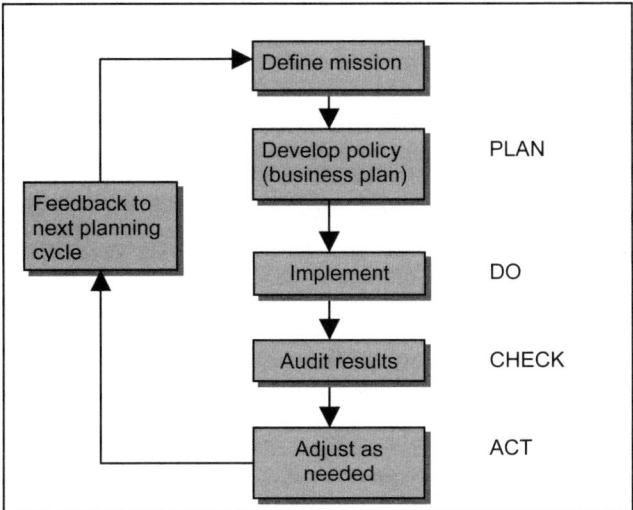

The conventional methods of strategic planning and strategic implementation tend to be marred with problems. Many strategies fail to deliver for a variety of reasons including, amongst others:
- Poor communication of goals – people working in total darkness.
- Moving the goal post – too many disruptions and changes in direction.
- Pursuit of pet projects – short-term goals to the detriment of long-term competitiveness.
- Cost is the key driver for results at the expense of real improvement opportunities.
- Goals developed in remoteness from the process.
- Voice of customer not really captured.
- Achievements are not sustainable.

On the other hand, QPD is focusing on sustainability and building strengths for increased competitiveness. While this process focuses on results, it only does so by continuously improving the processes concerned so that repeatability of performance and consistency can be ensured.

QPD introduces discipline, conveys the same goal at all levels and ensures goal congruence or real alignment. Unlike management by objective (MBO), which focuses on individual performance and follows a rigid hierarchical route of line of authority and responsibility, QPD follows a process route and measures team performance. Unlike MBO, QPD is not concerned with the "one leap at a time" type of approach, the effect is to focus on continuous improvement to optimise process capability, to learn from mistakes, to capture winning practices and ideas and to manage quality pro-actively.

The relationship between QPD and performance management is better illustrated in Figure 5.3. Perhaps the best description of quality policy deployment is the process by which congruence can be achieved and the "what to do" and "how to perform" questions can be answered. Performance measurement on the other hand measures motion, action and value added contributions. The business delivery process (BDP) reflects all the recommended effects which add value to the end customer, driven by a thorough understanding of customer requirements and process capability.

Figure 5.4 on the other hand describes the two activities of QPD and performance measurement in terms of:

1. *Process management*: this is a senior management responsibility, deciding on the right things to do, developing the right objectives and communicating them at all levels in the right way.
2. *Performance measurement*: quality improvements take place through team efforts and a multi-functional approach. Performance measurement therefore becomes the responsibility of process workers who have the ultimate task of carrying out the necessary improvements.

Figure 5.4 also highlights the fact that quality policy deployment and performance measurement have to focus not just on deficiency areas and negative gaps but also on pro-active quality and the protection of competitive advantages. Benchmarking therefore becomes very relevant at two levels:

1. Strategic benchmarking: to develop goals and critical success factors (CSFs) through a thorough understanding of customer requirements and process capability.
2. Operational benchmarking: to optimise process capability at all levels through the introduction of new practices, methods learned from leading organisations.

An example of a quality policy deployment process

This is a process described in Hronec (1993) who presents QPD as a model of seven key elements:

1. Strategy – its development and communication supported by having the right reward mechanisms in place, training and also reliance on benchmarking for doing the right things in the right way.
2. Goals.
3. Critical processes.
4. Output measures.
5. Key activities.
6. Process measures.
7. Implementation.

Figure 5.3 Integrating the voice of the customer with the voice of the process for goal congruence

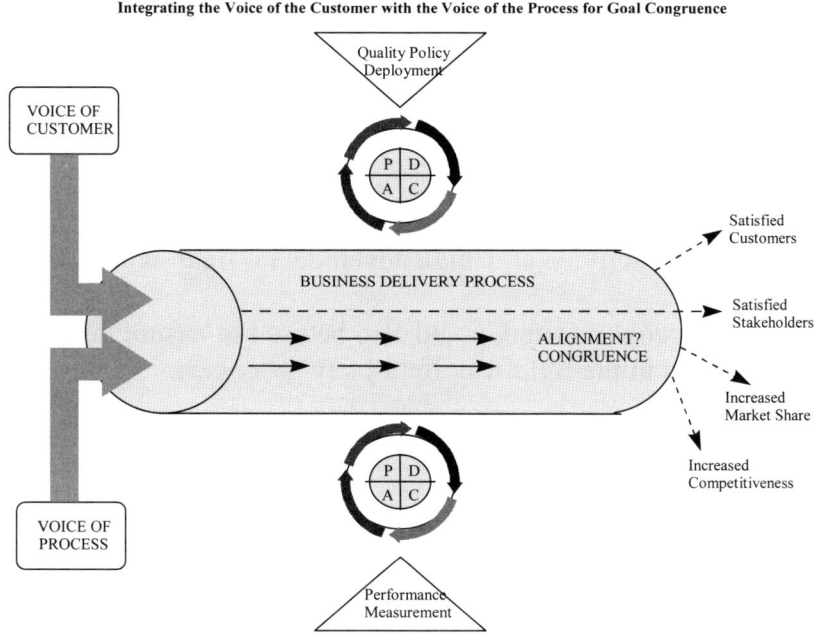

Figure 5.4 Integrating process management and performance measurement

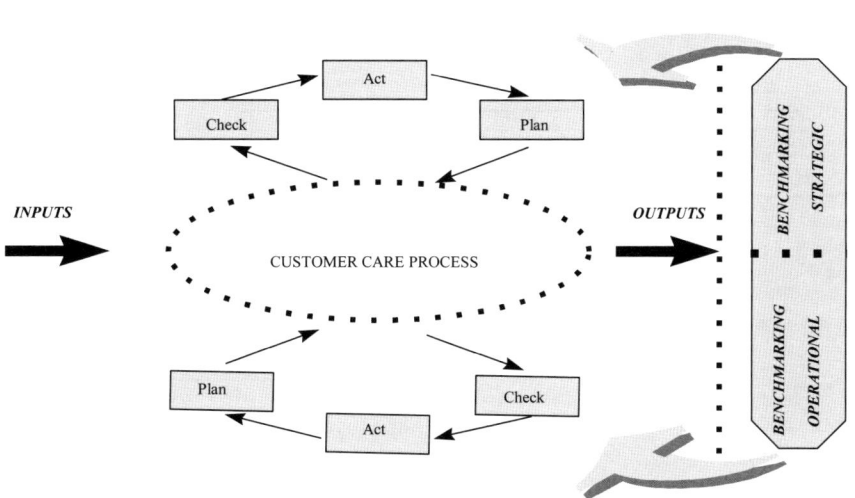

Best Practice Organisational Excellence

The "quantum performance measurement model", as it is referred to, is dynamically driven by continuous improvement (i.e. PDCA cycle). As Figure 5.5 illustrates, the corporate objectives could be to maintain customer loyalty through rapid product introduction.

The goals/CSFs could be to:
- Increase speed to market by 50 per cent over the next two years.
- Develop two new products each year.
- Get 25 per cent of company profits from new products in two years.

These goals are then cascaded down to all key activities and critical processes. Performance measurement and improvement start, therefore, once key performance measures have been developed (i.e. to capture core activity and high leverage in areas which impact most on customer satisfaction).

Soft measures, which are people related, could also be used to ensure that the right people with the required skills are used in the right way for all key processes.

Figure 5.5 Example of quality policy deployment process

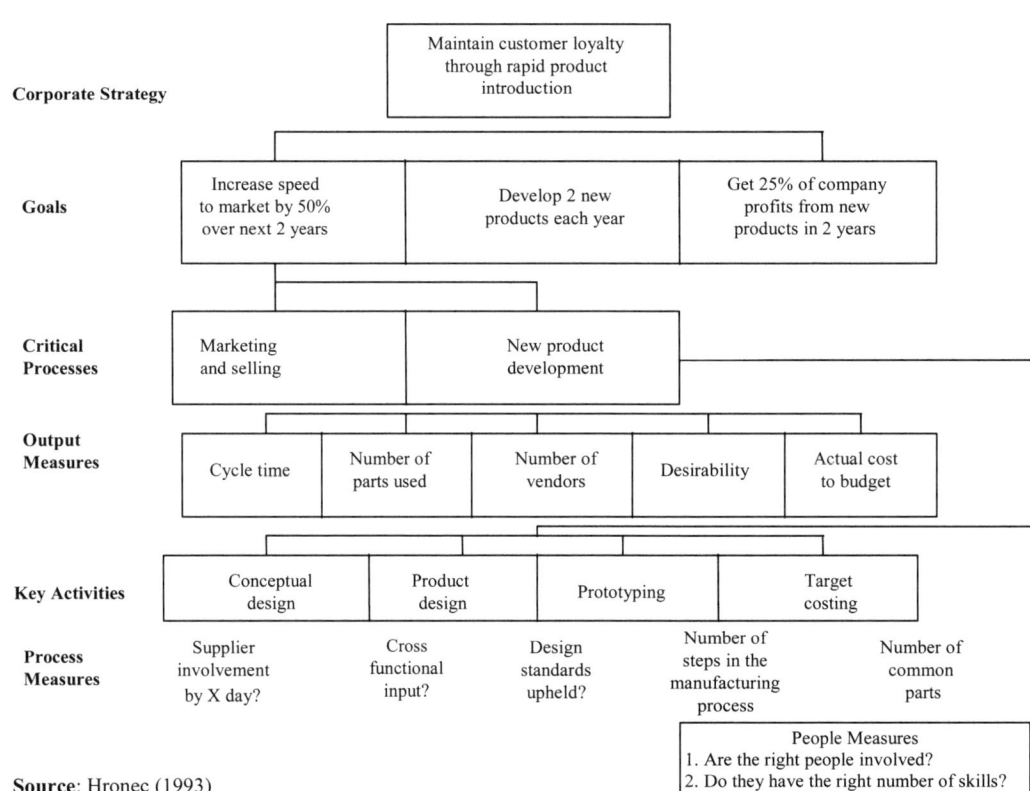

Source: Hronec (1993)

Defining quality policy deployment

Policy management is the vehicle by which business plans are put together and communicated at all levels of the organisation. Policy management is the translation of *hoshin kanri* as it is known in Japan: *hoshin* means direction; *kanri* means deployment/administration/management.

Rank Xerox defines policy deployment as follows:

> A key by which Rank Xerox can articulate and communicate the Vision, Mission, Goals and Vital Few Programmes to all employees. It provides the answers to the two questions: "What do we need to do?" and "How are we going to do it?"

At Rank Xerox, quality policy is used as a process by which company values and goals are translated into activities which, when carried out, can achieve the desired results.

Policy deployment is the propagation of a cycle where "whats" and "hows" are worked out at a very senior management team level (e.g. "What" = CSF = Be No. 1 supplier to major retailers by 1995; "How" = by focusing on on-time delivery, speed/quality of response, level of service). The "hows" can then become "whats" at the next management level, and so on. In this way performance measurement becomes an application which can be seen at major process level, sub-process level, activity and task levels.

Examples of quality policy deployment models

Procter and Gamble

The company, which was founded in 1837 by William Procter and James Gamble, is a global leader in areas such as health care, food, beverage, laundry, cleaning and beauty care products, amongst others. It employs over 100,000 people world-wide and has operations in 53 countries.

Procter and Gamble adheres to the TQ principles. It started implementing TQM in 1983 through a bottom-up approach. TQM is, however, endorsed by senior managers at the highest level, including the chairman and chief executive who argues that (Bemowski, 1992):

> Total quality, because of its focus on benchmarking customer and consumer satisfaction, is basically an insurance policy for sustaining competitive advantage over the long term, even when a company might not, at any given time, have a blockbuster advantage over the others. Total quality is the very essence of our long-term growth strategy.

P&G recognises that strategy development and implementation is a serious business. There is awareness of the various pitfalls of strategic implementation, reported by a 1989 Booz Allen study of strategy development and implementation (Huston, 1992). The study concluded that, of the respondents:

- 73 per cent of managers believed that implementation is more difficult than development;
- 72 per cent thought that it would take more time;
- 64 per cent believed that it impacted more on performance;
- 64 per cent of management lacked implementation skills;
- 75 per cent stated that employees misunderstood roles;
- 75 per cent maintained that groups did not co-ordinate;
- 48 per cent criticised inadequate measures for strategy achievement;
- 45 per cent said there was internal competition;

- 40 per cent stated there was insufficient employee involvement and commitment; and
- 85 per cent thought that implementation was the part of the strategy over which managers had least control.

As Figure 5.6 indicates, P&G is very serious about how they implement strategy. They use a four-stage approach. The process itself covers five key elements which include:
1. Strategic intent.
2. Year targets.
3. Annual deployment plans (based on each year's objectives, goals, strategies and measures (OGSM).
4. Management reviews.
5. Results feeding back to learning.

The whole process of strategic deployment is reinforced by a positive deployment of TQM. It is, however, recognised that TQM by itself does not lead to the production of winning strategies. There has to be a strong presence of management leadership. This was highlighted by P&G's chairman and CEO, who argues that (Bemowski, 1992):

> Total quality does not guarantee that companies will produce winning strategies. Winning strategies have to come from the minds of the leaders.

Figure 5.6 A four cycle approach to implementation of strategy

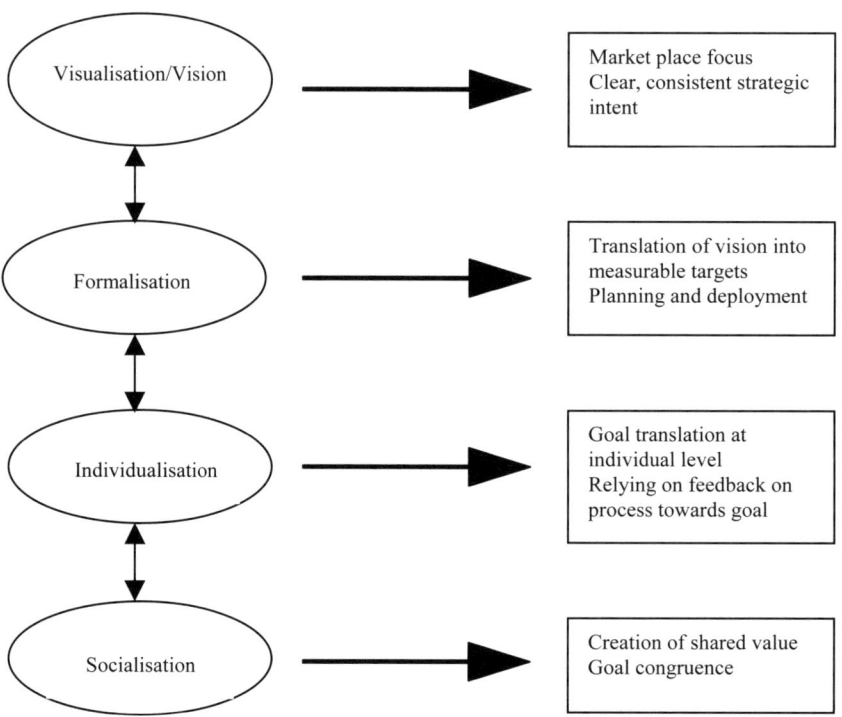

An example of quality deployment at P&G. Figure 5.7 illustrates quality policy deployment (QPD) at the Soap Sector of P&G. The process consists of three stages:
1. the long-term vision;
2. strategic development; and
3. strategic deployment.

The third stage (strategic deployment) is perhaps a revolutionary addition from conventional methods of strategy implementation. In addition to clearly specifying how goals are to be measured, how competitive advantages are measured and how progress is tracked, a shadow set of questions are asked to ensure that organisational capability is strengthened through the deployment process and that lessons learned are used to ensure more effective strategic deployment. Organisational capability is achieved through management reviews and visits conducted for purposes such as ensuring the quality of results, to assess strengths and weaknesses of organisation capability, to ensure that there is a goal congruence and total alignment within the organisation and finally to use the learning captured for future strategic planning.

Figure 5.7 Quality policy deployment

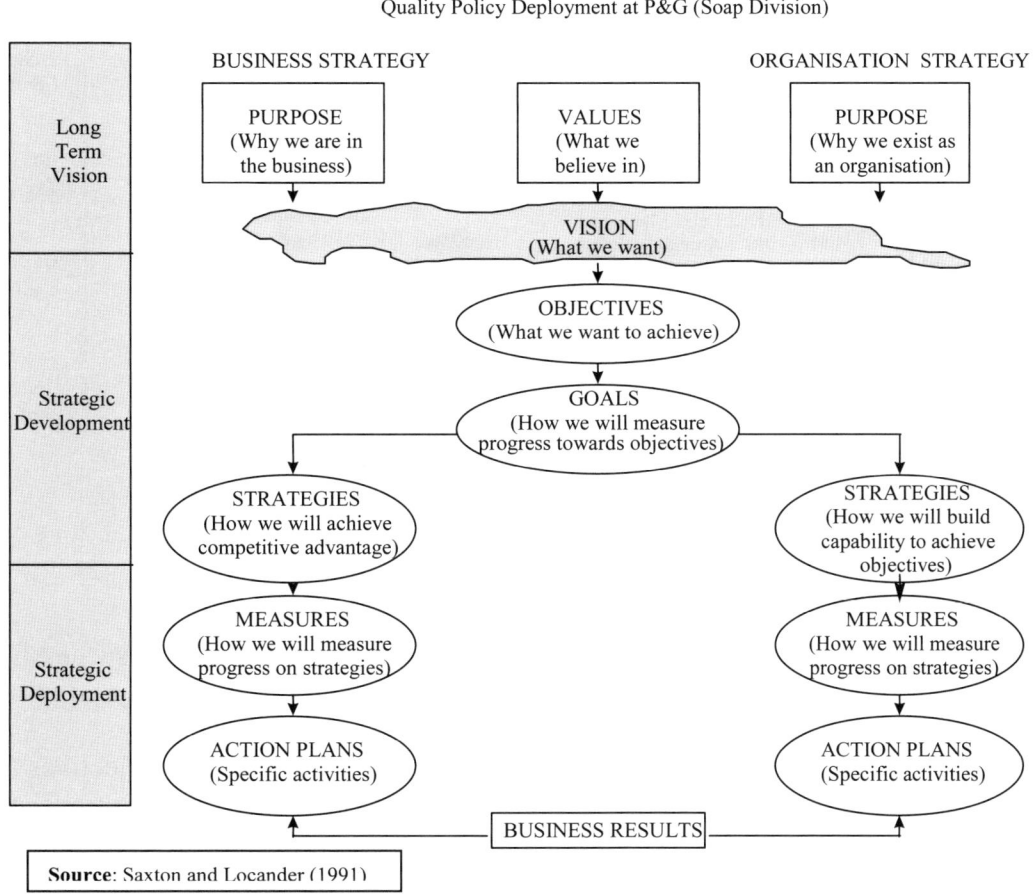

Komatsu Ltd

This company is one of the world's leading producers and suppliers of industrial machines. The product range includes over 300 different types and the market served represents a wide variety of customers including construction and industrial machinery. The Osaka plant which won the Deming prize back in 1964 employs 2,000 people and manufactures bulldozers, hydraulic excavators and underground machinery.

Figure 5.8 illustrates quality policy deployment at Komatsu Ltd (Catherine and Daniel, 1991).

Figure 5.8 Quality deployment process

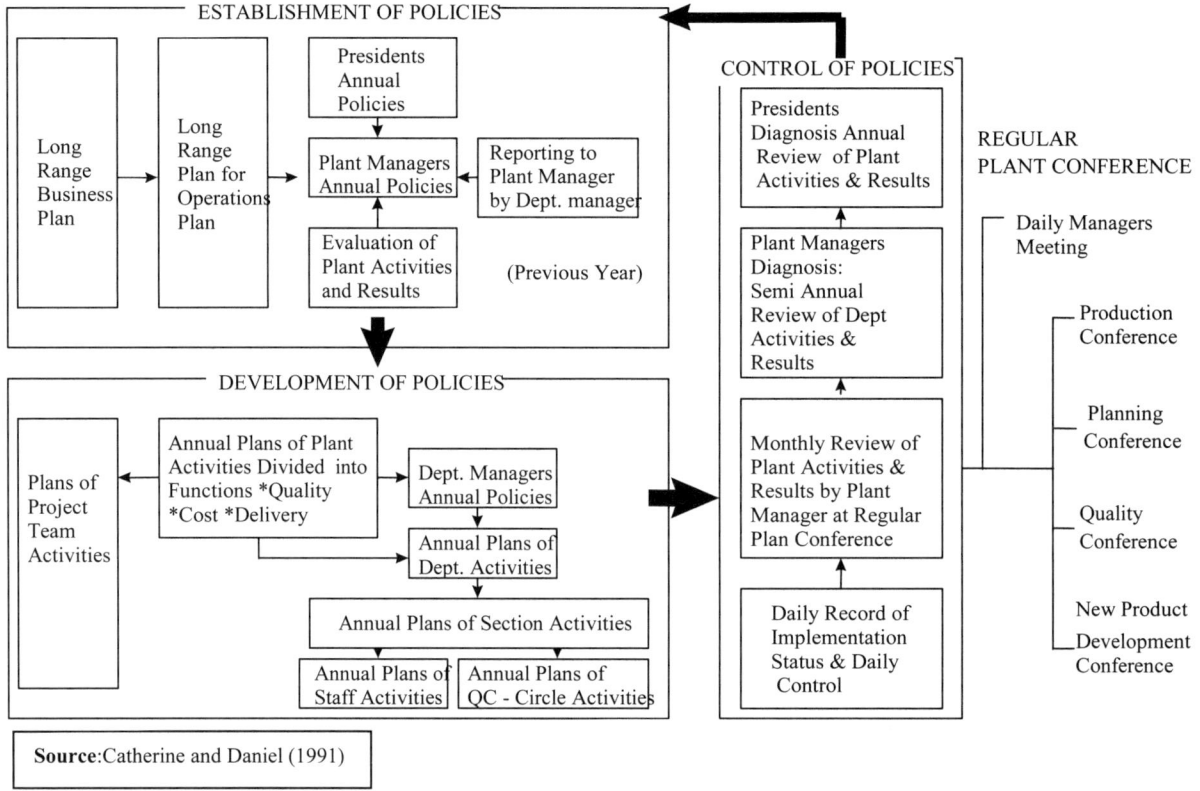

Excessive effort is placed on planning in a rigorous manner, this is the key to successful goal translation. Quality policy in this context is very similar to previous cases analysed in that the PDCA cycle tends to be used extensively:

1. *Plan stage*: establishing policies and deployment of various objectives to all functions. This is done through a focus on external customers and the translation of their needs into tangible goods and services.
2. *Do stage*: the translation of company goals at all levels in the organisation, including individual employees.

3. *Check stage*: regular monitoring of progress and performance checks to ensure that goals are still achievable.
4. *Act stage*: feedback from performance and results achieved, including new learning that can be used for the development of the next batch of goals.

Hewlett-Packard

This company manufacturers and sells electronic products which are used in the computer industry and also for measurement purposes. The products manufactured are widely used and include hardware equipment, peripheral equipment, printing equipment and software systems including networking.

Quality at H-P started in 1978, an inspiration coming from Japan, at the Yokagawa H-P Plant, a joint venture with Japan. The Yokogawa H-P Plant won the Deming Prize in 1982 as a result of its excellence in quality. At the heart of the quality drive with H-P is measurement in all areas. Some of the customer related measures include (Carter and Edmonds, 1988):

- Response time: the time from the first customer call to the arrival of the customer engineer at the customer's site.
- Repair time: the time it takes the engineer to repair the customer unit.
- System downtime: the total elapsed time from the customer call to the unit being repaired.
- Turn around time: the elapsed time from the unit arriving at the service centre to it being repaired.

Managing quality at Hewlett-Packard takes place through *hoshin kanri* (a literal translation is "shiny metal pointing direction"). As illustrated in Figure 5.9 the process uses the PDCA cycle and goal translation takes place through various stages.

The benefits of QPD include:

- Relying on QPD gives senior management a disciplined approach to planning and highlights the importance of goals and measures.
- It encourages regular reporting and provides managers with the right documentation that enables them to set future plans, implement them and review their outcomes.
- *Hoshin kanri* ensures that TQM implementation succeeds and the various efforts deliver.
- It constantly reminds people of the importance of customers and relying on measurement and action.

The motto at Hewlett-Packard is "That which is measured gets better, but that which is measured and reported gets better faster".

Rank Xerox Ltd

Hoshin kanri is a key process at Rank Xerox Ltd. It is used for creating synergy among the various functional areas and, hence, optimise capability to deliver, but also to convert all customer needs (explicit and non-expressed) into value added contributions.

Rank Xerox deploys quality policy at all levels of the organisation and integrates QPD with employee appraisal.

Although the process is deployed in a top-down fashion, there is active participation at all levels, to ensure that goals are delivered. In order to gain company wide commitment, Rank Xerox relies on a process called "catchball", which essentially means that there is negotiation using facts and hard data to resolve differences and disagreements during the deployment of company goals. Like playing " catch", employees and managers can throw data and information at each other so that goals are accepted and people are committed to delivering them.

Figure 5.10 illustrates quality policy deployment at Rank Xerox Ltd. Similarly to previously discussed processes, Rank Xerox used the PDCA cycle for planning, implementing and taking necessary actions.

Rank Xerox is discussed in depth as a case study in Chapter 14.

Figure 5.9 Quality policy deployment process at Hewlett-Packard

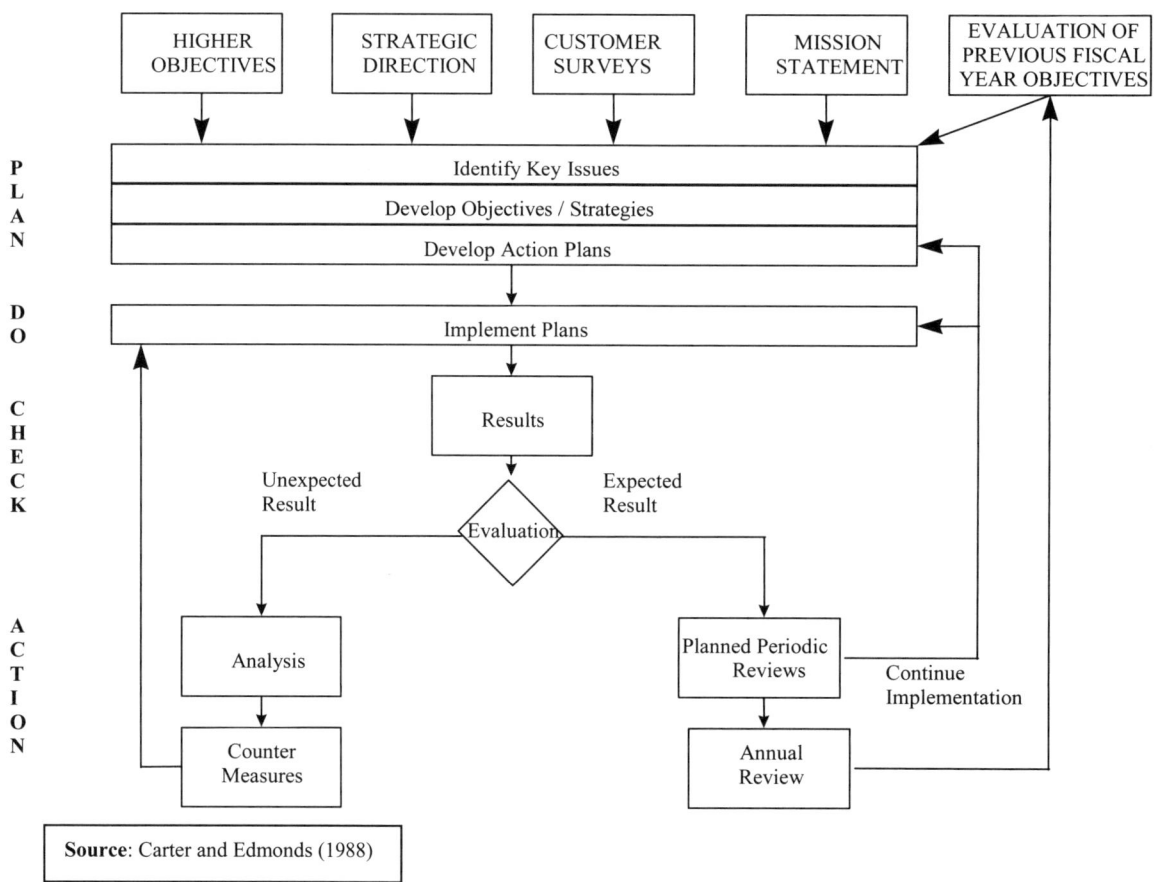

Figure 5.10 Quality policy at Rank Xerox

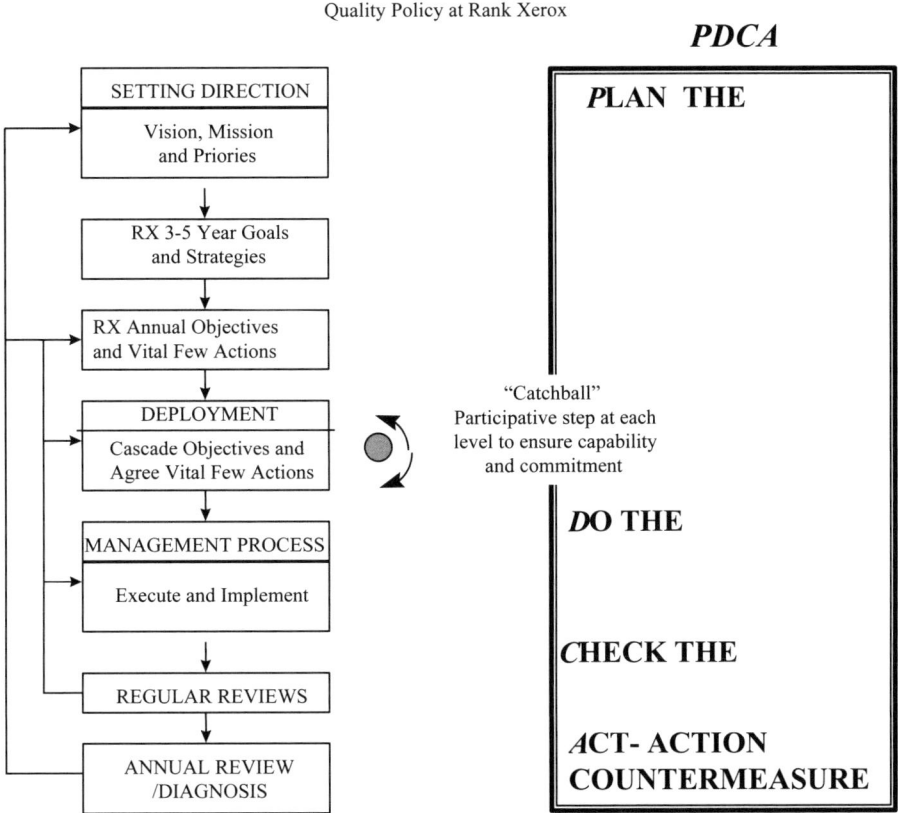

Florida Power & Light
The first non-Japanese company to have won the Deming Prize, in 1989, FP&L employs over 14,000 people and has over three million customers. FP&L uses Japanese techniques very extensively to deploy the quality effort.

FP&L used the techniques of Japanese quality gurus such as Dr Asaka who, in 1985, made the management realise the importance of quality policy deployment. The Japanese have always believed that quality has to be managed strategically and unless all the efforts are deployed for the same goals and in the same direction, there will be very little impact. Goal congruence is therefore a vital task for managers to achieve in their quest for directing people towards successful performance standards.

Table 5.1 illustrates the way QPD is deployed at FP&L. First, it was determined that the vital priorities needing improvement were:
- sales and service quality;
- delivery;
- safety; and
- price.

FP&L has developed a set of objectives, indicators and improvement targets for each measure. Similar to Rank Xerox, FP&L uses "catchball" to communicate and ensure commitment. The process is cascaded down to all levels, function-department-section-individual. The power of QPD at FPL is seen in its ability to instigate discipline in planning and in taking action to ensure that goals are achieved.

Table 5.1 How QPD is deployed at Florida Power & Light

		Short-term plans		Quality categories			
	Objectives	Indicators	% improvement targets	Sales and service quality	Delivery	Safety	Price
1.1	Improve the cost of electric service	a. Distribution service availability (customer minutes)	8		0		
		b. Transmission service unavailability (customer minutes)	13		0		
		c. Substation service unavailability (customer minutes)	9		0		
1.3	Improve customer satisfaction	Number of customer complaints to the FPSC/thousand customers (excluding current diversion)	12	0			
2.1	Improve the safety and competitiveness of nuclear power	a. Automatic trips (1991 St Lucie only)	100			0	
		b. Equivalent availability (1991 St Lucie only)	13		0		
		c. Turkey Point dual unit outage duration (days)	N/A		0	0	0
		d. O&M cost variance to budget	0				0
		e. Capital expenditure variance to budget	0				0
3.4	Improve employee safety	a. Number of lost time injuries per 100 FPL employees	19			0	
		b. Number of doctor cases per 100 employees	13			0	
4.1	Improve O&M cost per PWH and achieve budget security and quality	a. O&M C/h WH	N/A				0
		b. O&M cost variance to budget	0				0
4.3	Establish fossil unit reliability, availability and maintenance targets and develop programmes to achieve those targets	Equivalent forced outage rate (%)	18		0		0
4.4	Provide adequate energy supply capacity and maintain the energy of the delivery system during the Turkey Point emergency diesel generator (EDG) outage in an economical manner	MW required to ensure reserve margin 18>15%	N/A		0		0

References

American Supplier Institute (1989), *Policy Management – Executive Briefing Manual*, American Supplier Institute, Michigan.

Bemowski, K. (1992), "Carrying on the P&G tradition", *Quality Progress*, May, pp. 21-5.

Carter, P. and Edmonds, T. (1988), "Service quality at the Hewlett-Packard Company", in Spechler, J.W. (Ed.), *When America Does It Right*, Industrial Engineering and Management Press, Norcross, GA.

Catharine, G.J. and Daniel, M.J. (1991), *Customer Satisfaction through Quality – An international Perspective*, The Conference Board of Canada, Ottawa, Ontario, Canada.

Hronec, S.M. (1993), *Vital Signs Using Quality, Time and Cost Performance Measurements to Chart Your Company's Future*, AMACOM, New York.

Huston, L.A. (1992), "Implementing change – executing strategy at Proctor & Gamble", *Strategic Direction*, No. 84, October, pp. 28-30.

Saxton, J. and Locander, W.B. (1991), "A systems view of strategic planning at Proctor & Gamble", in Stahi, M.J. and Brunds, G.M. (Eds), *Competing Globally Through Customer Value*, Quorum Books, New York.

Yoji, A. (1990), "An introduction to quality function deployment", in Akao, Y. (Ed), *Quality Function Deployment – Integrating Customer Requirements into Product Design and Productivity*, Free Press, Cambridge, MA.

Appendix 5.1 Policy and strategy exercise

You have just been appointed Head of Strategic Planning for a large international computer manufacturer and one of your first tasks is to conduct a comprehensive review of the various sources of competitor and non-competitor data used by the business for accuracy, completeness and value for money ahead of the next strategy review. The people who report directly to you have already compiled a short list of six sources which the company uses:

1. Industry associations.
2. Benchmarking clubs.
3. Media.
4. Visits to sites.
5. Direct co-operation via telephone, reports, correspondence etc.
6. Consultants.

Before proceeding to the next stage of your comprehensive review you need to consider the advantages and disadvantages of each source of data as this may be critical at a later stage when evaluating the cost benefit.

Your task is to take each of the six main sources and compile a list of the perceived advantages and disadvantages of each source to enable the review to proceed to the next stage.

Policy and strategy exercise – suggested solution

Table 5.2 Policy and strategy exercise – suggested solution

	Advantages	**Disadvantages**
Industry association	Peer group Formal and comparative information Regular information and trends Early warning system for problems *Ad hoc* studies Regular meetings to update data	May not be best in class Traditional Formal data oriented Costs Comparability of data
Benchmarking clubs	Like minded individuals Focused agendas Sharing of survey data Performance oriented Means to close gap Cost effective	May not be best in class Who starts the process rolling? Only areas of common interest Who acts as facilitator? Who compiles comparisons? Becomes a club Who controls membership in terms of quality and numbers?
Media	International best in class Comparative and informative Investigative Cost effective	Are the press always to be believed? Lack of focus – no control over the information Cannot determine availability of information Vested interests
Site visits	Seeing is believing Not restricted to peer group Processes rather than data See it as it occurs	Industrial tourism Lack of data Variability Time
Direct co-operation	Can involve more than just peer group Informal relationship – *ad hoc* issues Processes/information rather than data Specific information Structures/soft skills Culture/decision making Best in class	Only one for one Trade mentality Mutually beneficial or competitive? Narrowness of comparisons (*Continued*)

Consultancy	Neutrality	Best in class?
	Experience	Organisations selected on basis of willingness to pay
	Consultants identify peer group	
	Bring like minded individuals together	Time scale lengthy
	Legwork	Data rather than information
	Provides benchmark on costs for other exercises	Consultants gain real knowledge
		Costs
	Focuses discipline of measurement	Becomes regularised on time and format
	Comparisons against best, average and worst	
	Can lead to dissemination of all data	
	Provides contacts which can be cultivated	

Chapter 6
People management: the key asset

Introduction
The era of organisations trying to achieve competitive advantage by putting heavy emphasis on technological know-how (automation, computerisation) is almost over. All except for a remaining few have realised that technology has become more affordable and most importantly easily transferable. The "perceived" competitive advantage resulting from the use of technology has further been eroded as business becomes more global, markets get saturated and demand is outstripped by supply.

As the core of competitive advantage will be innovation and creativity driven, organisations are beginning to focus more on people management. The softer aspects of performance include things such as sharing of common goals (vision), professionalism, teamwork, recognition, people creativity and productivity, learning individuals, etc. Treating people (employees) as the key major asset (more important than the customer – as it is the employees who ultimately design, manufacture, and deliver products/services that delight customers!) and developing their untapped potential will be the right way forward for securing effective competitiveness. Perhaps the phrase "human resource management" (HRM) was coined in the 1980s to reflect this importance and how the management of people should be placed at the strategic heart of competitive business approaches. This shift in trend can also be seen in the mission statements, quality policies and strategies of organisations. As Walt Disney once said, "You can dream, create, design and build the most wonderful place in the world... but it requires people to make the dream a reality" (Blocklyn, 1988).

Tyson and Wicher (1994) concluded in their post-recession study of HRM in 30 companies in the UK that HRM has changed as a consequence of recession with three distinctive trends:
1. More flexible approaches to human resource strategy.
2. Contributions to the business strategy through levers of strategic change; employee and management development, employee relations and specific organisational development strategies aimed at engaging hearts, minds and particular behaviours (all of which are people related).
3. A more strategic role for the HR specialist whereby they are expected to be more business-led, cost conscious and flexible.

Marketing, production and financial managers have long been forced to justify in a systematic way the costs of their activities by comparing them with the overall performance measures of other organisations. Timely enough now, HR managers are beginning to be asked to evaluate the value added effects of HR practices on organisational products and processes given the intensifying nature of the competitive business world, economic recession and the increased emphasis on cost reduction, quality and excellence in many organisations. This could indicate the end of an era of adjustments in HR policies and practices being based solely on intuition rather than a more systematic and methodological assessment based on performance measures. Hiltrop and Despres (1994) define performance measures in the field of HRM as a range of activities and approaches that allow organisations to attract, retain and mobilise a

critical mass of human talent. Morgan (1992) outlines three approaches in developing an effective performance monitoring system in HRM:
1. Adopting a stepwise procedure (similar to scientific methods). It begins with collecting as many measures as possible, then eliminating measures whose potential benefits are outweighed by the expense or difficulty in collection. Then a system is developed for consistently collecting, analysing and interpreting their meaning in the realm of HR strategy. This method risks being abandoned when there is difficulty in collecting, analysing and interpreting the measure both in terms of cost and time and the danger of "creeping numeration" – the temptation to turn every measure deemed relevant into a crucial part of an official measurement system.
2. Identification of key performance indicators associated with specific HR practice. The rationale is to keep things simple and to avoid information overload. This method risks being too superficial in that not enough information is collected to understand why specific outcomes have occurred or for lessons to be learned.
3. Benchmarking. This denotes a comparison with selected performance indicators from different organisations considered to be "best in class". This method is gaining popularity and requires careful selection and manipulation of comparison measures.

Glanz and Dailey (1992) explain that benchmarking HR practices serve a number of purposes:
- Enable an organisation to calibrate how it is delivering HR practices by comparing it with excellent organisations. It will then be able to identify areas where its practices are within or outside a norm. This can be translated into a measure of how effectively HR meets the needs of the business.
- Enable an organisation to learn from others thus creating a "learning mentality".
- Create a need for change by building a strong case through the best practice of others.
- Enable HR managers to set direction and priorities by examining repeatedly occurring themes among companies that can be used to frame and focus the HR function.

Critical factors for people management
One of the most difficult challenges facing HR professionals is developing specific criteria (performance measures) which define effectiveness in HR activities. In this regard, there exist two schools of thought:
- Monitoring the costs and benefits of human resource activities (attraction, selection, retention, development and utilisation of people in organisations) in economic terms. The underlying assumption to this belief is that the ultimate measure of HR effectiveness is the "bottom line". Even though this approach has the advantage of being simple and easily understood, it fails miserably to provide guidance when implementing effective HRM programmes. A more comprehensive and detailed means of assessing performance and how it compares with other organisations is needed.
- Measuring the set of HR practices delivered within an organisation and the contribution of each practice to the overall competitive advantage of the organisation. Schuler (1984) introduced a model which links competitive advantage to organisations that have identified and developed specific activities in six categories of HR practices; planning, staffing, training and development, appraisal,

compensation and union-management relations (see Appendix 6.1 for the key HR performance indicators). These indicators can help managers to evaluate how their HR practices relate to both operational and strategic levels of the enterprise and at the same time compare the effectiveness of HR practices and policies between organisations.

A number of studies have been carried out to link specific HR practices and organisational effectiveness in terms of financial performance, productivity, product quality, innovation etc. The idea behind this is that when an indicator goes up or down, actions can be taken to minimise or maximise the impact by changing the relevant practice.

Kravetz (1988) studied the correlation between financial results and human resources progressiveness (HRP) in 150 US companies. HRP is defined as:
> the extent to which an organisation is operating in concert with the current and future workplace, rather that experimenting with radical programmes or spending exorbitant amounts of money on HR programmes. A company high in HRP understands the critical importance of people to the bottom line and operates with this in mind.

An organisation's score on the HRP index is measured through a 50-item questionnaire covering the following nine areas of HR practices and policies:
1. Degree of openness of communication.
2. Degree of emphasis on people in the company culture.
3. Degree to which management is participative.
4. Emphasis on creativity and excellence in the workplace.
5. Extensiveness of career development and training.
6. Effectiveness in maximising employee job satisfaction.
7. Degree of recognition and reward for good performance.
8. Usage of flexitime and part-time employment.
9. Degree of decentralisation and flattened management hierarchy.

The results showed that HRP was significantly correlated with financial success over a five year period. Kravetz concluded that highly progressive companies enjoyed significantly higher sales growth, profit margins, equity growth and earnings per share growth.

Schuster (1986) conducted a similar study examining the relationship between HRM performance as measured by human resource index (HRI) and organisational effectiveness. He attempted to develop a reliable and practical instrument to be used as a benchmarking tool. He used six practices which were related to the general management philosophy which Peters and Waterman termed as "attention to employee needs":
1. The assessment centre approach to personnel selection.
2. Flexible or "cafeteria" approach in reward systems.
3. Productivity bonus plans.
4. Goal-oriented performance appraisal.
5. Alternative work schedules.
6. Organisational development.

Schuster found a meaningful relationship between the six HR practices and financial performance, which was consistent with that of Kravetz.

Assessment of best HR practices
Based on a self-assessment framework which highlights the importance of "people" for effective TQM implementation, a benchmarking exercise was carried out for the purpose of

identifying "best practice" in HRM. Structured interviews were carried out with five companies in the UK (two fast moving consumer goods companies and three service-related companies). These companies were approached on the basis of their active involvement in total quality initiatives. They are not, however, winners of prestigious quality awards, such as the EQA. The five companies studied to identify areas of best practice in HRM are:
1. Elida Gibbs Ltd.
2. Post Office Counters Ltd.
3. Nationwide Building Society.
4. National Westminster Bank.
5. Birds Eye Walls Ltd.

The framework adopted includes the following five areas:
1. History of TQM implementation:
    - Reason for implementation.
2. Leadership:
    - Visible involvement in leading quality management.
    - A consistent TQ culture.
    - Recognition and appreciation of efforts/successes of individuals/teams.
    - Support of TQ by provision of appropriate resources/assistance.
    - Involvement with customers/suppliers.
    - Active promotion of quality management outside the organisation.
3. People management:
    - TQ – opportunity or threat?
    - Sharing and communication.
    - Teamwork, participation and empowerment.
    - Training and development.
    - Trust, feedback, treatment and recognition.
    - Appraisal system.
4. People satisfaction:
    - How is it being measured?
    - Feedback and action plan.
5. TQ journey – the way ahead:
    - Main barriers in TQ implementation.
    - Main elements that will aid TQ progress.
    - Next steps in TQ journey.

Benchmarking HRM: a cross-industry analysis
Elida Gibbs Ltd (EG)
Elida Gibbs Ltd is the UK's largest manufacturer of mass market toiletries based in Leeds (single site factory) with 850 factory employees and 38 production lines. It is part of the Unilever Group and produces a wide range of leading brands of toothpaste, deodorants, hairspray, shampoo and skin-care products. The current turnover is over £180 million per year.

The company's mission statement is "the leader in all it does". The leadership goals are to be the leader in:
- its market;
- customer service;

- employee care and development;
- speed of operations; and
- business results.

In order to achieve the above mission, its approach is total competitiveness through total quality; continuous improvement in satisfying the needs of consumers and customers better than the competitors. This can only be achieved by the disciplined application of total quality practice throughout the business.

Leadership. The change programme was driven by the board members acting as the Executive Steering Group. Training programmes for employees were attended by at least one board member or senior manager. Managers' role model behaviours were fostered through several programmes:
- Cascaded awareness of TQ through training.
- Practical involvement in improvement initiatives.
- Adoption of management competencies in a "management development review" focusing on leadership, employee development and team building skills.
- Department lead teams chaired by heads of departments acting as reference points for assistance/information about TQ initiatives and co-ordinating local recognition works by teams/individuals.
- Monthly team briefings.
- "Walk the job" – enhance communication outside formal circles.

There are various types of recognition/appreciation:
- *Money rewards*: through the performance pay scheme which links individual's reward to company measures (determined by the board and related to corporate goals) and local measures (suggested by individuals/teams related to their areas of work which in turn support the company's goals).
- *Local recognition*: managed through the department lead teams to make recognition a stimulating part of everyday work. It is based on the principles of non-monetary reward and is locally awarded; based on flexibility, being discretionary and "fun" (e.g. quality badge, meals, radios, theatre tickets, visits, appreciation letter).
- *Corporate recognition*: given through personal contact (presentation or through newsletter). A Chairman Innovation Award was introduced to encourage innovative ideas. Winners, selected by the Chairman himself, receive a trophy with wide publicity. It is open to all, both individuals and teams.

Training is a major feature of the TQ cultural change and as such a budget of 1.3 per cent of turnover is given annually (about four times more than UK industry average). External learning of TQ best practice is encouraged which takes the form of overseas study tours, sponsoring TQ lectureship in a local university, membership of the Inter-Company Innovation Group and membership of the DTI "Inside UK Enterprise" scheme and inter-company TQ networking.

People management. In the quest to become a world class company, EG is determined to build excellence through its people:

Only through people can we achieve our goals. We are committed to:
- help everyone develop to their full potential;
- encourage commitment and involvement;
- train people in the skills they need;
- reward achievement and contribution to reaching our goals;
- provide a safe and attractive work environment.

The TQ initiative is not seen as a threat to the employees (message from trade union representatives). In fact, it is seen as an opportunity and efforts are made to constantly revive TQ approaches.

Recognising people as the critical success factor in the change programme, a powerhouse to drive change was set up directly responsible to the board. An Employee Development and Communication Group (EDGG) (consisting of the personnel director and a senior representative of each core business) was given three main tasks:
1. Improve operational performance by developing programmes such as TQ techniques, training, appraisal system, etc.
2. Support managers in carrying out their new roles of learning and people development (there is no training department).
3. Build communication mechanisms to ensure that the workforce is informed, involved and committed.

People development is the core of the change programme. It focuses on two parallel strands, i.e. identifying the core skills necessary to increase operational effectiveness and employee personal contribution and building a learning culture. In developing this culture, it invested heavily in training, i.e. 1.3 per cent of turnover and has exceeded the training target of six days/year/member of staff. Staff perceptions of a learning culture are changed through the following approaches:
- learning opportunities are on an open basis; no approval needed from managers;
- advisory service provided about learning opportunities;
- facilities for both private and group study; and
- skills training is available both at the plant and on external courses.

The focus of this activity is the on-site Learning Centre which addresses the approaches mentioned above. From the feedback report of Investors in People assessment, it was noted that the Learning Centre acted as a catalyst to the development of a learning organisation (a phrase commonly used in this company – becoming a learning organisation is the goal of the company's People Development Programme) and not just a collection of resources. In 1994 it introduced a scheme called "Gateway Initiative" providing enhanced advice and guidance for employees to create their own personal action plans, thus taking ownership of their own learning and self-development. It became one of the first companies to gain accreditation in Investors in People in 1991 and again in 1994. Employees are gaining NVQs, completing up-skilling training programmes and signing on for "open learning" schemes.

Communication is essential in cascading down the company's vision and goals. Methods used are company consultative committees, monthly team briefings, including the one given by senior managers, newsletters, fact sheets, videos and bulletin boards.

Effective teamworking is shaped through a total productive maintenance programme. It provides the opportunity for employees to take on new tasks – multi-skilling. Team members become more involved in putting a stop to major breakdowns by doing the maintenance themselves and thus improving line efficiencies.

Empowerment with the aim of meeting and exceeding both company and personal goals is also much encouraged. It allows teams and individuals to take greater ownership and responsibility within their own areas of work.

Employee surveys have been instrumental in finding out views of staff on issues to be later considered in the company's plans and development. In fact the suggestion of a Learning Centre and providing a child-minding service came through this channel. Self-assessment using the EQA model is also carried out to gauge the performance of the overall TQM implementation besides recognising any improvement opportunities. Appraisal systems for the management and non-management groups include self-appraisal and upward appraisal.

The company gets very good support from the trade union representatives. They were among the first to get training in TQM and they helped the management to set up selection criteria for jobs. They give due consideration to both the interests of the company and its members – partnership in the workplace.

People satisfaction. At EG a bi-annual employee attitude survey is carried out by independent agencies. Results from the survey are given to the employees via a special edition of a newsletter which includes the action plans agreed by the board to address employee concerns. Other surveys are carried out as and when necessary.

The results from Investor in People assessment are also used as a feedback mechanism for people satisfaction. Results from the 1994 feedback report show a very positive response, especially in the areas of corporate culture, people management, the learning organisation and the future.

TQ journey – the way ahead. The main barriers to effective TQ implementation are:
- Inadequate level of education and vocational skills among general workers as a result of state education system. Therefore more resources are needed to even out this disadvantage as compared to other European neighbours. This makes the TQ information implementation more difficult in the face of intense competition, especially from Europe.
- The way of working in the corporate culture. Traditional thinking and the existence of managers to control, impose and direct things make it difficult for the new TQ way of working which involves involvement, empowerment, trust etc.
- Constantly changing customer expectations have put pressure on employees to cope. New ways of doing things, constantly challenging the normal way of working makes working-life unpredictable. This is very different from the way of working in the 1960s and 1970s.

The main elements that will aid TQ progress are:
- Recognising people as the greatest asset. It is the objective of the company to create "a workforce of fully aware and involved individuals who make a real contribution to the way the company is run and have the opportunity to progress with it".
- Commitment to being a leading learning organisation, placing high value on individual employees and the organisation's learning.
- Continuing to build on the successful innovations of the past in the spirit of continuous improvement.

Central Services Group, Post Office Counters Ltd (CSG)
CSG was created as a result of reorganisation in 1993 of Post Office Counters Ltd. It is an internal supplier of expert services and central operations serving some 20,000 outlets in eight regions throughout the UK. It is divided into seven separate divisions: business services consultancy, client transaction processing, finance executive, human resources consultancy, property holdings, systems consultancy and audit.

On reorganisation, it was decided that the organisation should be customer-focused, recover costs but not be a profit centre and emphasis should be on cost containment/reduction rather than increasing overall levels of support.

TQM was launched for the whole organisation; the "Customer First" programme with its new mission and vision embracing the following principles:

- customer focus;
- management by fact;
- people based management; and
- continuous improvement.

Leadership. Leadership is being made the key driver of the cultural change and in particular it must be clearly visible "at the top". Team leaders receive feedback on leadership behaviours through a management behaviour feedback system, with input from team members, every six months. From this, team leaders are able to understand team expectations better and to achieve improvement (helping to produce a consistent approach to leadership throughout the organisation).

A framework for recognition has already been agreed. Divisions are responsible for the implementation of recognition plans which reflect local circumstances and actual preferences of people in the divisions. To maintain an emphasis on the issue of recognition, it has become a permanent item on the agenda in the monthly review meetings between the MD and his heads of divisions. The progress of the impact of recognition is measured through staff attitude surveys supplemented by local diagnostic research.

Generous training opportunities are given to staff (especially in "professional" areas) in upgrading their knowledge and skills to the benefit of both the organisation and the individuals. Involvement with customers/suppliers is organised through the process of preparing service level agreements (SLA) in which team leaders are involved in structured discussions with customers/suppliers. Joint improvement activities are also encouraged as a follow-up from the SLAs prepared.

People management. People management is a key issue for CSG, as spelt out in the principles of its TQM initiative. The ability of its people to focus on the needs of the customers and having the necessary knowledge and skills to fulfil them is crucial. Divisions have differing skill needs and the management of people must therefore be tailored to individual needs within an overall framework common to the organisation. Based on staff attitude surveys, focus group discussions and "listening-in" sessions, the objectives of people management for 1994/1995 were:

- promote empowerment culture;
- improve two-way communication;
- sustain focus on how teams support their customers;
- promote involvement of all teams in quality improvement activities;
- improve processes for identifying training and development needs;
- train new staff quickly in "Customer First"; and
- equip staff with consultancy skills to support the organisation's customer focus.

To improve forward planning, resource planning process was introduced in forecasting posts and staff levels as a planning tool suitable for use at team, division and organisational levels. This will assist in the training need analysis and succession planning.

Individual objectives are agreed in a two-way process and are reviewed and updated at half-yearly counselling sessions. It is a common practice in some areas to have monthly one-to-one reviews of objectives. Individual objectives are based on a direct cascade of team and business targets with input from the appraisee and increasingly input from the customers through the agreed service level agreements (SLAs).

Training and development are part of the resource planning process. Besides giving priority to the needs of job skills, personal advancement leading to professional skills is offered with the local managers deciding which professional training is appropriate. New entrants are given training in "Customer First" within the first three months so that they are able to be a member of quality improvement teams as soon as possible.

Teamwork is one of the key values of the organisation, "to work successfully with other business units to strengthen business performance". Team leaders play a very important role in inculcating this culture and are solely responsible for giving training to their team members. Cross-functional teams are active, especially in the drafting of SLAs. Members of teams have a say in their leader's management style and behaviour by giving feedback through the management behaviour and style review.

Based on feedback from employees, an empowerment model has been developed and a team-based empowerment workshop is currently being piloted to introduce and encourage a culture of empowerment in the organisation. This culture is not new to the organisation, the people themselves are already empowered to act on any improvement opportunities. Even though officially there are 65 quality improvement projects (QIPs), there are numerous other initiatives going on along QIP lines which have not been registered.

Communication is central to an organisation as large and diverse as CSG. Each division has its own communication plan based on the recommendation of best practice by the central communication team. Forms of communication are monthly newsbriefs, talking shop sessions, upward feedback ("listening") sessions, focus group discussions and staff attitude and local diagnostic surveys. Feedback and action plans from the communication process are again communicated through these various media. In this organisation, face-to-face communication is preferred as it is more effective and able to support leadership commitment.

People satisfaction. People satisfaction is being measured in various ways:
- annual group attitude survey (questionnaires);
- local diagnostic surveys (both qualitative and quantitative method);
- focus group discussions;
- individual division initiatives; and
- indirect monitoring through turnover and absenteeism levels.

The next steps in the TQ journey are:
- to become a process-based organisation where all continuous improvement activities will evolve around process mapping; and
- based on the business excellence model (EQA self-assessment model), efforts will be focused on improving enablers, and thus achieving the desired results.

Nationwide Building Society
The Nationwide Building Society operates over 700 branches throughout the UK, employing around 5,600 workers. In the late 1980s it merged with Anglia Building Society in an effort to strengthening the capital base. Prior to the mid-1980s, running a building society was relatively easy. After the introduction of the Building Society Act in 1986, building societies were allowed to extend their business to provide a range of other financial services beyond that of principally providing mortgage loans, thus competing with other commercial banks and financial institutions. They were also allowed to increase their capital resources by incorporating as joint-stock companies; issuing shares to the public and securing listing on the stock exchange.

Leadership. Top management involvement in the QM initiative was very much visible to staff (although in different ways). Divisional directors were champions of quality in their respective divisions. Issues on "best practice" (the first project undertaken was internal benchmarking for best practice within the newly merged organisation) have always been highlighted by directors at every opportunity they have to address their staff.

Leadership and appreciation were shown in various ways to both performing teams and individuals. Team bonus and Exceeding Expectation Awards are given to teams and individuals respectively. High performance branches become members of the Diamond Club and the ranking will determine in which quartile of the diamond the branch is positioned. Quality managers were appointed at every regional office to co-ordinate and facilitate improvement projects.

People management. It is stated in the organisation's corporate plan that one of the success criteria is its people: "this company is the place where I want to work". This is also reflected in the mission and values on people. The company:
- engages staff in rewarding employment;
- gives them the aspired working life style; and
- employs people above industry average standard and pays well.

Communication is always seen as a big barrier, especially when operating in 36 areas. Messages from the top are cascaded down through area managers and branch managers. Procedural changes are communicated through office instructions and benefit changes through the HRM division and Staff Association. The CEO meets the employees through corporate videos (presenting the corporate plan once a year) and roadshows. Talkback sessions are also held where staff are invited to informal gatherings with a team of the top management, and staff can ask any questions pertaining to the running of the business. This seems to be the most effective form of two-way communication. Top management people spend time at the branches talking to staff and customers and giving feedback on improvement opportunities. A newsletter is produced and involvement from all parties throughout the UK is maximised.

Area managers are empowered to carry out any improvement projects they see fit. However, involvement in QITs is optional, but peer pressure is being used to influence others to take part in QITs.

Training and development is agreed on a competency framework and almost all training is carried out in-house either in area offices or at the central training centre.

People satisfaction. People satisfaction surveys are carried out in various ways; annual staff attitude surveys covering all staff. Results are analysed and given to top management. Feedback is given through the normal communication channel.

The next steps in the TQ route for the organisation are:
- Taking the "temperature" of its TQ initiatives and its quality policies, readdressing problem areas and redefining the roles of TQ initiatives as an integral part of all business activities, and sending the right signal to the staff so that "the future is more certain".
- Standardising the approach to TQ initiatives so that they can be properly monitored and benchmarked both internally and externally. Certainly the launch of an "Operational Excellence Programme" based on the EQA self-assessment model within the organisation is the first step towards achieving this aim.

The Nationwide Building Society is discussed as a case study in Chapter 14.

UK Branch Business at NatWest Bank (UKBB)
UKBB NatWest Bank is one of the big five high street banking institutions operating over 2,000 branches throughout the UK. It is one of the six business units within the group: retail

banking, corporate banking, cards, mortgage, insurance brokerage and life insurance and investment. The vision of the organisation is:

> Becoming First Choice for our customers, our staff and our investors by becoming world class in the following areas:
> - financial perspective;
> - customer perspective;
> - internal quality; and
> - organisational development.

In order for the vision to be achieved, the Service Improvement Programme (SIP – a TQM approach programme) was launched in mid-1993. The programme was developed to tackle various problems the organisation was facing. It is defined as "meeting or exceeding customers' requirements at the lowest cost to ourselves". It is about a better service without increasing cost and providing the desired level of service at a lower cost. It provides the link between the vision and the results which need to be achieved. It was stressed that SIP is different to previous initiatives in that:

- It is focused on key business objectives.
- It is driven by specific targets and results.
- It is to be delivered at all levels with major commitment from all levels.
- Implementation and ownership are at a local level.
- It is part of an integrated series of change activities.

Leadership. Leadership of SIP is being demonstrated by managers in four key areas: commitment, leading a team, recognition and communications. The programme is led by the senior management level (Executive Level Steering Group) which has ultimate responsibility for the programme. It is then cascaded down at regional/directorate level and branch level. Leadership commitment and visibility are good (as reflected by an employee satisfaction survey – 68 per cent). Every possible opportunity (meetings, conferences, newsletters, etc.) was seized by the management to stress the importance of SIP.

Managers were trained to manage SIP and then to take on the role of training others. All managers are responsible for implementing service action team (SAT) activities – the targets for improvement are linked to the cascaded goals set out by the very top steering committee. An "empowerment" environment is created whereby SATs are given freedom to decide, act and respond to ideas that will lead to improvement. "Work shadowing" and "role swapping" activities are introduced whereby subordinates work with immediate bosses to have more of a bird's eye view of the business and bosses assume the role of subordinate to have a feel of the problems faced by them respectively. This has managed to melt away the traditional bank manager's image of "do as I tell you" in the eyes of the workers.

Recognising the importance of communication, the managers themselves took a proactive role in opening up new communication channels between various parts of the business, to aid in understanding and exchanging improvement ideas among them, which is something that never existed before. Managers are now more open in their way of managing the business. Subordinates' roles as team members are valued by giving them a say in the behaviour and style of management and by taking part in the upward appraisal system.

All the various working relationship initiatives have resulted in the breaking down of the "bureaucratic" way of doing things in the banking industry. The SIP infrastructure created support and is seen as promoting improvement activities rather than getting in the way.

People management. People management is one of four areas monitored in the SIP on a balanced business scorecard (BBS) approach under the organisational development heading. It seeks to monitor staff attitudes and skills, and how these effect progress of the SIP.

Involvement and participation of all staff based on a teamwork approach is very much encouraged at all levels throughout the business. As such, within six months after the launch of SIP, over 1,200 improvement ideas were collected. An "empowerment" environment has been created whereby employees are involved and made responsible in the setting up of objectives, identifying improvement opportunities, drawing up improvement plans and measuring progress.

Communication is considered one of the most important factors of SIP's success. It is done through newsletters, e-mail facilities, notice boards and weekly 30 minute staff meetings where suggestions, grievances and feedback are discussed.

Recognition forms part of a culture within the organisation. It is given regularly and consistently by everyone, with the managers taking a leading role. Types of recognition practised are:

- verbal or written thanks;
- managers asking employees for ideas/opinions/information;
- information sharing (passing information to other departments);
- expanding participation (assigning special projects); and
- managers taking personal interest in employees' efforts.

Personal development of staff is discussed and agreed by both parties based on skills and knowledge needed to carry out activities that will ensure personal/team objectives (based on the four quadrants of BBS – financial, customer, internal quality and organisational development – will be met.

People satisfaction. People satisfaction is measured mainly from the annual employee satisfaction survey which is done in-house. Each division is given the freedom to ask any questions relevant to their environment, but core questions decided by the steering committee are included, so that cross-comparisons can be made. Other methods used are team meetings and annual staff appraisal.

The main elements identified to aid TQ progress are:

- A powerful leadership figure who can keep the spirit of continuous improvement at the top of the organisation's agenda and is able to embody that spirit within himself.
- Efforts in TQ initiatives must be team-based to utilise the synergistic effect of group working and to effectively spread the SIP message throughout the organisation.
- Effective communication that will aid vision, understanding, plans, suggestions etc. Information which is shared and understood will create a harmonious environment for the SIP culture to grow.

Birds Eye Wall's Ltd (BEW)
Birds Eye Wall's Ice Cream is a business within Birds Eye Wall's. It produces ice cream only, with 1,500 workers on a manufacturing site situated in Gloucester. The company's mission statement is "Working Together For The Best". To enable long-term success in a rapidly changing and increasingly open European market, it sets out to achieve the following:

- rapid innovation;
- high quality;
- excellent customer service;
- lowest possible costs; and
- profitable growth

In the organisation, the words "total quality" were not formally introduced to workers. However, there were initiatives introduced which embrace the concept of TQ. This organisation is very cost-conscious. It was with this in mind that the first initiative called Excel was introduced in 1987. It was very much top-down driven, aimed solely at reducing cost, and much success was achieved through the relatively easy way of "cutting the fat out". After that another initiative was introduced called Line Performance Improvement (LPI), again to reduce cost by increasing efficiency and reliability. It was not until mid-1994 that another initiative called Teamworking was introduced. This is driven by the harnessing of knowledge and creativity of all employees, enabling them to make effective contributions through ongoing development of teams across the site, continuously improving the factory. The emphasis now is on exposing the latent human resource capability.

Leadership. Management supported the latest initiative by creating eight facilitator posts whose jobs were to mentor, facilitate and encourage teams in their improvement programmes. Budgets for training (both internal and external) and staff development are generously allowed.

The most recent attitude survey result has yet to be published, but there is a strong feeling among workers that even though they have seen lots of "fads" before, the Teamworking initiative is rather different. The leadership commitment and visibility is very much seen and felt by all employees.

People management. The Teamworking initiative is people-based. In trying to achieve the company's mission of working together for the best, it is in the company's interest to keep its people committed, confident and competent.

The company believes in "organisation drives behaviour". Therefore, in making Teamworking a success, an empowerment culture is developed through changes in the structure and the nature of the jobs. A manufacturing manager is now responsible for performance improvement of one to three production lines, working in three shifts. A manufacturing unit is like a "mini-factory", responsible for the operation and improvement activities to achieve company objectives. It is also responsible for the equipment performance and development of its people. The managers have flexible working time (can be present at any shift) and ultimately performance will be measured in terms of quality, safety, output efficiency, team and individual competencies, costs and attendance. Improvement ideas are generated from among the team and are not being imposed, therefore resulting in ownership, commitment and motivation towards improvement activities. Resources and support are made available to all teams in fulfilling their responsibilities.

Training and development is one of the strong points within the organisation. The company has twice been recognised as Investors in People. Managers and team leaders are responsible for the training of their subordinates. Personal learning plans for managers are made to develop competencies especially in handling people. Any training required (core or non-core skills) can be applied for through team leaders, and if agreed, will be fully paid for by the company.

The annual appraisal system is an agreed one, based on objectives of the team (team-based) with a bonus scheme attached to it.

Communications within the teams is through regular team meetings, performance review meetings, team briefings, resource meetings and action teams. Other forms of communication are noticeboards, company newsletters, house journals and internal TV service.

People satisfaction. This is done quantitatively through attitude surveys (every 18 months) and qualitatively through various methods of communication.

The next steps in the TQ journey for the company are:
- Further improvement in the Teamworking initiative with wider people involvement and a clearer empowerment environment.

- Focus on the development of first line managers as true leaders in the Teamworking initiative.
- Structural changes in personnel policy to create an environment conducive to the Teamworking initiative (seven days operation, PRP and competency based personnel within a team).

Assessment method used

In order to identify areas of best practice, a scale of 0-5 was developed and the various companies involved were scrutinised from the point of view of:
- degree of presence and application of criteria covering leadership, people management and people satisfaction;
- determination of benchmarks in the three criteria mentioned above.

The scoring system was based on various models of assessment. The aggregated scores are illustrated in Table 6.1. In this part of the study it was felt necessary to disguise the names of the five companies involved, in order to preserve any sensitivities.

Table 6.1 Aggregated scores

	Company				
Benchmarking criteria	A	B	C	D	E
Leadership					
Top management commitment	4	5	4	4	4
Recognition/appreciation policy	5	4	4	4	2
Resources/assistance support	4	5	3	3	4
Aggregate score for leadership	13	14	11	11	10
People management					
Policy in PM	5	5	4	3	3
Management structures supporting PM policy	5	3	3	2	2
Training and development	5	4	3	3	4
Involvement	4	5	3	3	4
Communication	4	5	4	3	4
Empowerment	5	4	3	3	4
Teamwork	4	5	2	3	4
Appraisal system	4	5	2	2	2
Aggregate score for PM	36	36	24	23	27
People satisfaction					
Methods used	4	5	3	3	3
Feedback mechanism and action plan	4	5	4	3	3
Aggregate score of PS	8	10	7	6	6
Total score	57	60	42	40	43

Discussion of practices exhibited
CSG had demonstrated competencies and was the benchmark in the following areas:
- Top management commitment – visibility of leadership being continuously felt by employees with MD and all heads of division spending about 10 per cent of their time on listening sessions with every QIT at least once a year.
- Resources/assistance support – TQM implementations generously supported by eight quality support managers and even having a benchmarking manager to facilitate and coach TQ activities. Training opportunities are provided in abundance to employees for knowledge and skill upgrading.
- Policy in people management – clearly written principles in managing its TQM programme "Putting the Customer First", of which people based management is one of them. CSG also produces yearly people management objectives (based on various feedback mechanisms from employees) which can be used by both the management and the employees to assess how "committed" CSG is in its principle of people based management.
- Communication – each division has customised its own communication plan based on best practice recommended by the central communication team.
- Teamwork – key value in the organisation, where cross-functional teams work together to strengthen business performance. The team leader is responsible for inculcating team culture and solely responsible for giving training.
- Appraisal system – a well developed individual appraisal system, both at staff level and management level (upward appraisal). Team objectives form part of individual objectives and are increasingly being applied to service level agreements (objectives prompted by customer requirements). Frequent reviews of objectives are held.
- Methods used to gauge people satisfaction – various methods are employed; qualitative and quantitative, face-to-face and in written form; direct and surrogate measures.

Equally well, Elida Gibbs Ltd is a leader in the following areas:
- Recognition/appreciation policy – timely given and includes local recognition (departments are empowered to give recognition – flexible, discretionary and "fun") and corporate recognition (given by the Chairman with wide publicity).
- Management structures supporting PM policy – set up employee development and communication group with tasks to develop, support and monitor programmes that are people-related (recognising people as a CSF in the TQM change programme).
- Training and development – determined to create a learning organisation culture with excellent learning facilities (on-site learning centre) and personal development programme scheme.
- Feedback mechanism and action plan in PS – results from surveys are given to employees via special edition newsletters which include action plans agreed by the board to address employee concerns.

Some conclusions
Benchmarking of HRM practices is so critical, not just for identifying improvement opportunities and thus being able to draw action plans, but also to enable organisations to attract, retain and mobilise a critical mass of human talent for successfully achieving business objectives. Holt (1994) concluded in his study that HR benchmarking is a valid and powerful

technique, and should be a continuous activity. This fact is further supported by the emergence of various benchmarking in HR forums – data sharing consortia:
- in Europe; initiated by Rank Xerox called Best in Europe (Williams, 1993);
- in the USA; called Benchmarking HRD Forum, under the auspices of the American Society for Training and Development (Ford, 1993);
- in Australia; called Australian Human Resource Benchmarking Programme under Saratog Institute (NRMA Australian Quality Award 1992 submission); and
- in Japan; the practice of benchmarking in HRM (Zairi, 1995) happens through *shukko* (external transfer of employees between companies) and through industrial co-operation (e.g. *zaibatsus*).

From this study, it can be concluded that people management is essential in effective TQM implementation. People management can be analysed through three headings and sub-headings namely:
1. Leadership:
    - top management commitment, recognition/appreciation, policy, and resources/assistance support.
2. People management:
    - policy in PM, management structures supporting PM policy, training and development, involvement, communication, empowerment, teamwork, appraisal system.
3. People satisfaction:
    - methods used, feedback mechanism and action plan.

References

Blocklyn, P.L. (1988), "Making magic: the Disney approach to people management", *Personnel*, December, pp. 28-35.

Tyson, S. and Witcher, M. (1994), "Getting in gear: post-recession human resource management", *Personnel Management*, August, pp. 20-3.

Hiltrop, J.M. and Depres, C. (1994), "Benchmarking the performance of human resource management", *Long Range Planning*, Vol. 27 No. 6, pp. 43-57.

Morgan, J. (1992), "Human resource information: a strategic tool", in Armstrong, M. (Ed.), *Strategies for Human Resource Management*, Kogan Page, London.

Glanz, E.F. and Daily, L.K. (1992), "Benchmarking", *Human Resource Management*, Vol. 31 Nos 1 and 2, pp. 9-20.

Schuler, R. (1984) "Gaining competitive advantage through HRM practices", *Human Resource Management*, Vol. 23 No. 3, pp. 241-55.

Kravetz, D. (1988), *The Human Resources Revolution: Implementing Progressive Management Practices for Bottom Line Success*, Jossey-Bass, San Francisco, CA.

Schuster, F. (1986), *The Schuster Report: The Proven Connection between People and Profits*, Wilkey, New York.

Holt, B. (1994), "Benchmarking comes to human resources", *Personnel Management*, June, pp. 32-5.

Williams (1993), "Fair comment", *Personnel Today*, March, p. 27.

Ford, D.J. (1993), "Benchmarking human resource development", *Training and Development*, June, pp. 37-41.

Zairi, M. (1995), "Understanding the practice of benchmarking in Japan: the significance of the human element", The European Centre for TQM Report No. 95/10.

Appendix 6.1 Key HR performance indicators

Recruitment and selection
- Number of long-term vacancies (over six months)/ total number of jobs.
- Average length of time to fill vacancies.
- Proportion of vacancies filled internally through promotion, demotion or lateral movements of personnel.
- Average time spent in job or function per employee.

Training and development
- Number of trainee days/number of employees.
- Total training budget/total employee expenditure.

Compensation and rewards
- Total compensation cost/total revenues.
- Basic salary/total remuneration.
- Number of salary grades/employees.

Employee relations
- Number of resignations/total headcount per year.
- Average length of service per employee.
- Rate of absenteeism.
- Average length of absence per employee.
- Number of supervisors and managers per employee.

Overall HR management
- Total revenue per employee.
- Total headcount this year, compared to last year.
- Proportion of part-time employees to total number of staff.
- Employment cost/total expenditure.
- Number of HR professionals per employee.
- Age distribution of employees.

Appendix 6.2 People management exercise
Mortgage Express
Market and product range
Mortgage Express is part of the Lloyds TSB Group with a staff of 280 and offers a range of mortgage loan products. It operates as a self-contained company within the group, selling products directly to the public or through mortgage intermediaries. Operations are conducted from a central base rather than through a branch network and funding for loans is raised through the money markets.

Business growth was exceptional and by 1990 mortgage assets had grown to £3 billion and there were over 50,000 customers. This was followed by a collapse in the housing market and a strategic decision was taken to stop taking on new mortgages and to withdraw from the market over the following two to three years. The company was loosing money through increasing bad debts, particularly as its customer base was in southern England, the area most affected by falling prices, and by 1992 losses had exceeded £70 million. By 1993 this position had been reversed. Mortgage Express was making a profit and business results, people and customer satisfaction had continued to improve.

Strategy was reviewed in light of the turnaround in the business and a decision was taken to expand the business by taking over responsibility for a number of smaller mortgage businesses which the group had acquired.

Mortgage Express is a niche mortgage provider seeking to meet the specific individual needs of different customers. Today it competes in chosen markets and concentrates on parts of the market where its innovative products and risk management capabilities provide it with competitive advantage.

Launch of total quality initiatives
The quest for quality began in 1991 at a time when employee motivation was at its lowest due to the downturn in the market, redeployment of existing sales staff, reengineering of processes and change due to upgrading of management information systems.

Restoration of employee motivation was critical to the business and a MORI poll on employee opinion was commissioned to quantify the extent of the problem and prioritise areas for improvement.

A commitment to quality by the management team was evident as resources were deployed in the training of everyone in the tools and techniques of total quality by 1991. Mortgage Express then progressed to its first assessment in 1992 using the EFQM.

Quality is now an integral part of the business, through extensive promotion at every opportunity. The high profile of quality is evident from board meetings to team briefings.

Mission and vision
The mission for Mortgage Express was redefined in 1993 to make total quality the driving force:
   To be recognised as a top quality company, using the EFQM model to help achieve four key strategic goals:
   1. Maximising the long-term value for the shareholder.
   2. Providing customers with a first class service.
   3. Enabling all employees to achieve their best.
   4. Achieving a top quality rating using the business excellence model.

The vision at Mortgage Express is to be recognised as the company for customers with individual needs: "We will do this by providing innovative, value for money products and world class service delivered by the best people".

The values at Mortgage Express are:
- Teamwork – everybody matters and has a valid point of view.
- Integrity – we are open, honest and fair in everything we do.
- Recognition – we praise achievement and celebrate success.
- Quality – we deliver what we promise and constantly seek to improve.

To ensure awareness throughout the business every employee has a copy of the mission and value statements in a document called "The Way Ahead".

Quality policy
Quality is central to the Mortgage Express mission and is given a high profile throughout the business by the top management team. Quality is seen as a significant contributor to the turnaround in the Mortgage Express fortunes.

Evolution of the process
Following the extensive training in total quality tools and techniques in 1991, which launched total quality at Mortgage Express, a quality improvement team was formed in 1992 to help integrate total quality into the culture of the business.

Quality became established as a regular item at each monthly board meeting and team briefings to raise the level of quality awareness and the importance which management places on its application.

In 1993 the business excellence assessment revealed a need for a unifying vision that would be shared by all employees. Activity then centred around redefining the mission and values to make total quality the driving force. Unlike the previous occasion, this activity involved all the workforce and gained their commitment through involvement.

The quality message is reinforced by the MD, who makes total quality a constant theme of his keynote speeches at the annual staff conference. An opportunity is taken to recognise achievement, review progress and target areas for specific focus in the months ahead.

Continuous improvement
A continuous improvement culture is evident with Mortgage Express as each year it measures performance, assesses leadership effectiveness and plans and implements improvements.

With total quality as a key item on the monthly team briefings, areas for improvement and best practice are being constantly researched and implemented. Total quality workshops are used as part of the quarterly management briefings to drive the continuous improvement message at the top level within the business.

Mortgage Express maintains a high quality profile by being a key member of the British Quality Foundation and the Industrial Society Quality Club. It also participates in the Royal Mail Benchmarking Forum and two mortgage lender benchmarking consortia to challenge its own processes and search for best practices which will lead to improvement.

Key benefits and achievements
The most significant benefit has been the ability to turnaround the business from loss to profit in a short period of time. Much of this can be directly attributed to the focus on total quality management and has resulted in record of profits of around £38 million in 1994 and 1995, in just two to three years.

Next steps and future challenges
The financial services sector is undergoing extremely competitive threats from new entrants normally associated with other industry sectors such as retailing and leisure. Mortgage Express's capacity for innovation and change will be challenged by many of these new players but, through its commitment to continuous improvement and a strong quality culture, it is well positioned to weather the storm.

Exercise
You have been appointed the HR director at Mortgage Express and your first task is to develop a progressive HR strategy for the next five years. Other parts of the business have been involved in this process and now you are about to draft the high level strategies which support the mission, vision and values of the company.

The exercise requires you to draft approximately eight high level strategies from the information which you have in this case study documentation.

People management exercise – suggested solution
Mortgage Express – high level human resource strategies:
- Develop system for assessing future manpower needs, handling redeployment and redundancies.
- Develop creative and flexible employment policies, including use of short-term contract, seasonal and part-time employees, and outsourcing high risk processes such as information technology.
- Introduce remuneration packages to retain and recruit people.
- Establish a training capability to provide personal development opportunities and meet the business skill needs.
- Develop and improve our systems for job definition, objective setting, performance measurement and appraisal.
- Improve health and safety management.
- Upgrade the employee communications process to create an environment of trust and understanding.
- Involve everyone in improving the business through learning.

Chapter 7
Resource management: the key sources of "improvement progress"

Information processing and decision making
The concept of information processing has been defined as the process of gathering, interpreting and synthesising information in the context of decision making and task management. This process is vital, because whatever information is derived from gathering, interpreting and synthesising becomes included in the process of decision making. The quality of information will undoubtedly have an "impression" on the decision outcome.

A review of the recent literature on communication aspects reveals that among the different aspects of information processing requisites are: amount of information; and timing of information. Different tasks will have different complexities which demand different informational treatment in making decisions on those tasks. Tasks which are not complex and are routine will not demand much effort in processing information and making decisions.

The quantity, timeliness, sources and richness of information are basic requisites of information processing. The quantity and quality of information have been seen to have an influence on the effectiveness of decision making. Daft and Lengel (1986) ranked media channels according to their information-carrying capacity. The richness of the medium is determined by the cues that it provides and by the immediacy of feedback to the receiver. Face-to-face discussions, telephone conversations, various electronic material and numerical documents are ranked according to the richness of their information transfer. Media characteristics of accessibility, frequency and quality were examined by Fann and Smeltzre (1989) where they found that managers used information sources that were informal and accessible at both the start-up and stable stages of organisational development.

Creating and embodying knowledge stems from processing of information, as Nonaka (1991) stated:

> Successful organisations seem to be consistently creating new knowledge, disseminating it widely throughout the organisation, and quickly embody it into new technology and products. These organisations want, not only to process objective information, but also to "tap" the tacit and often highly subjective insights, intuitions and hunches of individual managers and making those insights available for testing and use in the organisation as a whole.

The value and usefulness of information to a manager is also an important issue. Managers tended to use more information if it was deemed technically adequate, confirmed prior expectations, and when working closely with researchers (Deshpande and Zaltman, 1982), 1984)

In studying decision making, it would be useful to examine not just the decision, but the steps leading to it. There are three distinct stages in the decision process, first described by John Dewey (1910): What is the problem? What are the alternatives? Which alternative is the best? Similarly, Hogart (1980) extended and outlined the process as structuring the decision problem, acquiring information, processing it, and then making a decision.

Marketing management and information processing

The marketing management structure, developed by Procter & Gamble in 1972, became a structural norm for consumer companies to adopt. With the successful results by P&G, other companies began to adopt it without hesitation into their organisational structure (Low and Fullerton, 1994). The structure worked well, especially in companies having multiple marketing or product lines to manage, where there was a homogenous market, and in an era when advertising had its greatest impact. Marketing managers were seen as "little managers" running their own companies, pulling together other functions and contributing to the performance of their marketing.

There seem to be major debates on the usefulness and relevance of marketing management in meeting present competitive and dynamic market conditions. Increased trade power, fragmented media, shorter product development cycles, declining marketing loyalty, consumers moving away from supermarkets, and investors' expectations (Skenazy, 1987; Shocker et al., 1994) have influenced the rethinking and reorganising of the view of marketing managers' roles.

Some major consumer companies like Pepsico, Purex, Eastman Kodak and Levi Strauss have even abandoned the marketing manager structure totally (*Business Week*, 9 June, 1973). A more recent and similar response to such shifts in the structure was reflected in the UK, which began to view the structure as an "outdated organisational system" and ill-suited for today's environment (*Marketing UK*, 1990). Another element in the changes in the marketing manager structure is the influence of major changes in overall managerial styles and organisational design. Companies now "re-engineer" themselves by radically reshaping work processes (Hammer and Champy, 1993), downsize by slashing layers of middle management, or farming out key tasks on an *ad hoc* basis (Low and Fullerton, 1994). Others have still retained the marketing manager structure, but shifted major decisions like trade promotions to sales and pricing, and product development to manufacturing. This is a reflection that market changes demand decisions to be taken by people close to the activity.

Within the consumer products companies, marketing managers are facing new, shifting views of their existence and the role to play. Companies faced with increasing power of the retailers are forcing the marketing managers to be more in touch with what happens out in the market rather than handling corporate activities (Low and Fullerton, 1994).

Statement of purpose and significance of the study

The general purpose of the research by Noor (1996) was to produce a model of information processing for fast moving consumer goods (FMCG) manufacturing companies. The model to be developed was based on the examination of information processing behaviours of marketing managers in Malaysia and comparing outcomes with best practices in information processing found within organisations operating in the fast moving consumer goods sector in the West. The prime purpose of this research was:

- To develop a model which can be used to assess the level of information processing requirements in a FMCG manufacturing organisation.
- To study the relationship and effects of task characteristics and task environment as the prime influence on the perception of uncertainty, which in turn affects information processing requirements of marketing managers.
- To explore and test the effects of managerial experience as an individual characteristic of information processing.
- To determine how the interplay between managerial experience, the characteristics of tasks and the task environment affects information processing requirements.

- To develop a benchmarking framework and guidelines for best practice in information processing in a FMCG manufacturing environment. The purpose is to compare and analyse specific aspects of various information processing between UK and Malaysian FMCG manufacturers.

The context used in this study is the decision-making process, and the use of information by marketing managers.

Significance of the research study

Decision making based on information which affects the performance of marketing related activities is of prime importance to any organisation. Marketing managers have the responsibility of making good decisions to ensure that their products remain valid and competitive to the market. Managers will need relevant information for decision making in order to be strategically competitive, find new markets, produce new products and respond quickly to competitors' strategies.

Very little research on managerial experience and information processing in enhancing marketing decisions has been conducted. The research area which is not fully addressed by previous research is the interaction effect of managers' characteristics and decisions or task characteristics on decision making (Payne, 1982). It is this interaction that defines the area within which decisions are made (Newell and Simon, 1972).

The purpose of this research is to characterise the relationship between information processing requirements and their predictors. Such a characterisation will give the marketing theorists and researchers an additional insight and, the researcher believes, some sensible grounding on which to base further inquiry into the issues regarding information processing and marketing management.

According to a recent publication by Shocker *et al.* (1994), the area of research on marketing management that needs to be explored is the impact of information technology and information on the marketing management system and the marketing manager's job – and how the job is changing as decisions are decentralised and involvement in those decisions is broadened, both inside and outside the company. As Sinkula (1994) suggested:

> There exists an expansive and untapped body of thought on organisational learning that is undergoing active scrutiny by our friends in organisation sociology, organisational behaviour and psychology. Introducing this thinking to scholars who are curious about marketing knowledge development could foster an innovative way of discerning how organisations process information as they attempt to make sense of their markets. Such insights can lead organisations to better utilisation of market information, learning that is avaricious truth, and better market performance.

Details of the research study and its outcome are covered in Noor (1996).

An integrated model of information processing

The model described in Figure 7.1 has resulted from a detailed and comprehensive investigation which examined information processing in the context of marketing managers working in organisations operating in the fast moving consumer goods (FMCG) sector.

The model is based on best practices resulting from a comparative analysis between Malaysian manufacturing organisations and model organisations operating in Western Europe. The model suggests that decisions, and information derived from information processing, are integrated and shared amongst other processes in order that the whole business process is working in concert towards satisfying customers' needs.

Process represents a value chain, including operational and support processes starting from the process of analysing the customers' needs right through to the process of selling the product. The model is represented through the following levels.

Level 1. Top management process
Top management formulation of business direction, policies, philosophy and strategic intention, identification of the critical success factors (CSFs) needed for competing in the FMCG environment. At this level, the top management will be the provider of strategic information of directions and guidelines for the whole business process.

Level 2. Analytical processes
At this level, information pertaining to analysis of customers' needs and wants is passed on to the process of generating ideas and concepts of satisfying those customer needs. Marketing process plays an important role in providing initial inputs into the product developments, synergising customer needs, and the management of the product when launched in the market place.

Level 3. Operational processes
The next process will be in the development, testing and analysis of the product in order to ascertain its worthiness and viability in satisfying the customer. Once the product is considered potential and viable, the manufacturing process will begin the mass manufacturing of the product and making sure all the product qualities are in place.

The distribution process is responsible for selling and distributing the product, making it accessible and available to the customers. The after-sale support process makes sure that the distributors and retailers are full supported, stocked and well-informed.

The surveillance and analysis process monitors customers' trends, tastes and requirements which are vital information to be passed back to the other processes, so that reformations and product modifications can be done to meet such changes. This process also monitors movements of its competitors, and other external environmental influences.

It is noted that each of these processes is processing and managing its own information while performing its tasks. The information is passed along to other processes, providing an integrated system of information sharing.

Level 4. The supportive processes
This level comprises the financial, IT and business services and human resources, which are supportive processes that assist the operational processes in managing their tasks efficiently and effectively.

Level 5. Benchmarking for best practice process
All the levels and processes are each benchmarked for best practice. This will provide the encouragement for learning new practices, knowledge, initiatives for continuously improving the whole business process. This adds the dimension of dynamism into the whole business process.

Conclusions

Using information processing and benchmarking for best practice is not a new management tool. As described by Marvin Patterson (1993), HP director of R&D, Hewlett-Packard has used information processing in its product development based on the principle of an "information assembly line". HP realised that the biggest impact on customer satisfaction and return on investment comes from the time it takes to develop and introduce new products, measured from the time it takes HP to recognise the business opportunity. The effectiveness of this approach is heavily dependent on the robustness of the information processes available. HP has made use of information from information processes to improve its time to market. Products became more viable and costs were reduced when time was removed from the supply chain/manufacturing process and applied to brand development.

Research and theory in the area of marketing information processing are still in a very early stage and only a few empirical studies have been carried out. The success of information processing in marketing and other functional areas can be investigated through exploring best practice in the context of organisations using such approaches which yield superior performance. As best practice and benchmarking are incorporated into information processes and also into other operational and supportive processes, there will be a greater scope for research investigation.

Figure 7.1 Information processing and integration between other processes

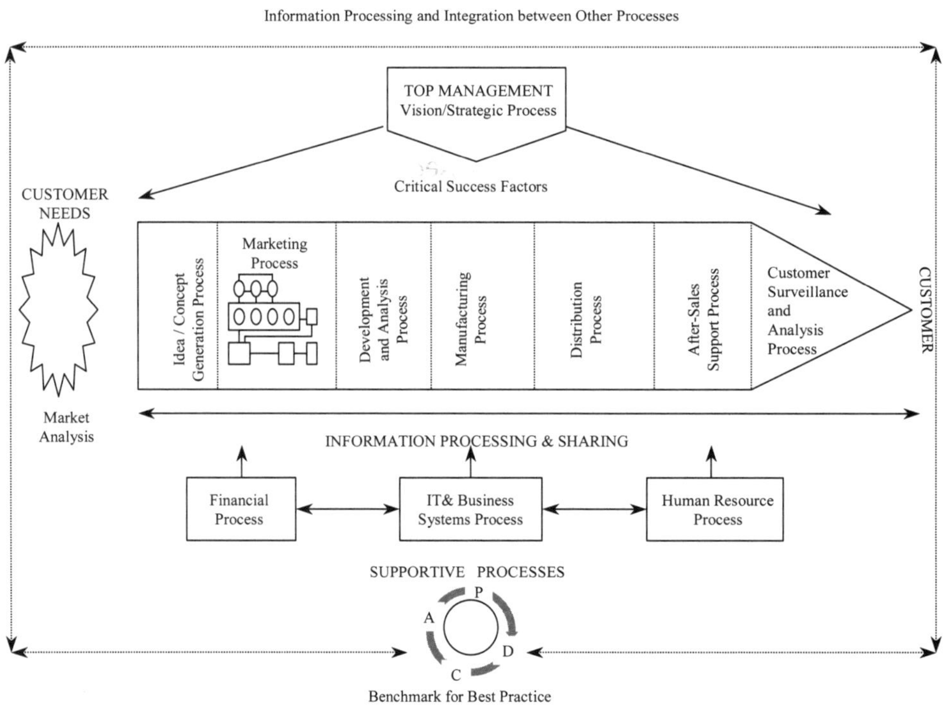

Supplier partnerships – a perspective

Managing supplier relationships in a modern business context is no longer considered as a "distraction" from doing important tasks, on the contrary, this is one of the most critical areas for superior competitiveness. For those companies that manage their suppliers effectively, this is a core competence. Supplier management in the 1990s is no longer the function of the "buying" or "purchasing" manager, it is a corporate wide activity which relies on a cross-functional, process based, approach where suppliers become an integral element of the value adding chain.

Strategic management has to take into account supplier issues at various levels, to ensure that goals are achieved and supplier performance is compatible with company objectives. Perhaps two issues need to be considered from the outset in developing strong partnerships with suppliers:
1. supplier evaluation and selection; and
2. supplier management.

Supplier evaluation and selection
Supplier evaluation and selection is not merely a financial consideration, or a functional consideration. Very often organisations consider suppliers who can be "bolted on" to their existing culture, or alternatively, the option is given to suppliers who are more likely to consider changing and radically re-engineering their processes to fit their customer requirements. Visionary organisations, however, may even consider internal changes and internal re-engineering in order to capture full potential from their relationships with their key suppliers. Unlike traditional approaches to supplier evaluation, some of the models suggested cover various aspects:
- financial issues;
- organisational structure and strategy;
- technology; and
- business credibility and other factors.

Supplier management
The management of suppliers in a modern business context is not "transaction based" but process focused. The spirit of continuous improvement has to be linked to the optimization of external processes, such as supplier management. Cost reduction should not overshadow wider benefits in the areas of quality improvement, responsiveness, flexibility, innovation and involvement in problem solving. Some of the issues which need to be addressed during the development of close relationships with suppliers should include:
- consistent payment of invoices;
- long-term commitment to suppliers;
- early involvement of suppliers;
- consideration of suppliers' feed back; and
- supplier access to key people.

Effective supplier management has also to be dependent on some "hard necessities" such as:
- a clear definition of requirements;
- a selection of qualified suppliers;
- an agreement of quality assurance;
- a provision for the settlement of disputes;
- incoming inspection control; and
- the receipt of quality records.

Effective supplier partnership models are only those where human bonds are established at all levels through commitment, positive communications, openness and willingness to share knowledge and expertise and joint vision development. Some of the recommended

approaches in facilitating the process of effective partnership development through team building include:
- identifying the willingness to embark on a partnership enhancing process;
- identifying mutual issues;
- selecting participants;
- selecting realistic expectations;
- fashioning ground rules;
- structuring, monitoring, and managing the problem solving process;
- avoiding and managing conflict;
- considering an outside facilitator-consultant;
- gaining resolution and ensuring actions are taken; and
- learning from experience and planning the continuation.

Examples of best practice
The following examples provide pioneering and effective practices of supplier-customer partnerships. The models highlighted represent integrated approaches, usually driven from a top-down, strategic perspective and exhibiting interactions at various levels. These case studies do also show the power of total quality management and how a commitment to continuous improvement can help forge better links. At the heart of all quality drives is the emphasis on performance measurement and action taking.

Lucas Automotive
Supplier development process. Lucas Automotive has responded to competitive challenges by changing its relationships with suppliers, in an attempt to match the best in the world. Following a successful pilot project in the firm's heavy duty braking division, sourcing reforms were brought in at Lucas Group plants world-wide.

For European manufacturing companies generally a 1 per cent cut in spending on materials can give a financial benefit equal to a 8-10 per cent increase in sales. Companies have traditionally placed a heavy emphasis on negotiating the lowest price from their suppliers. A new approach was designed, emphasis was placed on quality to reduce costs throughout the sourcing process. In its drive to improve product development lead times and quality, and cut total acquisition costs, Lucas decided to concentrate on a limited number of very close partners. These links covered aspects of planning, engineering, manufacturing and finance. This required a commitment from the most senior level.

The greatest opportunities were at the design stage where it was considered that suppliers could assist in the task of achieving the optimum design for manufacture. Suppliers were involved with the product design team as opposed to making a product from a drawing. As the suppliers' responsibilities have increased, more of Lucas' own engineering resources have been released. The strategic process of supplier partnership development involves three phases:
1. *Phase 1: research.* This lasts for four to six weeks and is carried out by interview and literature search. The main tasks are to:
    - Analyse current and future spending.
    - Determine the structure of the supply industry.
    - Understand the technology available to suppliers.
    - Build an initial model of the total acquisition cost.
    - Long-term saving opportunities are also worked out.

2. *Phase 2: evaluate.* Evaluating suppliers lasts between six to eight weeks. The characteristics required of a supplier will vary according to the item being bought. Suppliers are assessed, according to their different technologies and skills, against the required characteristics and a world class benchmark.
3. *Phase 3: structure.* After establishing the implications of the partnership with those short-listed suppliers, the co-makers are selected and the supply relationship structured. The long-term nature of the relationship means that it is vital that the co-maker should achieve world class performance levels. Benchmarking helps to define where cost reduction efforts should be concentrated. Joint targets are set and improvement plans approved. This process takes two to three months. Lucas is examining changes to some of its structures and skill levels to take account of the new arrangements. But the following remains to be done:
    - strengthening Lucas's ability to help co-makers with improvement programs;
    - extending to co-makers, the benefits Lucas has obtained on raw materials and service; and
    - developing supplier groups to optimise product design and spread best practice.

Achievements. The benefits achieved for the customer, the supplier and the mutual benefits are set out in Table 7.1.

Table 7.1 Customer benefits, supplier benefits and mutual benefits

Customer benefits	Mutual benefits	Supplier benefits
Fair price	Equitable pricing based on open book cost modelling	Fair margin
No double tooling cost	Scale economics	Increased volumes
Long-term agreement	Less uncertainty	Better forecasting
Less component variability due to single source	Better quality	Clearer understanding of requirements
Lower long-term cost of acquisition	Long-term perspective	Encourages investment
High support and responsiveness	Increased mutual dependence	Not forced to be a "yes" man

British Telecommunications Ltd
Philosophy. Major purchases are carried out centrally where an increasing number of corporate agreements are being set up. Supply opportunities also exist through local procurement units and, on a sub-contract basis, through BT's main contractors. In addition, BT has several subsidiaries and associated companies, each with their own purchasing units. With such buying on a large scale, it is important that the company gets value for money, which is why emphasis is placed on quality, reliability and price. Quality is the cornerstone of BT's strategy. It is of equal importance to its customers who recognise that price is important, but quality is crucial. As BT operates at the forefront of technical change in an increasingly competitive market, it is vital that the position of both the customers and BT is safeguarded by buying only those goods and services which represent value for money. For this reason, a

close relationship with suppliers is essential. Such a partnership is founded on trust, co-operation, support and, above all, continuous improvement.

Supplier requirements. As the partnership develops, the supplier will need, at various stages, to:

- Show commitment to meeting the requirements of ISO 9000 and to introduce systems such as electronic data interchange and bar coding.
- Discuss problems in an open and timely manner.
- Participate in joint quality improvement projects.
- Co-operate in comprehensive monitoring of performance.
- Provide information on whole life costs.
- Identify and improve any process which might harm the environment.

BT expects its suppliers to have high quality, reliable goods and services, first class delivery to schedule and excellent support services. BT prefers to buy proprietary services against international standards, leaving design questions to the suppliers, instead of issuing detailed product specifications.

For a successful partnership, commitment is required from both sides, hence BT ensures that:

- the professionalism of its staff will be used to purchase goods and services in a way which meets the European Community legislation, and is fair to all participants;
- it gives a better view of its forward plans so that suppliers can invest in quality improvement, product capacity and development with great confidence;
- it provides better feedback on overall performance;
- it clearly defines the requirements; to help with this BT has rationalised its internal processes; and
- it continues its company wide total quality management programme, supported by ISO 9000 accreditation.

Supplier development process. Initial enquiries are addressed to a central contact place. A potential supplier will be invited to provide information on the company profile, goods/service range, financial accounts and quality assurance structure. This will be studied against the requirements of BT's qualified supplier list. A vendor appraisal will be conducted prior to issuing invitations to tender.

Quality standard. BT's quality standards are applied according to the type of item to be bought and to the degree to which it affects BT's service to its customers. They are classified into sectors as follows:

- Sector 1: covers low risk purchases for internal consumption, cash transactions, vehicles and energy needs. The quality standards required are that the products conform to standard terms and conditions.
- Sector 2: covers items like personal computers, computer maintenance, tools, most engineering stores, freight services, underground work etc. In addition to Sector 1 requirements, the supplier is expected to be committed to ISO 9000, and have a pro-active approach to quality.
- Sector 3: covers goods and services that directly impact on the service imparted to BT customers. In addition to Sector 2 requirements, joint quality improvement programmes and vendor ratings are used to monitor and measure supplier and product performance.
- Sector 4: covers critical purchases vital to the operation of BT's core activities and encompasses switching, transmission and network management computing. Quality

standards require suppliers to participate in reliability improvement programmes to comprehensive whole life costing studies.

BT also has additional generic standards addressing issues like the environment, human factors, safety etc.

Nissan
Philosophy. The advent of Japanese companies, like Nissan, into the European automotive industry influenced a radical shift in customer-supplier relationships. The traditional adversarial relationship has given way to closer co-operation. This is because manufacturers now realise the importance of the supplier's contribution to competitiveness. Competitiveness could not be achieved in the 1990s by the original equipment manufacturers (OEMs) alone; more success will be achieved if their suppliers are aligned to their strategic visions. The effectiveness depends on the supplier's ability with respect to the following:
- Insight into the market, customer and competitive needs.
- Flexibility and responsiveness to competitive thrusts.
- Efficiency in the use of combined assets.
- Elimination of any non-value added activities in the chain.
- Adoption of a vigorous culture of "continuous improvement".

The increasing trend is to source a greater proportion of components from outside, thus reducing the amount of vertical integration. The trend is for the manufacturer to become a designer and assembler of products; unlike traditional European mass producers which do not retain a high proportion of value chain in-house, and are not involved in the detailed design. This means that the supplier has a very high profile at Nissan.

Nissan tends to source sub-assemblies from a few suppliers rather than sourcing components which comprise the lower levels of the bills of materials. This enables Nissan to pay more attention to fewer suppliers. The costs that would be associated with dealing with a large number of suppliers are eliminated and more attention can be paid to the remaining suppliers in terms of helping them, and monitoring their performance. Suppliers who used to cater to the lower levels of bills of materials are eliminated. They now comprise the second tier suppliers and are managed by their customer who supplies the sub-system to the final assembler.

This facilitates a close relationship between the customer and supplier. This close relationship does allow more security for the suppliers, but it makes their operations more visible and exposed to the customer demand for continuous improvement in terms of cost, quality and delivery.

The main reason stems from the need to be cost competitive. The increased proportion of sourced components gives the opportunity to reduce costs in several ways. The responsibility of the cost for holding stock is transferred to the supplier. This statement might imply that the supplier now holds the inventory, but this only occurs if the supplier's manufacturing system is inefficient and no assistance is given to rectify this. There is also a demand for the supplier to be cost competitive and pass on any productivity savings to the customer. Since the proportion of components that is sourced externally is increasing, the supply chain is the largest area which can be improved upon. This is achieved by allowing the customer to examine the costing structure of the supplier, and then working together to reduce costs. The supplier is integrated into the production schedule in order to reduce the cost of stock-holding.

Another aspect of cost saving is that of specialisation. The supplier no longer produces to a given design. Instead the supplier is given the required performance and cost parameters and a free rein to develop the product. The trend is for the supplier to build sub-assemblies. This reduces research and development costs. In-house engineering staff levels can be reduced and the supplier's technical expertise can be utilised.

Supplier development process. Nissan represents the present benchmark in the UK for customer-supplier relationships in the European automotive industry. It has only 160 suppliers compared to Rover which has 350 suppliers. Nissan has introduced to the UK its supplier quality assurance system, which is similar to that which it implements in Japan.

The supplier development process comprises two stages:
1. The pro-active stage. This stage consists of agreeing to standard terms of price, quality and delivery, and adhering to them. The emphasis is on proper and thorough project management and planning. This stage is where a new supplier is being initiated, or a new component/model is being introduced.
2. The reactive stage. This stage involves the process of continuous improvement. Kaizen teams undertake improvement projects. The emphasis is on people involvement. These teams are not management driven, problem solving task forces. In a similar vein, Nissan embarks on a programme of supplier development by giving direct assistance towards quality and productivity improvement. Targets are set and the benefits are shared by both parties. Sometimes Nissan finances capital equipment required for substantial improvements on very easy terms.

Nissan has been very successful with its suppliers through forging a close working relationship, systematically to plan, do and improve. Suppliers may not make high profits, but they make profits which are stable and certain. Nissan's claims of being the benchmark in distinguishing its supply quality system from other manufacturers rely on the fact that good planning and project management are required.

Supplier performance assessment. An evaluation questionnaire is used by Nissan to address the following areas:
1. Management.
2. Quality manual.
3. Drawing/document and specification control.
4. Control of purchased material.
5. Control of process/finished parts.
6. Calibration of gauge and test equipment.
7. Control of non-conforming products.
8. Machine control.

The auditors involved write their comments and score these aspects accordingly. Provision is made on the form for the suppliers to reply and, where necessary, to record what pertinent action is to be taken and time scales for corrective actions to be implemented.

Kodak
Kodak's dedication to total quality management in the manufacture and supply of all its products and services extends from the market place, through manufacturing to its suppliers. Kodak recognises that its quality objectives cannot be cost effectively achieved without ensuring consistent quality of incoming materials and services. To achieve this, the company has found it mutually beneficial to enter into a quality partnership with key suppliers to

achieve continuous improvement in the quality of supplies to Kodak. This forms the basis of the Kodak "Quality First Supplier Programme".

The "QI" programme is a structured programme, co-ordinated by the purchasing department, in which key suppliers are invited to work closely with the relevant Kodak users and buyers in improving the quality, and value for money, of the materials and services they supply.

The programme identifies and tackles individual areas of opportunity for improvement on a project priority basis. This is accomplished through small dynamic teams, involving the skills and resources of supplier personnel in conjunction with the Kodak purchasing and user departments. Working together, these team efforts are directed towards total quality improvement in all aspects of their business relationship. Sharing of information, co-operation, trust and mutual understanding are fundamental to the programme and create a climate in which the supplier is encouraged to employ innovative methods of problem solving and quality control which will enhance the quality of the product/service supplied.

Supplier development. The characteristics of an ideal Kodak supplier are defined as follows:
- Products are 100 per cent correct and reliable.
- Deliveries are always on time.
- Quantities delivered are always correct.
- Deliveries occur frequently to minimise stock carried by the user.
- The supplier provides appropriate response to urgent requirements.
- If something goes wrong, there is total commitment to rectifying it as soon as possible.
- There is competitive product pricing.
- Invoices and documentation are free from errors.
- The supplier is totally open and honest about his processes, his costs and pricing methods.
- The supplier works with Kodak to improve performance continuously.

Supplier development is conducted in a series of progressive stages. The supplier is accorded a particular status during each stage. These are defined as follows:
1. Potential. This stage is where quotations and samples are provided for various specifications and trials are conducted.
2. Accredited/approved. Visits are made to suppliers and specifications are agreed and set. Limited business is conducted and the supplied products are subjected to inward inspection. After this stage, a formal system of awards is implemented. This comprises three different levels of achievement. To qualify for these awards, a supplier would be expected to participate in a quality management programme that entails regular buyer/client/supplier quality team meetings to achieve the following:
   - Identification of opportunities for improvement.
   - Establishment of appropriate improvement projects and goals.
   - Measurement, monitoring and review of progress.
3. Level 1 (preferred) – Quality First Preferred Supplier Certificate. This is the basic level award and demands that high levels of conformance to specifications and supply are consistently maintained and no significant failures occur over a defined period – normally six months or a year. Performance should be monitored by means of a checklist or a performance matrix. Separate criteria are used for materials and services.

4. Level 2 (product control) – Silver Award/Service Award. To qualify for awards at this level, a quality team (QT) should be appointed. In addition to the criteria for Level 1, confidence in a supplier's ability to consistently meet requirements is such that Kodak's incoming inspection and testing of goods is dispensed with. This state is referred to as "product control" and responsibility for conformance rests solely with the supplier. Quality of design enhancements and other quality improvement should be realised by meeting the quality team's continuous improvement objectives. Nominations for a Silver Award must be accompanied by a performance matrix (see the Kodak case study in Chapter 14) and additionally a "self-audit checklist" completed by the QT, unless the supplier has a recognised third party accredited quality system (i.e. BS 5750).

   Service providers will have proven their ability to provide a significantly high level of service over a sustained period and have been judged to provide a fault free service. The supplier will have reached goals and objectives set and monitored by the quality team. The quality team will also have completed the "self-audit checklist", unless third party accredited.

5. Level 3 (process control) – Gold Award/Service Excellence Award. In addition to the criteria for Level 2, the supplier utilises statistical quality monitoring and data analysing techniques to control all the key process parameters and has a minimum process capability (Cpk) of 1.3 for these parameters. This state is referred to as being in "process control". Nominations to this level also require a satisfactory formal assessment of the supplier's quality systems by Kodak quality control specialists, unless third party accredited. In addition, a high level of pro-activity and dedication to continuous improvement should be evident (i.e. exceeding the criteria).

   Service providers are expected to provide outstanding contributions in all areas of the business relationship, being pro-active in proposing improvements to goods, services, methods and design. Again, all continuous improvement objectives and goals should be exceeded and there is the requirement to have a satisfactory assessment of the supplier's quality systems.

Supplier performance measurement. The key result areas that Kodak addresses when assessing suppliers are:
- Quality of conformance to specifications.
- Quality of design.
- Quality of service.
- Statistical process control.

The tool to measure these dimensions is a performance matrix. This is the primary means of tracking progress in a Kodak Quality First Supplier Programme. The matrix is used for:
- benchmarking current performance;
- establishing the quality team objectives and goals;
- monitoring on-going progress;
- communicating progress within the team and to Kodak/vendor management; and
- summarising the programme for award nomination purposes.

Various performance dimensions are assessed on a scale of 1-10. These dimensions should satisfy certain criteria to ensure that they are fair.

Expectations. Suppliers can expect from Kodak:
- Early involvement in the design and establishment of its requirements.
- Early involvement in the optimisation of the production process.
- Realistic and understandable specifications.
- Accurate forecast of Kodak's needs and early sharing of pertinent information.
- Timely payment.
- Open, timely and accurate communications of any change in plans and requirements and any less than satisfactory condition in any phase of the customer/supplier interface.
- Involvement in, and support for, joint customer/supplier improvement activities.
- Recognition for meeting or exceeding Kodak quality objectives.

Kodak expects from its suppliers:
- Commitment to continuous improvement.
- Conformance to contract agreements: on time delivery, delivery to proper location, proper qualities, proper labelling, packaging etc.
- High quality, invariant products and services which meet the specification and require no receiving inspection and extra cost.
- Co-operative management.
- Mutual sharing of the benefits achieved as a result of supplier/customer team improvements.
- Open, timely and accurate communication of any process change and any less than satisfactory condition in any phase of the customer/supplier interface.
- Supplier management that is committed to exploring "state of the art" technologies in their field of endeavour.

Achievements. The achievements gained by Kodak's suppliers are:
- increased effectiveness;
- lower total cost;
- increased business opportunities; and
- formal recognition by Kodak.

The achievements gained by Kodak are:
- optimum product design;
- increased effectiveness;
- strengthened long-term relationships with suppliers;
- receipts conform to specifications; and
- lower total cost.

Ten golden rules of supplier partnerships based on best practice
The various cases discussed cover specific areas thought to be very pertinent and critical for effective partnerships with suppliers. Drawing on "best practice", there are ten areas to be considered in the development of effective partnerships with suppliers:

1. Supplier quality statement, demonstrating visible commitment to work effectively with suppliers.
2. Integration of supplier development in company quality policy: to determine visible commitment towards building a long-term, lasting relationship with suppliers.
3. Defined supplier characteristics or requirements. The working relationship with suppliers has to be very explicit and based on expectations and outcomes.
4. Structured development strategy: a strategy of how suppliers are going to be developed and integrated as partners.
5. Supplier performance measurement: the use of various indicators to monitor overall supplier performance against set targets and agreed parameters.
6. Extent of performance measurement: measurement should cover both hard and soft aspects and also short-term and long-term issues. Measurement should also be seen as a trigger for continuous improvement and not a controlling mechanism for blame and reprimand.
7. Defined supplier expectations: partnerships are based on a win-win situation and as such customers need to be sensitive to the expectations of their suppliers.
8. Defined statement as customer/partner: similarly, suppliers need to explicitly indicate their visible commitment to the development of partnerships.
9. Structured supplier merit schemes: supplier efforts in meeting and exceeding quality standards need to be recognised, to encourage their innovation and creative potential.
10. Achievements: achievements must be recorded and publicised internally and externally.

Financial resources – the vital lifeblood
Finance has been described as the vital lifeblood of a business as it enables organisations to meet their daily operating overheads and make substantial capital investment in fixed assets such as plant and machinery. Managing financial resources effectively will ensure that wealth is created for the business, cash is readily available to enable the business to operate and an adequate return is achieved from an investment, having taken into account all the potential risks. The importance of effective resource deployment is demonstrated in a quote from a previous winner of the European Foundation for Quality Management Award:
> The efforts of strong leadership, strategy formulation and business planning are wasted unless resources are effectively deployed (High Performance Technology).

Financial resources are always finite and, therefore, the more effective their management, the greater the funding available to that business. Within the private sector funding is restricted by:
- The amount of unissued share capital. This is the difference between the issued and authorised share capital and, therefore, represents the additional funding the company can access by issuing those remaining unissued shares. Ultimately the company is constrained by a company's authorised share capital.
- The ability to generate sales revenue from its trading or provision of service. Innovative product features and service improvements need to generate increased sales revenue either directly through pricing or indirectly through cross-selling of products or services.
- The availability of cash balances. Bank and cash balances provide the most liquid form of assets for the business and these are directly affected by the size of the debt and turnover of the debtors. Having generated sales the company must manage the

outstanding debt to avoid an adverse impact on liquidity from late receipt of funds and potential reduction in profitability from bad debts.
- Disposal of fixed assets, provided there is some monetary value left in the asset at the time of disposal.

Similarly in the public sector, financial resources are restricted by:
- The size of funding from the public sector provider such as central or local government. This constraint mirrors the private sector's share capital constraints.
- The potential sponsorship to be gained from the private sector providers. Again, this is similar to the "ability to generate sales revenue" in the private sector.
- The availability of cash balances, as in the private sector.
- Disposal of fixed assets, as in the private sector.

Scope of financial management
Within the context of business excellence, financial management focuses on the key areas of financial strategy formulation, budget review, capital investment decision making and the cost of quality.
- The financial strategy formulation is where the organisational direction and tactics are integrated into the financial requirements necessary to fund their future operations. Achieving an organisation's mission requires a clear strategy and focus on the critical issues. The tasks and activities undertaken in support of this mission require funding either in the form of operating costs or capital expenditure and therefore require a financial strategy which will deliver the appropriate funding when required.
- Having established the business strategy a budget is required to evaluate the precise funding requirements across the business. Budget holders will be accountable for "managing" the funds in their area of operations, making changes to reflect the dynamics of the market and explaining any variance.
- Business requests for capital expenditure require a methodology for evaluation as funding is limited and managerial decisions have to be taken based on the "best case scenario". Investment in new plant and machinery, premises, motor vehicles and office equipment requires extensive use of funds and needs to be made with a medium to long-term confidence that their purchase will add value to the business. Therefore the business will need appropriate investment decision making tools and techniques in order to make the right decision.
- Financial resources can be significantly increased through the effective management of the cost of quality. Poor quality results in higher operating costs through wastage and rework together with the negative impact on sales which is attributable to customer dissatisfaction. Businesses which focus on reducing the cost of quality not only increase their financial resources but also improve their competitiveness.

Leadership and financial management
The determinant of success has traditionally been measured solely by reference to an organisation's financial results, but increasingly a more balanced approach is being adopted in line with the pioneering work undertaken by Kaplan and Norton (1992) on the balanced business scorecard. This balanced approach recognises financial results are the final outcomes from the actions taken and that by focusing on more upstream measures such as customer satisfaction, innovation, process efficiency and people satisfaction financial results will automatically improve. Higher customer satisfaction leads to increased sales turnover,

improved people satisfaction leads to more innovative improvement ideas together with improved profitability arising from lower turnover and absenteeism.

> Talented people adding value and delighting loyal customers in turn enable us to achieve excellent business results and provide sustained shareholder value (Texas Instruments).

Leadership has a vital role to play in balancing the needs of all stakeholders and providing a focus for the business. Texas Instruments demonstrates this through their "Golden Circle", shown in Figure 7.2.

Figure 7.2 "Golden Circle" at Texas Instruments

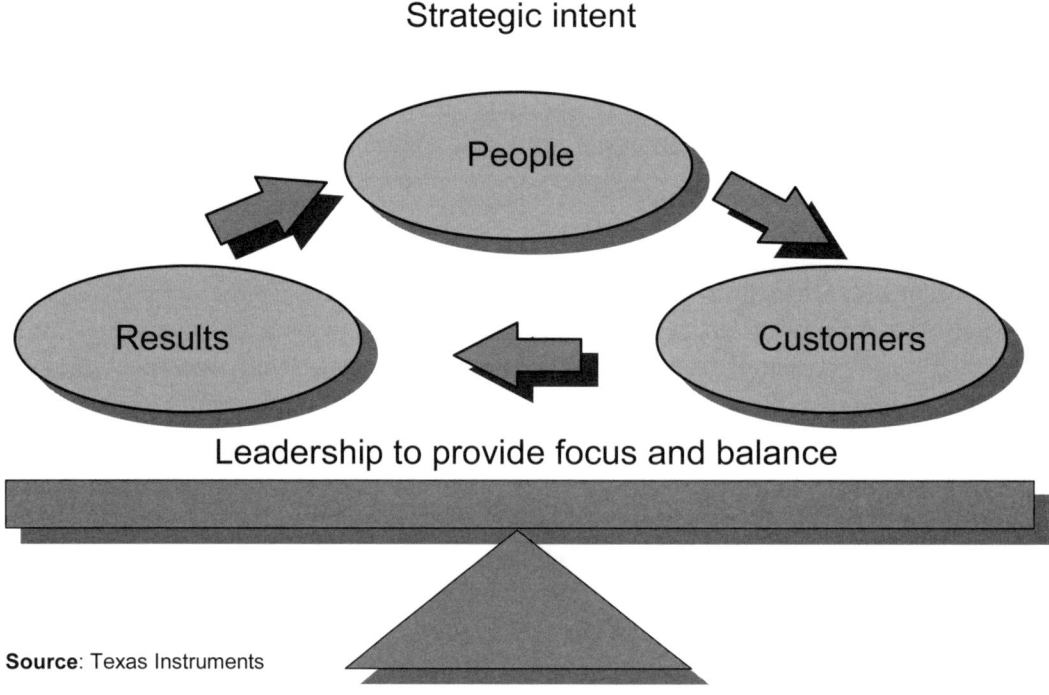

Source: Texas Instruments

The leadership role in providing the focus and balance of the customer, shareholder, people and management needs is determined by reference to the organisation's strategic intent. Focusing on the strategic intent of the business will ensure that an organisation's finite resources are effectively deployed on the "vital" requirements of the business.

Financial management process
The process for managing the financial resources requires the high level strategic goals to be broken down and aligned to the operational structure of the business. Collectively these goals will achieve the high level goals but breaking them down enables responsibility to be assigned, achieving local accountability.

At Texas Instruments, strategic goals are translated into profit from operations (PFO) goals and then broken down by business and region to ensure an equitable contribution is made to each of the corporation's goals.

The long range financial plans are compiled in the second quarter each year and cover a five year period with input from a variety of sources including:
- Customer satisfaction – surveys and complaint analysis.
- Performance requirements – internal standards and external benchmark data.
- Technology trends – external developments within the industry.

- Product roadmaps – system and process analysis.

A net revenue plan is constructed and structured by region and business entity to form a business wide plan. The process also includes a review of the previous year's assumptions and strategies as well as capital expenditure and space models. Customer satisfaction priorities are included at this early stage to ensure that they are fully understood.

Manufacturing capability is assessed by considering:
- technology requirements;
- packaging requirements;
- yields;
- product performance.

The outcome from this process is that the manufacturing capability and customer satisfaction outcome can be optimised and aligned to the computed net revenue plan. This is then used to construct a total financial plan in which several options are evaluated against market penetration and organisational goals.

Management teams are in place at each level to review and amend financial strategies so that they are aligned with the business and shareholder goals. These teams are also supported by a finance team which assists in the review and improvement of business systems, processes and organisations.

Review and improvement of financial strategies and practices
The reviewing of financial strategies and practices is a critical element in the practice of financial management due to the financial vulnerability of organisations and dynamics of the market place. At D2D the "cash" is monitored on a daily basis:
- Review payment terms – are the cash terms agreed with customers both competitive and effective to ensure the company's liquidity position is not adversely affected?
- Monitor debtor and creditor days – having agreed the payment terms, are debtors paying within the agreed time frame? Any imbalance between the time allowed for debtors to pay and the time allowed by creditors for payment can impact on the company's liquidity.
- Minimise inventory holdings – the holding of stock adversely impacts on the organisation's cash flow together with the factory space used for storage of the products. Also the products run the risk of becoming obsolete and scrapped if they are held for too long and so their management is critical to the profitability and cash flow of the business.

In addition to the daily cash review, a forecast review for each site is compiled covering the next six weeks. The review is conducted per site and consolidated at company level to assess the cash strength of the company as a whole. Current pricing of products and services is reviewed in line with competitors, together with progress towards reducing costs on a monthly basis.

Monthly reviews are conducted on specific cost reduction activities at company and local levels and include feedback from the organisation's customers and suppliers. The sales and marketing activities, together with the proposals, are also subject to a monthly review.

Quarterly reviews of product costs are conducted both at customer and company levels, along with current market price reviews, business evaluation process and quote reviews.

Cost of quality

Management is often unaware of the organisation's own cost of quality and consequently fails to manage the financial funds effectively. Research has shown that an amount equal to 25 per cent of sales turnover may currently be lost though poor quality, thereby reducing a company's competitiveness through reduced margins. The costs therefore represent a high level of expenditure to both the individual organisation and the economy at large.

There are a number of models which organisations can use to measure their cost of quality and focus their improvement activity:

- The simple cost of non-conformance is calculated by identifying the costs associated with the error, wastage, putting things right etc.
- The prevention, appraisal, failure (PAF) model attempts to "classify" costs according to their different nature:
    - Prevention costs – any action taken to investigate, prevent or reduce the risk of non-conformity or defects.
    - Appraisal costs – cost of evaluating the achievement of quality requirements.
    - Failure costs – cost of non-conformity, both internal (discovered before delivery to the customer) and external (discovered after delivery to the customer).
- Feigenbaum's model advocates that quality costs should be expressed as a ratio against sales turnover, production costs or the value of material used.
- Juran advocates a recognition of costs under three distinct classifications:
    - Tangible factory costs – scrap, rework, inspection.
    - Tangible sales costs – cost of handling customer complaints.
    - Intangible costs – costs that can only be estimated, such as customer goodwill, delays caused by stoppages, loss of staff morale.
- An advantage claimed for this model is that it allows for inclusion of internal benefits such as reduced stock and fewer lost opportunities.
- A process cost approach can be adopted by flowcharting the process, identifying the key process steps and the parameters that are monitored in the process. The cost of conformance for each stage can be measured or estimated and key areas for process improvement identified. High non-conformance cost at any particular step in the process may indicate a requirement for further expenditure on failure prevention activities.

The PAF model has received much criticism:
- Classification of costs under these headings will always be difficult. Design reviews may be considered a prevention, appraisal or failure cost.
- Almost everything in a company has something to do with quality.
- A range of manufacturing and production engineering functions, which are integral to ensuring product quality, are never included in any schedule of costs.
- Research in Japan shows that high productivity and quality are the result of thorough and professional production engineering aimed at simplicity and this is integral to the method of business management, not a separate quality activity.
- Timing of costs such as "warranty" are not recognised in the model, for example production may take place in Year 1 but warranty work takes place in Year 2. To be useful the data needs to be offset against the period in which production took place.
- Quality costs cut across the business rather than residing within functional areas and so require comprehensive accounting systems, which often do not exist, to "track" these costs adequately.

- PAF focuses on cost reduction and ignores the positive contribution to sales volume and price that improved quality can provide.
- The model implies an acceptable quality level as a result of trade off between prevention, appraisal and failure costs. This is incompatible with never ending improvement philosophy.
- Disagreement exists on how accurate the figures should be, from total accuracy to being determined by the use which will be made of them.
- Many firms which have achieved substantial reduction in quality costs have done so by increasing expenditure on prevention.
- No account is taken of management time taken in "fire fighting" (a major UK bank estimated 49 per cent of its employees' time is wasted in this way).

Reducing the cost of non-conformance requires a thorough process understanding and neither the PAF or process costing model (PCM) fully integrate both the quality costs and benefits of quality improvement.

Evaluation of investments
The size of funding required for capital investment dictates a professional approach to its appraisal before a commitment is made:

> The process of evaluating proposed investment in specific fixed assets and the benefits to be obtained from their acquisition: the technique used in the evaluation can be summarised as non-discounting methods (simple pay-back) return on capital employed and discounted cash flow methods (discounted pay back, yield net present value) (Chartered Institute of Management Accountants).

Capital investments have two key features:
1. substantial initial cost; and
2. medium to long-term income generation;

and therefore must be considered both in terms of current liquidity to fund the acquisition and the effect which the asset will have on future revenues (income less on-going maintenance). For example, new plant and machinery costing £25,000 will be funded either from current cash balances, loans, new capital issue or leasing arrangements. If the plant and machinery has a useful life of ten years, during which time additional revenues totalling £250,000 and maintenance costs of £25,000 are incurred, then there will be an apparent paper profit of £200,000 over the life of the asset.

However, consideration will need to be given to other factors such as:
- Inflation – the "time value of money" will result in future sales being "worth" less than the same amount would be worth today.
- Taxation – changes in capital allowances, corporation tax and other fiscal requirements will impact on future cash flows.
- Sensitivity analysis – impact of changes in sales volume, prices, variable and fixed costs. How far can these go before they become an element of risk for the project?
- Capital rationing – it is impossible to fund all requests, so how is capital rationed and alternative proposals considered?

Pay back
> The period, usually expressed in years, which it takes the cash inflows from a capital investment project to equal the cash outflows. The decision between two or more projects is usually based on the shortest pay back time. Pay back is commonly used as a first screening method and is a rough measure of liquidity and not of profitability (Chartered Institute of Management Accountants).

An example is given in Table 7.2.

Table 7.2 An example of pay back

Year	Cash flows	Cumulative inflows
0	(30,000)	
1	5,000	5,000
2	10,000	15,000
3	12,000	27,000
4	12,000	39,000
5	12,000	51,000
6	10,000	61,000
7	8,000	69,000

$$\text{Pay back} = \text{Year 3} + \frac{30{,}000 - 27{,}000}{12{,}000 \ (\text{Year 4 inflow})}$$
$$= 3.25 \text{ years}$$

Net present value
> The value obtained by discounting all cash flows and inflows attributable to a capital investment project by a chosen percentage, e.g. the equity's weighted average cost of capital (Chartered Institute of Management Accountants).

Net present value (NPV) is the price today of funds received at some time in the future, e.g. £1,000 received in three years time will be valued at a sum less than £1,000 for today's value. It is, in effect, reverse compound interest received on savings.

Four items of data are required:
1. What is the principal or present value?
2. What is the final amount received?
3. What is the annual interest rate?
4. How many years?

For example, £1,000 at an annual rate of 10 per cent in three years will be valued at £751 for today's price:

$$\text{Today's price} = \frac{£1{,}000}{[1 + 0.10 \ (10\% \text{ as a decimal})]^{3 \ (\text{no. of years})}}$$
$$= £751.31$$

The advantage of this approach compared to just taking gross amounts is that the impact on future cash flows can be more realistically established. Because NPV is concerned with cash flow and not profitability, depreciation is excluded from the investment calculation.

Internal rate of return
> A percentage discount rate used in capital investment appraisal which brings the cost of the project and its future cash inflows into equality (Chartered Institute of Management Accountants).

In simple terms, internal interest rate (IIR) is the interest rate which results in an NPV of nil. Where the IIR is higher than the cost of capital (cost of funding) then it will be worth further consideration. NPV is preferred to IIR as a method of investment appraisal because it is concerned with the absolute difference between the cost of an investment and the return from the investment, whereas IIR is concerned with the relative measure of the return. Consequently the impact on cash flow in terms of outlay and future revenue is not fully taken into account. Hence the potential from reinvestment arising from substantial cash inflow is acknowledged in NPV but not in IIR.

Accounting rate of return (ARR)
This is a ratio sometimes used in investment appraisal which is analogous to the return on capital employed ratio. Unlike net present value and internal rate of return the ratio is based on profits as opposed to cash flows. It is represented by the formula:

$$\text{ARR} = \frac{\text{Average annual profit from investment}}{\text{Average investment}} \times 100$$

This is a non-discounting method of appraisal which springs from the prime ratio of return on capital employed. It is particularly useful if the organisation is more concerned with profitability than liquidity. An example is given in Table 7.3.

Table 7.3 Non-discounting method of appraisal of projects X and Y

	Project X	Project Y
Investment (£)	10,000	10,000
Profit year 1 (£)	1,000	3,000
2 (£)	2,000	2,000
3 (£)	3,000	1,000
Total profits (£)	6,000	6,000
Average annual profit (£)	2,000	2,000
Accounting rate of return (%)	40	40

Clearly project Y is preferable due to the timing of the profits, although both show the same ARR.

The criteria used for investment decision making will largely be determined by the type of industry concerned, for example within manufacturing, criteria for consideration would include:
- customer requirements;
- competitive strengths;
- lifetime revenues;
- key milestones;
- detailed cost projections;
- market price assumptions;
- financial summary of cash flow.

Within the service sector the following criteria are used:

- Minimum return on investment of 17.5 per cent.
- Minimum of 140 per cent of costs recovered within 18 months.
- Product launches to specify:
    - forecast take up;
    - margin;
    - costs;
    - fees;
    - income;
    - bad debt risk.
- Product delivery to specify:
    - time;
    - cost;
    - specification.

Through effective management of an organisation's financial resources, more can be achieved from the same resources. However, effective financial management is much wider than bottom line results, it must consider the needs of all interested parties including customers who purchase the products and services, shareholders who invest in the company, management who take decisions about deployment of resources and employees who make the product or deliver the service. It is only by balancing the requirements of all those needs in line with the strategic direction of the company that effective financial management can be obtained.

The case studies of Rank Xerox, Custom Research Inc. and Kodak, presented in Chapter 14, discuss the management of financial resources, data and information and suppliers, respectively.

References

Daft, R.L. and Lengel, R.H. (1986), "Organisational information requirements, media richness and structural design", *Management Science* Vol., 12, pp. 554-69.

Deshpande, R. and Zaltman, G. (1982), "Factors affecting the use of marketing research information: a path analysis", *Journal of Marketing Research*, Vol. 19, February, pp. 14-31.

Deshpande, R. and Zaltman, G. (1984), "A comparison of factors affecting researcher and managers perceptions of market research use", *Journal of Marketing Research*, 21 February, pp. 32-8.

Dewey, J. (1910), How We Think, D.C. Health & Company, New York.

Hammer, M. and Champy, H. (1993), *Re-engineering the Corporation*, Harper Business, New York.

Kaplan, R.S. and Norton, D.P. (1992), "The balanced scorecard – measures that drive performance", *Harvard Business Review*, Vol. 70 No. 1, January-February, pp. 71-9.

Low, G.S. and Fullerton, R.A. (1994), "Brands, brand management, and the brand managers system: a critical-historical evaluation", *Journal of Marketing Research*, Vol. 26, pp. 173-90.

Marketing UK (1990), "Brandstand", 22 March, p. 27.

Newell, A. and Simon, H.A. (1972), *Human Problem Solving*, Prentice Hall, Engelwood Cliffs, NJ.

Nonaka, I. (1991), "The knowledge creating company", *Harvard Business Review,* November-December.

Noor, N.M. (1996), "Information processing in fast moving consumer goods companies: an empirical study of best practice", dissertation, School of Management, University of Bradford.

Patterson, M. (1993), in Zairi, M., "Best practice in brand management development", internal report, Bradford University.

Shocker, A.D., Srivastava, R.K. and Ruekert, R.W. (1994), "Challenges and opportunities facing brand management: an introduction to the special issues", *Journal of Marketing Research*, Vol. 41, May, pp. 149-58.

Sinkula, J.M. (1994), "Market information processing and organisational learning", *Journal of Marketing*, Vol. 58, pp. 35-45.

Skenazy, L. (1987), "Brand managers shelved? Professors offer alternative for changing market", *Advertising Age*, Vol. 58, No. 29, p. 81.

Appendix 7.1 Management of resources exercise

You are employed as a management consultant with a specialist expertise in benchmarking. A number of your clients have undertaken internal, competitive and functional benchmarking for sometime but are now wanting to proceed to generic benchmarking as they have been advised that it is from this type of benchmarking that best in class improvements can be identified.

You are required to advise the following clients on who may be suitable partners for their benchmarking activities:

- Client 1: an airline wishing to optimise its fleet of airplanes by reducing the amount of time they are grounded due to the cleaning process between flights. Who would be a suitable benchmarking partner?
- Client 2: a car producer wishing to increase efficiency in the distribution of cars from its factory to various dealers throughout the country. Who would be a suitable benchmarking partner?
- Client 3: a high street bank is experiencing problems with dissatisfied customers having to wait in queues for service. Who would be a suitable benchmarking partner?
- Client 4: a cosmetics company has received complaints from customers concerning its lipstick holders which do not open and close properly causing inconvenience. Who should it benchmark with to reduce production variability?

Exercise: identify a suitable benchmarking partner from a different industry sector for each of your four clients and indicate the process similarities which may exist between them.

Management of resources exercise - suggested solution

Table 7.4 Suggested solution

Client	Benchmarking partner	Process similarities
1. Airline company	Formula 1 pit crew team	Fast turnaround time Teamwork Leadership Training
2. Car producer	Supermarket chain	Central point to multi point locations Logistics Loading Transport
3. High street bank	Fast food supplier	Fast moving queue Training Offering fixed products from a menu Problems are taken away from the main line
4. Cosmetics company	Weapons manufacturer	Gun barrel precision Manufacturing equipment set up Training in process control

Chapter 8
Business process management: the key driver for continuous improvement

Introduction
The literature on business process re-engineering, benchmarking, continuous improvement and many other approaches of modern management is very abundant. One thing which is noticeable, however, is the growing usage of the word "process" in everyday business language. This suggests that most organisations adopt a process-based approach to managing their operations and that business process management (BPM) is a well-established concept. Is this really what takes place? On examination of the literature which refers to BPM, it soon emerges that the use of this concept is not really pervasive and what in fact has been acknowledged hitherto as prevalent business practice is no more than structural changes, the use of systems such as EN ISO 9000 and the management of individual projects.

What is a process?
A process is an approach for converting inputs into outputs. It is the way in which all the resources of an organisation are used in a reliable, repeatable and consistent way to achieve its goals.
  Post Office Counters Ltd for instance define a process as:
  A related series of actions, directed to the achievement of a goal, that transforms a set of inputs into desired outputs, by adding value.

Essentially there are four key features to any process (*Bulletpoint*, 1996):
1. a process has to have predictable and definable inputs;
2. it has to have a linear, logical sequence or flow;
3. a set of clearly definable tasks or activities; and
4. a predictable and desired outcome or result.

What is business process management?
BPM is a structured approach to analyse and continually improve fundamental activities such as manufacturing, marketing, communications and other major elements of a company's operation.
  Essentially, BPM is concerned with the main aspects of business operations where there is high leverage and a big proportion of added value. Business process management has to be governed by the following rules, so that major activities are properly mapped and documented:
- BPM creates a focus on customers through horizontal linkages between key activities.
- BPM relies on systems and documented procedures to ensure discipline, consistency and repeatability of quality performance.
- BPM relies on measurement activity to assess the performance of each individual process, set targets and deliver output levels which can meet corporate objectives.

- BPM has to be based on a continuous approach of optimisation through problem solving and reaping out extra benefits.
- BPM has to be inspired by best practice to ensure that superior competitiveness is achieved.
- BPM is an approach for culture change and does not result simply through having good systems and the right structure in place.

The importance of accredited quality systems

Accredited quality assurance systems such as EN ISO 9000 are essential, but perhaps not enough by themselves, in providing a culture based on process management. Quality systems are widely acknowledged as a staring point and a key element for the implementation of total quality management (Oakland and Porter, 1994; Porter and Parker, 1993; Price and Chen, 1993). Various companies have reported the real value of quality assurance systems such as EN ISO 9000:

- Carnaud Metalbox plc found that the ISO 9000 registration process provided the foundation on which a quality culture was built and helped the company move on in developing the total quality process (Oakland and Porter, 1994).
- Tioxide Group Ltd found that the registration programme pushed quality to a much higher profile in the company as everyone was actively involved in the process. In addition, Tioxide saw itself in a better position to meet the specific requirements of customers (Oakland and Porter, 1994).
- Esso Research Centre (UK) found that the use of the discipline of a recognised industry accreditation, such as ISO 9000, helped to install the quality process into the site culture.
    The systematic approach as stipulated under the various elements such as calibration and maintenance of laboratory equipment, staff training, and sample management assist in minimising errors and increase the incidents of "right first time" (Price, 1990; Thiagarajan, 1996).
- Nissan Motors UK, Federal Express and Club Med view operating standards as an important requirement in the quality stakes. They do not, however, see the need to have a recognised industry accreditation.

In many cases, however, registration to internationally recognised quality assurance systems, such as ISO 9000, is not done by choice, but can be a necessary requirement imposed by customers' minimal requirements. The common message which seems to be coming out from discussions is that quality assurance systems can assist in the development of a process-based approach to competitiveness since former principles place emphasis on doing the "right things" "right first time" and to continue doing the same in a consistent, repeatable and predictable manner.

The importance of quality structure

Structure is often described as one of the "hard" elements of modern management. Although extremely important in the setting up of a BPM based culture, structure on its own is incapable of changing the culture of the organisation in order to do what the "blue prints" may be recommending. This is an area of great controversy, the proponents of business process re-engineering (BPR) through information technology means have suggested that this is the quickest and most effective way of bringing about change. Referring to their model of integrated management based on the 7Ss, Peters and Waterman (1982) have presented the following analysis:

> In retrospect, what our framework has really done is to remind the world of professional managers that "soft" is hard. It has enabled us to say, in effect, all that you have been dismissing for so long as intractable, irrational, intuitive, informal, organisation can be managed. Clearly, it has as much or more to do with the way things work (or don't) around your companies as the formal structures and strategies do.

Further, to make it explicitly clear that focusing on structural changes alone is not enough for inducing an effective process-based culture, Waterman *et al.* (1980) have presented the following justification:

> Our assertion is that productive organisation change is not simply a matter of structure, although structure is important. It is not so simple as the interaction between strategy and structure, although strategy is critical too. Our claim is that effective organisational change is really the relationship between structure, strategy, systems, style, skills, staff, and something we call superordinate goals.

The 7Ss model is sometimes referred to as the "happy atom". It reflects the following characteristics:

- Multiplicity of factors – all influence how organisations behave.
- Interconnectedness of variables – progress can be achieved by giving attention to all areas.
- All seven variables act as a driving force – at particular points in time, one or more of the seven "Ss" will emerge as the most critical variable(s).

In the process of implementing total quality management, the type, role and usefulness of structure was found to vary from organisation to organisation (Black, 1993). It has also been suggested that differences in structural approaches may reflect cultural differences (Smith, 1994). Structure is a sub-servant of strategy and has to be assessed and reviewed in line with corporate objectives:

- In BP Chemicals the structure which served the purpose of introducing TQM has been dismantled and changed as the programme moved from the planning to educational, to the implementation phase (Stark, 1990).
- In Thomas Cork SML the high-powered quality council set up at the outset to oversee the introduction of total quality was disbanded and its function taken over by the management committee once the quality initiatives got off the ground (Oakland and Porter, 1994).

The importance of strategy
The achievement of a BPM culture depends very much on the establishment of total alignment to corporate goals and having every employee's efforts focused on adding value to the end customer. This is acknowledged by many authors (Olian and Rynes, 1991) and all quality gurus. Deming (1986), for instance, through the first of his 14 points, "strive for consistency of purpose", stresses the need to link quality efforts within an organisation to a larger sense of corporate purpose. The objectives of an organisation are best communicated to all employees through a formal process of policy and strategy development and deployment. In fact many strategies fail to deliver because what is planned and what is implemented are not the same (Zairi, 1995; Easton, 1993). It is acknowledged very widely that policy deployment and implementation processes are difficult to implement (Groocock, 1986).

Examples of effective management of strategic processes have a lot in common:

- Rank Xerox Corp when making the commitment to adopt TQM in 1984, articulated a simple and direct quality policy and communicated it to all employees (Coleman, 1991).
- Grundos has ensured that a quality policy is central to its efforts to win a sustainable competitive edge. Typically, it is found that the quality policy, strategy, goals, vision/mission and values are contained within the larger quality policy.
- Procter and Gamble, through its CEO, has made strategic planning a management leadership role (Bemowski, 1992; Davidson, 1995).
- Mitel Telecom Ltd UK views the publishing of its quality policy as the first evidence of its commitment to quality improvement.
- Southern Pacific Airlines, in implementing continuous quality improvement, has emphasised that a strong and clear leadership statement of mission and strategy is essential. This statement must make clear that quality is the strategy.

World class organisations, such as Procter and Gamble, NEC Japan, Komatsu, Unilever, Hewlett Packard, Rank Xerox, Florida Power & Light, in the process of ensuring success in developing, communicating and reviewing strategic plans at all levels, have heavily depended on a structured planning process termed: quality policy development (Zairi, 1994). The latter is defined at Rank Xerox as:

> A key process with which Rank Xerox can articulate and communicate the vision, mission, goals and vital few programmes to all employees. It provides answers to the two questions: What do we need to do? And how are we going to do it? (Zairi, 1994).

At NEC Japan the quality policy deployment process (called *Hosin Kanri*) starts with the CEO setting the long-term policy in line with the aims and philosophy of the corporation (Smith, 1994).

The importance of process management
Kanji (Edson and Shannahan, 1991) argues that almost, if not all, organisational activities are considered as processes which cut across traditional functional boundaries. The functional approach creates barriers to achieving customer satisfaction. It allows control points between departments to be vulnerable to organisational "noise" (Edson and Shannahan, 1991) such as "turf protection" and poor communication. In contrast, however, the process-based approach improves customer focus and avoids the limitations by managing by vertical functions (McAdam, 1996).

Best-in-class organisations have recognised the need to move away from the traditional functionally-based approach, to managing through a set of clearly-defined customer driven processes. This is certainly the case of Rank Xerox (Coleman, 1991), BIM (Snowden, 1991), ICL and Shell Chemicals UK (Sinclair, 1994).

The following are examples of world class organisations where a radical change from a functionally-driven to a process-based approach took place.

Elida Faberge Ltd
Elida Faberge is a leader in personal products, part of Unilever plc, with famous brands such as Sure, Lynx, Brut, Impulse, Organics, Timotel, Ponds, Vaseline, Mentadent, Signal. Elida Faberge Ltd relies very much on TQM principals in the running of its operations. Numerous benefits were achieved from the use of TQM, such as:
- reduction in changeover time;
- improved teamwork; and
- reduction in NPD cycle time.

The driving themes of total quality are:
- continuous improvement;
- the importance of the customer;
- empowerment of employees; and
- business activities as processes.

Elida Faberge decided to undergo a radical change for the creation of a business process management culture, driven by the following factors:
- During the 1990s, a number of key challenges started to face the company, which resulted in the need to improve its service to retain customers.
- The need to move to a European manufacturing centre.
- The need to move to a European then global innovation centre for deodorant/fragrance products.
- The need to "right size" the company, to improve productivity and competitiveness.

Three cross-functional teams were created, each led by a director and facilitation was provided by a consultant. The results led to the creation of:
- New organisation based on five core processes, including business planning/strategy as one of the core processes (Figure 8.1).
- Re-alignment of senior management responsibility.
- Responsibilities are based on natural boundaries between processes (not functional boundaries which cut across processes).

Rank Xerox Corp. (Bulletpoint, *1996)*
- Moved from being a manufacturer of copier, printer and fax products to a provider of document tools and services.
- Appreciated that processes are liberating and empowering rather than constraining.
- Focused on core processes to become customer focused and more efficient and effective.

Figure 8.1 Business process management at Elida Faberge

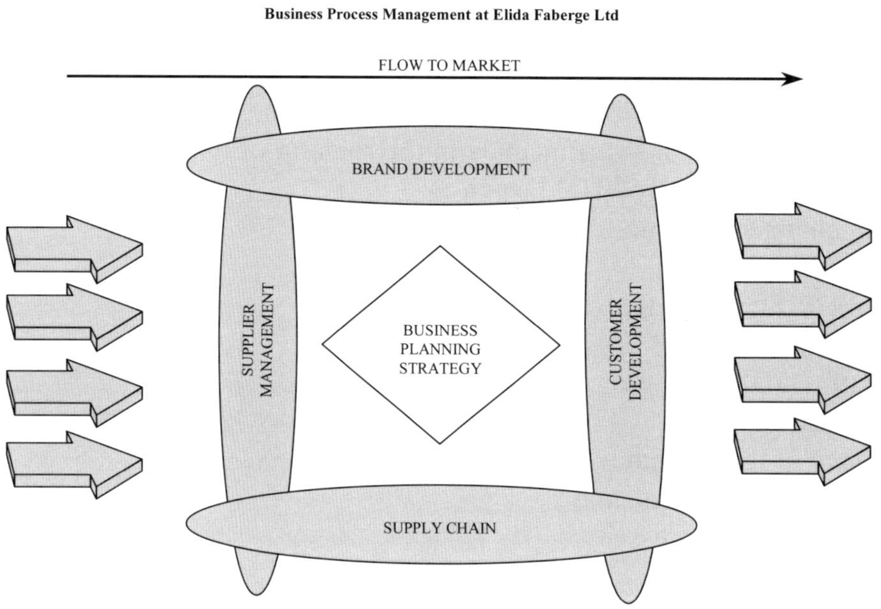

*British Telecom (*Bulletpoint, *1996)*
- Changed from technology-based divisions to customer sector and international market-based divisions.
- Moved from managing through a project-based approach by focusing on the management of risk to effective planning, continuously improving routine processes, eliminating waste and duplication and learning from previous experience and injecting innovation and best practice.

*SmithKline Beecham (*Bulletpoint, *1996)*
- Realised that the customer has changed, and therefore decided to move away from the doctor-driven approach.
- The four traditional divisions: pharmaceuticals, consumer health care, animal health, and clinical laboratories were reorganised into three key areas: care delivery, care management, and care coverage. Each has many layers of sub-processes.
- The big task now is to ensure that each process is mapped, documented, with performance measures and attains a consistent, repeatable and predictable performance.
- SmithKline Beecham has recognised that it will take many years (at least five) to become a full process-oriented organisation.

Building a culture based on process management: examples of best practice
The previous discussion has shown that an effective approach to change management has to rely on a combination of soft and hard aspects of organisational systems. In particular, if a business process management culture is to ensue, there has to be a systematic approach to designing, prioritising, managing, controlling and monitoring business processes that can lead

to superior competitive standards. Performance, therefore, is very much dependent on the dynamism generated and the degree with which organisations can develop their capabilities to compete in the market place.

There are numerous examples of methodological approaches covered in the literature. One of the most comprehensive frameworks is perhaps the one recommended by Harrington (1995) "The process breakthrough methodology".

The process breakthrough methodology
Essentially this approach consists of five major phases which are subdivided into 27 key activities. Table 8.1 illustrates the breakdown of the various key activities.

Table 8.1 The process breakthrough methodology

Phase	Key activities
Organising for quality	Defining critical business processes
	Selecting process owners
	Defining preliminary boundaries
	Forming and training process improvement teams
Understanding the process	Flowcharting the process
	Preparing the simulation model
	Conduct a walk-through
	Performing process cost and cycle time analysis
	Implementing quick fixes
	Aligning the process and the procedures
Streamlining the process	Process redesign (focused improvement)
	New process design (process re-engineering, process innovation, big picture analysis)
	Benchmarking the process
	Improvement, cost and risk analysis
	Preferred process selection
	Preliminary implementation plan
Implementation, measurement and controls	Finalised implementation plan
	New process implementation
	In-process measurements
	Feed-back systems
	Poor quality cost
Continuous improvement	Major breakthrough in performance
	Process improvement must continue
	Natural work teams or department improvement teams take over

Harrington (1995) reports that by subscribing to sound systematic methodological approaches, such as the one he initiated and illustrated in Table 8.1, business process improvement can be made to work effectively and lead to positive results. He reported the following examples:
- McDonnell Douglas:
    ○ 20-40 per cent reduction in overheads;
    ○ 30-70 per cent inventory reduction;
    ○ 5-25 per cent material cost reduction;

- 60-90 per cent quality improvement;
- 20-40 per cent administrative cost reduction.
- Federal Mogul: reduction in NPD cycle time from 20 weeks to 20 business days, leading to 75 per cent reduction in throughput time.

Harrington (1995) acknowledges that business process management is fundamentally a senior management responsibility. They have the task of determining the right vision for the organisation and the top strategic priorities, designing the right processes, breaking down walls and barriers to effective performance, and putting in place the key enabling factors for all employees to make optimum contributions.

Harrington (1995) argues that:

> The process, and the system which controls it, represents the real problem facing business today, not the people who work within the boundaries set for them by management. Employees must work within the process and management must work on the process. The improvement efforts and their supporting systems must be directed at the process and not the individual. This means that all functions must work together to optimise the efficiency, effectiveness and adaptability of the total process.

Rank Xerox approach to process improvement and management

Rank Xerox Ltd is known for its leadership in total quality management. Its achievements are reflected by its superior competitive position in the market place and the large number of prestigious awards and major accolades that the company has won over the years. What propels the quality improvement effort within Rank Xerox is an initiative called "Leadership Through Quality" which represents an integrated philosophy with the following key areas of focus:

- A goal for Rank Xerox to attain and maintain.
- A strategy to enable Xerox to achieve its competitive advantage.
- A way of working or process to use for managing operations of the business at all levels.

Leadership Through Quality is based on the use of key tools including:

- the problem solving process;
- the quality improvement process;
- the benchmarking process; and
- the self-assessment process (business excellence certification model).

The last two will not be discussed in the context of this chapter, however the problem solving process, which is illustrated in Figure 8.2, is used to enable people to close gaps in performance and to analyse problems, develop solutions and put action plans together (Zairi, 1996). Rank Xerox is discussed in more detail as a case study in Chapter 14.

Figure 8.2 The problem solving process

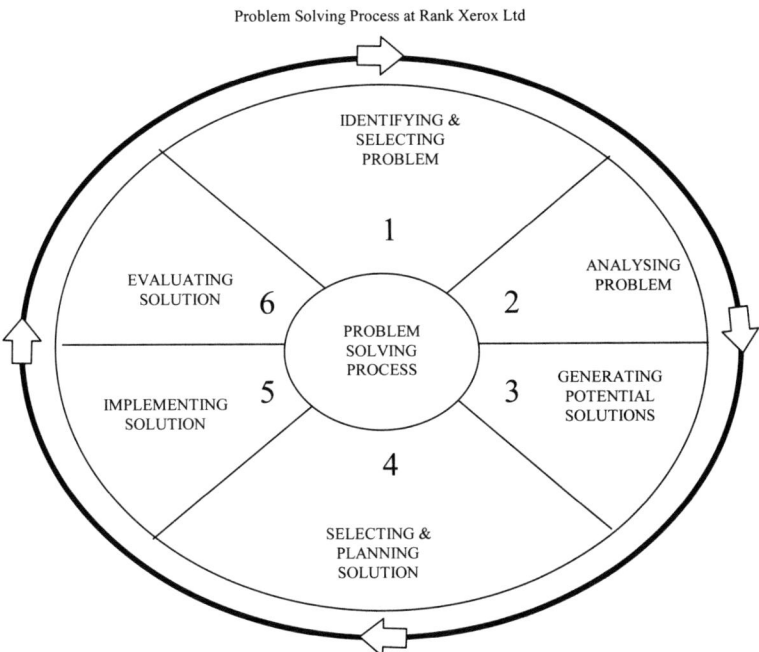

The quality improvement process. This is a more pervasive tool, it is not just related to internal problems. It focuses more on process routes for products and services, which are delivered to the end customer. It is therefore customer related. Table 8.2 illustrates the differences between the problem solving process (PSP) and the quality improvement process (QIP). Although the differences are very apparent, the two approaches are complementary and the use of one will trigger the utilisation of the other.

Table 8.2 The difference between the problem solving and quality improvement processes at Rank Xerox Ltd

When to use problem solving	When to use quality improvement
There is a gap between what is happening and what you want	You need to improve the quality of a particular, currently existing output
You want to move from a vague dissatisfaction to a solvable, clearly defined problem	You do not have agreed-upon customer requirements for an output
You are not sure how to approach an issue	You are about to produce a new output

The QIP process has nine steps which are grouped into planning, organising and monitoring stages (Figure 8.3):
1. Identify output – the team brainstorms and defines the desired output.
2. Identify customer – refers to customers of the desired output, outcome of using the QIP (often internal customers).
3. Identify customer requirements – stems from stage 2, and will prompt the project team (suppliers) to work closely with customers (beneficiaries of the output) to define what is required and therefore how it is going to be delivered.

Best Practice Organisational Excellence

Figure 8.3 Quality improvement process

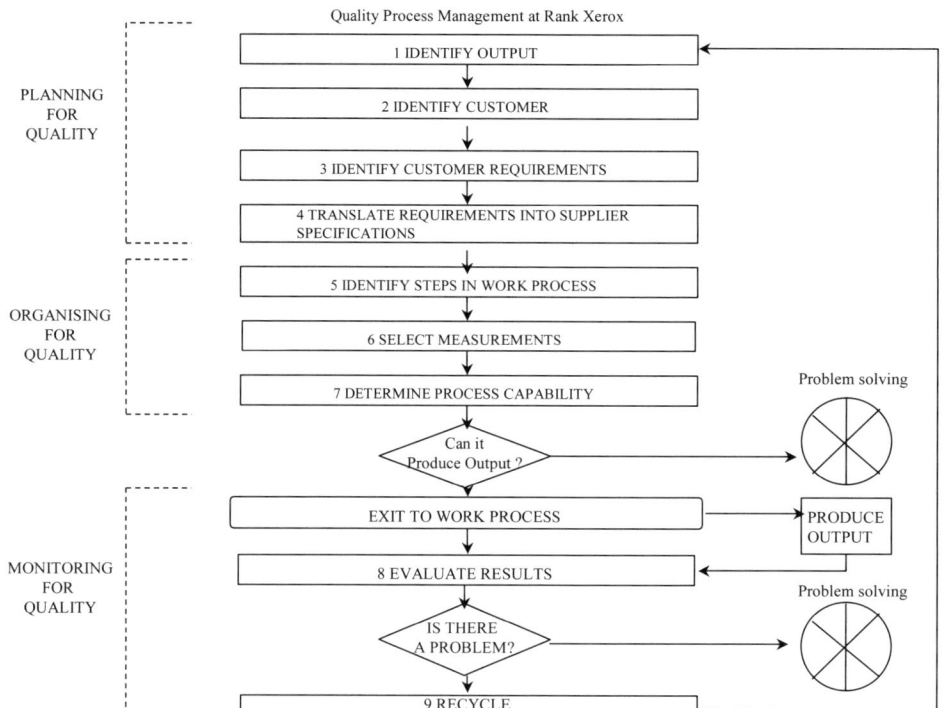

4. Translate requirements into supplier specification – all requirements are put into measurable and achievable deliverables.
5. Identify steps in the work process – a step-by-step approach to how the output is going to be produced needs to be developed, using perhaps existing work procedures and guidelines and producing a flow chart.
6. Select measurement – measures need to be selected to assess before, during and after scenarios, and also measures need to be designed for continuous monitoring and prevention purposes.
7. Determine process capability – this is to test the recommended process and to ensure that it can do the "right things" "right first time". Otherwise the team can use the PSP to fine-tune the process for full capability to deliver customer requirements.
8. Evaluate results – this is to answer the following two questions:
    - Did the process work?
    - Did the results of what we did meet customer requirements?
9. Recycle – this is for continuous monitoring following changes in customer requirements and for exploiting best practice and new learning opportunities.

Process management methodology at Ford Motors
Ford introduced a new process management approach in 1992, called quality operating systems (QOS). Ford felt there was a need for an operating system to guide improvement and optimisation efforts. The following arguments were put forward in an internal document:

> Ford trained thousands of our people in the quality engineering tools and we developed Q-1 facilities only to find we needed more. QOS was the management "glue" that improved our success with our customers.

QOS is defined as a systematic, disciplined approach that uses standardised tools and practices to manage business and achieve ever increasing levels of customer satisfaction. QOS relies on the following sets of policies for its effective implementation:
1. The assembly and analysis of existing data into a system of key process and result measurables which are correlated and can be quickly reviewed and acted upon.
2. A set of standardised management practices and system standards which maximise performance through a total systems approach.
3. A set of standardised tools and methodologies for implementing continuous and breakthrough improvements in both manufacturing and non-manufacturing applications.
4. The establishment of effective communication links between all people in the system through cross-organisational uniformity.

Figure 8.4 illustrates the QOS process at Ford. The quality operating system at Ford Motors is a generic process which can be applied in manufacturing and non-manufacturing operations. It is based on eight steps driven by continuous involvement of all employees and the principle of plan-do-check-act. The reported benefits of QOS include:
- providing senior management with a tool to determine the correlation between customer expectations and company results;
- enhancing empowerment; and
- combining the power of the team dynamics and management authority.

Process management at Post Office Counters Ltd
Post Office Counters Ltd (POCL) has over 25 million customers. In the late 1980s, it appreciated the need to introduce quality into its business operations. In 1989, the "Customer First" initiative was launched. Customer First was defined as:
> We manage the business in a way which continually focuses on the customer and harnesses everyone's commitment.

The business process improvement (BPI) methodology was introduced as a structured approach which will assist with the simplification and streamlining of business processes thus leading to the efficient and effective use of resources such as facilities, people, equipment, time and capital.

BPI has three major objectives:
1. Making processes more effective – producing the desired results.
2. Making processes more efficient – minimising resources use.
3. Making processes adaptable – being able to meet changing customer and business needs.

Similarly to Rank Xerox, POCL uses a quality improvement process (QIP) as a problem solving process, used within functions and across functions. Figure 8.5 illustrates the QIP at POCL. The business process improvement (BPI), however, starts and ends with customer needs identification and their fulfilment to customer satisfaction. BPI:

Figure 8.4 Quality operating system at Ford

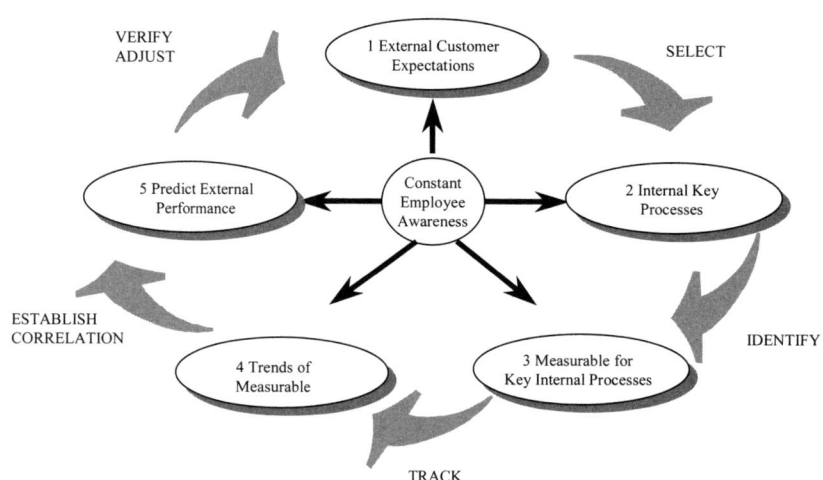

- provides a structured approach for focusing improvement activity on external customer satisfaction and business objectives;
- has a measurement framework which is clearly positioned; and
- emphasises the use of in-process measurement and display, especially promoting service level agreements.

Figure 8.6 illustrates the BPI at Post Office Counters Ltd, which consists of five phases each with a specific purpose described in Table 8.3.

Sustaining business process management – some guidelines

It is evidently clear that business process management is an approach which is all encompassing and is dependent on strategic elements, operational elements, use of modern tools and techniques, people involvement and, more importantly, on a horizontal focus which will best suit and deliver customer requirements in an optimum and satisfactory way.

The development of a culture based on business process management can be greatly assisted by using total quality principles, a systematic methodology, a problem solving or quality improvement process which can help with delivering local solutions within functions or across functions, the use of performance measures for monitoring inputs, outputs and the control of each process, and a culture of continuous improvement based on learning from within, and outside, the organisation.

Figure 8.5 Quality improvement process at POCL

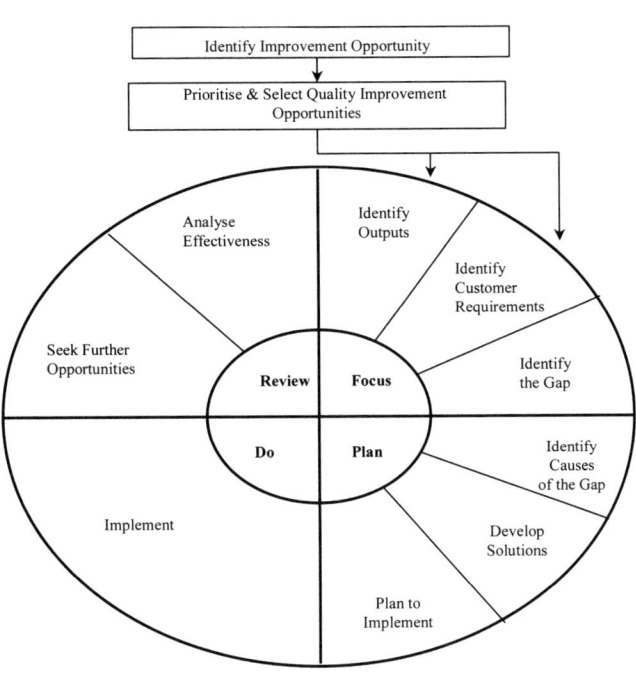

Figure 8.6 BPI at POCL

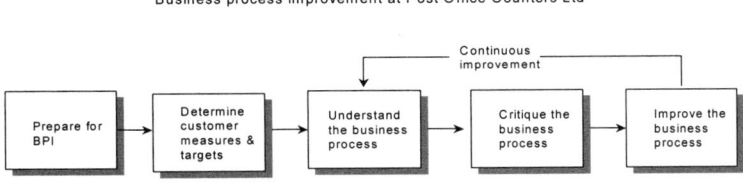

The following are proposed as a set of rules which can assist in the development of a business process management culture:
- Business process management is the way in which key activities are managed, and continuously improved, to ensure consistent ability to deliver high quality standards of products and services.
- Business processes are the critical and all encompassing activities of design, manufacture, marketing, innovation, sales and other activities, which deliver quality to the end customer.
- Process management also refers to the way companies constantly strive for excellence and how they stimulate innovation and creativity for process improvement and optimisation.

- Business process management also includes activities which refer to supplier quality management issues.
- The management of processes is conducted through performance measurement for setting targets for improvement and also for measuring product/service capability, process capability, supplier capability and efficiency/effectiveness aspects in terms of cycle time, quality standards, costs, etc.
- Business process management, through continuous measurement and improvement, will determine effectiveness of process design for streamlining and simplification. It ensures the introduction of best practice through benchmarking information and is based on valuable inputs from customers.
- Process management challenges practices (i.e. the dynamic aspects of each process and its behaviour) as much as the performance of each process (its output/metrics). Further, process management seeks to strengthen continuously all activities through the introduction of best practice, to ensure that internal standards of performance are competitively acceptable.
- Business process management relies on a systematic methodology supported by a problem solving methodology to strengthen newly designed processes, to reinforce the linkages between various functions and to ensure that optimum performance can be achieved.

Case studies, presented in Chapter 14, of Royal Mail, Ritz-Carlton and D2D discuss quality improvement, business process structure and business process management, respectively.

Table 8.3 Purpose of each phase of BPI at POCL

Phase	Purpose
Prepare for BPI	To ensure the success of BPI effort by building understanding and commitment
Determine customer measures and targets	Define success criteria for the BPI effort
Understand the business process	To understand all dimensions of the current business process
Critique the business process	To determine the best solution(s) to improve the quality and efficiency of the business process
Improve the business process	To implement changes that will improve the effectiveness and efficiency of the business process

References

Bemowski, K. (1992), "Carrying on the P&G tradition", *Quality Progress*, Vol. 25 No. 3, pp. 51-4.

Black, S.A. (1993), "Measuring the critical factors of total quality management", unpublished PhD Thesis, University of Bradford Management Centre, Bradford, UK.

Boyer, S.M. (1990), "TQM and new product development", in Oakland, J.S. (Ed.), *Proceedings of the 3rd International Conference on Total Quality Management*, IFS Publications Ltd, Bedford, UK.

Bulletpoint (1996), "Creating a change culture – not about structures, but winning hearts and minds", sample issue, pp. 12-13.

Carman, J.M. (1993), "Continuous quality improvement as a survival strategy: the Southern Pacific Experience", *California Management Review*, Vol. 35 No. 3, pp. 118-32.

Coleman, R. (1991), "People and training – the progressive evolution of a training strategy in support of the implementation of total quality management", in Oakland, J.S. (Ed.), *Proceedings of the 4th International Conference on Total Quality Management*, IFS Publications Ltd, Bedford, UK.

Davidson, A.R. (1995), "Quality management – do we believe in it 'totally'?", in Kanji, G.K. (Ed.), *Total Quality Management Proceedings of the 1st World Congress*, Chapman & Hall, London.

Deming, W.E. (1986), *Out of the Crisis*, University Press, Cambridge, MA.

Easton, G.S. (1993), "The 1993 state of US total quality management: a Baldrige examiner's perspective", *California Management Review*, Vol. 35 No. 3, pp. 32-54.

Edson, J. and Shannahan, R. (1991), "Managing quality across barriers", *Quality Progress*, February, pp. 45-7.

Groocock, J.M. (1986), *The Chain of Quality*, John Wiley, Chichester.

Harrington, J.J. (1995), *Total Improvement Management – The Next Generation in Performance Improvement*, McGraw Hill Inc., New York.

McAdam, R. (1996), "An integrated business improvement methodology to re-focus business improvement efforts", *Journal of Business Process Re-Engineering and Management*, Vol. 2 No. 1, pp. 63-71.

Oakland, J.S. and Porter, L.J. (1994), *Cases in Total Quality Management*, Butterworth-Heinemann, Oxford.

Olian, J.D. and Rynes, S.L. (1991), "Making total quality work: aligning organisational processes, performance measures and stakeholders", *Human Resources Management*, Vol. 30, pp. 303-33

Peters, T.J. and Waterman, R.H. (1982), *In Search of Excellence*, Harper and Row, New York.

Porter, L.J. and Parker, A.J. (1993), "Total quality management – the critical success factors", *Total Quality Management*, Vol. 4 No.1, pp. 13-22.

Price, F. (1990), *Right Every Time*, Gower Publishing Co. Ltd, Aldershot.

Price, M. and Chen, E.E. (1993), "Total quality management in a small, high-technology company", *California Management Review*, Vol. 35 No. 3, pp. 96-117.

Smith, S. (1994), *The Quality Revolution*, Management Books 2000 Ltd, Didcot, UK.

Stark, J.A.L. (1990), "Experience of TQM at BP Chemicals", in Oakland, J.S. (Ed.), *Proceedings of the 3rd International Conference on Total Quality Management*, IFS Publications Ltd, Bedford, UK.

Sinclair, D.A.C. (1994), "Total quality-based performance measurement: an empirical study of best practice", unpublished PhD Thesis, University of Bradford Management Centre, Bradford, UK.

Snowden, D. (1991), "Business process management and TQM", in Oakland, J.S. (Ed.), *Proceedings of the 4th International Conference on Total Quality Management*, IFS Publications Ltd, Bedford, UK.

Thiagarajan, T. (1996), "An empirical study of total quality management (TQM) in Malaysia: a proposed framework of generic application", PhD Thesis, Bradford University Management Centre, Bradford, UK.

Waterman, R.H., Peters, T.J. and Philips, J.R. (1980), "Structure is not organization", *Business Horizons*, June, pp. 14-16.

Zairi, M. (1994), *Measuring Performance for Business Results*, Chapman & Hall, London.

Zairi, M. (1995), "Strategic planning through quality policy deployment: a benchmarking approach", in Kanji, G.K. (Ed.), *Total Quality Management: Proceedings of the 1st World Congress*, Chapman & Hall, London.

Zairi, M. (1996), *Effective Benchmarking – Learning from the Best*, Chapman & Hall, London.

Appendix 8.1 Business processes exercise

Using the background and data for D2D in the case study in Chapter 14 you are to assume the role of managing director at D2D and one of your key tasks is to conduct a high level review of the core processes and their associated measures of success ahead of the management review meeting next week.

You are required to identify the key core processes which you would expect to see (maximum of 12) together with the appropriate measure of success for each of your processes. The background information above, together with your awareness of the industry, should provide you with the necessary insights into products, business size and culture necessary to undertake this task.

Business process suggested solution

Table 8.4 Critical processes and related success factors

Critical process	Related success factors
System, product and service delivery, including customer satisfaction and performance measurement, for each of their six business streams	Total solution capability Product quality Service quality Time to market Preferred partner
Prospective customer/strategic partner identification	Organisational capability
Competitive technology status and benchmark identification	Organisational capability Time to market Lowest cost of ownership
People satisfaction – Investing in People process	Organisational capability
Process improvement reviews	Process quality
Supplier partnership improvement	Procurement capability Lowest cost of ownership
Cost reduction	Lowest cost of ownership
Self-assessment	Technical capability
Recognition	Organisational capability Preferred partner
Deployment	All success factors

Chapter 9
Managing performance outcomes for business excellence

Introduction

The EFQM and MBNQA models both stress the importance of managing business results in an integrated fashion and using wider stakeholder analogy. The EFQM model, for instance, awards 500 points to the results section, which covers:
- Customer satisfaction: customers' perception of the organisation's products, services and customer relationships. Additional measurements relating to the satisfaction of the organisation's customers.
- People satisfaction: people's perceptions of the organisation. Additional measurements relating to people satisfaction.
- Impact on society : society's perception of the organisation. Additional measurements of the organisation's impact on society.
- Business results: financial measurements of the organisation's performance. Additional measurements of the organisation's performance.

The MBNQA model, on the other hand, allows for 450 points on the business results section, which covers:
- Customer satisfaction results (130 points).
- Financial and market results (130 points).
- Human resource results (35 points).
- Supplier and partner results (25 points).
- Company-specific results (130 points).

The wealth of any business organisation is therefore determined by the degree of sophistication and comprehensiveness of the performance measurement systems used. The following section describes two different approaches, which are balanced, well-integrated and give an internal/external perspective to the measurement effort.

The GAO performance measurement model

This model was developed by the General Accounts Office (Zairi, 1994) to study the impact of TQM on bottom line results (Figure 9.1). This model has all the key elements for business excellence:
- leadership;
- quality systems;
- internal quality measurement;
- external quality measurement;
- customer satisfaction and retention measurement; and
- business results measurement.

Further, the GAO model allows for feedback and continuous improvement to keep performance enhancements and competitive standards improving.

The balanced scorecard model
This useful model of performance measurement (Kaplan and Norton, 1992) is based on a 12 month research project on 12 leading companies. The model is referred to as the "balanced scoreboard", and covers all areas critical to business competitiveness. It addresses four sets of issues:
1. Customer perspective: the premise is that all businesses exist to satisfy customer requirements. To succeed, they have to start with customer needs and not with the needs of the organisation itself. Measurement has to be externally focused, with external data including service, quality, responsiveness and cost.
2. Process capability: building capability internally is essential to becoming competitive. Optimisation of process performance in terms of quality, speed, delivery, cost and synergy through cross-functional activity and teamwork is essential.
3. Focus on innovation: modern competitiveness is based on fulfilling customer requirements through creativity and innovation. Building a learning organisation where people productivity is the main focus and there is the belief in learning through improvement is essential. The consideration of people as the main asset is crucial as is the measurement of employee satisfaction and employee attitude.
4. The financial perspective focusing on the shareholder: shareholders are another set of customers, and value added to shareholders must be tracked continuously. Delivering performance which would satisfy shareholders has to be looked at in an overall context of corporate business objectives. Sound strategies tend to blend short-term and long-term impact with the view of optimising delivery to customers, shareholders and the organisation itself.

Figures 9.2 and 9.3 illustrate the balanced scorecard model and an example of its application, respectively. The usefulness of this model lies in its ability to put strategy and vision first, rather than control. It supports:
- teamwork;
- empowerment;
- continuous improvement;
- the implementation of quality principles;
- the use of tools and techniques for improvement; and
- innovation through continuous improvement and a focus on the end customer.

For a more detailed discussion see Zairi (1994).

An integrated model of total quality-based performance measurement
The model presents measurement within the overall management process. The model consists of five levels: strategy development and goal deployment, process management and measurement, performance appraisal and management, break-point performance assessment, and reward and recognition systems.

Best Practice Organisational Excellence

Figure 9.1 The GAO performance measurement model

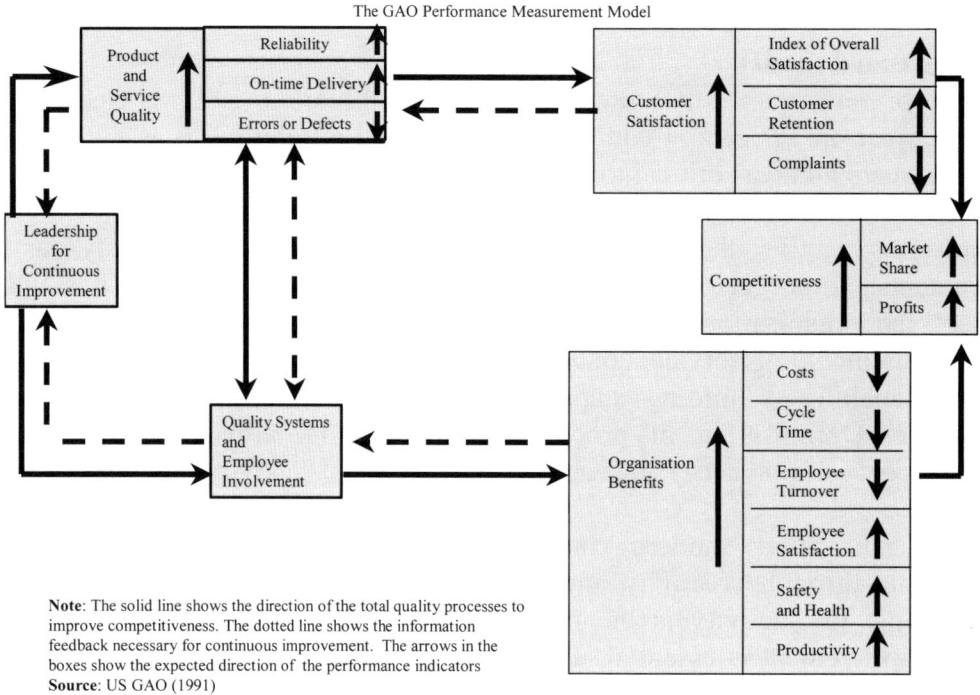

Figure 9.2 The balanced business scorecard model

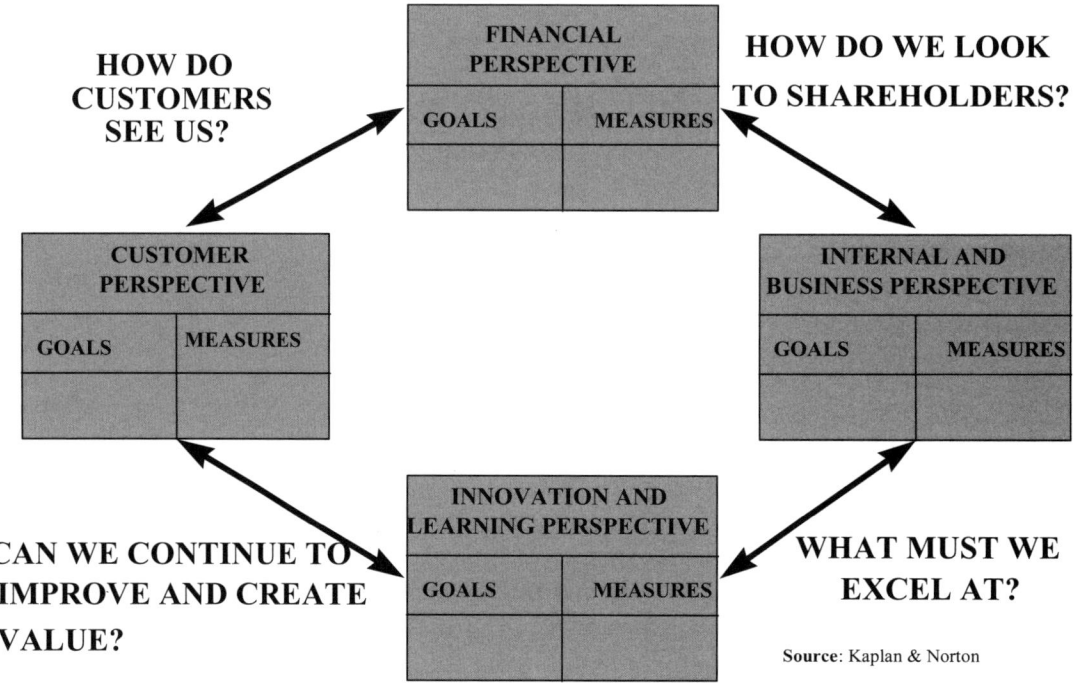

Figure 9.3 Balanced business scorecard example

An Applied Example of the Balanced Scoreboard Model in Electronics

FINANCIAL PERSPECTIVE	
Goals	Measures
Survive	Cash flow
Succeed	Quarterly sales growth and operating income by division
Prosper	Increase market share and ROE

CUSTOMER PERSPECTIVE	
Goals	Measures
New products	Percent of sales from new products
	Percent of sales from proprietary products
Responsive supply	On time delivery (defined by customer)
Preferred supplier	Share of key accounts purchases
Customer partnerships	No. of co-operative engineering efforts

INTERNAL AND BUSINESS PERSPECTIVE	
Goals	Measures
Technology capability	Manufacturing geometry vs competition
Manufacturing excellence	Cycle time
	Unit costs
	Yield
New product introduction	Actual introduction schedule vs plan

INNOVATION AND LEARNING PERSPECTIVE	
Goals	Measures
Technology leadership	Time to develop next generation
Manufacturing learning	Process time to maturity
Product focus	% products that equal 80% sales
Time to market	New product introductions competition

Definition of terms

Before examining the model in detail, it is useful to formally define the terms used in the model. The following terms are generally applicable to the model:

- Performance measurement is "the process of determining how successful organisations or individuals have been in attaining their objectives" (Evangelidis, 1992). Total quality based performance can be defined as the measurement of non-financial performance at all levels within the organisation (including individuals, teams, processes, departments and the organisation as a whole), with a view to the continuous improvement of performance against organisational objectives.
- Performance measurement systems are "the numerical or quantitative indicators that show how well each objective is being met" (Pritchard *et al.*, 1991).
- A performance measurement system is "a systematic way of evaluating the inputs, outputs, transformation and productivity in a manufacturing or non-manufacturing operation" (Oakland, 1993). A total quality-based performance measurement system can be defined as a system that integrates the measurement of non-financial performance at all levels within the organisation with a view to the continuous improvement of performance against organisational objectives (Sinclair, 1994).
- A target can be defined as the pre-determined desired level of performance against each measure.

The following terms are specific to each level of the model:
1. Strategy development and goal deployment:
    - Critical success factors (CSFs) are "The limited number of areas in which results, if they are satisfactory, will ensure successful competitive performance for the organisation" (Rockart, 1979).

- Key performance indicators (KPIs) are the actual measures used to assess quantitatively performance against the critical success factors. There should be at least one CPI for each critical success factor.
2. Process management and measurement. It is suggested that process performance measures should include measures of inputs, process and outputs. Outputs from a supplier form the inputs to the next customer. It is therefore only necessary to define process and output measures:
    - Process measures "monitor the activities of a process and motivate people within a process" (Hronec, 1993).
    - Output measures "report the results of a process, often to management, and are used to control resources" (Hronec, 1993).
3. Performance appraisal and management. Performance appraisal and management includes the two linked elements of performance management and performance appraisal:
    - Performance management is "a systematic, data-oriented approach to managing people at work that relies on positive reinforcement as the major way to maximise performance" (Daniels and Rosen, 1988). Performance management refers to the management of individuals and teams on a frequent and ongoing basis.
    - Performance appraisal is "the process by which organisations establish measures and evaluate individual employee's behaviour and accomplishments for a finite period of time" (De Vries, 1986).
4. Break-point performance assessment can be defined as the measurement of any performance criteria that is intended to identify significant gaps in current performance, and thereby motivate activities to improve performance so as to reduce or eliminate the gap (Sinclair, 1994). Break-point assessment includes both internal (within the organisation) and external (involving sources outside the organisation) measurement techniques.
5. Reward and recognition are the financial and non-financial consequences given as a result of superior performance (Sinclair, 1994).
    - Rewards are the financial consequences given as the result of measurably superior performance.
    - Recognition includes all non-financial consequences given as the result of measurably superior performance.

Strategy development and goal deployment
The first "level" of the performance measurement system model is the development of organisational strategy, and the consequent deployment of goals throughout the organisation. Steps in the strategy development and goal deployment process are (Sinclair, 1994):
1. Develop a public mission statement based on recognising the needs of all organisational stakeholders (customers, employees, shareholders and society). This includes mission statement, vision statement, quality policy, and corporate values.
2. Based on the mission statement, identify those factors critical to the success of the organisation achieving its stated mission (i.e. identify critical success factors of CSFs). CSFs should represent all stakeholder groups (customers, employees, shareholders and society).
3. Define performance measures of each CSF, i.e. key performance indicators (KPIs). There may be one or several KPIs for each CSF. In some cases, organisations may

define CSFs and KPIs separately, such that CSFs are themselves set to be constant (see, for example, Kodak's key result area approach as discussed in the Kodak case study in Chapter 14), or they may be identical to CPIs, and therefore be expected to change over time. Definition of KPIs should include:
- Title of KPI.
- Data used in calculation of KPI.
- Method of calculation of KPI.
- Sources of data used in calculation.
- Proposed measurement frequency.
- Responsibility for the measurement process.

4. Set targets for each KPI. If KPIs are new, targets should be based on customer requirements, competitor performance or known organisational criteria. If no such data exists, a target should be set based on best guess criteria. If the latter is used, update the target as soon as enough data is collected to be able to do so.
5. Assign responsibility at the organisational level for achievement of desired performance against KPI targets. Responsibility should rest with directors and very senior managers.
6. Develop plans to achieve the target performance. This includes both action plans for one year, and longer-term strategic plans.
7. Deploy mission, CSFs, KPIs, targets, responsibility, and plans to macro processes (core business processes). This includes the communication of goals, objectives, plans, and the assignment of responsibility with appropriate individuals.
8. Manage organisational processes (see level 2 of the model).
9. Measure performance against organisational KPIs, and compare to target performance.
10. Based on this comparison, identify areas with high leverage for improvement, and update action plans.
11. Communicate performance and proposed actions throughout the organisation.
12. At the end of one year compare organisational capability to target against all KPIs, and begin again at step 2 above.
13. Reward and recognise superior organisational performance.

Strategy development and goal deployment are the responsibility of senior management within the organisation, although there should be as much input to the process as possible by experts in the areas and employees generally, in order to achieve "buy-in" to the process. Strategy development and goal deployment (level 1 of the performance measurement system model) is shown diagrammatically in Figure 9.4.

It should be noted that financial performance is seen as a result of performance against non-financial KPIs, as suggested by Walsh (1989) and Kaplan and Norton (1992). The only aspect of financial performance that is cascaded throughout the organisation is the budgetary process, which acts as a constraint rather than a performance improvement measure, as suggested by Euske *et al.* (1993).

The difference between the KPIs at the process and organisational level is due to the deployment of organisational KPIs. Not only measures but also CSFs, plans and responsibility are cascaded to the process level. As such the process is nearer to the quality policy deployment (QPD) approach, suggested by Zairi (1994) and Oakland (1993).

Figure 9.4 Performance measurement system model level 1

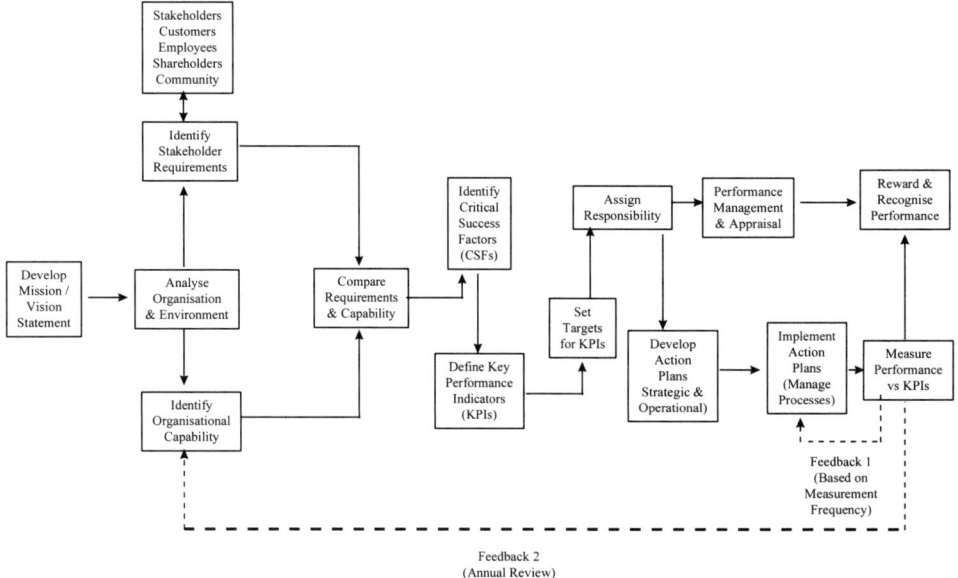

Process management and measurement

The second level of the performance measurement system model is process management and measurement. Steps in process management and measurement are (Sinclair, 1994):

1. If not already completed, identify and map processes. This information should include identification of:
   - process customers and suppliers (internal and external);
   - customer requirements (internal and external);
   - core and non-core activities; and
   - measurement points and feedback loops.

2. Translate organisational goals and action plans and customer requirements into process performance measures (input, in-process and output). This includes definition of measures, data collection procedures, and measurement frequency.
3. Define appropriate performance targets (based on known process capability, competitor performance and customer requirements).
4. Assign responsibility for achieving performance targets.
5. Develop plans towards achievement of process performance targets.
6. Deploy measures, targets, plans and responsibility to all sub-processes.
7. Operate processes.
8. Measure performance against process KPIs, and compare to target performance.
9. Use performance information to:
   - implement continuous improvement activities;
   - identify areas for improvement;
   - update action plans;
   - update performance targets;

- redesign processes (where appropriate);
- manage the performance of teams and individuals (performance management and appraisal) and suppliers;
- provide leading indicators and explain performance against organisational KPIs.

10. At the end of each year, compare process capability of customer requirements against all measures, and begin again at step 2.
11. Reward and recognise superior process (including sub-processes, and teams) performance.

The above process should be managed by the process owner, with inputs wherever possible, from the owners of sub-processes. Process management and measurement (level 2 of the performance measurement system model) is shown diagrammatically in Figure 9.5.

The process outlined should be used whether an organisation is organised and managed on a process or functional (departmental) basis. If the organisation is functionally organised, the key task is to identify the customer-supplier relationships between functions, and for functions to see themselves as part of a customer-supplier chain (Oakland, 1993).

Performance measures. Whilst some organisations measure performance along the same dimensions as at the organisational level, using some kind of balanced scorecard approach, other organisations monitor performance across different dimensions according to the process. At all organisations, however, measurements can be identified as input (supplier), in-process, and output (or results).

Summary. Process management and measurement has been well-documented in the literature on TQM. However, at the case study organisations, there were great differences between the levels of management of processes, as opposed to the management of functions. Cross-functional performance measurement is a vital component of the removal of "functional silos", which have potential for sub-optimisation and failure to take account of customer requirements (Hall *et al.*, 1991).

Performance appraisal and management
The third level of the performance measurement system model is the management of individuals. Steps in performance appraisal and management are (Sinclair, 1994):

1. If not already completed, identify and document job description, based on process requirements and personal characteristics. This information should include identification of:
   - Activities to be undertaken in performing the job.
   - Requirements of the individual with respect to the identified activities, in terms of experience, skills and training.
   - Requirements for development of the individual, in terms of personal training and development.
2. Translate process goals, action plans and personal training and development requirements into personal performance measures.
3. Define appropriate performance targets based on known capability and desired characteristics (or desired characteristics alone if there is no prior knowledge of capability).
4. Develop plans towards achievement of personal performance targets.
5. Document steps 1 to 4 using appropriate forms. Documentation should include space for results of performance appraisal.
6. Manage performance. This includes:

- planning tasks on a daily/weekly basis;
- managing performance of the tasks;
- monitoring performance against task objectives, using both quantitative (process) and qualitative information on a daily and/or weekly basis;
- giving feedback to individuals of their performance in carrying out tasks;
- giving recognition to individuals for superior performance.

7. Formally appraise performance against range of measures developed, and compare to target performance.
8. Use comparison with target to:
   - identify areas for improvement;
   - update action plans; and
   - update performance targets.
   Redesign jobs (where appropriate). This impacts step 1 of the process.
9. Update documentation.
10. After a suitable period (ideally more than once a year) compare capability to job requirements, and begin again at step 2.
11. Reward and recognise superior performance.

Figure 9.5 Performance measurement system model level 2

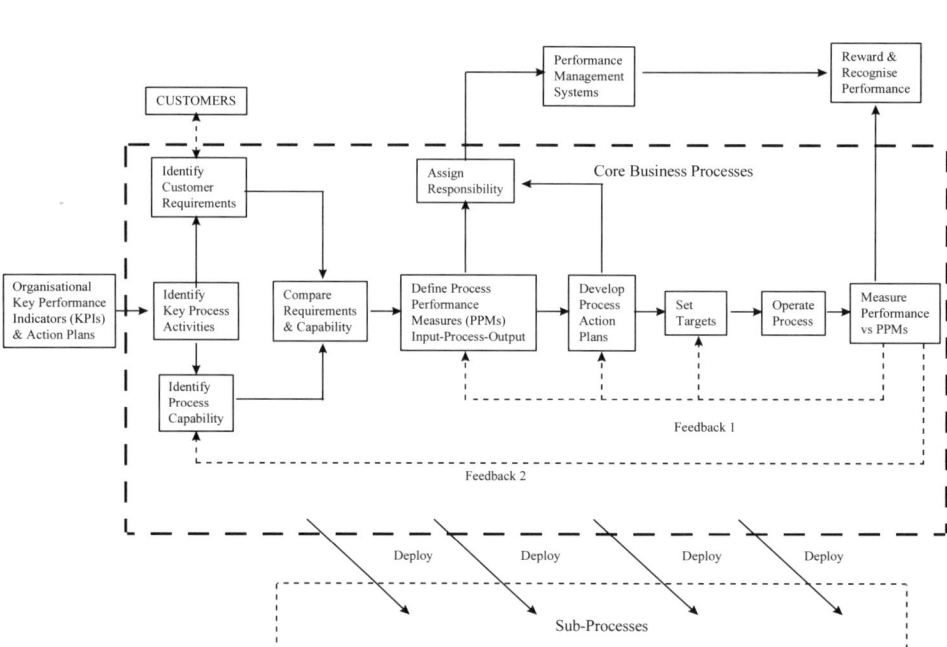

The above activities should be undertaken by the individual whose performance is being managed, together with their immediate superior. Performance appraisal and management is shown diagrammatically in Figure 9.6.

The major differences between TQ and non-TQ approaches in the management of individuals appear to lie in the reward for effort, as well as achievement, and consequently the different measures used (Hutt, 1994), the use of performance management in TQM (Daniels and Rosen, 1988), the use of information in continuous improvement, and to reward and recognise performance in TQ-organisations (Zairi, 1994) and the attempt to manage teams in TQ-organisations (Longenecker *et al.*, 1994).

The case study organisations attempted to measure a combination of process/task performance (effort and achievement) and personal development. The frequency of formal performance appraisal is defined by the frequency of the appraisal process (generally with a minimum frequency of six months). Most organisations recognised that this period was probably too long, but none suggested that they would increase the frequency. Between formal performance reviews, organisations rely on performance management techniques to manage individuals.

Figure 9.6 Performance measurement system model level 3

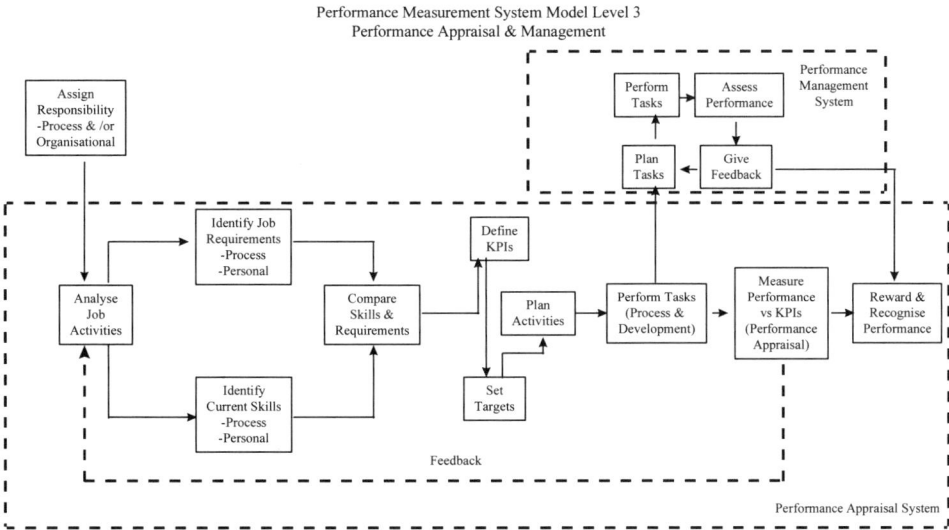

"Break-point" performance assessment
The fourth level of the performance measurement system model is break-point assessment. The steps in break-point performance assessment are as follows (Sinclair, 1994):
1. Identify the need for assessment. Identification of the need for assessment will come from:
   - poor performance at the organisational or process levels against KPIs;
   - identified superior performance of competitors;
   - customer inputs;
   - the desire to direct better the improvement efforts; and
   - the desire to concentrate attention on the need for performance improvement.
2. Identify mode and technique of assessment. This involves determining whether the assessment should be carried out internally within the organisation, or externally, and the type of assessment that should be carried out. Some techniques are purely internal (e.g. self-assessment), whilst others (e.g. external benchmarking) involve obtaining information from sources external to the organisation. The choice depends on:
   - How the need for assessment was identified (see step 1).

- The aim of the assessment. If the aim is to improve performance relative to competitors, external benchmarking may be a better option than internally measuring the cost of quality.
- The relative costs and expected benefits of each technique.
3. Carry out the assessment.
4. Feed results into planning process at the organisational or process level.
5. Determine whether to repeat the exercise. If it is decided to repeat the exercise, the following points should be considered:
   - frequency of assessment;
   - at what levels to carry out future assessments (e.g. organisation-wide or process-by-process); and
   - decide whether the assessment technique should be incorporated into regular performance measurement process, and if so, how this will be managed.

Three major differences between break-point assessment and other measures of performance are:
1. Break-point assessment exercises are generally new to the organisation, or are carried out less frequently than other measurement exercises.
2. Break-point assessment often requires the use of a level of resources greater than that normally associated with performance measurement.
3. Break-point assessment techniques give a broader view of performance than most individual measures.

Break-point performance assessment (level 4 in the performance measurement system model) is shown diagrammatically in Figure 9.7.

Techniques identified for break-point assessment at the case study organisations include: quality costing, self-assessment (against Baldrige or European Quality Award criteria), benchmarking (internal or external), customer satisfaction surveys, quality function deployment (QFD) and activity-based costing (ABC).

The use of the techniques as outlined differs from that suggested by most authors in two respects:
1. The integration of break-point assessment techniques into the overall performance management process.
2. The recognition that such techniques can move from being "break-point" techniques to being simply another organisational or process performance measure.

Reward and recognition systems
Reward and recognition form an output of performance measurement at the organisational, process (including suppliers), and performance appraisal and management (including performance related pay and performance management) levels (Sinclair, 1994). Reward and recognition appear to often be "bolted-on" to the management process. They are included in the performance measurement system model, since it would appear that all the case study organisations have attempted to innovate in this area.

Summary
The overall performance measurement system model can be shown as a series of complementary PDCA cycles, as shown in Figure 9.8. It should be remembered that each cycle operates at a different frequency, and within each cycle there will be individual cycles

for each measure. The frequency of the cycle is dependent on organisational level, frequency and criticality of the measurement.

The budgetary control process is separated from the outlined performance measurement system. The information in the performance measurement system is used in performance improvement, whereas budgetary control acts as a constraint within which performance is managed. This finding was also suggested by Euske *et al.* (1993).

Validation of the model
The model developed on the basis of the analysis of the case study data needed to be validated for its practical applicability (Sinclair, 1994). The aims of the survey were to:
- confirm that the model is in use at organisations which have implemented TQM; and
- compare performance measurement in TQ and non-TQ organisations.

Sample selection
Questionnaires were sent to a random sample of 500 organisations. It was not possible to ensure that the sample included a balance of TQ and non-TQ organisations, since this information is not documented. It should also be remembered that there is little agreement on which organisations can truly be defined as "total quality" even when they claim to have implemented TQM.

Figure 9.7 Performance measurement system model level 4

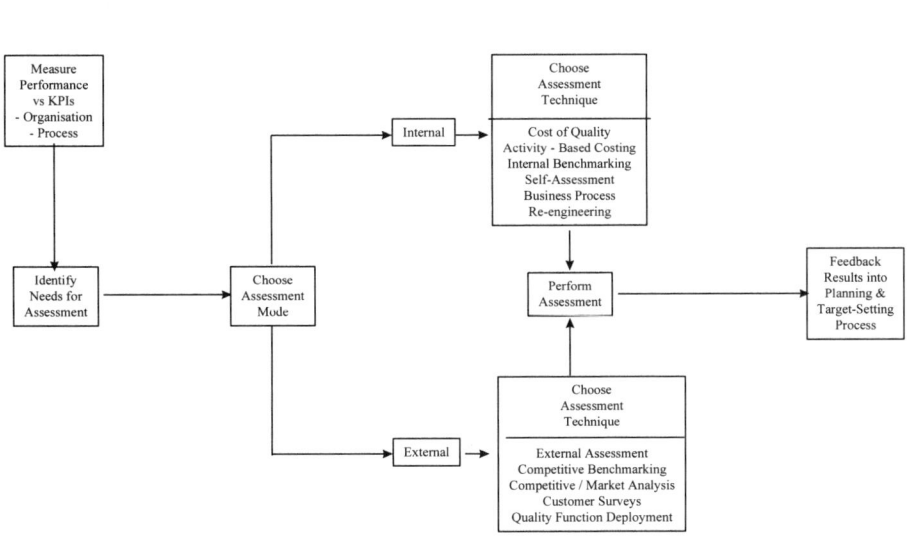

Analysis of responses
In total, 115 usable responses were returned, giving a response rate of 23 per cent. Of these, 95 organisations (83 per cent) had implemented TQM, while 20 (17 per cent) had no TQM process. The division between manufacturing and services was almost even, with 58 manufacturers and 57 services responding. The division of TQ and non-TQ organisations by industry was almost even. Of the 95 TQ organisations, 49 (52 per cent) were manufacturers

and 46 (58 per cent) were services. Of the 20 non-TQ organisations, nine (45 per cent) were manufacturers and 11 (55 per cent) were services.

Figure 9.8 Performance measurement system model

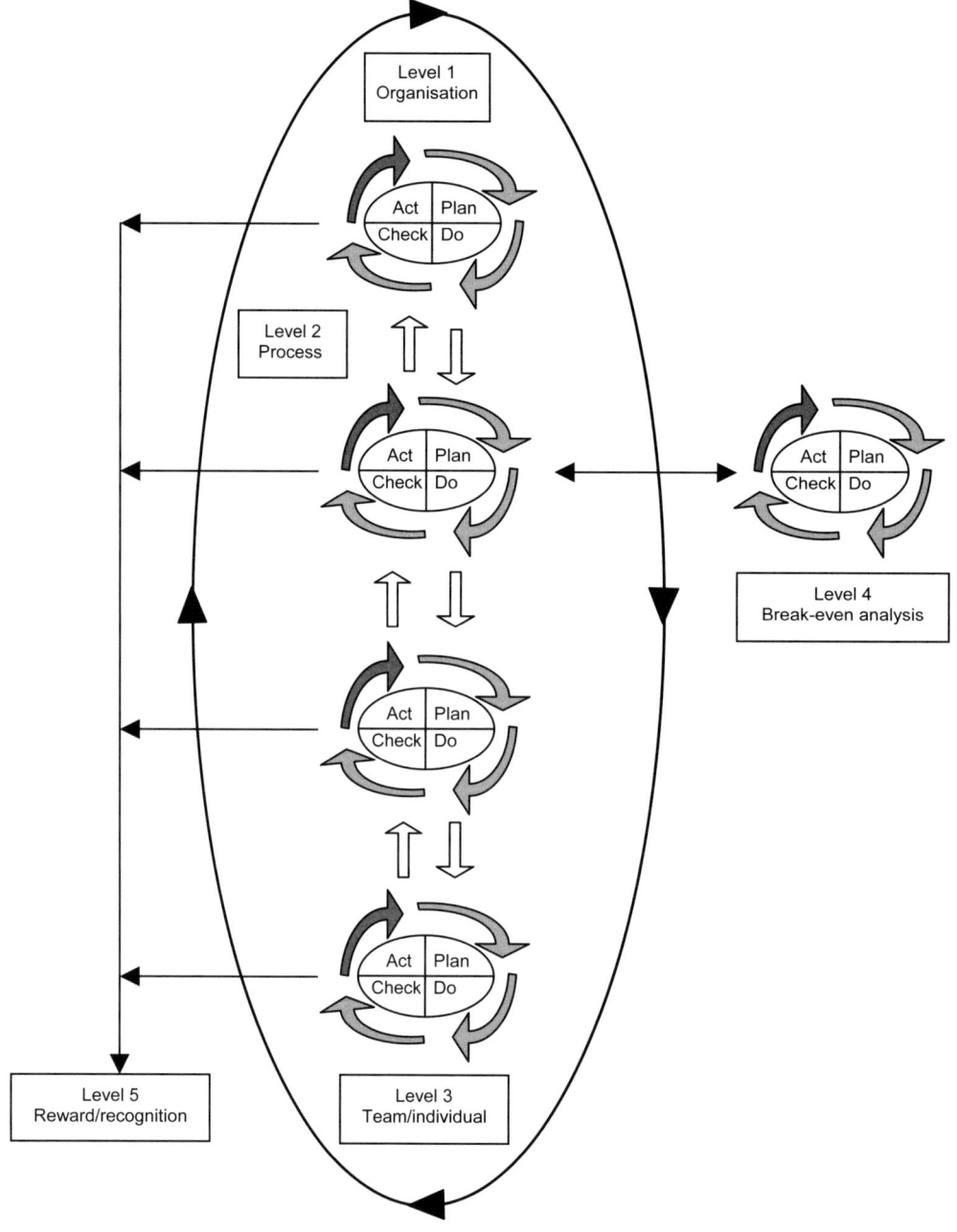

Of the organisations that had implemented TQM, the average experience of use of TQM was 3.8 years. The majority of organisations (77 or 81 per cent) had less than five years' experience of TQM, although four organisations had at least ten years' experience of TQM. Manufacturers had, on average, one year more experience of TQM than services, with 4.2 years compared to 3.1 years.

In the following discussion of the survey, findings are generally descriptive, since the small number of non-TQ respondents (and difficulty defining true "TQ" organisations) precluded meaningful inferential statistical analysis (Sinclair, 1994).

Strategy development and goal deployment
In the first section of the questionnaire, respondents were asked to identify which of a number of strategic management practices had been implemented by their organisation. The hypothesis was that TQ organisations were likely to have implemented a wider range of the formal strategic management practices identified at the case study organisations.

Analysis of the data showed that, apart from the production of a mission/vision statement, TQ organisations in the sample are approximately twice as likely as non-TQ organisations to have implemented the strategic planning practices identified in the case study organisations. This includes development and communication of strategic objectives, the development of critical success factors (CSFs) and key performance indicators (KPIs), and the assignment of responsibility for strategic objectives.

Respondents were then asked to identify the purposes for which performance measurement is used in their organisation. Purposes included measurement of organisational, process/functional, team and individual performance, goal alignment, continuous improvement, benchmarking and opportunity identification.

Analysis of the data on performance measurement related to the strategy development and goal deployment level of the performance measurement system model identified clear differences between TQ and non-TQ organisations. TQ organisations are more likely to have formal strategic management processes based on the use of critical success factors and associated KPIs than non-TQ organisations. It should be remembered that such formal strategic control processes are associated with more effective performance measurement systems. The tentative conclusion that can be drawn from the above analysis, therefore, is that performance measurement systems in TQ organisations are likely to be more effective than in non-TQ organisations.

Process management and measurement
Respondents were asked to identify which aspects of processes have been identified, defined and documented. TQ organisations were found to be more likely to have mapped and documented all aspects of processes (core and sub-processes, process owners, suppliers and customers, measurement frequency and performance targets) than non-TQ organisations. This is particularly the case in manufacturing organisations.

Respondents were asked to identify the individuals responsible for developing measures, setting performance targets, and actually measuring performance. Data analysis showed that in TQ organisations responsibility for defining measures and measuring performance rests with process owners and their immediate superiors to a greater extent than for non-TQ organisations. In non-TQ organisations, responsibility rests to a greater extent with higher management. This suggests that the performance measurement at TQ organisations is a more participatory process than at non-TQ organisations, where the process appears to be more top-down.

Performance management systems
Respondents were asked to identify which of a range of performance management techniques were used in their organisation, including the use of performance appraisal, performance management, team management, the reward and recognition of teams and individuals, and linking the performance of processes and people.

TQ organisations were found to use performance measurement in performance appraisal, performance management, and linking people and processes more widely than non-TQ organisations. TQ and non-TQ organisations use performance measurements in team management and reward and recognition in similar proportions.

TQ organisations appear to use performance measurement more widely than non-TQ organisations in the management of individuals. This supports the findings from the case study organisations, and also those found by Schneier et al. (1991), who suggested that performance management is of vital importance in the management of TQ organisations.

Break-point performance assessment
Respondents were asked to identify which of a range of break-point assessment techniques were used by their organisations. Techniques were separated into internal (involving resources and data within the organisation) and external (sources or data from outside the organisation).

Data analysis showed that TQ organisations generally use the range of internal break-point assessment techniques more widely than non-TQ organisations, particularly quality costing, self-assessment, business process re-engineering, and process capability analysis. Activity-based costing is used in similar proportions by TQ and non-TQ organisations.

As for internal techniques, TQ organisations generally use all external break-point assessment techniques (competitor/market analysis, benchmarking, customer surveys and quality function deployment) more widely than non-TQ organisations.

Effectiveness of performance measurement
Respondents were asked to rate the effectiveness of performance measurement within their organisation. Data analysis showed that quality organisations rated performance measurement to be more effective than non-TQ organisations at the 5 per cent level of significance.

Summary
The model developed was based on best practice performance measurement identified at the case study organisations. The survey was designed to examine some elements of the model. Despite the lack of statistical significance, due to the small number of non-TQ organisations responding, some general conclusions can be drawn about performance measurement at TQ and non-TQ organisations (Sinclair, 1994):

- TQ organisations use a wider range of formal strategic management techniques than non-TQ organisations. TQ organisations appear to use non-financial performance measurement much more widely than non-TQ organisations at the organisational level.
- TQ organisations manage processes more than non-TQ organisations.
- TQ organisations use a wider range of performance measures at the process level than non-TQ organisations.
- TQ organisations use a wider range of break-point assessment techniques than non-TQ organisations.
- TQ organisations use non-financial performance measurement for more purposes than non-TQ organisations. As such they generally use "fact-based" management more widely than non-TQ organisations.
- Performance measurement in TQ organisations appears to be more effective than in non-TQ organisations.

It is possible for non-TQ organisations to develop effective performance measurement systems. However, the nature of performance measurement systems at TQ organisations is different from non-TQ organisations. Also, it appears the TQ organisations are more likely to develop a truly effective performance measurement system than non-TQ organisations. In particular, the need to integrate strategic objectives, customer requirements, process capability and individual involvement is seen as vital for effective TQ-based performance measurement systems. The model developed allows for the introduction of an integrated performance measurement system, whereby all levels of the organisation, and all measurements, are focused on the continuous improvement of processes towards increased customer satisfaction.

No attempt has been made to identify a prescriptive list of measures at each level of the performance measurement system model. Flexibility in the face of changing competition, and customer requirements, is vital if performance measurement is to remain supportive and not become an inhibitor of organisational change (Brignall, 1993). The model therefore incorporates regular reviews of the measurement processes at all levels, in order to ensure measurement is modified in line with changes in the competitive environment.

References

Brignall, S. (1993), "Performance measurement systems as change agents: a case for further research", *Warwick Business School Research Papers No.72*, ISSN 0265-5976, Warwick Business School Research Bureau.

Daniels, A.C. and Rosen, T.A. (1988), *Performance Management: Improving Quality and Productivity through Positive Reinforcement*, Performance Management Publications Inc., Tucker, GA.

De Vries, D.L. (1986), *Performance Appraisal on the Line*, Centre for Creative Leadership, Greensborough, NC.

Euske, K.J., Lebas, M.J. and McNair, C.J. (1993), "Performance management in an international setting", in *Proceedings of the 16th Annual Congress of the European Accounting Association*, Turku, Finland, 28-30 April.

Evangelidis, K. (1992), "Performance measured performance gained", *The Treasurer*, February, pp. 45-7.

Globerson, S. (1985), *Performance Criteria and Incentive Systems*, Elsevier Science Publications.

Hall, R.W., Johnson, H.T. and Turney, P.B.B. (1991), *Measuring Up: Charting Pathways to Manufacturing Excellence*, Business One Irwin, Homewood, IL.

Hronec, S.M. (1993), *Vital Signs: Using Quality, Time and Cost Performance Measurements to Chart Your Company's Future*, Amacom, New York.

Hutt, G. (1994), "Incorporating quality objectives into performance appraisal systems", *TQM Magazine*, Vol. 6 No. 1, pp. 8-12.

Kaplan, R.S. and Norton, D.P. (1992), "The balanced scorecard-measures that drive performance", *Harvard Business Review*, January-February, pp. 71-9.

Longenecker, C.O., Scazzero, J.A. and Stansfield, T.T. (1994), "Quality improvement through team goal settings, feedback, and problem solving", *International Journal of Quality & Reliability Management*, Vol. 11 No. 4, pp. 45-52.

Oakland, J.S. (1993), *Total Quality Management*, 2nd ed., Heinemann.

Pritchard, R.D., Roth, P.L., Jones, S.D. and Roth, P.G. (1991), "Implementing feedback systems to enhance productivity: a practical guide", *National Productivity Review*, Winter, pp. 57-67.

Rockart, J.F. (1979), "Chief executives define their own data needs", *Harvard Business Review*, March-April, pp. 81-93.

Schneier, C.E., Shaw, D.G. and Beatty, R.W. (1991), "Performance measurement and management: a tool for strategy executive", *Human Resource Management*, Fall, Vol. 30 No. 3, pp. 279-301.

Sinclair, D.A.C. (1994), "Total quality-based performance measurement systems: an empirical study of best practice", PhD Thesis (unpublished), Bradford University.

US GAO (1991), *Management Practices*, Report/NSIAD-91-190, General Accounting Office, May.

Walsh, F.J. (1989), "Current practices in measuring quality", *The Conference Board Research Bulletin*, No. 234, The Conference Board Inc., New York.

Zairi, M. (1994), *Measuring Performance for Business Results*, Chapman & Hall, London.

Chapter 10
Managing customer satisfaction

Creating a customer-focused culture
Nowadays being customer-focused has to be accepted as a bare necessity to conduct business and as some would say, it is the licence to practice only. Organisations need to indicate that they are truly focused on their customers through deeds and actions. This really means that:
- Customer-focus is not necessarily statements on paper.
- These statements will have to be examined in terms of their appropriateness and the degree of seriousness and discipline from senior managers to instigate a culture of customer-focus.
- Customer-focus is a statement of intent. It signals that the organisation is willing to challenge the status quo and embrace new concepts and management disciplines adopted by world class organisations.
- It also means creating new systems, procedures and guidelines and adhering to the theme of servicing customers to people's best ability, by doing the right things right first time and on time.
- Customer-focus is an evolutionary rather than revolutionary process. It is painstaking and requires patience and great perseverance.
- Finally, customer-focus is really a state of mind rather than an absolute concept which indicates optimised performance and reaching the pinnacle of success.

One of the most basic questions that is never asked is who is the customer or, even more embarrassingly, what is a customer? Customers are the purpose of what we do and rather than them depending on us, we very much depend on them. The customer is not the source of a problem, we should not perhaps make a wish that customers "should go away" because our future and our job security will then be jeopardised. Mr Leon Bean, the founder of an organisation called L.L. Bean based in the USA selling mail catalogue camping equipment, defines a customer as:
> Someone who has needs and it is important for us to meet his needs profitably both for him and ourselves.

Many organisations go to great lengths to remind all of their employees of the importance of customers with statements of the importance of delighting the customer as a necessity to maintaining and ensuring business survival; honouring all of the pledges and various commitments made, as in the case of Ritz-Carlton Hotel, being determined not to lose a single customer.

Every organisation has to ensure that the process of identifying all of its customers is well-disciplined and very much adhered to. We often forget for instance the importance of internal customers and how much they impact on the quality of service finally offered to the customer. Of course focusing on the external customer is the right thing to do and ultimately it is external customers who pay for our goods and services. Internal customers are also real, they represent the value chain and through the levels of synergy generated from involving each of our employees, we will then be in a position to impact on the internal customer with the desired effect. As the saying goes, "you are only as good as your weakest link in the chain". Furthermore, as far as external customers are concerned, they need to be closely studied and their needs closely identified and translated. Segmentation will ensure that the organisation is delivering high volumes through the principle of mass customisation.

Customer-supplier relationships
The creation of customer-supplier chains is an important task, otherwise the internal fragmentation will adversely affect the external customer. Essentially, every person employed is both a customer and perhaps a supplier too. Through a process of translating the customer-supplier chain at all levels, better focus can be achieved and ultimately all work carried out will be of value. This approach avoids duplication, misunderstanding, confusion, waste, sub-optimisation and miscommunication.

Customer satisfaction is very often a misused and abused expression. Many organisations use it as a casual approach to state that their customers are happy and satisfied with the levels of service rendered and the products and services purchased. The process itself of course requires discipline and has to be based on factual information, measurement and regular communication. More importantly their needs vary with time and we need to be aware of this fact. Furthermore, customers cannot be compared across the board. In addition, one has to realise that we cannot use yesterday's means to serve tomorrow's needs. Service provision and customer satisfaction are relative states and not absolute ones.

Focusing on customers is the right thing to do and most important thing to do. Good performance, profitability and growth are important to a business. On the other hand, job security, good pay, good job prospects, promotion and a bright future are most important to employees at all levels. These are all heavily dependent on an organisation's ability to fulfil all of its customers' needs to their full satisfaction. There is a lot of research which directly links customer satisfaction to increases in profitability levels and sales. On the other hand, customer satisfaction is found to greatly impact business, corporate image and gaining new customers through direct recommendations.

Customer satisfaction versus dissatisfaction
Managing customer dissatisfaction will definitely lead to increases in customer satisfaction. British Airways, for instance, through dealing with complaints effectively, has realised that this impacts very significantly on the retention levels.

Essentially customers will only express their repurchasing intentions through the most recent experience they have had with a company. More importantly, customers take a keen interest in how a company goes about providing services to them and they compare with others to satisfy their own minds that the company is up to date and uses the most current means, which are compatible with those of the best providers. Furthermore, they will be curious about the systems, procedures and processes in rendering services to them and, of course, in the service industry, sectors such as the airline industry, everything is transparent and customers will observe the anomalies and shortcomings almost immediately.

There are numerous studies that have looked at the impact of customer satisfaction on repeat purchase, loyalty and retention. They convey similar messages in that:
- Satisfied customers are more likely to share their experiences with other people to the order of perhaps five or six people. Equally, dissatisfied customers are more likely to tell another ten people of their unfortunate experience.
- Furthermore, it is important to realise that many customers may not complain and this will differ from one industry sector to another.

- Lastly, if people believe that dealing with customer satisfaction/complaint is costly, they need to realise that it costs as much as 25 per cent more to recruit new customers.

Achieving customer-focus

What does it take to achieve customer-focus? How do we know that we are focusing on the right attributes? What determines customer satisfaction? What should we give them and which area should we prioritise? None of these questions are easy to answer and will always be difficult to answer. Customers are individuals and will judge their providers on different criteria and assess their performance in a wide variety of ways which are meaningful and important to them.

In the airline industry for instance, all travel attributes are extremely important. Customers, of course, would like their journey to be smooth, comfortable, and the whole experience to be very enjoyable. Of course, aspects such as safety will be on everyone's mind, but this is a basic requirement that every airline company has to address and would not be the reason why customers buy from one operator or another. Other attributes will impact differently on individual customers. For some, for instance, time is important, for others food and on-board entertainment, for others perhaps it is the comfort of the seats. But in all of these aspects the impact on the customers has to be consistent and that is where the challenge of being customer-focused starts.

Achieving and maintaining an effective customer-focused culture would, therefore, require consideration of the following:
- First, being customer-focused means that the company is attempting to get closer to its customers, know them better, be clearer about their needs, be aware of what concerns they may have, and have a feel for their future needs.
- It is also very important to get some direct feed back on how well the company is doing from the customers' perspective. Sometimes profitability and increases in business are extremely poor measures and it could well be that the reasons are incidental rather than deliberate.
- Customer-focus means that the company is in a position to assess the adequacy of current approaches for fulfilling its customer needs and to know what new services, products and innovations are required in the future.
- Customer-focus means that through concentrating on its customers, a company can identify its strengths and weaknesses and assess its performance from a competitive perspective.
- Finally, the external feedback is the echo of a company's efforts and the "acid test" for determining whether it is doing the right things. The process also gauges employee performance and the most appropriate reward and recognition systems.

Measurement of customer satisfaction

The measurement of customer satisfaction is not dissimilar from one industry to another. Whether a company is selling commodities or flight tickets is not necessarily going to affect how customer satisfaction ought to be measured:
- Value as perceived by the customer is a very important measure. Customer differentiation is often associated with how they perceive the value of purchasing from one provider as opposed to another.
- This will impact on the satisfaction level received as a result of value perception.

- There are some hard tangible aspects related to quality of products and services that the company is supplying.
- Some measures assess long-term loyalty and retention.
- Price is only one parameter and in most instances does not represent the dictating factor in customer choices.

A study from Tarp Europe indicates the effect resulting from satisfaction and dissatisfaction of customers. It is very clear that customers' intentions of buying again from the same supplier are greatly enhanced by how satisfied they are. On the other hand, customer dissatisfaction greatly reduces the commitment of buying again from the same organisation. In the airline industry, for instance, good service is rewarded by a significant commitment to repurchase again, while dissatisfaction reduces that commitment significantly to 33 per cent (Table 10.1).

Table 10.1 Impact of satisfaction on propensity to buy again

	Satisfied %	Dissatisfied %
Car hire	91	46
Consumer goods	95	38
Telecom (business)	95	36
Air travel	94	33
Petrol retailing	95	61
Financial services (USA)	73	17
Source: Tarp Europe		

One way of measuring the effectiveness of an organisation's approach to customer-focus is by referring to the Kano model. Essentially this model is based on two distinctive aspects (Figure 10.1):
 1. what an organisation does internally and the capability it builds to serve customers; and
 2. the degree of impact it creates on its customers through quality and service delivery.

The challenge for any organisation is to optimise its process capability and ability to deliver value to the customer and, of course, it is also to optimise the impact it creates on customer satisfaction.

Professor Kano (1993), the Japanese management expert, who developed this model, argues that customer-focus can be measured through three dimensions of quality:
 1. The first dimension is referred to as basic quality. This dimension is the licence to practice. It is taken for granted and customers do not speak about it. For instance, planes are expected to fly safely; restaurants are expected to serve hygienic food; computer manufacturers are expected to supply working computers; car manufacturers/dealers are expected to sell cars which are reliable and not faulty.
 2. The second dimension of quality is referred to as performance quality. In this instance the customers choose what to buy and where to buy from because of some additional criteria. For instance, we buy a ticket from a particular airline because they provide a direct flight, they serve the best food and their prices are favourable compared to other airline carriers. So if the airline concerned excels in all of these factors, the customers' reaction is going to be "I am happy/satisfied with what I have

experienced and received but I am not sure about tomorrow". If, however, the provider fails to deliver on this expected and differentiated dimension the customer is once again going to be angry.

3. The third dimension of quality is known as the delight factor. This dimension is above the line, unspoken and unexpected quality. If the customer does not get it, then it does not really matter. However, the more it is provided to the customer, the more delighted they are going to be and, therefore, the more committed they are going to be to the company. For instance, if when flying with a particular airline, we are told on the plane that for our next flight we will get 50 per cent discount and we will be provided with two complementary nights in the best hotel of any city of our choice, we are definitely going to consider flying with the same airline again.

One of the issues which does not really get treated seriously by senior managers is the management of customer complaints. Of course, it is to be expected that customer complaints are not something to be excited about, but they are however very real and their absence does not mean that a company is doing well and that customers are happy. On the other hand, their presence does not mean that a company is not doing the right things.

As the Chairman of British Telecommunications, Sir Ian Valance once said, "Customer complaints are the Voice of the Customer and one way of preventing total complacency". Encouraging customers to complain and provide impartial and objective feedback is not a bad thing. If a culture of customer-focus is to ensure improvement there has to be some direct input from the customer on whether the formulae put in place are working well or not. A company cannot brand itself as a customer-focused organisation if this does not carry the seal of approval from its customers.

Figure 10.1 The Kano model

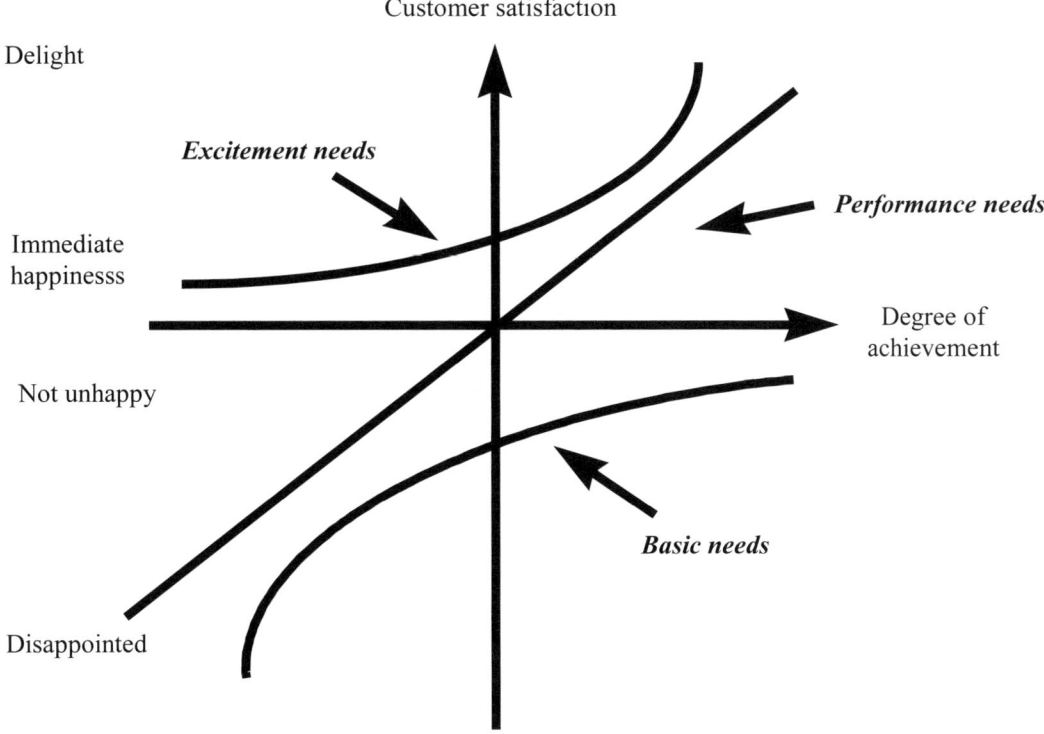

Many customers, in most industries, do not complain. In some industries, the proportions are much higher, perhaps due to the fact that volume is much higher or because the use of services/products is on an occasional basis only (Figure 10.2).

There is a serious message relating to non-complainant customers. Non-complainant customers are those who may have written off the poor performing provider and have made up their minds about buying from them ever again. The severity of the problems they have experienced will of course accentuate their decision not to deal again with the particular organisation concerned. If they complain and their complaints are not resolved, the intention of repurchase will be very low. If they have their complaints dealt with, that increases their commitment to purchase again from the provider concerned, and if their problems are resolved promptly and effectively this raises the commitment level to buy from them even higher. It therefore goes to show that dealing with complaints effectively and swiftly does have major benefits (Figure 10.3).

Essentially the intention of repurchasing is greatly affected by problems experienced and if customers do not experience problems or have their problems dealt with effectively then this increases the loyalty factor tremendously.

Customers tend to amplify their compliments or complaints to other people. If an organisation does it right first time then the customer is going to be their best marketing manager. On the other hand, if customers receive a raw deal and a terrible experience they will make sure that as many people as possible know about it. Figure 10.3 indicates the significance is related to the regularity with which customers use the product/service.

Figure 10.2 Many customers do not complain

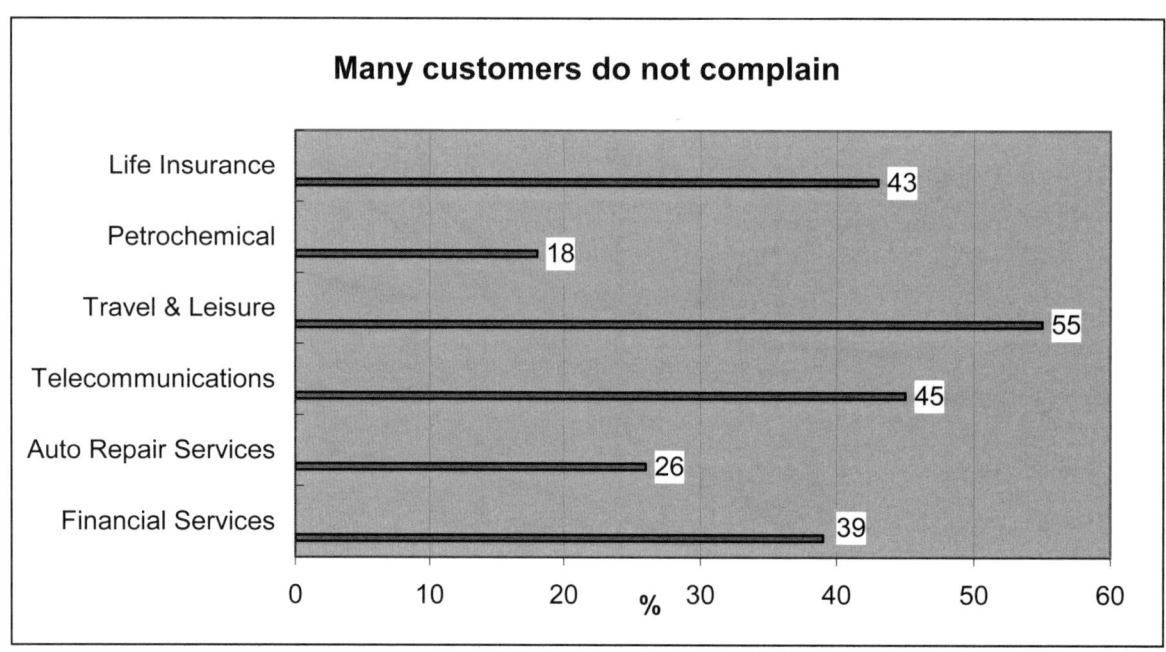

Figure 10.3 How many unhappy customers will buy again from the same company?

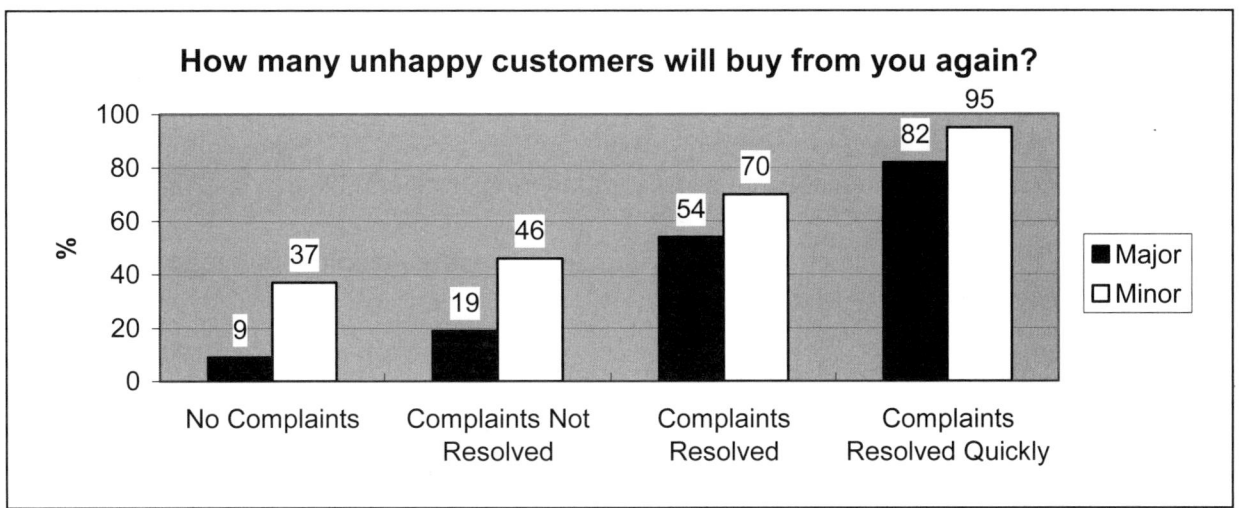

Customer satisfaction performance measurement models

Being customer-focused means that the company is constantly having a dialogue with its customers, serving them, anticipating their needs, measuring their satisfaction levels and, of course, dealing with their complaints. As far as the latter is concerned there is a need to have a proper and systemised process. The example in Figure 10.4 is based on the Rank Xerox approach. The model depicts real empowerment to handle customer complaints as closely as possible to the source. If this does not resolve it, then it is referred to the next level then the next level and it could even escalate to corporate level. Every time there is delay, however, and the matter is referred upwards, this will impact on the customer and add to their frustrations and it adds cost since more and more people have to leave important tasks to investigate the matter

When a company provides customer service there are some basic rules that ought to be observed. These are in many instances pure common sense. As the saying goes, " common sense is not so common":

- All employees need to be reminded of the importance of customers and who they are.
- All employees need to learn to listen, emphasise and support the customer as far as practically possible.
- Individually, all employees need to strive to do better than expected in pleasing customers.
- If the customer has experienced inconveniences or is having a problem, employees need to help them and resolve any issue they may encounter.
- Being civil, polite and saying thank-you are important when serving customers.

Figure 10.5 displays best practice adopted from the financial services sector as an example of what it takes to provide excellent service quality:

- When providing a service such as selling tickets, holiday bookings, travel arrangements etc. employees need to be aware that there are tangible aspects that the customer will be studying such as the way they dress, the way the branch office looks, the way information is displayed etc.

- The service provided will also have to be reliable. For example, the booking system needs to be accurate, up and running all the time; otherwise the customer will not trust the company and will avoid it in their future requirements.
- Being responsive when providing the service means dealing with disruptions, long queues, manning counters etc.
- The people at the front dealing with customers have to convey assurance, look competent, be knowledgeable and should demonstrate enthusiasm and their liking of the job.
- Finally, since service provision is a human transaction, employees need to empathise and show sensitivity to the customer.

Figure 10.4 Rank Xerox closed loop escalation process

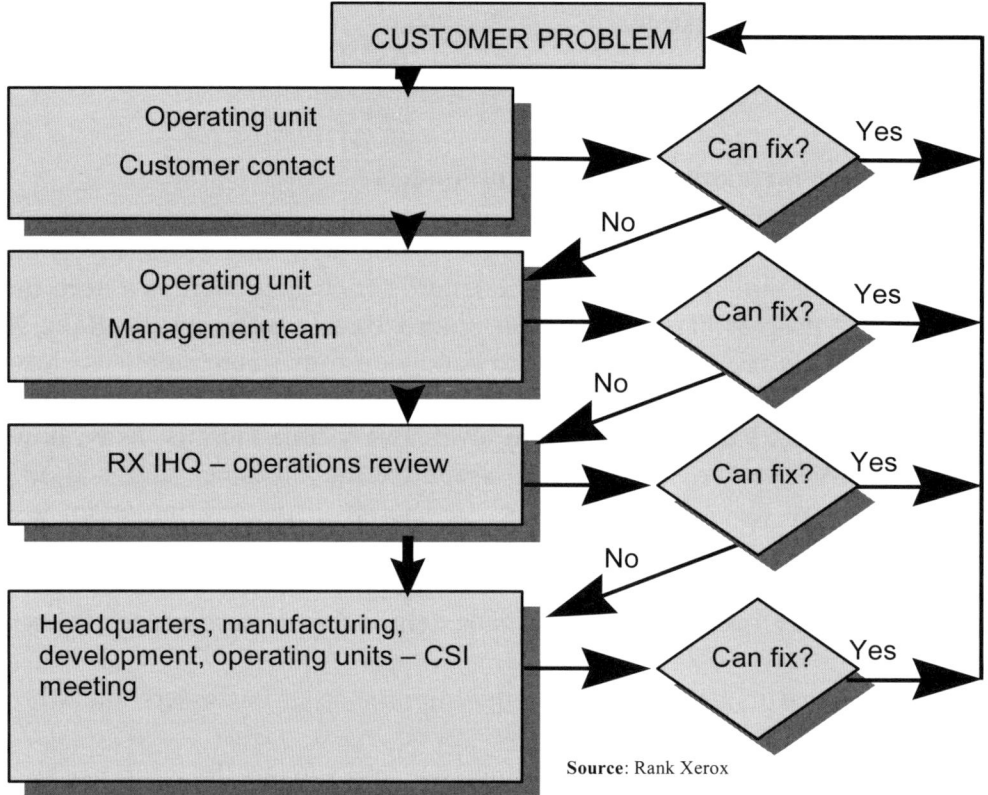

Source: Rank Xerox

Beyond satisfaction: customer loyalty and retention

Customer loyalty and retention can never be achieved unless there are consistent and sustainable satisfaction levels. This obvious statement is important to re-iterate for a wide variety of reasons:

- Customers do not become loyal to an organisation just because they receive high quality products and services. Customers commit to providers who generate high value by adding high value service to what is expected.
- Various research studies have come to similar conclusions in that only high levels of customer satisfaction can generate customer loyalty.
- Customer satisfaction is not generated through "occasional contact" via questionnaires and surveys, but rather through a dedicated effort to establish

continuous communications on products/service quality, complaints, future intentions etc. Through regular study and analysis of data and information received, customers can be better understood and their needs more appropriately met.

- Satisfaction of customers is a useful approach to ensuring that high competitive impact is generated thorough focusing on the 20 per cent of the population that impact 80 per cent of a particular company's success.

Figure 10.6 illustrates the customer pyramid model which helps organisations to focus on their customers who bring significant financial benefits and sustainable competitiveness. Harris (1999), who proposed the pyramid model, argues that:

- The largest part of a marketing department's budget is allocated to non-company customers.
- From 5 per cent to 30 per cent of all customers are able to ascend the pyramid's levels and the most important motive is their total satisfaction.

Gorman (1997), on the other hand, presents a useful template for categorising customers and determining the value/loyalty aspects (Figure 10.7). He argues that there are three tiers of customer:

1. Safe valuable (with scenarios of safe but lesser valuable customers).
2. Battle valuable (predicted to leave or are close to leaving with two more scenarios of less value).
3. Lose valuable (most valuable who have left plus lesser valuable ones).

Gorman's point is that every organisation needs to focus on its most valuable customers. A loss of 10 per cent of this segment will have a more significant impact on profits that a loss of 10 per cent elsewhere (Figure 10.7).

Figure 10.5 Service attributes – best practice approach

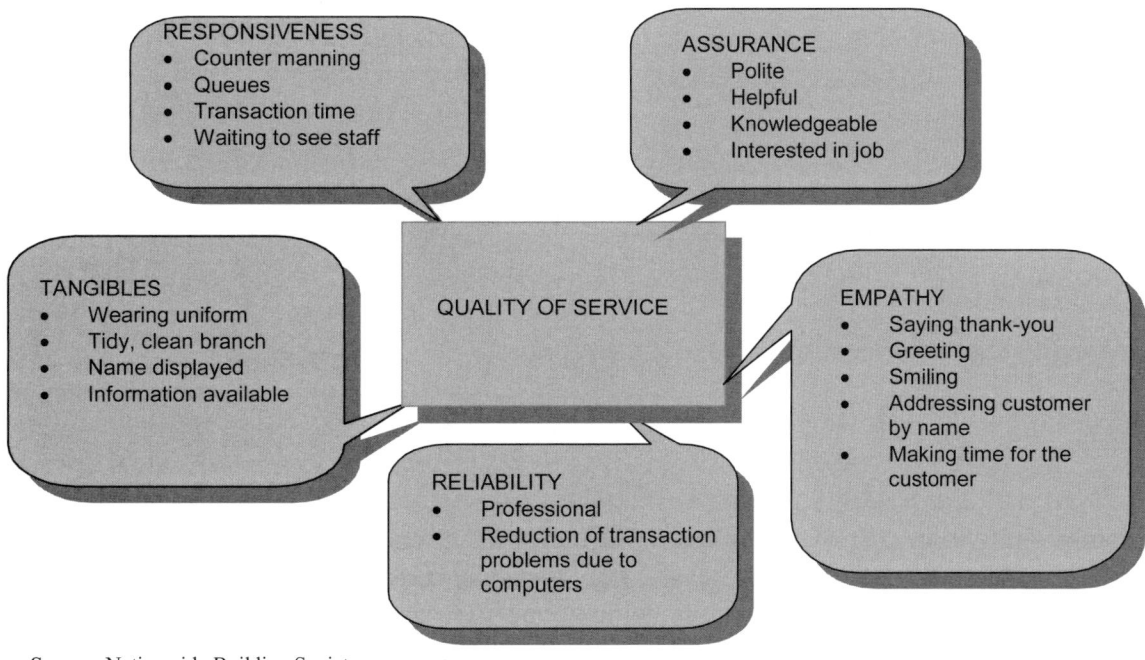

Source: Nationwide Building Society

Best Practice Organisational Excellence

Figure 10.6 How to manage customer loyalty: the customer pyramid model

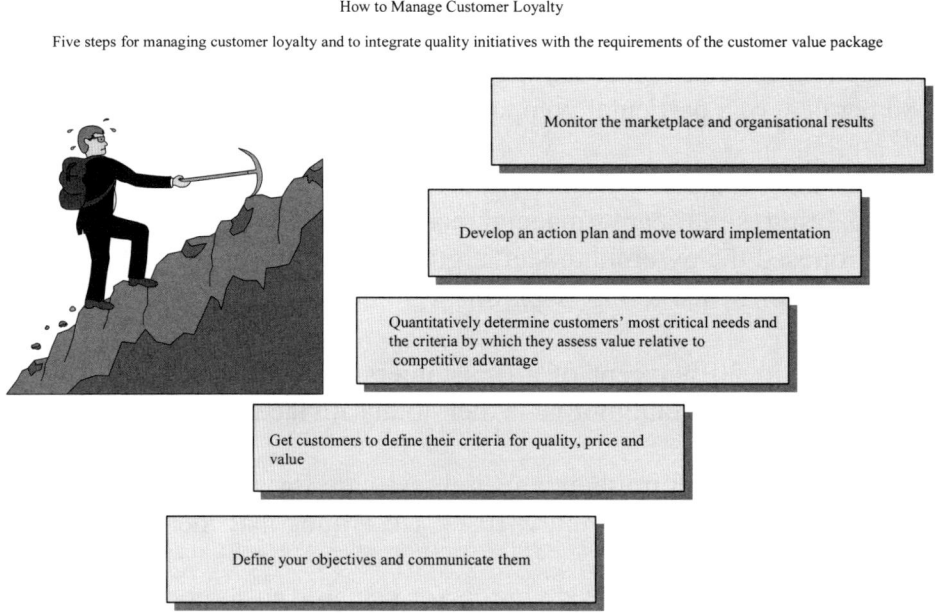

Figure 10.7 The value/loyalty matrix

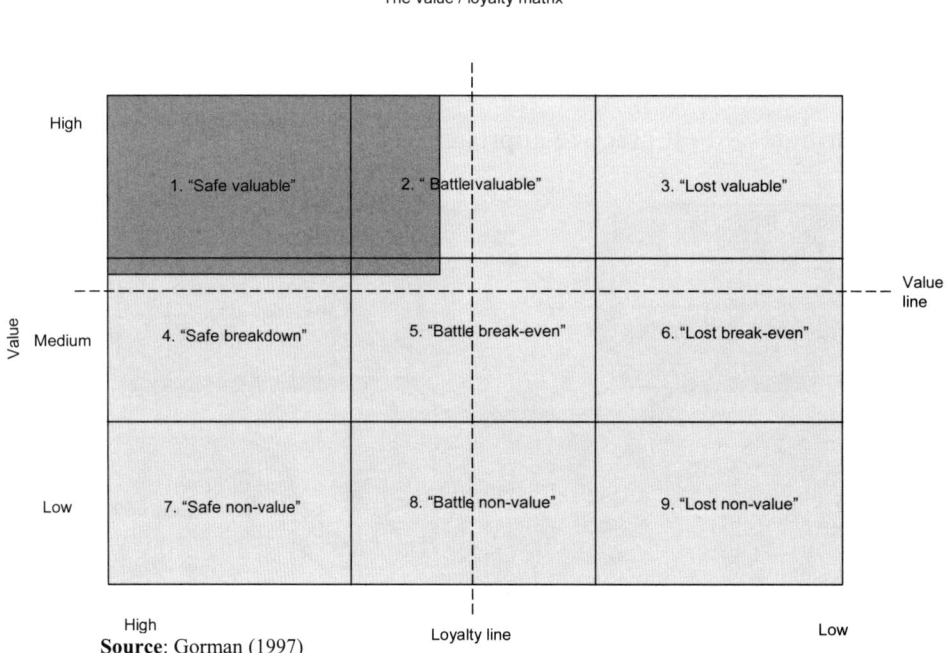

Source: Gorman (1997)

Customer retention and loyalty is heavily driven by the word "value", which is described in a consistent but wide variety of ways. For instance, Gorman (1997) describes value as: "Something the customer perceives as being a worthwhile addition to the product".

Harris (1999) on the other hand describes it as: "The relationship between all the benefits of the acquisition or use of the product and experience (what is received) and its cost (what is paid)" (see Figure 10.8).

Figure 10.8 Customer value determinants

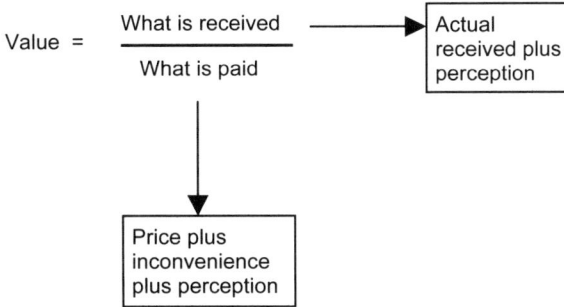

Fredericks and Salter (1998), on the other hand, have identified that customer value is affected by three factors: quality, price and image, which have to be assessed relative to competition.

Achieving value-driven customer loyalty will require not only approaching each of the three factors mentioned above as "processes" that are well-understood and managed, but also that the organisation's systems, processes, etc., which deliver the outcomes to the customers, are well managed and constantly optimised.

Previous experience and external factors can also influence the degree to which customers commit to long-term relationships. These are factors over which the providers concerned have no direct control.

Fredericks and Salter (1998) conclude that:

> Customers perceive that they are receiving superior value when a company provides products and services that represent a better combination of what is received for what is paid relative to purchases from competitive companies in similar markets.

Customer loyalty and retention are outcomes of understanding the principles of value creation and the factors that impact or affect the former. It is therefore important to re-iterate the following key messages:
- Value is related to perceived quality.
- Quality is related to price. Quality is measured by other non-price-related attributes such as service support.
- Company image drives customers' beliefs and perceptions of what they are getting.

Harris (1999) in relation to creating high value and achieving customer loyalty and retention, argues that:

> This is only possible by understand the latent (unspoken or hidden) needs of customers and the emerging strategies of competitors or others providing similar services to the market. This is achieved by delivering value as the only secure trust factor between a provider and a customer. With trust built on delivery or value, long-term loyalty will be attained.

Some final thoughts on customer-focus
- Being customer-focused means having a clear service strategy which is deployed with vision, purpose, goals and targets. This process may start with some basic questions on the reasons why a service is offered in the first place: how the company plans to provide it; how the company goes about providing it and who is responsible for which areas, etc.

- To support the process of developing a customer-focused culture there are some key drivers, based on best practices and used to measure business excellence at world class level:
  - The first stage is perhaps to know who the customer is and use a wide variety of means to gather information on all customers.
  - It is also important to learn about market dynamics, competition, threats and opportunities amongst other things.
  - It is important for employees to know what is required of them and what pressures are on them, which will help in deciding on how they should go about creating focus on the customers.
- Being customer-focused means that employees do not shy away from asking questions on service quality standards, satisfaction levels, future intentions, complaints etc. Creating a dialogue with customers and developing a closed loop system which continuously monitors how employees perform in the eyes of customers, how they grow and develop as a customer-focused organisation and how they use an innovative spirit to keep customers interested in the company is an absolute must.
- The dialogue that employees create with customers has to be based on a strong system which constantly seeks views, gathers feedback, assesses future needs, handles issues, puts action plans in place, monitors satisfaction levels and drives forward to guarantee loyalty factors and retention of all customers.

Customer satisfaction is discussed in the case studies of Rank Xerox and Nationwide Building Society in Chapter 14.

References

Fredericks, J.O. and Salter II, J.M. (1998), "What does your customer really want", *Quality Progress*, January, pp. 63-8.

Gorman, B. (1997), "The measurement of customers' perceived value", *Strategy*, No. 16, August/September, pp. 12-14.

Harris, M. (1999), "Service quality: nothing but value your services can generate more value than your products", *Competitive*, Vol.7 No. 4, February, pp. 1, 5-6.

Kano, N. (1993), "A perspective on quality activities in American firms", *California Management Review*, Vol. 35 No. 3, pp. 12-31.

Chapter 11
Managing people satisfaction

People – the most valuable asset

Organisations are looking increasingly closely at their approach to people satisfaction so that the full potential of their employees can be realised. The organisations which "care" for their people tend to produce exceptional results because the two are intrinsically linked:

> People who feel good produce good results and people who produce good results feel good (High Performance Technology).

People who are doing the right things demonstrate the right behaviours and act as role models for others to emulate within the business. Recognition plays an important role in this process, as identified by the Chief Executive Officer at Milliken, "Managers must take time to identify and recognise the right people and behaviours".

Process for managing people satisfaction

At Xerox, motivation and satisfaction of its people are key business priorities and are the responsibility of local management teams within the operating units. Surveys are conducted to identify people's level of satisfaction and provide management with areas in which improvement may be required. Although individual units had operated their own surveys in the past, a company-wide approach is now in operation. Data from the survey respondents is presented to managers, giving overall satisfaction improvement for the year and performance against targets by country and by parameter. Improvement objectives are set on an annual basis at local level with reference to the relevant data from the satisfaction survey. The improvement targets then form part of the individual manager's objectives for the coming year. Individual operating unit objectives for overall satisfaction have been introduced as part of the closed loop process.

Feedback of the results to employees is given in each operating unit as part of the closed loop management process. Quality improvement teams then conduct root cause analysis on the main findings before making recommendations for improvements.

At High Performance Technology the process is managed through an employee opinion survey. Employees are asked to respond to a series of questions as favourable, neutral or unfavourable.

A focus on good communication is seen as central to maintaining a high level of employee satisfaction and this is achieved through three key activities:
1. Twice yearly business briefings for staff.
2. Twice yearly line development unit briefings for all people.
3. Team meetings for all appropriate people to be held at least monthly.

There are seven feedback mechanisms (see Table 11.1) used to provide a comprehensive analysis of people satisfaction within the company. The mechanisms are both on-going in the form of meetings and at fixed intervals through employee satisfaction surveys.

Table 11.1 Communication feedback mechanisms

Mechanism	Frequency	Communication
Employee survey	Annually	People to management
Divisional business briefing	Twice yearly	Management to people
Development unit briefing	Twice yearly	Management to people
Team meetings	Monthly	Two way
Investing in People (IIP)	Annually	Two way
Absenteeism	Checked each quarter	Management information
Accident rate	Every divisional safety meeting	Management information

Royal Mail managed its people satisfaction process, first, by conducting research, which indicated that employees' perceived needs can be classified into the following seven areas:
1. Job security.
2. Communication.
3. Training and career development.
4. Pay.
5. Recognition.
6. Employment conditions.
7. Involvement.

The employee opinion survey is confidential and conducted by an external independent organisation to maintain an objective and independent view. Results are presented with a commentary and then broken down to a local level if there are more than ten responses.

The output from the survey is externally benchmarked using comparative data which is available through membership of the Opinion Survey Forum, a group of UK companies undertaking surveys.

The Mortgage Express approach to people satisfaction is gained through an employee opinion survey which is undertaken to measure progress towards targets and compare each key measure to the UK norm. A response rate of 81 per cent has been achieved, which is above the 70 per cent norm for such surveys.

A similar process operates at D2D where an annual employee opinion survey is conducted to help focus the organisation in meeting people's expectations. There are 42 questions under five sections:
1. Work objectives, appraisal and development.
2. Management style and communications.
3. Pay, benefits and conditions.
4. Quality and customer care.
5. Satisfaction with D2D as an employer.

At TI Europe, employee satisfaction is integral to the business and measured using an employee opinion survey. The questions used have been aligned to those used by other companies, which have enabled direct comparatives to be made and benchmarks established for those participants.

The internal assessment is undertaken through "The Partnership" report. Undertaking this in-house has reduced the cycle time and administration time involved and given management ownership of the closed loop survey process.

Consistency and simplification of approach have been the foundation for TNT's approach to obtaining feedback on employee satisfaction. The questions used in its employee survey require an assessment of always, often, sometimes, seldom or never for each:

1. Our most senior managers are committed to developing people.
2. Their commitment has been made known to all our employees.
3. Employees at all levels are aware of the broad aim and vision of the company.
4. People at all levels know how they can contribute to our success.
5. We have a process for regularly reviewing the individual training and development needs of each of our employees.
6. We develop the skills of our existing employees to help achieve our business objectives.
7. Our managers ensure that everyone is aware of the range of development opportunities open to them.

Corning, a former winner of the Malcolm Baldrige Award in the USA, recognises a direct link between satisfaction and the well-being of its employees. This has led to attention being paid to the general welfare of its people. Furthermore, safety was found to be a key factor when determining satisfaction and consequently has been given high prominence throughout the business, together with facilities which are offered for health and fitness.

The measures of people satisfaction

At Rank Xerox employee satisfaction parameters cover eight broad areas:

1. overall satisfaction;
2. career development;
3. pay;
4. team spirit;
5. communication;
6. objectives and performance;
7. training; and
8. work environment.

These measures are supplemented by indirect measures of employee satisfaction, which are gained through the measurement of absenteeism and attrition. Attrition is measured for all levels irrespective of the reason for leaving.

Overall employee satisfaction is compared to the national norm by individual country and the objective set is to reach norm status in all operating units. This will be achieved through sharing of best practice with those operating units which are currently above their national norm.

The employee satisfaction closed loop management process drives continuous improvement and is pervasive across the whole of the company. It is coupled with the establishment of company-wide objectives. The power of the process is in the involvement of the people.

Similarly, High Performance Technology has identified the measures of satisfaction in 15 key areas:

1. work environment;
2. health and safety provisions;
3. job security;
4. communications;
5. appraisal and target setting;

6. training and retraining;
7. career development;
8. job requirements;
9. reward schemes;
10. recognition schemes;
11. management style and effectiveness;
12. employee conditions;
13. empowerment;
14. involvement; and
15. understanding of the organisation's mission, values, vision and strategy.

Like Rank Xerox, High Performance Technology has set a target for the organisation to be at the UK norm in each of the measures. Eleven additional measures are used to gauge employee satisfaction level:
1. levels of training and development;
2. involvement in improvement programmes;
3. recognition of individuals and teams;
4. absenteeism and sickness;
5. grievances;
6. staff turnover;
7. accident levels;
8. recruitment trends;
9. improvement suggestions received;
10. use of the organisation provided facilities; and
11. industrial relations.

Raising the level of quality perception within the business is a key target and to achieve this four key actions have been taken:
1. commitment to the UK Quality Award for the next year;
2. introduction of a new system of raising quality improvement ideas, dELTA;
3. putting together a team to raise awareness of the business model; and
4. launching a poster campaign to raise awareness of the business model and its owners.

Within the service sector, Mortgage Express targets employee satisfaction as part of every manager's personal objectives and is one of the four elements that determine bonuses for directors and managers. National norms are obtained from the Independent Survey Research, Institute of Personnel and Development and the Confederation of British Industry and targets are set against them. Eleven main measures are determined from the survey:
1. environment/health and safety;
2. job security/satisfaction;
3. communications;
4. training, appraisal and development;
5. reward and recognition;
6. management style and effectiveness;
7. terms and conditions of employment;
8. employee involvement and empowerment;
9. mission, vision, values and strategy;
10. quality; and
11. teamwork.

Eight additional measures are used to establish employee satisfaction at Mortgage Express:
1. training provision;
2. involvement in improvement activities;
3. recognition;
4. absenteeism and employee turnover;
5. grievance;
6. health and safety;
7. further education; and
8. sports and social activities.

Best practices adopted for measuring people satisfaction
The following critical success factors have been identified from an analysis of the approaches adopted by the quality award winners in the UK and USA:
- Employee opinion survey is the main vehicle for obtaining data on employee satisfaction.
- Annual basis is the preferred frequency for undertaking a survey.
- External consultants are more frequently used to provide an unbiased and objective report on findings.
- Data is benchmarked to establish performance gaps and norms.
- Employee surveys include the following main topics:
    - management style;
    - working conditions;
    - rewards and recognition;
    - communications;
    - work environment;
    - training; and
    - understanding the company's mission, vision and values.
- Additional data sources for people satisfaction are:
    - training and development;
    - involvement in improvement programmes;
    - absenteeism and sickness;
    - grievance; and
    - recruitment trends.
- Data is displayed to show a trend over a three to five year period.

Additional best practices
At Rank Xerox managers received a two week intensive course of study and training to improve their effectiveness in career planning, following data received from the satisfaction survey. The following year's results showed an increase in satisfaction for this area. Quality improvement teams work on how to increase opportunities for teamwork following feedback from the satisfaction survey and this improved the following year.

Within High Performance Technology the work environment is an open plan office layout with only a minority of staff based in workshop or laboratory environments. Their health and safety provisions include a well-equipped occupational health centre staffed part time by a nursing officer and a significant number of fully trained first aiders and fire marshals. The low accident rates have been recognised by a certificate from the Engineering Employers Association.

People have at least one performance assessment and one training and development discussion a year to discuss their career aspirations, achievements, development achievements, development areas and training plans. An external consultant has been used to advise on careers.

Three significant employment conditions have been introduced over and above the basic remuneration:
1. comprehensive pension scheme;
2. 24 hour a day accident insurance; and
3. private health insurance.

Royal Mail has improved the levels of communication satisfaction through the provision of resources (employee communication manager), the growing expertise and management of the whole communication process and the development and deployment of a national "Understanding the Business Programme".

Quadrant has adopted a "Dedicated to our success" board in the restaurant, where thank-you letters signed by all the directors and managers in that area are displayed.

At TI Europe people's health is checked rigorously, in excess of legal requirements – free eye re-education, electrocardiograms and influenza vaccinations. Voluntary health and lifestyle improvement programmes exist at all TI locations. To improve communications within TI, all employees receive a special booklet entitled "Ethics in the Business of IT". The belief is that there are three ingredients essential to fostering an ethical environment: candour, trust and proper recognition.

Integration of people satisfaction data

At Rank Xerox and most of the quality award winning companies, a company-wide employee satisfaction survey is undertaken which provides consistency and a co-ordinated approach across the business.

In the USA, Corning integrates its health and safety initiatives into its overall planning process rather than adopting a stand alone approach for people satisfaction.

External benchmarking of pay and conditions has been undertaken with Hewlett Packard and DEC and this data has been integrated into the forward planning of the companies.

The measurement of people satisfaction is an integral part of the business at Royal Mail: "people management policies are developed to involve employees by satisfying the needs and expectations of people and increase customer focus".

People satisfaction is discussed in the case studies of Ulster Carpet Mills and Dana Commercial Credit in Chapter 14.

Chapter 12
Impact on society

Business and organisations have a privilege denied to ordinary mortals – they don't have to die. This makes them especially responsible (Charles Handy).

Focusing on community issues

It is interesting to note that at a time of global recession and great mergers, the business community has been more concerned with financial issues rather than social ones. In fact what is emerging very strongly, is a determination and commitment to address both environmental and societal concerns.

John Elkington (1999) argues that:

> Environmental reporting is now well-established, as of course is financial reporting. But further challenges lie ahead for companies looking to evaluate social indicators in such areas as community, employee and supplier relationships. The pressure for accountability, together with the significant expense of producing the data, will develop powerful pressures towards the integration of financial, social and environmental accounting and reporting.

He goes on to say that:

> Companies – and their stakeholders – will have no option but to address this emerging "triple bottom line". They will have to work harder to assess what really matters to them and which indicators will be seen by key stakeholders (including financial analysts) in assessing the triple bottom line performance of companies and sectors alike.

It is widely argued that the business ethos generally speaking has started to subscribe to the principle "show me" rather than just "trust me". Corporate social accountability and reporting is therefore seen as a key driver for engaging the wider community as an important stakeholder in business activity.

There are conferences and global events organised to promote this new principle. For instance, the World Business Council for Sustainable Development (WBCSD) and the Institute for Social and Ethical Accountability (ISEA), among many organisations, have staged conferences to debate the themes of social accountability and social responsibility. For instance, ISEA organised an important conference in January 1999 to address the following key areas:

- The concepts and principles behind organisational social reporting, accountability and sustainability and the business drivers for change.
- How the social reporting system is linked with existing financial, environmental and risk-reputation systems.
- The range of issues that can be included in a social statement and how organisations can embark on the process of social reporting.
- Techniques and methods to establish social reporting as a powerful audited system for improved market performance.
- The value of developing effective stakeholder dialogue to inform measurement and reporting strategies.

Focusing on community issues is not however a new concept. Many gurus in the TQM field have, for instance, stressed the importance of "stakeholders". Dr Edward Deming, as far back as 1946, argued that statistical quality techniques ought not to be limited to economic applications. Deming argued about the significance of social contributions that would emerge, through the application of quality tools and techniques (Jacques, 1999).

Deming's views were further stressed by Joseph Juran, who has often urged quality institutions, such as The American Society for Quality, to expand their mandates by placing more emphasis on rendering service to society (Juran, 1994).

Definition and meaning of corporate social reporting
A report on social reporting by Elkington *et al.* (1998) describes in a useful way, the various meanings of corporate social reporting. In short, this concept covers social, ethical accounting, auditing and reporting; a little bit more than just philanthropy. The report argues that companies like BP and United Utilities should measure, evaluate and benchmark their social activities. Furthermore, they should view the community's perception of them as a critical factor in their business success. The inter-dependency between ethics and social concerns is undisputed. Organisations have, first of all, got to operate with a high code of ethics so that everything else can follow on from this.

How to create optimum societal value-added?
The key drivers for adding optimum value to society and the communities in which specific business organisations operate are through having strong commitment to corporate and social governance, having an open dialogue with external stakeholders and having the determination to achieve environmental sustainability.

Nelson (1998) proposes an approach based on three elements, for building societal value-added. Table 12.1 illustrates how this can be carried out in practice.

Nelson (1998) argues that companies that have started to make real headway in the area of societal value-added tend to share four characteristics:
1. They rely on value-based, transformational leadership (i.e. sponsor-headed by the CEO and reflected in the company's vision/mission and value statements).
2. Cross-boundary learning (a commitment to learning, innovation and through networks and global partnerships).
3. Stakeholder linkages (mutual benefits through various modes of relationships).
4. Performance levers (use of a wide range of financial and non-financial performance measures, supported by auditing, verification, reporting and recognition systems).

Standards of social accountability and reporting
There are various principles and standards that the global business community has started to adhere to on a voluntary basis.

The CERES Principles
The CERES Principles are a ten point code of conduct on companies' environmental performance and accountability. Any organisation that pledges to endorse the CERES Principles will agree to monitor and improve its behaviour in the areas shown in Table 12.2.

Table 12.1 Creating societal value-added: a proposed approach

	Approach	Example of area of application
1.	Efficient and ethical pursuit of core business activities	Making environmentally and socially responsible decisions Investing in responsible sourcing, production, distribution by taking into account access to the poor Creating local jobs Paying taxes and royalties Implementing social human resource policies Adopting international accepted business standards Supporting technology co-operation
2.	Social investment and philanthropy	Offering training programmes to the community at large Running employee volunteering schemes for social or cause-related initiatives Business education projects Community health projects Sponsoring community development trusts Resource mobilisation and civic improvement
3.	Contribution to the public policy debate	Tackling obstacles to private sector development and responsible foreign investment Contribution to social and environmental policies and frameworks in areas such as education, training, local economic development, employment and environmental management Supporting progress for good governance, including anti-corruption initiatives and human rights standards

Other principles and standards
Some other standards are:
- Principles for Global Responsibility: Benchmarks for Measuring Business Performance.
- The CAUX Round Table: Principles for Business.
- The Business Charter for Sustainable Development: Principles for Environmental Management.
- Social Responsibility Initiative by the Foundation for Ethics and Meaning.

One of the organisations that is recognised as a leading example for its commitment to corporate responsibility is Levi Strauss & Co. Operating in over 60 countries, with a turnover in excess of $7 billion, Levi Strauss stresses values and social standards. According to its Chairman and CEO, Robert Haas:

> A company's values – what it stands for, what it believes in – are critical to its competitive success. Indeed, values drive the business.

Levi Strauss's mission statement is:

> To sustain responsible commercial success as a global marketing company of branded apparel, we must balance goals of superior profitability and return on investment, leadership market positions and superior product and services. We will conduct our business ethically and demonstrate leadership in satisfying our responsibilities to our communities and to society. Our work environment will be safe and productive and characterised by fair treatment, teamwork, open communications, personal accountability and opportunities for growth and development.

Levi Strauss was given several recognitions and awards for its commitments to global socially responsible practices.

Table 12.2 The CERES Principles

	Environmental area	Principles
1.	Sustainable use of natural resources	We will make sustainable use of renewable natural resources, such as water, soils and forests. We will conserve non-renewable natural resources through efficient use and careful planning
2.	Protection of the biosphere	We will reduce and make continual progress toward eliminating the release of any substance that may cause environmental damage to the air, water or the earth or its inhabitants. We will safeguard all habitats affected by our operations and will protect open spaces and wilderness, while preserving biodiversity
3.	Reduction and disposal of wastes	We will reduce and where possible eliminate waste through source reduction and recycling. All waste will be handled and disposed of through safe and responsible methods
4.	Energy conservation	We will conserve energy and improve efficiency of our internal operations and of the goods and services we sell. We will make every effort to use environmentally safe and sustainable energy sources
5.	Risk reduction	We will strive to minimise the environmental, health and safety risks to our employees and the communities in which we operate through safe technologies, facilities and operating procedures and by being prepared for emergencies
6.	Safe products and services	We will reduce and where possible eliminate the use, manufacture or sale of products and services that cause environmental damage or health or safety hazards. We will inform our customers of the environmental impacts of our products or services and try to correct unsafe use
7.	Environmental restoration	We will promptly and responsibly correct conditions we have caused that endanger health, safety or the environment. To the extent where this is feasible, we will redress injuries we have caused to the environment and will restore the environment
8.	Informing the public	We will inform in a timely manner everyone who may be affected by conditions caused by our company that might endanger health, safety or the environment. We will regularly seek advice and counsel through dialogue with persons in communities or our facilities. We will not take any action against employees for reporting dangerous incidents or conditions to management or appropriate authorities
9.	Management commitment	We will implement these principles and sustain a process that ensures the Board of Directors and CEO are fully informed about pertinent environmental issues and are fully responsible for environmental policy. In selecting our Board of Directors we will consider demonstrating environmental commitment as a factor
10.	Audits and reports	We will conduct an annual self-evaluation of our progress in implementing these principles. We will support the timely creation of generally accepted environmental audit procedures. We will annually complete a CERES report which will be made available to the public

Source: adapted from *Green Money Journal* (1996)

Best practice examples in social responsibility and accountability

Royal Mail and its focus on the community

As one of the largest employers in the UK, Royal Mail has made significant commitment to enhance its performance in community issues, to encourage and support employees in various community activities and to ensure that the whole corporate organisation acts as a good and responsible corporate citizen. Royal Mail North East, for instance, has two key aims in its community policy:
1. to support and encourage employees in their chosen community services; and
2. to demonstrate to the community that as a business, Royal Mail North East is committed to improving its environment and the opportunities available for the diversity of people who live in it.

The process of getting support for community-based activity is illustrated in Figure 12.1. A request sheet to apply for support is illustrated in Figure 12.2.

Royal Mail is discussed in detail in the case study in Chapter 14.

Figure 12.1 Support for community-based activity process

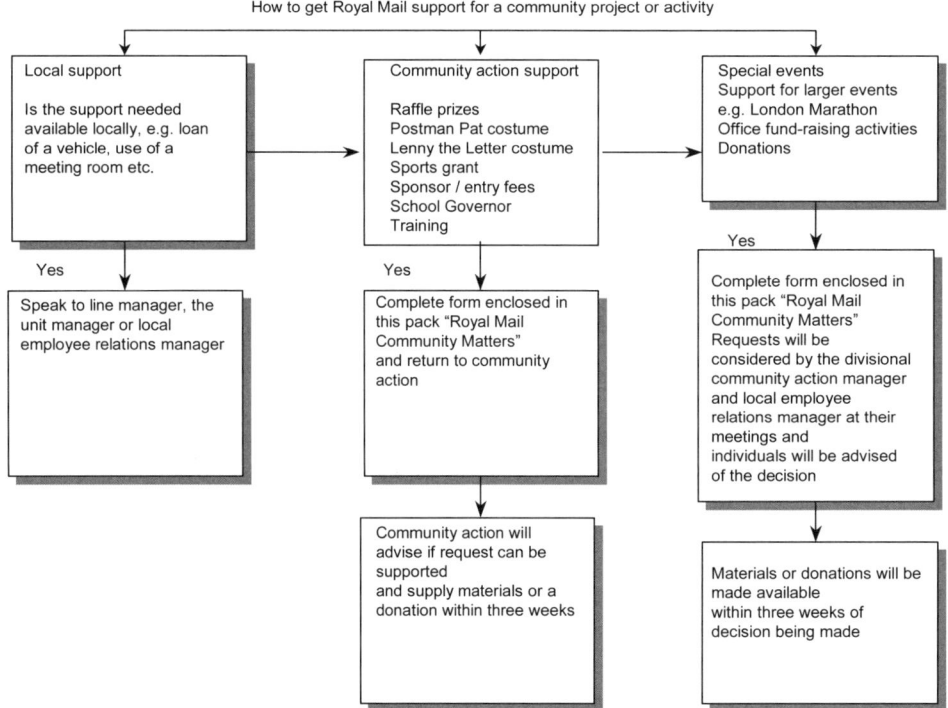

Lever Bros. Ltd

Lever employs people on the following principles in order to focus effectively on societal value added:
1. We recognise that our employment policy, not least the commitment to training and personal development and our emphasis on safety, health and environment, has a positive impact on the world outside the working environment.
2. We improve the well-being of society at large both by the generation of employment in companies which service and supply us and in our marketing activities.
3. We use a world class expertise base in human safety to ensure the consumer safety of our products.

4. We take great care to minimise the environmental impact on all our operations – from raw material procurement, product design, manufacture and distribution to use and disposal.
5. Lever has a long and proud tradition of involvement with the community. This originated when William Hesketh Lever first established Port Sunlight village to improve the living conditions and well being of his employees.

Figure 12.2 Community action support request sheets

```
                    Community Action
                    Special Event Support

1  Please give details of the project or event you would like support for, including the date


2  What type of support would you like Royal Mail to provide?


3  If you are raising money please give an estimate of how much you hope to raise?


4  What opportunities are there for publicity at the event?


5  Have you spoken to your Area Communications Manager or Courier about publicity for the event?
   Yes ☐   No ☐
        If you take photos of your event or activity please send them in. We would like to see them!
        Just put your name and address on the reverse so we can return them to you
```

Lever as a source of business/employment. As Figure 12.3 illustrates, Lever makes considerable expenditure in generating opportunities for industrial people and businesses in the communities where it has operations. Employment is generated in many areas including:
- Raw and packaging material suppliers.
- Packaging and process plan manufacturers.
- Distribution and transport providers.
- Market research and advertising agencies.
- Design and artwork agencies.
- Mechanical, electrical and civil contracts.
- Service and support agencies.

Figure 12.3 Lever's support for business and employment

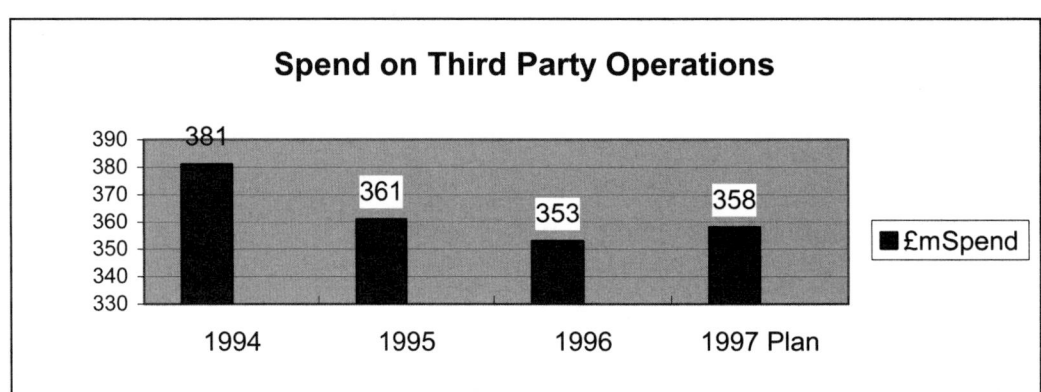

Environmental policies and activities. Lever is a founder member of ERRA (The European Recovery and Recycling Association) and has recently become a committed signatory to the AISE Code of Good Environmental practice, with specific European targets to be achieved in the next five year period.

There is involvement in various schemes including, for instance:
- The Merseyside Industrial Consumer Awards (MICA) offering solutions to business nominated problems.
- Supply of training/support to the introduction of Investors in People schemes in local schools.
- European Summer Placement Scheme which provides 10-12 week industrial placements for students from other countries in Europe.
- Factory tours specifically targeted at schools.

As far as community involvement programmes are concerned, these are founded on three principles:
1. The company devotes the equivalent of at least 1 per cent of its pre-tax profit to community involvement in the form of donations, time and materials (Figure 12.4).
2. Lever's involvement is targeted and focused on charitable work, supporting education, health and welfare.
3. Lever encourages direct contact between employees and the local community.

Figure 12.4 Lever's charitable contributions

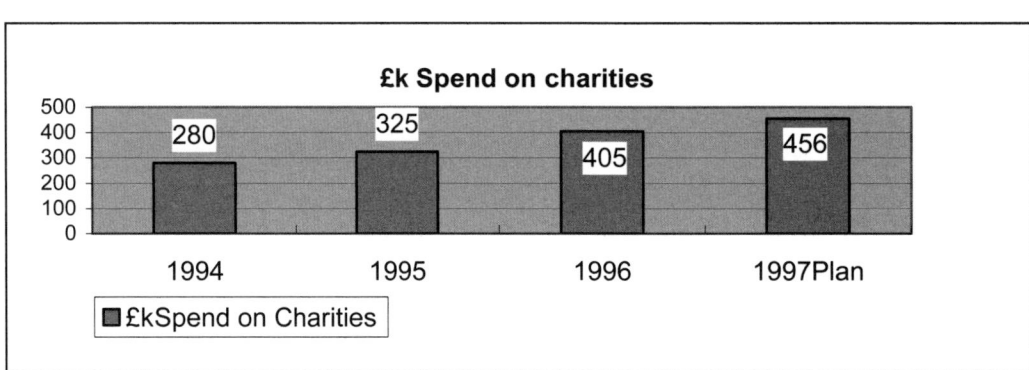

References

Elkington, J. (1999), "The link between accountability and sustainability – theory put into practice", Conference on the Practice of Social Reporting for Business, ISEA, Tuesday 19 January, Commonwealth Conference Centre, London.

Elkington J., Van Dijak, F., Delbe, C. and Terry, V. (1998), *The Social Reporting Report*, Sustainability Publications, 49-53 Kensington High Street, London.

Green Money Journal (1996), Fall, www.greenmoney.com/gmj/Fall96/htm

Jacques, M.L. (1999) "Applying quality concepts to community issues", *Quality Progress*, March, pp. 49-56.

Juran, J.M. (1994) "The upcoming century of quality", *Annual Quality Congress Proceedings*, ASQ, Milwaukee, WI.

Nelson, J. (1998), "Leadership companies in the 21st century: creating shareholder value and societal value", *Visions of Ethical Business*, No. 1, October, Financial Times Management, London, pp. 21-6.

Chapter 13
Benchmarking performance for business excellence

Introduction

A quest for quality and the pursuit of excellence in business practices and performance standards bring very tangible benefits. The link between a commitment to TQM and bottom line results is now beyond any doubt. Several studies have consistently indicated supporting evidence, using different industry sectors and in different parts of the world.

The Baldrige Index (fictitious index), for instance, was used in the USA to track the performance of finalists and winners of the MBNQA against the Standard & Poor's 500 Index. According to Harry Hertz, director of the National Institute of Standards and Technology (NITS) Baldrige National Quality Program, the "Baldrige Index" has outperformed the Standard & Poor's 500 Index for the third year running. He said that:

> While stock market performance is only one indicator of business success, this study demonstrates that a quality approach to running a business can be financially profitable and can lead to increased productivity, satisfied employees and customers and a competitive advantage (*US Department of Commerce News*, 1997).

The Baldrige Index 1996 study

A hypothetical sum of $1,000 was invested in a group of publicly traded site visited and winning companies. After adjusting for stock splits, the site visited applicants and winners, together with the group of whole companies visited and winners, performed as shown in Table 13.1. The results showed that:

- 48 publicly-traded site visited applicants, as a group, outperformed the S&P 500 by 2:1 thus achieving a 167.5 per cent return compared to a 83.3 per cent return for the S&P 500.
- The group of ten whole company site visited companies outperformed the S&P 500 by more than 2:1, thus achieving a 185.9 per cent return compared to a 83.8 per cent return for the S&P 500.
- The group of 35 site visited applicants without the winners outperformed the S&P 500 by 68 per cent, achieving a 138.3 per cent return compared to a 82 per cent return for the S&P 500.
- The six whole company site visited applicants without the winners did not outperform the S&P 500. This group achieved a 60.6 per cent return, while the S&P 500 achieved a return of 80.8 per cent.

Table 13.2 illustrates the results of the Baldrige winners and S&P 500 common stock comparison.

Table 13.1 Baldrige applicants and S&P 500 common stock comparison, 1990-1995

1990-1995	$ invested	Value 12/2/96	Change %
Site visited applicants			
Baldrige Index	16,387.98	43,838	167.5
S&P 500	16,387.98	30,032	83.3
Site visited, whole company applicants			
Baldrige Index	10,000	28,586	185.9
S&P 500	10,000	18,376	83.8

Table 13.2 Baldrige winners and S&P 500 common stock comparison, 1988-1995

1988-1995	$ invested	Value 12/2/96	Change %
Publicly-traded winners			
Baldrige Index	6,485.27	27,554	324.9
S&P 500	6,485.27	13,738	111.8
Publicly-traded, whole company winners			
Baldrige Index	5,000	24,008	380.2
S&P 500	5,000	10,481	109.6

Table 13.2 illustrates that:
- 16 publicly-traded winners, as a group, outperformed the S&P 500 by approximately 3:1, achieving a 324.9 per cent return compared to a 111.8 per cent return for the S&P 500.
- The group of five whole company winners outperformed the S&P 500 by 3.5:1, achieving a 380.2 per cent return compared to a 109.6 per cent return for the S&P 500.

Malcolm Baldrige National Quality Award, whole company winners used in the study were:
- Eastman Chemical Company.
- Federal Express Corporation.
- Motorola, Inc.
- Solectron Corporation.
- Zytec Corporation.

The calculation used for the subunits was: $1,000 (sum invested) × the percentage of the parent company's employee base that the subunit represented at the time it applied. Subunit winners used in the study were:
- Armstrong World Industries, Inc., Building Products Operations.
- AT&T Consumer Communication Services (now part of the Consumer and Small Business Division of AT&T).
- AT&T Network Systems, Transmission Systems Business Unit (now part of Lucent Technologies, Inc., Network Systems).
- AT&T Universal Card Services.
- Cadillac Motor Car Company (subunit of General Motors).
- Corning Telecommunications Products Division.
- GTE Directories Corporation.

- IBM Rochester.
- Texas Instruments Incorporated, Defense Systems and Electronics Group (now part of the Systems Group of Texas Instruments).
- Westinghouse Electric Corporation, Commercial Nuclear Fuel Division.
- Xerox Corporation, Business Products and Systems.

Although the "Baldrige Index" is fictitious, it does reflect the strength of world class organisations whose logging performance indicators are a reflection of the significant improvements carried out in all aspects of their business operations. Some of the leading performance indicators are covered in Appendix 13.1.

Further evidence that a commitment to TQM does ultimately impact on performance improvement and bottom line results is provided through the following examples:

- Federal Express, the first company to win the MBNQA, became the first US company to top the $1 billion in revenues within the first ten years and it has a commanding 43 per cent of the air express market.
- Motorola (a 1988 winner) achieved cumulative manufacturing cost savings of $5.5 billion from 1988 to the second quarter of 1994 and saw its stockholders' share value increase fourfold.
- Xerox (a 1989 winner) had a return on assets which was at a 15 year high and stock at a 20 year high.
- Wallace Co. (a 1990 winner) saw profits increase 7.4 times between 1987 and 1989 and this was directly attributed to quality successes. During that time absenteeism fell by 50 per cent and is now less than half the industry average.
- IBM Rochester (a 1990 winner) has increased productivity and through a TQ focus has improved the cost of ownership of its products to among the lowest in the industry.
- Solectron Corp. (a 1991 winner) increased its sales from $130 million to $1.455 billion and net profits from $4 million to $56 million. Its stock price has achieved an average growth of 82 per cent.
- Marlow Industries (a 1991 winner) increased its sales by 35 per cent; productivity by 33 per cent and work force by 60 per cent. Evidence that TQM does not result in a reduced work force and lower staff costs.
- Zytec (a 1991 winner) had sales per employee of $100,000 compared to an industry average of less than $80,000. Since 1988 it has achieved a 50 per cent improvement in manufacturing yield, a 26 per cent reduction in manufacturing cycle time and warranty costs down by 48 per cent. Product costs were also cut by between 30 per cent and 40 per cent depending on the product line.
- Ritz-Carlton Hotel Co. (a 1992 winner) used its quality management system to eliminate $75 million of waste through project improvement. Profitability is now best in its class among high grade hotels.
- Ames Rubber Corp. (a 1993 winner) achieved a 99.9 per cent quality and on-time delivery status through sharing its TQ techniques with its suppliers.
- AT&T (a 1994 winner) reduced the time taken to develop new products by 50 per cent and in the GTE Directories was the preferred supplier in 271 of 274 primary markets.

The Bradford study
The Bradford study (Zairi *et al.*, 1997) identified 29 companies within the UK which displayed characteristics associated with TQM. These characteristics included leadership, hard and soft elements. Nine measures were used to compare its performance with the median for the particular industry over the period 1991 to 1995. Results were also compared to the 1987 to 1991 findings and conclusions drawn.

The companies studied produced the following successes:
- 81 per cent were above the industry median for turnover per employee;
- 81 per cent of the companies produced a higher salary to turnover ratio than their peers;
- 74 per cent of the organisations remunerated their employees above the median for the industry;
- 65 per cent of the organisations produced above median profit per employee for their industry; and
- 62 per cent of the organisations had a higher net asset turnover than their peer group.

Four of the nine measures were marginally below the median for their industry, but this was expected as quality becomes institutionalised and more widespread. The performance gap between the 29 companies and others was much narrower than in 1991 now that many organisations have adopted TQM practices and behaviours, either in part or in total:
- 48 per cent more highly geared;
- 45 per cent profit margin;
- 47 per cent return on capital employed; and
- 48 per cent return on assets.

Further evidence that in Europe too, TQM can be demonstrated to have a direct impact on bottom line results is provided through the following examples.

Europe
D2D (a 1994 winner) has been able to reduce its lead times to as low as eight days for main frames which are configured to user requirements and a one day turnaround on personal systems which is on par with the industry benchmark. Profits increased by 50 per cent in the two years since it changed from the company with a captive supplier and prime focus on cost reduction rather than profit before tax to autonomous status.

Texas Instruments Europe (a 1995 winner) achieved a return on assets increase from 1.5 per cent in 1993 to 8 per cent in 1994. Semi-conductor revenues increased by 35 per cent, reversing a ten year decline and gaining market share of 5.7 per cent. Their annual running costs were down by $55 million. A 95 per cent delivery on time was achieved.

Alcatel Austria (a 1995 finalist) achieved an average 12 per cent sales growth and the return on sales is above industry sector average. Productivity per head has grown by 70 per cent since 1989. Its manufacturing rejection rates have declined by 53 per cent and component failures by 72 per cent.

Netas (a 1995 finalist) is a joint venture between Turkish PTT and Northern Telecom Canada (Nortell). A valuation on the Istanbul Stock Exchange indicated that it has increased by 11.3 times since its first quotation in 1993. This was against an Istanbul Stock Exchange index of 4.5.

United Kingdom

The British Quality Award (BQA) utilises the EFQM framework and is a much more recent innovation, with the first winners announced in 1994.

TNT (joint 1994 winner) in 15 years has grown from a £7 million per annum to £7 million per week organisation. Its commitment to quality has been a major factor in its success, although it has resisted the use of TQM jargon and regards the tools, techniques and behaviours as business as usual. Its commitment to customer satisfaction is evident when it claims that 99.4 per cent on-time delivery is still not good enough. It is this focus on the customer which has led to a 3,000 strong vehicle fleet, 8,000 staff and 300 locations. Their debtors came down from 7.5 weeks to five weeks and overdue debts from 20 per cent to 0 per cent in eight years. Alan Jones, the Chief Executive and Director at TNT, states that "you may not win but if you have beaten your previous best you have won a personal battle. That is the whole essence of continuous improvement".

Rover (joint 1994 winner) is Britain's largest motor manufacturer, producing around 500,000 small, medium and executive cars and specialist four wheel drive vehicles a year. It is a major employer with 33,000 people directly working for the company and a further 110,000 working in companies supplying production materials and services to the Rover Group. The purchase of Rover Group by BMW for £800 million in 1994 received mixed reaction, with the Prime Minister hailing it as a vote of confidence in British industry. The transformation of Rover has been outstanding and much can be attributed to its 16 year collaboration with Honda. John Towers, Rover's Chief Executive in 1995, stated "The Japanese philosophy is straightforward – get design of products and processes right". Its quality programme has evolved from quality awareness where a few champions try initiatives. Quality promotion follows with everyone striving to promote quality, but not all in the same direction. Then, development is where quality management becomes part of the business process and common goals are defined. Finally, quality empowerment evolves, where everyone is engaged in planned and voluntary self-sustaining improvement activity.

ICL HPT (1995 winner) now has 25 per cent of the UK large computer systems market and over 1,800 installed systems world-wide. Fifteen new business gains were achieved in 1993/1994 and confirmations have been received from existing customers such as Inland Revenue, British Gas and DHSS to maintain and upgrade their systems through ICL HPT.

Mortgage Express (1996 winner), in 1992, had losses of £70 million and was looking to withdraw from the market. A new Managing Director (MD) was appointed in 1991 to manage the winding down, but he decided to embark on a TQM journey. The MD could not offer staff a career as the future was uncertain but he could offer an opportunity for their own personal development. This focus on TQM, combined with an improvement in the market place, returned the organisation to profit in 1993 and it currently employs over 300 staff. Its performance measurement has focused on customer value, shareholder value and employee perceptions, all of which have significantly improved the bottom line results.

BT Northern Ireland (a 1996 finalist) has had turnover growth of 22 per cent in the last five years with costs only rising 4 per cent.

Lawson Mardon Plastics (a 1996 finalist) has had an average annual sales growth since 1991 of 15 per cent with a 10 per cent return on sales. Sales per employee were £80,000.

Ulster Carpets (1996 winner) produced a profit of £3.1 million on a turnover of £39 million in 1995. It won the Northern Ireland Quality Award in 1991 and is now ISO 9001 certified. The quality drive was re-launched in 1992 when suppressed market demand, due to a crumbling of the UK housing market, placed an ever higher premium on providing levels of customer service and product quality that the competition could not match. The "total customer satisfaction" programme, started in 1989, marked the beginning of a formal commitment to quality management techniques and involved the training of all 700 staff.

Satisfaction was developed to "delight" in 1991 so that any customer who is not delighted with the product during the first 60 days is able to have a refund irrespective of whether or not it is due to a company fault.

Business Intelligence commented that although award criteria are well defined and achievements are measured in detail the award system does not provide advice on how to achieve the objective. However, organisations based within the UK are committed to quality and are producing exceptional results.

D2D, TNT and Ulster Carpets are discussed in detail as case studies in Chapter 14.

Benchmarking performance for business excellence

The previous sections have clearly demonstrated that a commitment to TQM and continuous improvement can have a direct impact on bottom line results.

For any organisation aspiring to world class status, therefore, the potential for identifying gaps in performance and learning to use best practices can be made possible. This book outlines a huge catalogue of practices found to be embraced by winners and finalists of the most prestigious, international quality awards such as the European Quality Award and the Malcolm Baldrige National Quality Award (MBNQA).

Using data of winners and finalists of British Quality Award, European Quality Award and Malcolm Baldrige National Quality Award provides the basis for benchmarking organisational performance from an overall business perspective or criteria specific approach.

Overall business performance

Organisations have the opportunity to benchmark their self-assessment scores against the median of best-in-class companies in the UK, Europe and the USA. As Figure 13.1 illustrates, Company A's overall score has been benchmarked and this can assist senior management in reflecting on the overall performance and in positioning the state of maturity of their TQM programmes against world class standards. Figure 13.2, on the other hand, represents the degree of emphasis on the various criteria of the business excellence model. Each organisation can see whether it needs to focus more on the enabler side (building capability) or managing performance results (reaping the benefits).

Benchmarking individual criteria

Individual organisations also have the opportunity to benchmark their performance against each individual criteria of the business excellence model. Figure 13.3, for instance, illustrates how Company A performs against median scores of British Quality Award winners and finalists/applicants. Figure 13.4, on the other hand, shows how Company A fares against winners, finalists and applicants of the European Quality Award. Seniors managers can identify specific gaps in performance and therefore develop a series of specific action plans to close benchmark gaps.

Benchmarking against aggregate scores

It is possible to see the extent of the gap in performance by amplifying each specific score against the combined gaps from the BQA and EQA sets of data. Table 13.3 demonstrates how Company A fares against the median scores of the BQA and the EQA. The individual gaps in performance are then aggregated to look at the true extent in performance gaps.

Best Practice Organisational Excellence

Figure 13.1 Benchmarking Company A self-assessment score

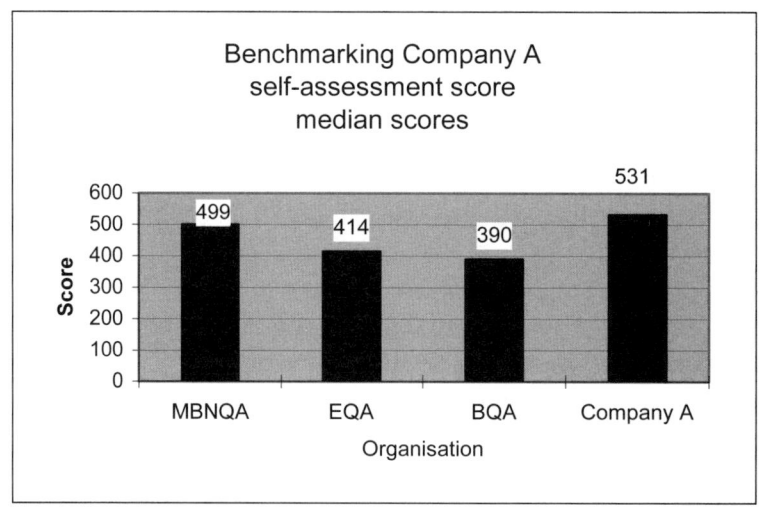

Figure 13.2 Plotting performance gaps

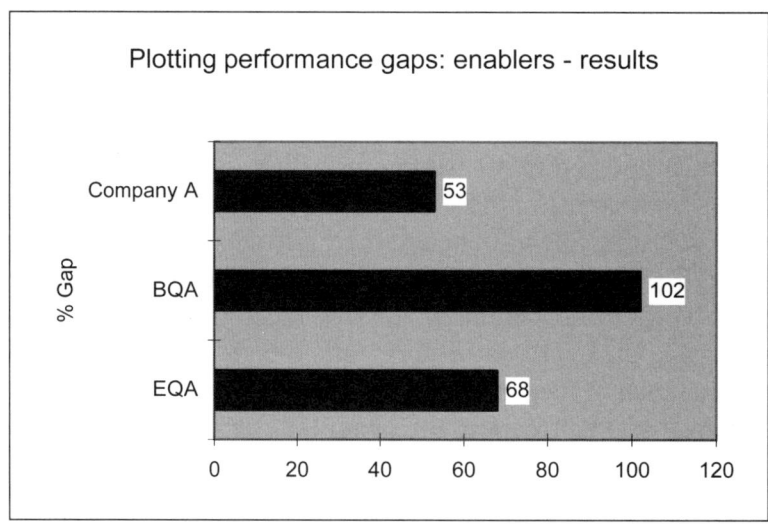

Figure 13.3 Benchmarking Company A vs BQA self-assessment median

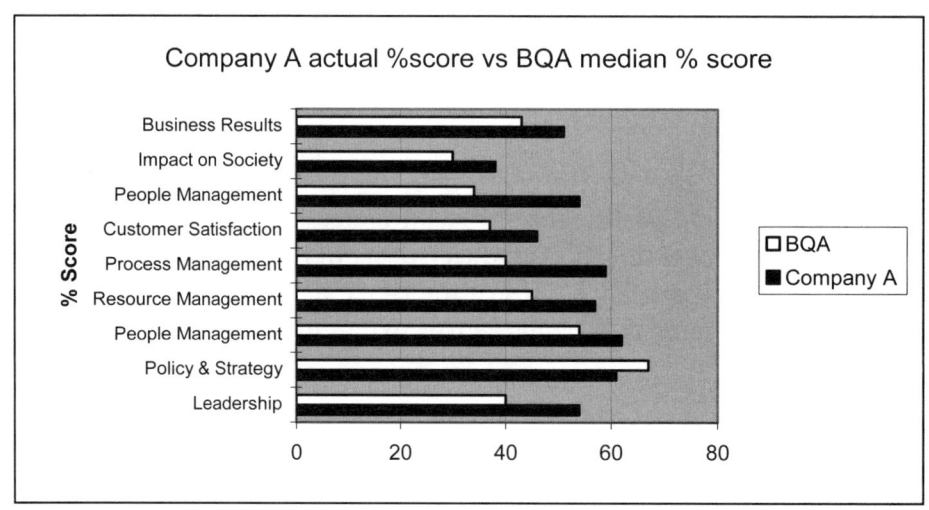

Figure 13.4 Benchmarking Company A vs EQA self-assessment median

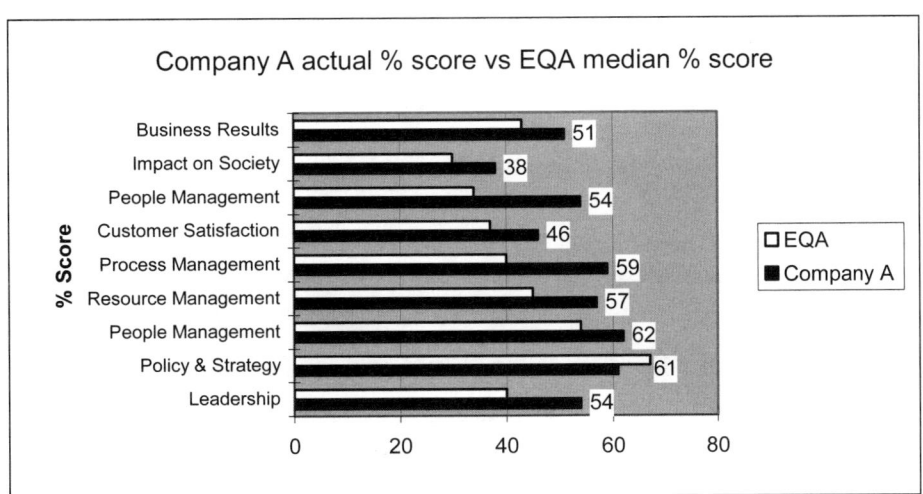

Table 13.3 Measuring performance gap for Company A self-assessment performance

	Company A	EQA	BQA	Gap 1 EQA-Co. A	Gap 2 BQA-Co. A	Total gap
Leadership	54	46	40	-8	-14	-22
Policy and strategy	61	48	67	-13	6	-7
People management	62	49	54	-13	-8	-21
Resource management	57	51	45	-6	-12	-18
Process management	59	47	40	-12	-19	-31
Customer satisfaction	46	45	37	-1	-9	-10
People satisfaction	54	40	34	-14	-20	-34
Impact on society	38	40	30	2	-8	-6
Business results	51	48	43	-3	-8	-11

As Figure 13.5 indicates, in the case of Company A, gaps in its performance have been aggregated and the amplified, true performance levels have been clearly identified. In this way senior managers can put in place a well-informed, accurate and factual action plan.

This benchmarking exercise will enable any organisation to answer the questions: what performance gaps are there against world class standards, where specifically are those gaps and also what is the extent of the gaps in question? Other sections of the book explain how performance gaps can be closed and what makes some organisations achieve world class status. A catalogue of best practices embraced by best-in-class organisations and extensive methodologies and approaches used by model companies which enable them to achieve winning performance scores are covered elsewhere in this book. Appendix 13.2 contains aggregate distribution scores for the BQA, EQA and MBNQA.

Figure 13.5 Measuring performance gap through benchmarking: aggregating gaps in performance from EQA & BQA data criteria

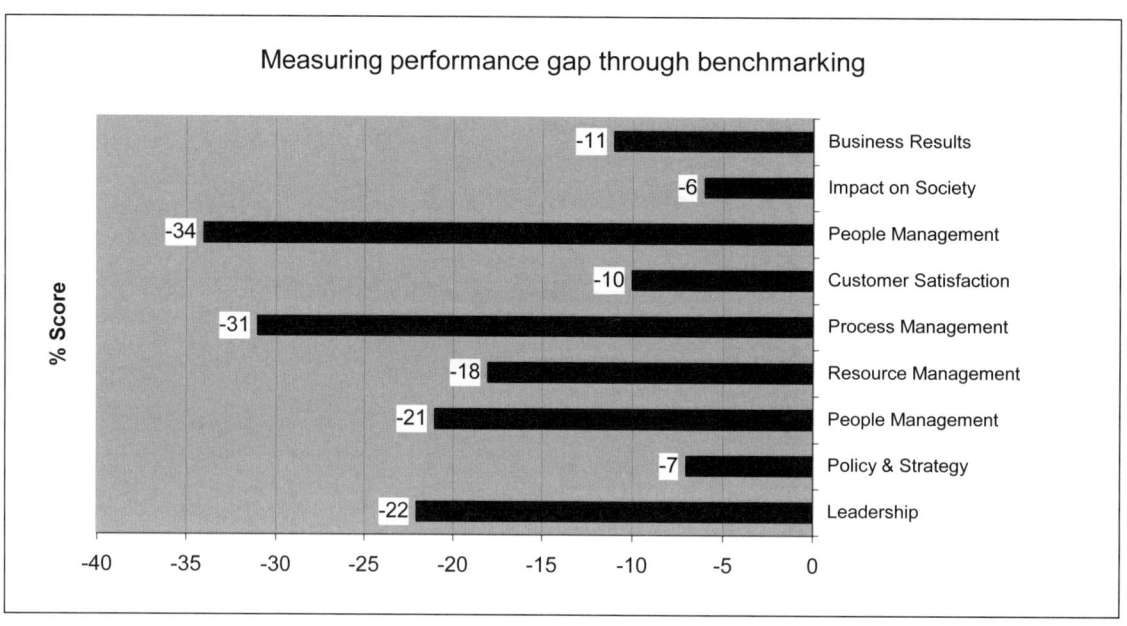

References

US Department of Commerce News (1997), "One more time: latest NIST stock study shows quality pays", NIST, April.

Zairi, M. *et al.* (1997), "Does TQM impact on bottom line results?", Part II Report, European Centre for TQM, University of Bradford, UK, January.

Appendix 13.1 Key successes for winners of the MBNQA

Table 13.4 MBNQA winning companies and their successes

Company	Key successes
Ames Rubber Corp. (1989-92)	55 per cent decrease in suppliers 50 per cent decrease in internal relations 48 per cent increase in sales per employee 22 per cent increase in on time delivery performance $3 million savings due to employee ideas 60 per cent decrease in customer complaints
AT&T Transmisson Systems Business Unit (1989-92)	Ten fold improvement in product quality 50 per cent decrease in new product development time 50 per cent decrease in manufacturing batch sizes 40 per cent decrease in inventories $400 million in cost savings 100 per cent increase in international sales
The Ritz-Carlton Hotel Co. (1989-91)	Three fold increase in TQM expenditures 67 per cent increase in supplier on time deliveries 47 per cent decrease in employee turnover 100 per cent increase in predetermination of repeat customer needs 6 per cent increase in employee satisfaction 8 per cent decrease in hours worked per guest room
Solectron Corp.	50 per cent decrease in average product rejection rate (1987-9) 10 per cent per year average cycle time decrease (1987-91) Ten fold decrease in part defect rate (1984-91)
AT&T Universal Card Systems (1990-92)	Ten fold increase in employees Five decreases in interest rate charged 40 per cent increase in calling card revenues amount Three fold increase in employee suggestions
Texas Instruments Defence Systems & Electronics Group (1987-91)	72 per cent decrease in customer-conducted quality audits Three fold increase in quality teams 62 per cent decrease in customer complaints 66 per cent decrease in an average design cycle time 56 per cent increase in revenue/employee 18 per cent decrease in suppliers
Cadillac Motor Car Co.(1986-89)	27 per cent and 71 per cent decrease in reliability/durability problems 29 per cent decrease in warranty related costs 16 per cent increase in customer satisfaction 29 per cent decrease in styling change time 56 per cent decrease in engineering changes 50 per cent decrease in parts and assembly times of many assemblies
Wallace Co. Inc.	77 per cent increase in market share (1987-90) 84 per cent increase in team participation (1985-90) 600 per cent increase in team participation 800 per cent increase in use of electronic data interchange systems among Wallace suppliers (1988-90-) 23 per cent increase in on time deliveries (1987-90)
Eastman Chemical Co. (1990-92)	50 per cent decrease in new product cycle time Eight fold increase in customer partnership terms 35 per cent decrease in warranty claims

(Continued)

	11 per cent decrease in product/process variability
Three fold increase in per cent complaints resolved in 24hr
Westinghouse Electric Corp. (1983-91)	50 per cent decrease in inventory (Electromar)
66 per cent decrease in design cycle time (Comm. Nuclear Fuel Division)
25 per cent decrease in product defects (Thermo King Division)
74 per cent increase in fuel rod manufacturing yields (Comm. Nuclear Fuel Division)
50 per cent decrease in design cycle time (Assemblies Division)
Ten fold increase in product reliability (Comm. Nuclear Fuel Division)
Federal Express Corp.	1,000 per cent increase in individual performance awards (1985-89)
223 per cent decrease in quality-failure index (1987-90)
71 per cent decrease in package expediting costs (1989-90)
Xerox Corp. (1985-90)	73 per cent increase in incoming supply quality
27 per cent decrease in service response time
78 per cent decrease in machined part defects
38 per cent increase in customer satisfaction
40 per cent decrease in unscheduled maintenance
17 fold increase in use of benchmark measures
Globe Metallurgical Inc. (1895-91)	367 per cent increase in firm productivity, revenue per employee 30 per cent higher than in industry average
63 per cent decrease in quarry truck loading time
Three times more training per employee than industry average
Zytec Corp.	50 per cent increase in manufacturing yields (1988-91)
26 per cent decrease in manufacturing cycle time (1988-91)
Ten fold increase in mean time between failures (1987-91)
50 per cent decrease in design cycle time (1988-91)
48 per cent decrease in warranty costs (1988-90)
IBM Rochester (1984-90)	47 per cent decrease in customer complaints
55 per cent decrease in product write offs
45 per cent decrease in engineering change costs
70 per cent decrease in cycle time for AS/400
35 per cent increase in revenue per employee
Milliken and Co.	72 per cent decrease in suppliers (1981-89)
77 per cent increase in ratio of production/management employees (1981-89)
60 per cent decrease in costs of non-conformance
32 per cent increase in on time deliveries
42 per cent increase in productivity (1981-89)
Marlow Industries Inc.	72 per cent decrease in suppliers
100 per cent increase in the quality training hours per employee (1988-91)
49 per cent decrease in costs of non-conformance (1989-91)
66 per cent increase in material production yield (1988-91)
100 per cent increase in team membership (1988-90)
75 per cent decrease in waste disposal needs (1988-91)
Motorola Inc. (1981-91)	150 fold improvement in in-process defects
$2 billion in cost savings due to quality improvements (1986-91)
97 per cent decrease in cycle time for cellular phones
90 per cent increase in cellular phone reliability
93 per cent decrease in returned order costs
62 per cent decrease in part count for cellular telephones

Appendix 13.2 Percentage distribution of scores
UK Quality Award percentage distribution of scores

Figure 13.6 Leadership category

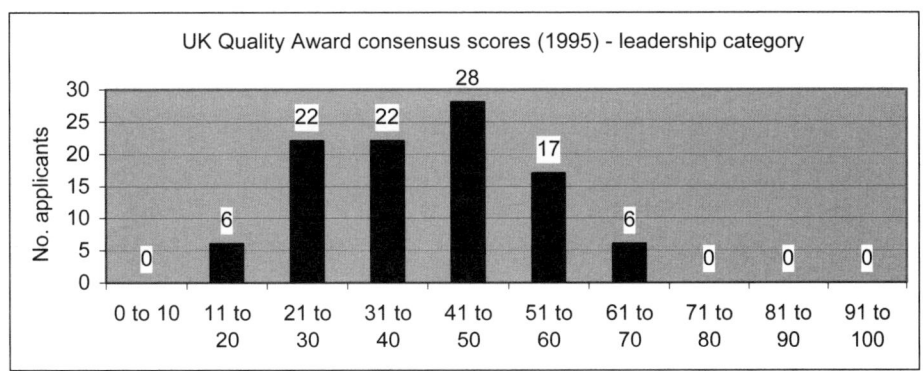

Figure 13.7 Policy and strategy category

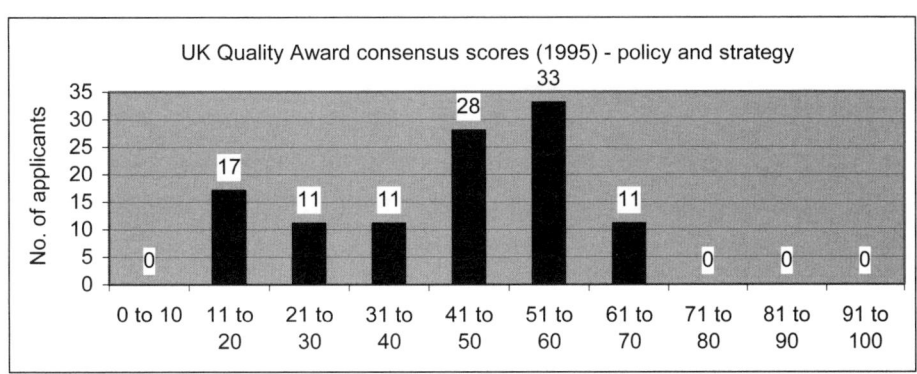

Figure 13.8 Resources category

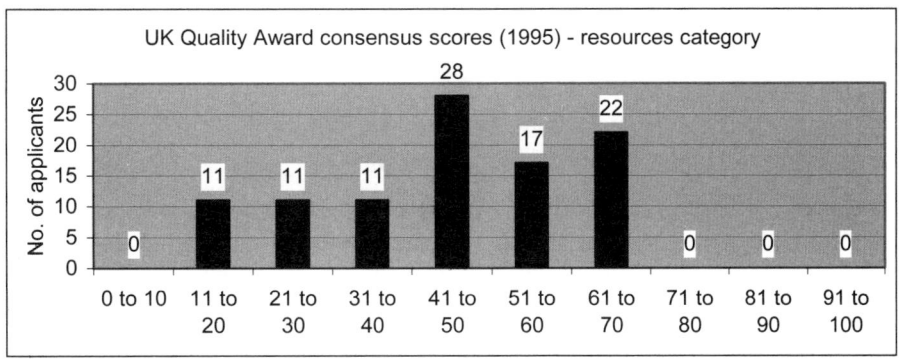

Best Practice Organisational Excellence

Figure 13.9 People management category

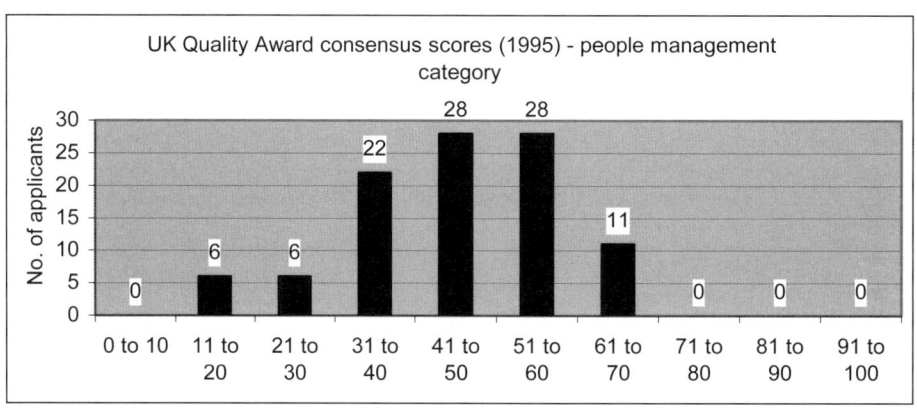

Figure 13.10 Process management category

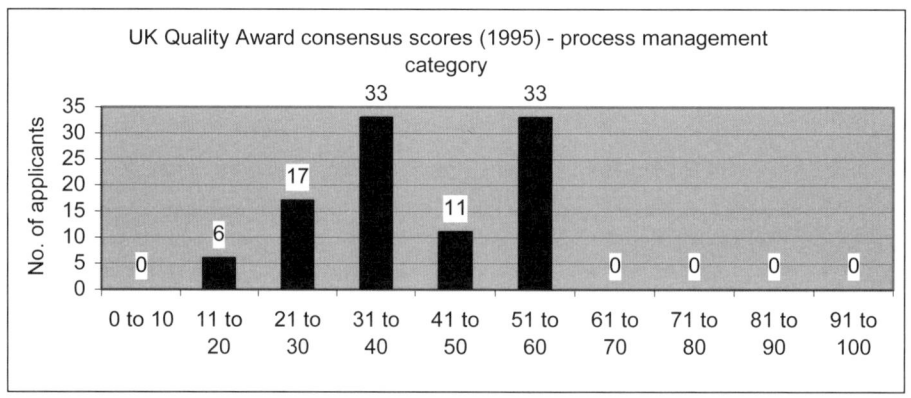

Figure 13.11 Customer satisfaction category

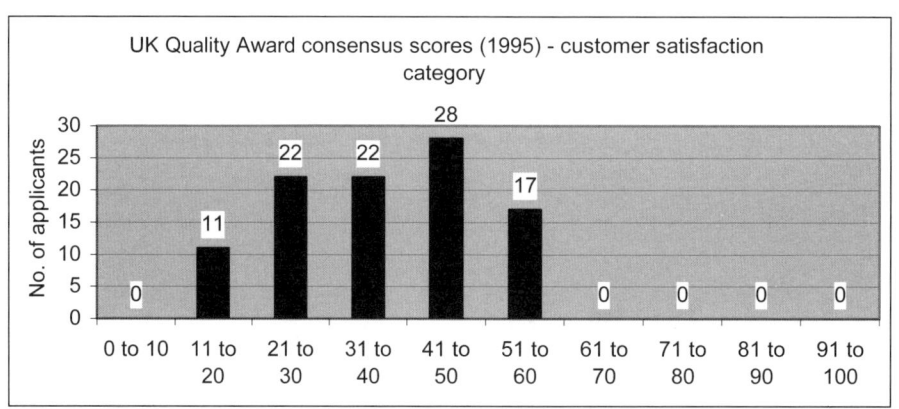

Figure 13.12 People satisfaction category

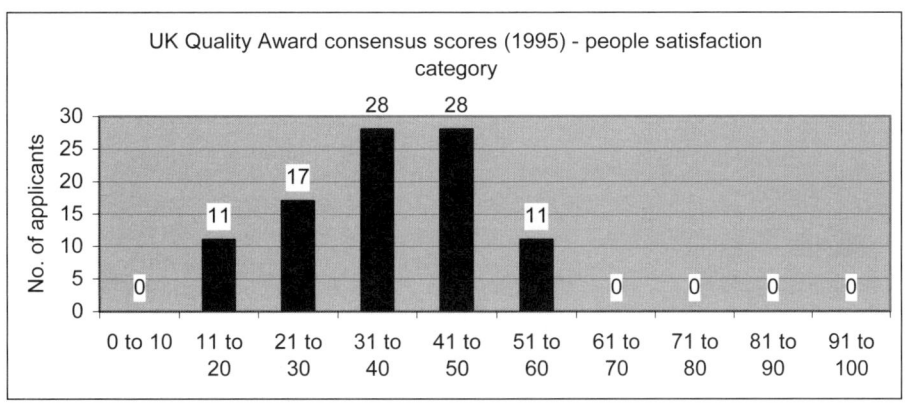

Figure 13.13 Impact on society category

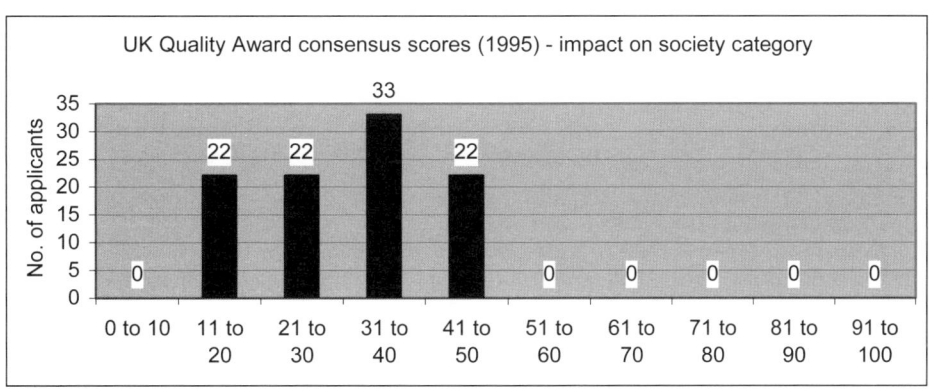

Figure 13.14 Business results category

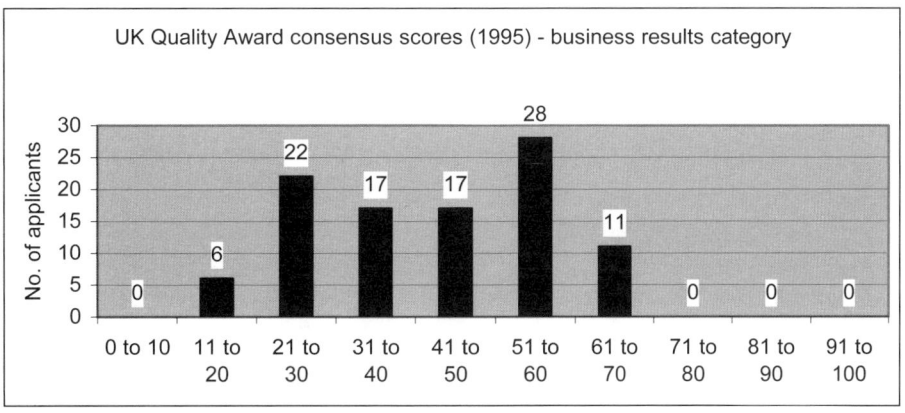

Best Practice Organisational Excellence

European Quality Award percentage distribution of scores

Figure 13.15 Leadership category

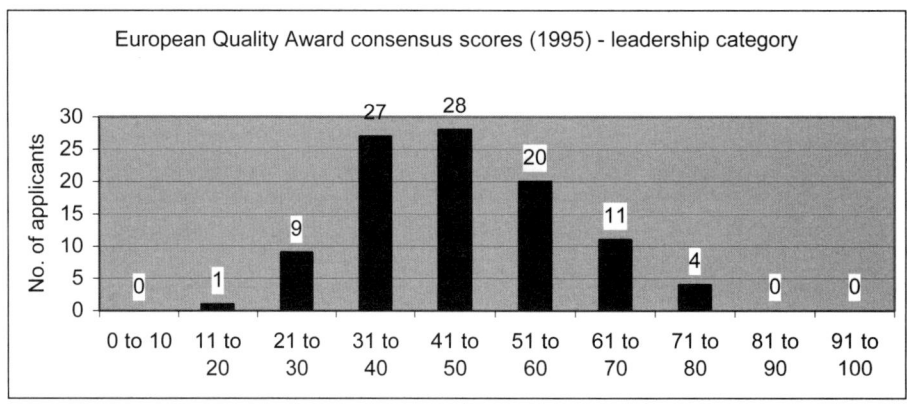

Figure 13.16 Policy and strategy category

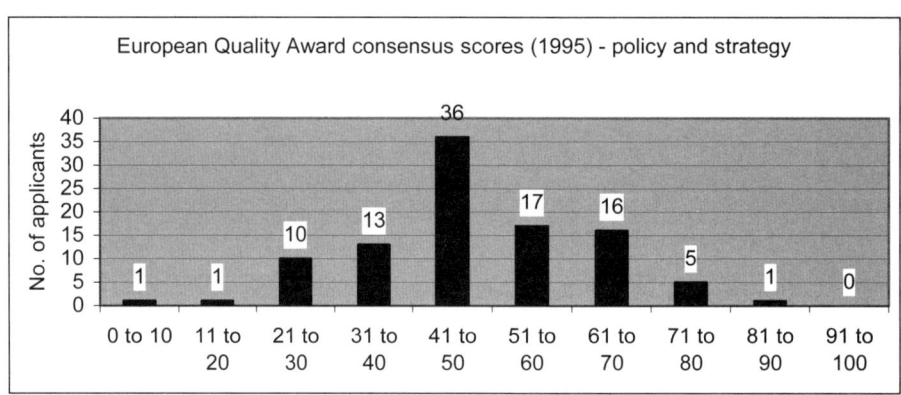

Figure 13.17 Resources category

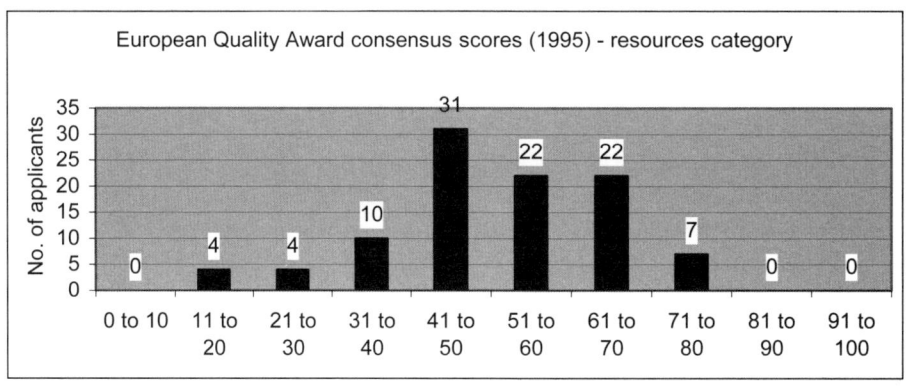

Figure 13.18 People management category

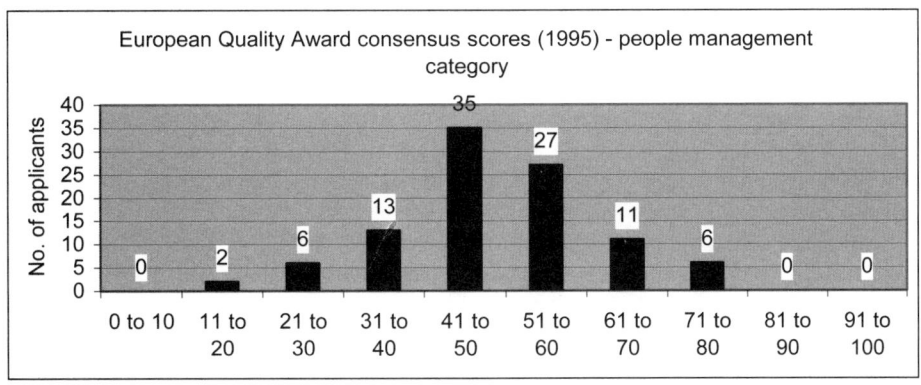

Figure 13.19 Process management category

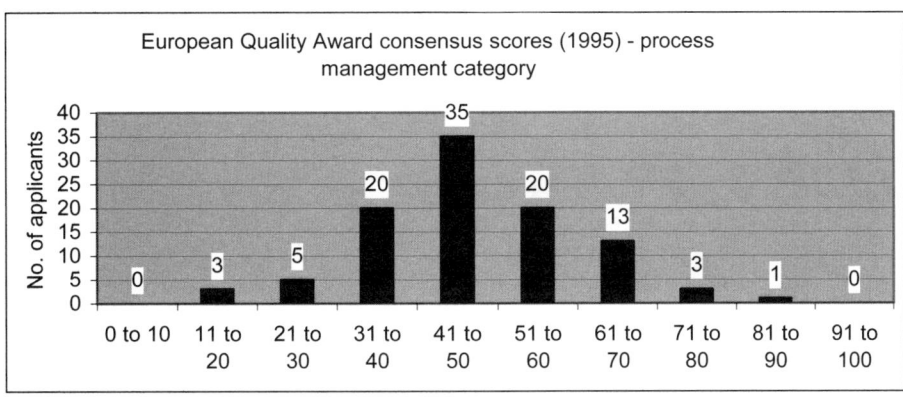

Figure 13.20 Customer satisfaction category

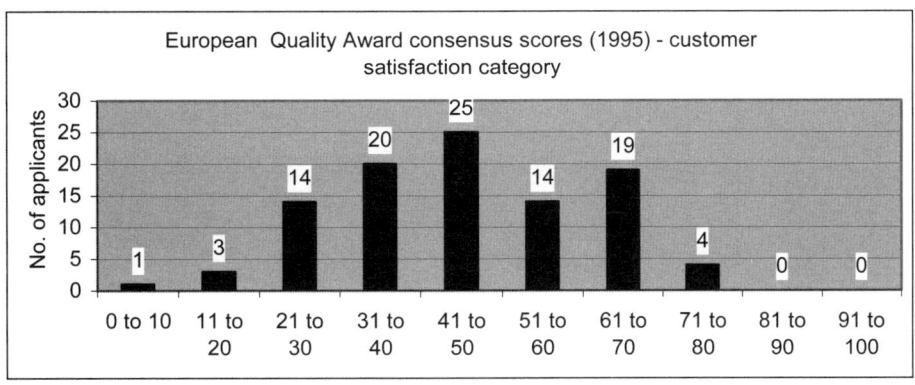

Best Practice Organisational Excellence

Figure 13.21 People satisfaction category

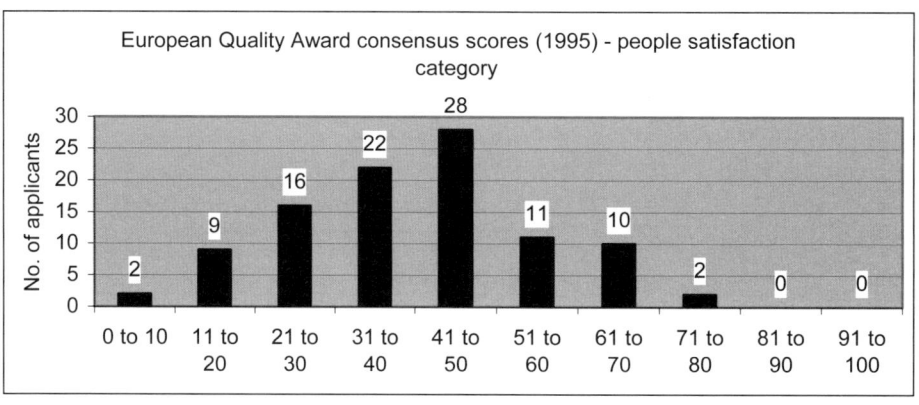

Figure 13.22 Impact on society category

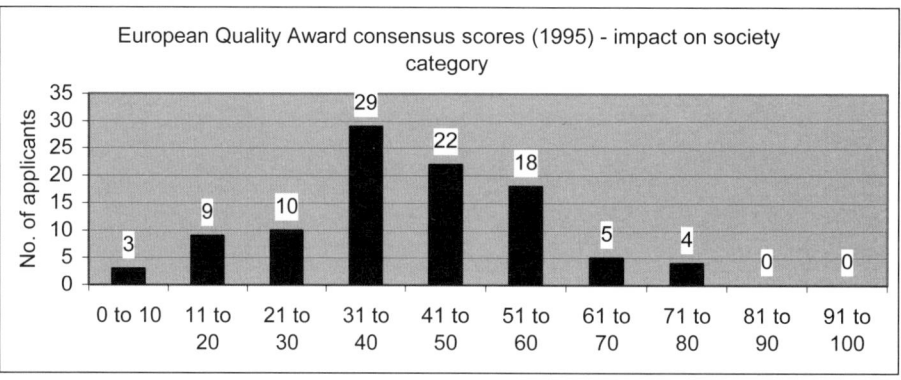

Figure 13.23 Business results category

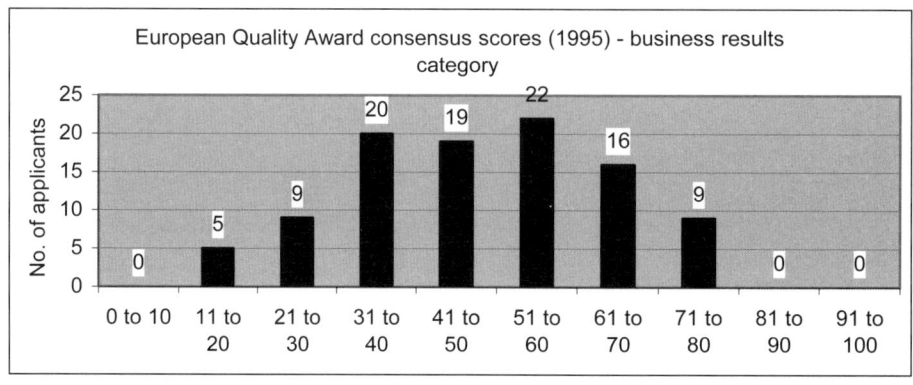

Malcolm Baldrige Award distribution of entry scores 1988-1992

Figure 13.24 1988

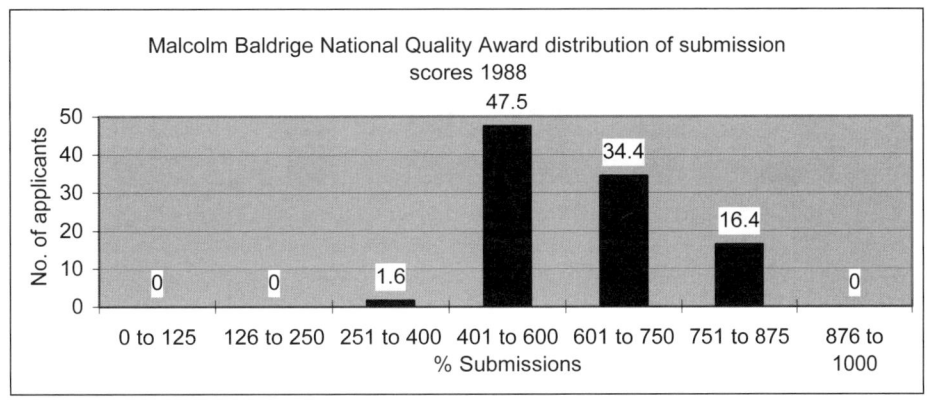

Figure 13.25 1989

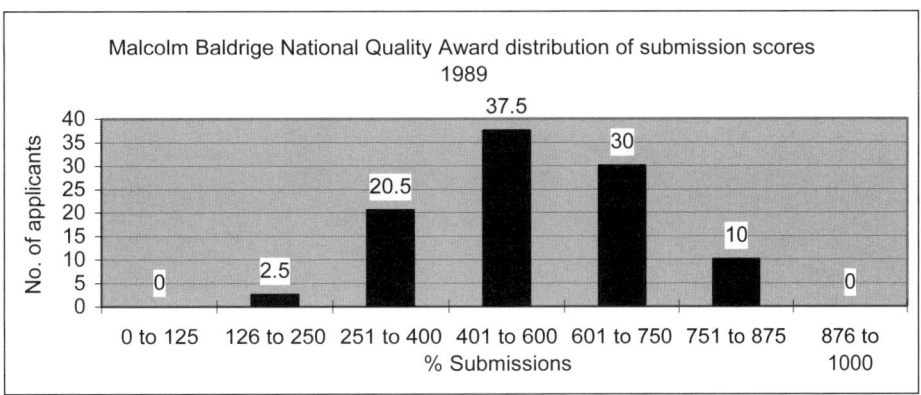

Figure 13.26 1990

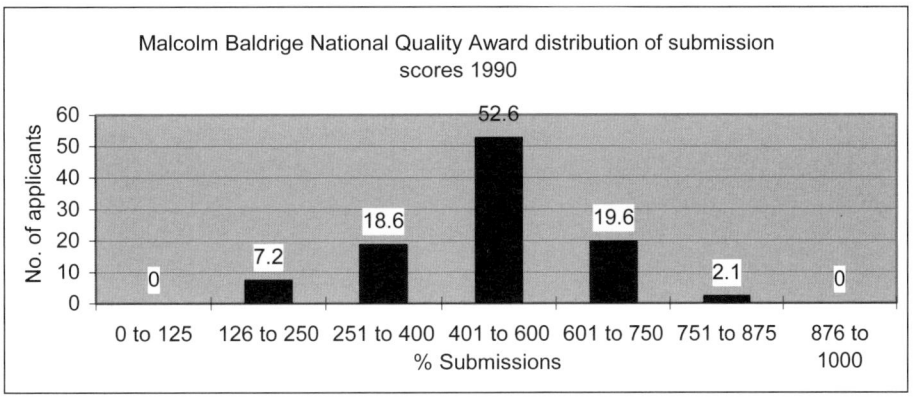

Figure 13.27 1991

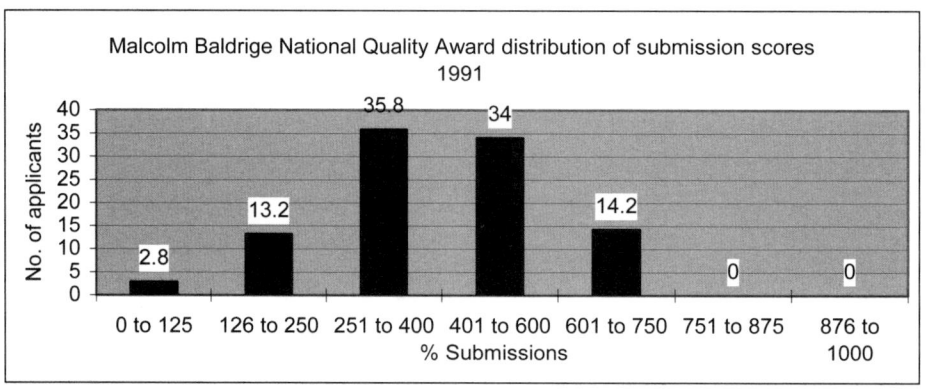

Figure 13.28 1992

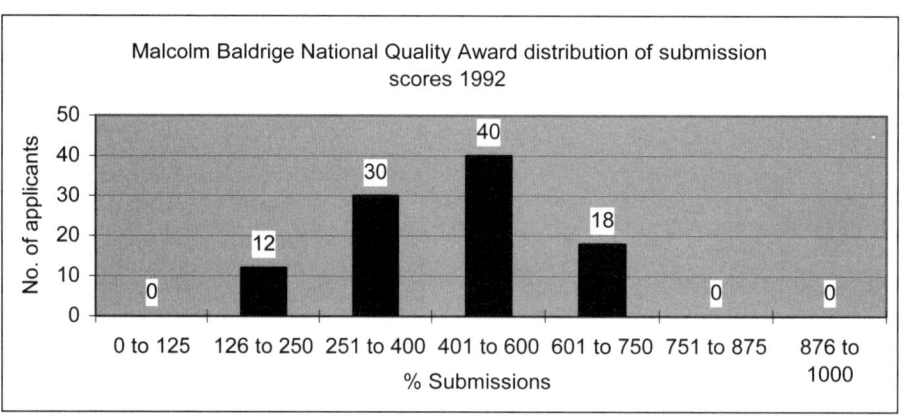

Appendix 13.3 Performance exercise

TNT operates in the very competive environment of parcel carriage and express carriage. TNT is discussed as a case study in Chapter 14. After reading the case study, complete the following exercise.

You have recently taken up a new role as Director of Finance at TNT and one of your first tasks is to review the way in which performance is measured. You have to draw up a list of financial and non-financial measures, but you need to keep the list of measures down to the "vital few".

From the information contained in the case study you are required to compile both financial and non-financial measures which you consider are most suitable and indicate alongside each one, who are the main beneficiaries of this information (shareholder – current or potential, customer, employee, management and/or supplier).

Suggested solution

Table 13.5 Financial and non-financial measures

	Shareholder	Customer	Employee	Management	Supplier
Financial measures	√			√	
Profit as percentage of turnover	√			√	
Budgeted profit as percentage of budgeted turnover				√	
Working capital				√	√
Liquidity				√	√
Net assets employed	√			√	
Non-financial measures					
Productivity – consignments per employee, unit costs			√	√	√
Pricing trends – price premium		√		√	
Product line – breadth of services		√		√	
Market share	√	√	√	√	√
Loss/damage statistics		√		√	
Vehicle accidents			√	√	
Five star performance rating					
Delivered on time		√	√	√	
Failures			√	√	
Delivered on copy notes, unmatched			√	√	
Misroutes			√	√	
Late trucks			√	√	

Chapter 14
Case studies

Rank Xerox
Market and product range
Rank Xerox was founded in 1956 with a specific purpose to manufacture and market reprographics and other office information equipment throughout the world. It has gained a reputation since that date for being a leading high technology company and has many pioneering inventions to its name in reprographics, workstations, laser printers, electronic printing systems and colour copiers.

The organisation achieved rapid growth with revenues of $53 million by 1959 and a major corporation with revenues of $4 billion by 1975. This rapid growth and market position was then challenged by the Japanese companies, particularly in the small, high quality, low priced copier sector and by the 1980s 80 per cent of all copiers in use throughout Europe were Japanese supplied.

The sharp decrease in revenue and profit growth together with a fall in return on capital from 19 per cent in 1980 to just 8.4 per cent in 1983 prompted the drive for quality as a means of survival. That strategy decision has been proven as today they are one of the top 150 companies in Europe, serving over 500,000 customers, employing 26,000 people in Europe, working with 400 component suppliers and earning revenues of £2.5 billion per year.

The extensive customer base represents every level of commercial, industrial and government organisation and the customers' different needs are met through a product range of more than 300 systems, including advanced information storage and retrieval technology.

Launch of total quality initiatives
A series of benchmarking studies undertaken in the late 1970s to determine the underlying reasons for competitor success from Japan triggered the need for total quality management if Rank Xerox was to survive in the future. The studies revealed that Rank Xerox was currently at a disadvantage in terms of cost and quality, together with being slower to introduce new products than its Japanese competitors. Consequently it was losing market share and in danger of going out of business.

The benchmarking studies and experience from Fuji-Xerox in Japan resulted in the Leadership Through Quality programme introduced in 1984 which, through various evolutions to take account of changing needs, is still running today. Initially the business focus was on product quality and cost but was redefined as establishing customer (internally and externally) requirements, and developing plans to meet those requirements.

Mission and vision
The Rank Xerox mission is an integral part of the business culture and therefore subject to review and continuous improvement in order to meet the changing needs of the business. Consequently in 1991 the mission was significantly revised to position them as The Document Company, meeting all the document management needs both electronic and paper of their diverse customer base. The mission statement is:

> Rank Xerox, The Document Company will be the leader in the European document market, by providing document services that enhance business productivity.

Quality policy

Senior executives in Rank Xerox were unified in their commitment to customer satisfaction through total quality management and so they developed the company quality policy. To ensure that the policy came to life and was more than just words, the main elements of the policy were communicated in terms of recognition and reward, standards and measures (processes), communication, management behaviours and actions, teamwork and training. The strategy by which these elements would be implemented was named Leadership Through Quality. The Rank Xerox quality policy is:

> Rank Xerox is a quality company:
> - Quality is the basic business principle for Rank Xerox.
> - Quality means providing our external and internal customers with innovative products and services that fully satisfy their requirements.
> - Quality improvement is the job of every employee.

The quality policy now forms the basis for both direction and the motivation of the company. At the same time the management team reaffirmed the company values, which are:

- We succeed through satisfied customers.
- We value our employees.
- We aspire to excellence in all that we do.
- We require premium return on assets.
- We use technology to develop product leadership.
- We behave as a responsible corporate citizen.

In 1991 the senior management committee, with input from the quality improvement teams, developed their values in line with company values in a document entitled "The Way We Work":

- Honesty: between ourselves and our customers and among ourselves at all times.
- Trust: in our peers, managers and subordinates to do the right thing.
- Respect: for our colleagues.
- Openness: in a free exchange of information and opinion between all employees.
- Professionalism: to maintain pride in our performance based on the continual application of knowledge, experience, expertise and dedication to the job in hand.
- Teamwork: strong individual contributions co-ordinated, agreed and implemented through teamwork towards a common goal.
- Initiative: the ability to develop and drive new ideas and approaches.
- Fun: "Laughter is a social act" (Bergson); "Laughter is man's special gift" (Rabelais).

Evolution of the process

Leadership Through Quality was launched in 1984 and remains the basis and branding for the quality drive throughout the business. Since that date the business priorities and focus have changed but the main thrust of Leadership Through Quality remains unchanged.

In 1987, three years after the launch of Leadership Through Quality, a major assessment was conducted, which resulted in the business priorities being changed to emphasise the importance of customer focus. The business priorities in 1985 were:

- Return on assets.
- Customer satisfaction.
- Market share.

From 1990 onwards they have been:
- Customer satisfaction.
- Employee motivation and satisfaction.
- Market share.
- Return on assets.

In 1989, a further major review of progress was conducted which resulted in the development of a quality intensification plan to sharpen the focus of the original quality plan and initiate the implementation of policy deployment. Later in 1990, progress against the plan was audited and specific areas for improvement within employee motivation and satisfaction were established.

In 1991 following continued self-assessments a Business Excellence Certification programme was launched which integrates business, quality planning and review across the company.

Continuous improvement
The quality strategy and operational performance are reviewed at monthly and quarterly business review meetings in the operating units. Performance against plan is measured in each of the priority areas and future activity focused accordingly. The importance of customer satisfaction is recognised at these meeting by its appearance as the first item on the meeting agenda.

As a leading exponent of benchmarking, Rank Xerox has gained an enviable reputation for its expertise and methodology. In order to prevent complacency, the company has benchmarked the benchmarking process to check its robustness, completeness, pervasiveness and overall effectiveness.

Self-assessment is adopted throughout the company through the Business Excellence Certification process which is itself subject to continuous improvement and refinement.

Employee objective setting
The setting of objectives (see Figure 14.1) provides employees with a focus for their activities over the medium term and an outline of the key deliverables which they are expected to achieve. The objectives are formalised and documented in the individual's performance review, to emphasise accountability and gain commitment to their attainment.

Alignment of individual goals to both the functional and organisational goals is essential to ensure consistency in effort throughout the organisation. With finite resources, the organisation must focus on the vital few goals and activity other than that which will achieve them can put the realisation of the vision in jeopardy.

Periodic reviews provide a feedback mechanism, both on an individual's performance and on progress towards the organisation's vision. The performance review process provides a dual role of reviewing individual achievement and identification of opportunities for improvement through a revision of objectives where appropriate.

Case studies

Figure 14.1 Employee objective setting

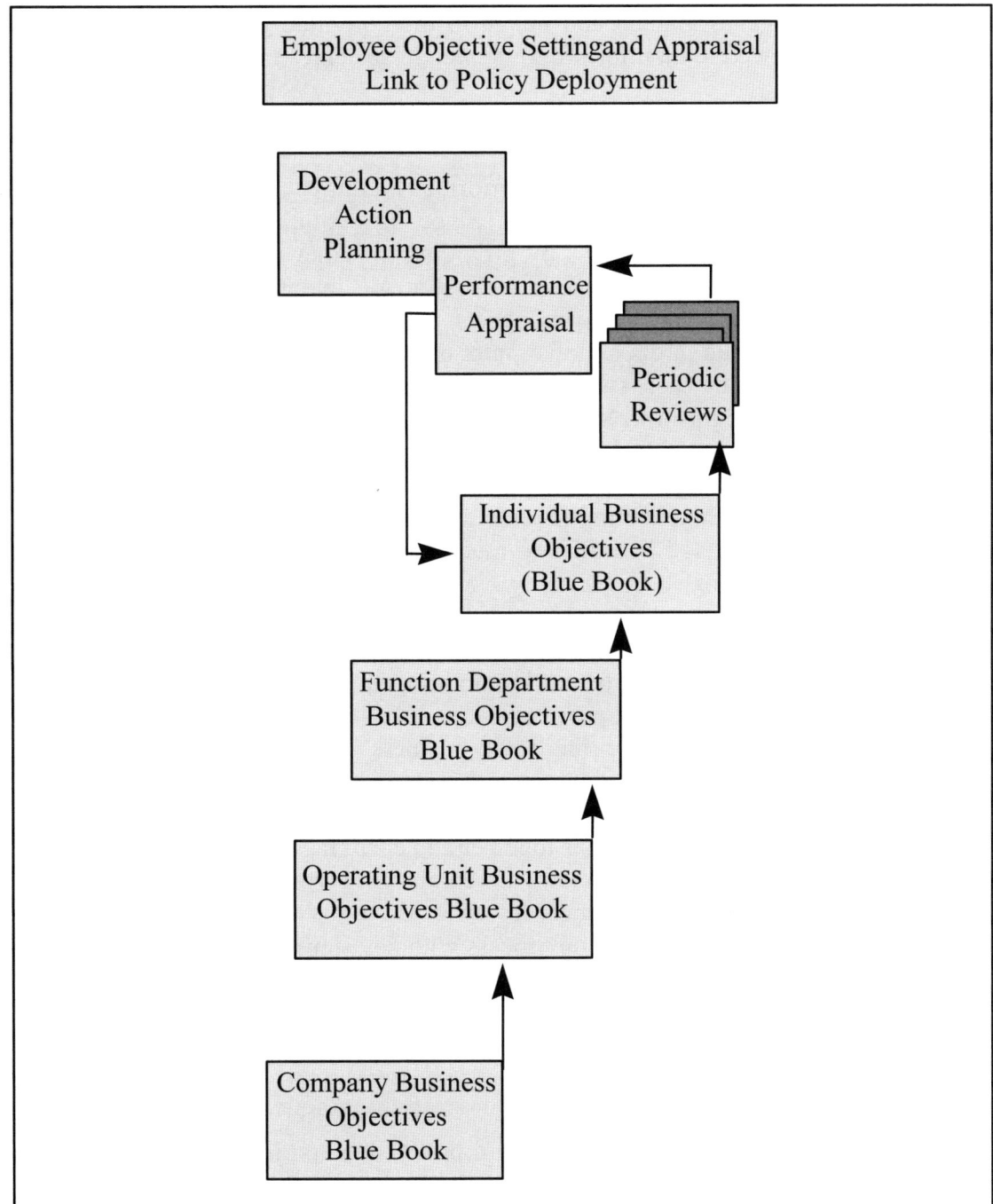

The employee objective setting process is lengthy throughout the business calendar year. The process begins in July when the company business objectives are set. These provide a path for managers throughout the business and simplify the alignment of individual and corporate goals.

In October and November the function and department objectives necessary to deliver the corporate goals are set. Each of the corporate objectives is reviewed in line with the function objectives to ensure that collectively they are sufficient and necessary to meet the corporate objectives.

Once the function objectives have been agreed, individual objectives are developed which support and deliver the function's objectives. The cascade of objectives process ensures that each "level" is aligned and linked to the corporate goals. Progress against the objectives is then reviewed to monitor progress, recognise achievement and realign objectives where appropriate.

Management of financial resources

Financial plans are prepared in line with the priorities and direction given through the policy deployment process within the organisation. Since its evolution, policy deployment has improved the strategic planning process by providing a framework for focusing on the key improvement actions necessary to achieve their strategic intent. Policy, values and vision provide the base from which company goals, objectives, strategy and priorities are established. These are then broken down into operating units, functions and individual objectives and actions with each subject to negotiation and review as part of the policy deployment process (see Figure 14.2).

The Xerox planning process delivers an integrated plan covering all aspects of the business with the relationship between business activity, sales, revenues, costs, assets and liabilities clearly defined. The planning process also ensures the correct balance between the income, expenditure, assets and liabilities to meet the needs of the shareholders, customers, people and management team.

Integration of the planning process is reflected in the reporting activity which ensures that only necessary data is reported and that it is reported at the right time to enable actions to be taken. The actual results are reported each month together with the rest of the year forecast and risk analysis through the outlook process.

The operational reviews cover the total business and these are supplemented by functional network reviews such as marketing, service, logistics, finance, quality and human resources. This ensures the appropriate environment for identification of common problems and their solutions by bringing specialists together and encourages internal benchmarking.

Annual international functional reviews are conducted across all operating units to focus on major issues and to supplement the local reviews.

The planning process is a closed loop process with key steps to:
- establish the optimum plan;
- identify variances from the plan;
- take corrective actions; and
- monitor results.

Variances between actual and planned results in profit, debtors, inventory and capital spend are identified and analysed for their impact on the organisation's cash requirements and appropriate is action taken to correct the situation.

Full deployment of the planning process across the organisation is attained through financial plans and targets which exist at all necessary levels in the company. Departmental budgets and personal targets are deployed and supported by information flows which give prompt feedback of results.

Figure 14.2 Management of financial resources

Management of Financial Resources

Policy Deployment → The Vision → The Business Plan 3 years → The Operating Plan 1 year ↔ Plan Reviews → Outlook Reporting This year ↔ Operations Reviews / Functional Reviews → Results Diagnosis

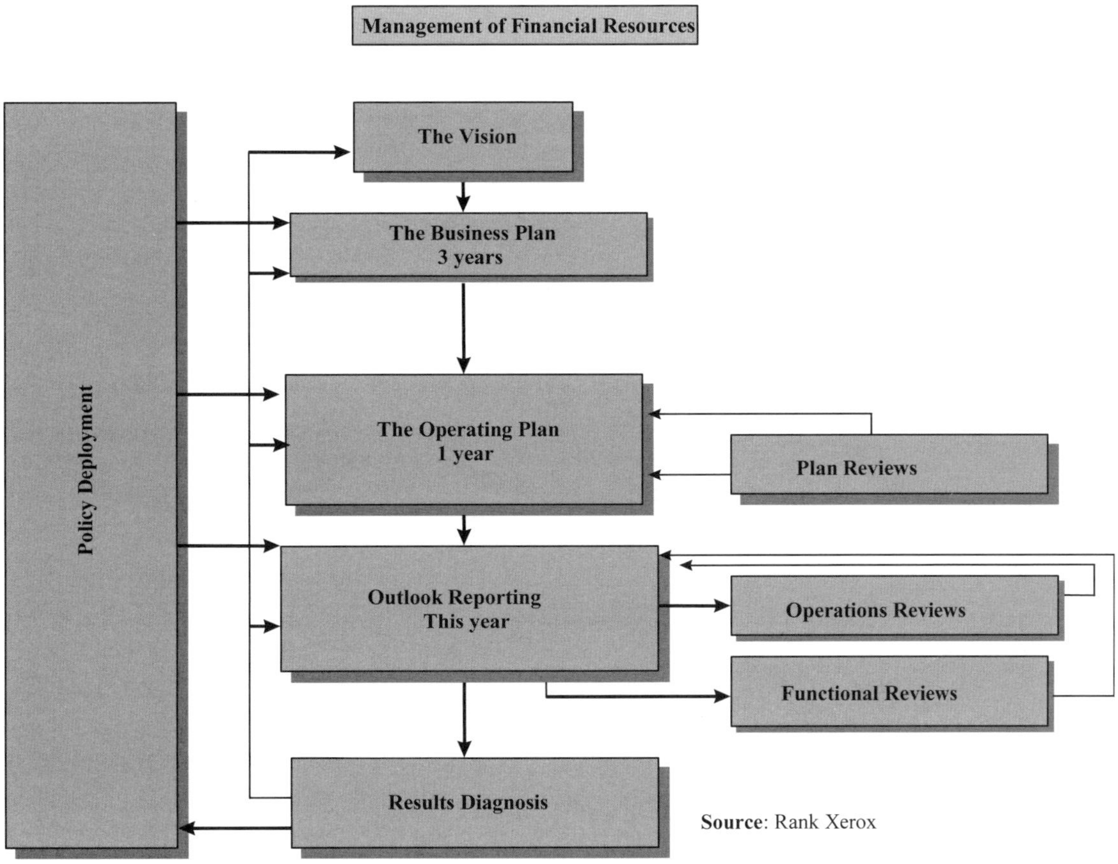

Source: Rank Xerox

Customer satisfaction – closed loop escalation process

At Xerox, customer satisfaction data is used to design new products as well as improve existing processes. This is effected through the five steps of a root cause analysis technique:

1. Generate a list of possible causes.
2. Identify which possible causes actually contribute to the problem.
3. Identify the root cause of the problem using Pareto, checksheets, solution effect.
4. Identify possible solutions.
5. Select and test solutions.

Listening to the customer enables an in-depth understanding of what the customer wants and using root cause analysis techniques enables solutions to be found and implemented to avoid reoccurrence of problems. The improvements arising require monitoring in terms of both their efficiency and ability to meet customer requirements (see Figure 14.3).

The organisation adopts an escalation process to enable the customer problem to be resolved to the complete satisfaction of the customer. If the problem is not resolved at the operating unit customer contact level then it is escalated to a higher level until referral to HQ where it is ultimately fixed. This process ensures that the problem is resolved at the nearest level to the customer as possible and only referred up if the decision is outside their jurisdiction. Figure 14.4 shows this closed loop process.

Figure 14.3 Customer satisfaction continuous improvement

```
                    Continuous improvement in customer satisfaction
```

[Diagram: cycle showing Voice of the customer → Root cause analysis → Actions developed → Implement and monitor → back to Voice of the customer, with Customer at the centre]

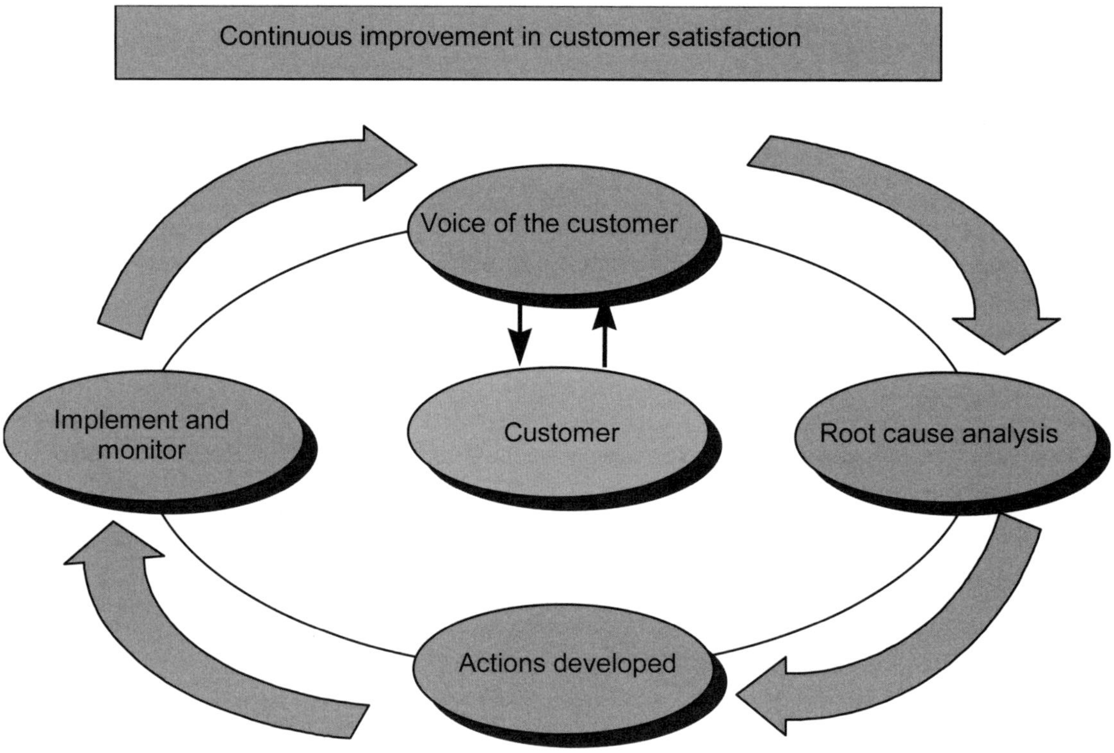

Source: Rank Xerox

Overall satisfaction measurement process
Having considered the need to understand customer requirements, managers require data and information in order to track progress towards company goals and refocus activity where milestones are not being met.

The most important parameter for Xerox in customer satisfaction is the overall satisfaction level and this is achieved by satisfying customers in all areas of importance to them (see Figure 14.5).

Customer satisfaction is measured at each stage of the product lifecycle including:
- when the product is purchased;
- during the sales experience at the time of purchase;
- in the administration at the time of purchase and any subsequent interaction with the organisation; and
- when receiving on-going service during their ownership of the product.

Each of these four parameters has a number of attributes which are evaluated by the customer both in terms of how well the company performed and how important each attribute was to the customer.

Xerox recognises that customer needs change over time and therefore variables are continually updated to reflect these changes. Research has indicated that organisations focusing solely on producing trend data are reluctant to change their variables but in not so doing miss the opportunity to measure what is currently important to the customer. Xerox attributes are continuously updated to reflect current needs of the customer, for example in 1989 a question was added about noise levels as a result of customer input.

Figure 14.4 Closed loop process

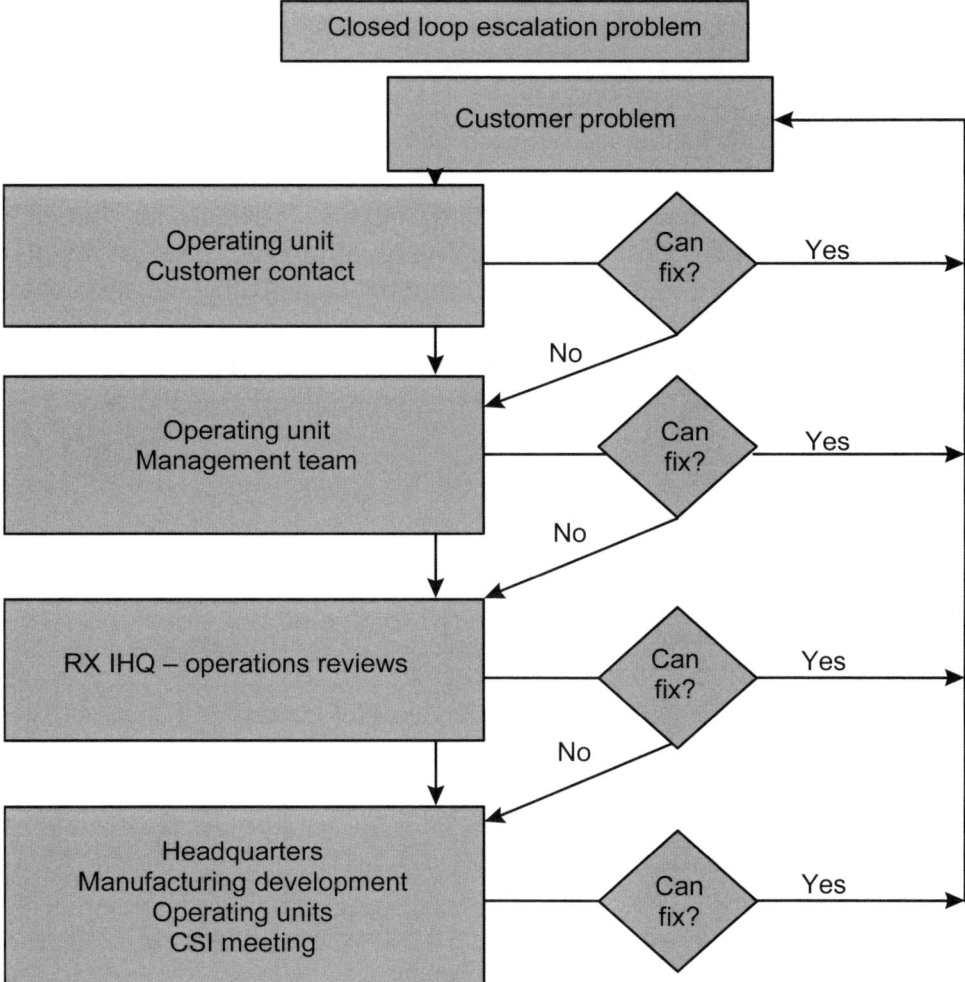

Focus on key measures
Having identified the interested parties and main headings under which results are tracked, Rank Xerox has a number of key measures:
- Profit is linked back to the plan for consistency and integration. Each unit has its own plan, is accountable for its variances and the information is used to adjust future performance expectations.
- Return on assets is the fourth business priority and the measure is used to challenge operating units in order to maximise their use of assets.
- With over 30 significant competitors in Europe, market share is a key measure. This is analysed by country and segment.
- Revenues are tracked over a ten week period to indicate trends. The gross revenue is split into a number of sources to identify strong and weak revenue producers.
- Gross margin is used to confirm that pricing and cost relationships are appropriate.
- Manufacturing costs are controlled against the plan and standards. Product costs are externally benchmarked.
- Every major expense element for each unit and function is planned and measured.

- Productivity is analysed by revenue and quantities sold per salesperson.
- Debtors are the main balance sheet current asset and are therefore managed carefully to ensure adequate future cash liquidity and profitability.
- Maintenance times and spares usage are measured per product and per engineer.
- Effectiveness in controlling the asset value of stock is measured in terms of days supply.
- Leasing companies have been established in each of the business units in response to customer demands.
- Operational effectiveness is measured in terms of quality – defects per hundred machines, quality standards, process control, delivery – on time, days of supply, cycle time reduction – from initial product conception to delivery and invoicing. Time to market – process delivery process, manufacturing – production lead times, logistics – ability to deliver is seen as a key efficiency indicator by customers. Customer service response times – response times are continuously monitored.

Figure 14.5 Overall satisfaction measures

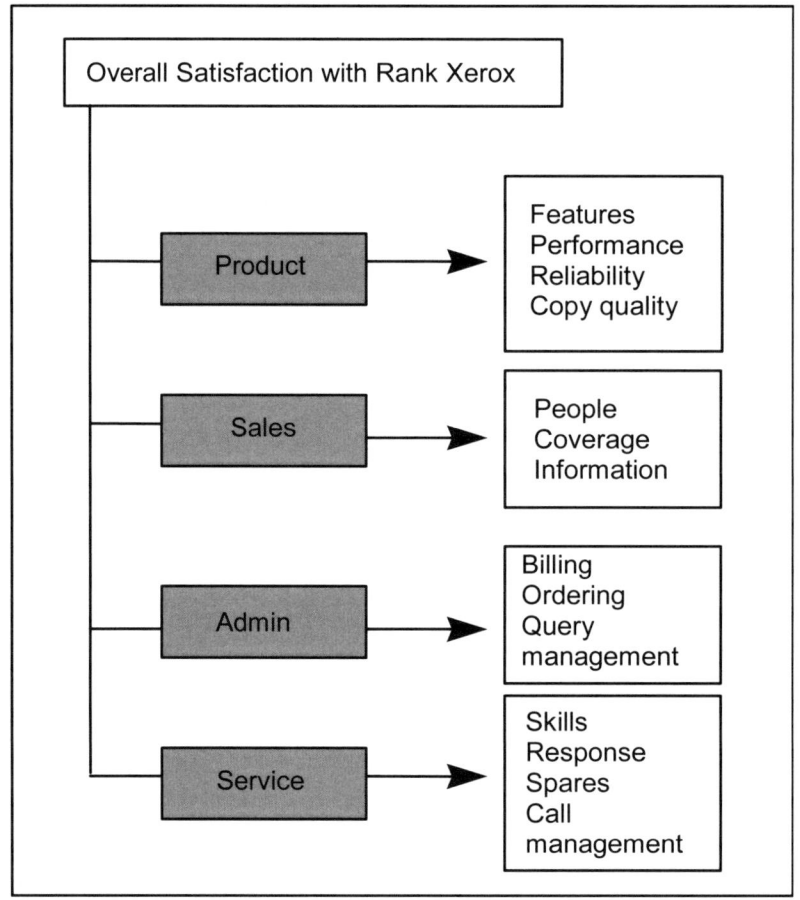

Kodak

Market and products

The motto at Kodak has always been "You press the button, we do the rest" and this reinforces the corporate view that photography should be made simple. George Eastman, the founder of the company, revolutionised the art of photography in 1900 with the launch of the Kodak Brownie camera. He registered it under the name of Kodak, a name he invented as it could not be easily mispronounced.

Product development led to models being designed for sound in 1929 and by 1932 the first 8mm amateur movie film was introduced. The quest for innovation and advancement at Kodak has continued ever since.

Quality development

Quality was officially launched at Kodak in 1982, first with inspirations from the teachings of Juran, and consisted of specific projects. By 1985, the teachings of Deming were included as the company launched its statistical process control on a company wide basis. The complete approach to total quality management began in 1989 when it became a part of the business and performance management.

Quality developed through four distinct phases:
1. People – where the focus moved away from control to empowerment. The internal customer concept was a key feature of this development.
2. Products – where the commitment to move away from a producer to a customer focus was developed. Measurement started to move away from internal to external measurement using such indicators such as cycle time reduction.
3. Management systems – an era where the company moved from an *ad hoc* and informal approach to creating a formal and enabling corporate discipline. Processes were documented and systems such as supply chain management evolved.
4. Kodak quality – the culture moved away from being too obsessed with cost to the detriment of quality as processes became controlled through consistency.

Ideal supplier characteristics

Kodak supports the view that suppliers are an important part of the manufacturing process and has found it mutually beneficial to enter into a quality partnership with key suppliers to achieve continuous improvement in the quality of supplies.

There is a structured programme, co-ordinated by the purchasing department, in which key suppliers are invited to work closely with Kodak users and buyers in improving the quality and value for money of the materials and services they supply.

Individual areas for improvement are identified on a project priority basis and improvement accomplished through small dynamic teams involving skills and resources of supplier personnel in conjunction with the Kodak purchasing and user departments.

The ideal supplier characteristics are:
- Error free products every time as returns waste time and inferior quality leads to customer dissatisfaction.
- On time deliveries as it is no good receiving stock late and halting the production line.
- The volume received should be just right as any excess can impact on storage space and cash flow and under-supply can affect the production line.
- Frequent supplies of stock are required if stock levels are to be kept to a minimum.
- If things do go wrong then suppliers must be devoted to resolving it immediately.
- Although not the only determinant, price must be competitive.

- Invoicing and other administrative documentation must be error free as time is otherwise wasted in resolving the errors leading to inefficiency.
- Openness is essential as reputations are at stake.
- Working together continuously to improve processes benefits both parties.

A series of development stages are used to raise the level of improvement expected from the suppliers and a particular status is given to them at each stage:
- Potential supplier – quotations and samples are provided for various specifications and trials are conducted.
- Accredited/approved – suppliers are visited and specifications are set and agreed. Limited business is conducted with the suppliers and products are subjected to inward inspection.
- Within the accredited/approved system there are three levels of supplier:
    - Level 1 (preferred): basic level award demands high levels of conformance to specification and that the supply is consistently maintained. Performance should be monitored by means of a checklist or performance matrix.
    - Level 2 (product control) Silver Award: need to appoint a quality team for this level so that Kodak's incoming inspection and testing of goods can be dispensed with. Responsibility for conformance tests rests solely with the supplier. Quality of design enhancements should be realised by meeting the quality team's continuous improvement objective. Nominations must be accompanied by a performance matrix and the self-audit checklist must be completed by the quality team, unless the supplier has a recognised third party accredited quality system. Supplies must have been fault free at the level 1 stage.
    - Level 3 (process control) Gold Award: supplier uses statistical quality monitoring and data analysis techniques to control all the key process parameters and has process capability for these parameters.

To become a supplier requires nomination and a formal assessment of quality systems by Kodak quality control specialists, unless the supplier has recently been third party accredited.

Nationwide Building Society
Market and products
Nationwide is the largest mutual building society and offers a range of financial services to its customers including banking, savings, mortgage and loan products. It has maintained that by remaining a mutual organisation, the customers are the shareholders and therefore potential conflict arising from balancing the needs of shareholder dividends with those of customer interest rates is avoided.

The organisation has an extensive branch network of approximately 700 branches together with a call centre for direct business, an Internet facility and an agency network to service its customers.

Quality development
A merger of the former Nationwide and Anglia Building Societies took place in the early 1990s to provide a capital base that would allow diversification into the current bank account and estate agency businesses. The former societies have different backgrounds, with one having developed through organic growth and the other through merger and acquisition.

The organisational culture was "confused" following the merger, diversification of business interests and increasing competition from new players in financial services. Branch staff in particular, felt isolated and committed to their individual job rather than to the corporation as a whole.

Staff "feared change" as they had worked in an environment where relatively little change had previously taken place and business had flourished. The queues for mortgage funds in the 1980s had been replaced with hard fought competition and new staff skills were required.

Service satisfaction attributes
Broad measures of customer satisfaction often provide managers with insufficient detail and consequently improvement activity is unfocussed. By "drilling down" customer satisfaction data under key service attributes, more meaningful information was obtained and enabled improvement activity to be focused on the important issues for customers.

Research had indicated that service attributes were collated under five headings (see Figure 14.6):
1. Responsiveness – how quickly was the customer served?
2. Assurance – how reassured did the customer feel?
3. Empathy – did the service provider make the customer feel welcome?
4. Tangibles – was the service provided in a business like environment?
5. Reliability – was the service offered in a professional and consistent way?

Drilling down of customer satisfaction into the key service attributes enabled the identification of the main drivers of satisfaction, which could subsequently be addressed through quality improvement.

The attributes identified were obtained by consensus between a number of major financial service organisations and sample testing of customers to rate a range of different criteria in terms of their relative importance. This syndicated market research was conducted by an independent market research organisation and provided a cost effective means of obtaining performance data and comparative information with other key players.

Research indicated that customer satisfaction was particularly influenced by:
- Confidence that the information given is accurate – savings and mortgages are particularly sensitive products and assurance that the correct information is being given is of paramount importance.
- Customers expect to be treated courteously – observing the usually friendly approach that is expected.
- Information must be consistent throughout the business and is a key problem for service providers as purchase and delivery often take place at the same time, unlike manufacturing.
- Customers want to know who they are dealing with and that the place of the service delivery is well kept.

Figure 14.6 Service attributes

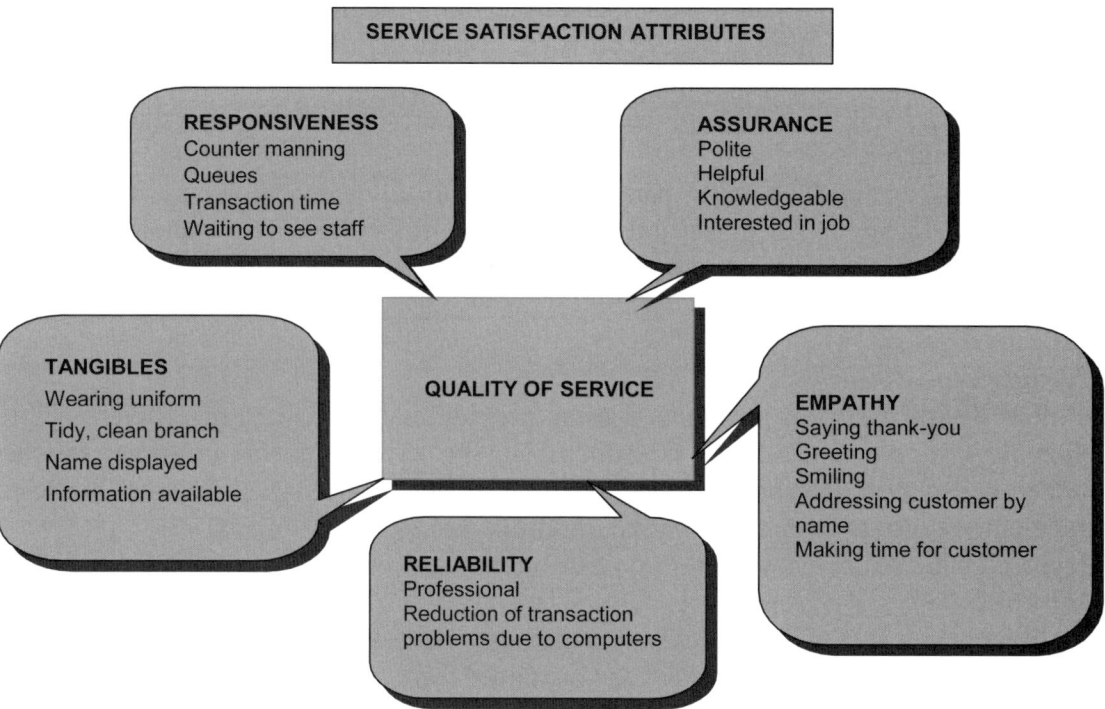

Source: Nationwide Building Society

Data was collected and produced on a quarterly basis for the participating organisations, providing a benchmark of current performance within the group and a trend over consecutive quarters. The data was collected by the independent market research organisation by interviewing a representative sample of customers from each organisation. The output from the interviews was consolidated into a report and presented to management by the market research organisation.

Following the management briefing, the detailed findings were located and transcribed into a more "user friendly" form for dissemination to front line staff. Accompanying the statistics and charts were best practices from previous research which could be adopted to improve performance in those key areas of customer dissatisfaction.

Communication was in a written form incorporating charts, words and "pictures" to appeal to all staff and each branch was responsible for constructing a branch improvement action plan to improve performance in these key areas of customer dissatisfaction. The plans detailed specific actions which the branch intended to take alongside each area of dissatisfaction to create performance improvement month on month.

Dana Commercial Credit

Market and product range

Dana Commercial Credit Corporation (DCC), a subsidiary of the USA Dana Corporation, is a provider of leasing and financing services to a broad range of commercial customers. The company was started in 1980 with a $2.5 million investment from its corporate partner and has grown to become the eleventh largest company among 22,000 US leasing companies with revenues of nearly $200 million and total assets of $1.5 billion.

DCC headquarters are in Ohio where most of its 550 people are located. The company is structured around its major product groups, each aligned to a different market sector:

- Passenger car.
- Light truck.
- Medium/heavy truck.
- Off highway.
- Industrial.
- Automotive distribution.
- Truck parts distribution.
- Off highway/industrial distribution.

Launch of total quality initiatives

Total quality was originally initiated by DCC's division operating committee members who attended a total quality leadership seminar in 1992 and concluded that it was a wake up call needed to improve management communications and teamwork. Following the seminar they decided that the business needed a focus and so they developed a vision statement along with the DCC service logo of "1^{st^3}". This signified the goal to be first in customer satisfaction, first in quality and first in knowledge.

Mission and vision

The senior management team developed the following mission and vision statements to provide a business focus for Dana:

- It is our vision to be the preferred, knowledge based, service oriented leasing company in our selected markets, both domestically and internationally.
- It is our mission to be first in customer satisfaction, by being first in knowledge and quality.
- Knowledge signifies that "People are our most important assets" who will provide value-added quality lease products and service processes. This approach will influence our customers to refer DCC to other people, which will result in earnings and growth, i.e. profit for our shareholders.

The vision and mission were then communicated to all 550 people within Dana through team meetings and various publications.

Dana's philosophy is that people are their most important asset and the purpose of the business is to earn money for their shareholders and increase the value of their investment.

Quality policy

The quality policy has been defined by the policy committee of the Dana Corporation and approved by the Board of Directors of Dana Corporation:

We believe that Dana people should accept only total quality in all tasks they perform. We believe in continuous improvement to ensure our products and services are the best value available anywhere.

Quality extends outside Dana to its suppliers and customers, with senior managers meeting regularly with both key customers and suppliers to ensure that objectives are being met.

Evolution of the process

Quality is seen as an integral part of the business and therefore its evolution has been part of the business development. Following development of the mission and vision, the key business drivers were identified and used as criteria for progress measurement:
- Knowledgeable people.
- Quality processes.
- Profit for shareholders.
- Customer satisfaction.

Continuous improvement

Performance excellence goals are the primary measures by which a commitment to continuous improvement can be judged. They are established during the strategic planning process and led by the product group managers. The performance excellence goals are reviewed on a monthly basis by the product group managers at the product group operating committees. Specific products are reviewed using a scorecard set of measures.
- Customer satisfaction.
- Internal performance.
- Competitor performance.
- Financial performance compared to "hellweek" forecast and human resource performance.

Winning the MBNQA stimulated Dana's primary objective of achieving continuous improvement and the management is committed to providing DCC with a competitive edge in the years ahead.

A commitment to learning is a key requirement as through knowledge Dana can differentiate itself from the competition. Management commitment to education is evident from the increased number of hours for education which each person now receives per annum (risen from 47 hours in 1992 to 58 hours in 1996).

Management are aware of their requirement to improve and specific areas on which to focus are gained from the total quality leadership culture survey conducted on a biennial basis, together with the annual feedback from the Dana Quality Leadership Award process and product group operating committees.

People satisfaction survey process

Dana has developed a survey approach to measure the level of people satisfaction within the company, with the assistance of external consultants to advise on the type and scope of questions to be used. The questions used are then linked to the Malcolm Baldrige National Quality Award criteria to integrate the two processes and identify process owners for areas in which improvements are required.

The survey is applied throughout the whole company from top through to middle management and other staff, ensuring that the satisfaction levels for all groups are taken into account. Planning is the first step in the process, where a date is agreed, the deployment approach detailed and the questions scoped. The second step is administrative, where the survey forms are distributed and collated on their return. Having received back the completed forms, the answers are analysed and interpreted using a variety of histograms and pie charts to identify "what" and "where" are the main areas of people dissatisfaction.

Following an analysis of the results the potential areas for improvement are classified as either short or long term. The short-term issues are action planned by a division operating committee for detailed consideration, with alternative scenarios debated. The proposed solution is then scheduled for action, taking into account all the implementation issues, and a communication plan devised to ensure that all staff and management are aware of the changes. Where appropriate, any changes which affect an individual's area of responsibility must be communicated effectively.

The next stage in the process is to consider the issues arising from the survey which require a long-term action plan. In a similar way to the short-term plans, alternative scenarios are considered, a proposed solution agreed and a communication plan devised to ensure that all staff and management are made aware of the changes together with how individuals' roles will change following this revision.

The final stage is to evaluate the effect of implementing these changes through the next people survey or by using alternative performance measures.

Ulster Carpet Mills

Market and product range

Ulster Carpet Mills, a subsidiary of Ulster Carpet Mills (Holdings) Ltd, was founded in 1938 by the father of the three current owners, Walter, John and Edward Wilson. The company operates from three manufacturing sites in Portadown, Northern Ireland, with marketing subsidiaries in France, Germany and other European markets. They employ a direct sales force within the UK, selling direct to retailers and contractor custom purchasers.

Ulster Carpet Mills Ltd is a manufacturer of high quality woven Axminster and Wilton carpets and the world's second largest producer of Axminster carpet. In addition to the stock ranges, the company specialises in supplying carpet custom designed and woven to customers' special orders. Advanced technology is used to ensure precision colour matching during production and in the warehousing of finished goods.

Launch of total quality initiatives

The total quality culture started to develop in 1983 when the company introduced quality circles into the manufacturing areas and became accredited to BS 5750 Part 2 in 1986.

In 1989/1990 all 730 people employed were given training in the first total quality programme "Total Customer Satisfaction". The "care woven in" motto was derived from one of the syndicate exercises used in this first total quality programme and has been adopted to emphasise the "care" for customers, people, suppliers and the community. Delivery of the total quality training is undertaken by all managers from the chairman down to demonstrate commitment to the quality drive within the business.

Mission and vision

The motto of "care woven in" is carried into the mission statement, which is shown in Figure 14.7. The company displays its value statements throughout the organisation and uses the company magazine to emphasise that the values are at the core of their strategy. The company values are shown in Figure 14.8.

Quality policy

The company's philosophy is that quality is of paramount importance and that it encompasses all aspects of the business including design, product development, production, quality of finished product and service to customers. A total quality master plan is integrated into the company's five year forward development plan and the philosophy that every employee is responsible for quality led to the successful dismantling of the quality department in 1992.

Evolution of the process

The total quality culture has evolved through a series of key milestones since 1980 (see Table 14.1), emphasising that quality takes time to develop and is a journey not a destination.

Continuous improvement

Business review meetings continuously evaluate progress towards plans and realign policy and strategy to reflect the changing needs of the market using feedback received from customers, employees and suppliers to highlight areas in which improvements are required.

The chairman and entire management team have demonstrated their commitment to continuous improvement by taking part in problem-solving teams and they were involved in improvement projects for some six months before the initial total quality training was carried out with the workforce.

Figure 14.7 Mission statement of Ulster Carpet Mills

MISSION

Our mission is to delight our customers in all that we do in every aspect of the product and service we provide

As a family controlled, professionally managed business, we will operate to the highest standards of integrity, quality and safety. All our resources will be totally focused on our commitment to care

Care for.....
OUR CUSTOMERS
the most important people whose total satisfaction is our success
OUR PEOPLE
working in harmony to delight our customers
OUR SUPPLIERS
in active and creative partnerships to meet our customers' wishes
OUR COMMUNITY
sharing in our success and benefiting from our care for the environment

Care woven in

Figure 14.8 Company values

COMPANY VALUES

We succeed through delighted customers
We value our employees
We aspire to business excellence through continuously improving all that we do
We use technology to develop product leadership
We behave as a responsible member of the community
We aim to achieve good financial performance

Communication

Underpinning the communication process (see Figure 14.9) at Ulster Carpets are three critical elements:
1. Briefing notes which provide a consistent message across the whole organisation rather than managers subjectively selecting items for communication, which leads to conflicting interpretations.
2. Communication meetings are planned as part of the business diary, rather than being "fitted into" other tasks. This ensures that all people hear the "news" on the same day.
3. A closed loop process for questions which "local" management cannot resolve ensures that all people fully understand the messages and their implications.

Table 14.1 Milestones in developing a total quality culture

Date	Milestones
1980	Company magazine launched
1982	Team briefing starts: Gold Sovereign Awards for 25 years service introduced Quality circles introduced
1986	BS 5750 (ISO 9002) registration achieved through BSI
1989	Total customer satisfaction – all 730 employees trained Problem-solving teams BSI Kitemark Employee survey starts
1990	Problem-solving employee teams Supplier appraisals Internal customer/supplier contacts introduced Customer surveys Open-plan offices
1991	Company workwear introduced Single status car park Safety year programme Gold Sovereign safety awards introduced Group working introduced
1992	Total customer delight programme Won Northern Ireland Quality Award Divisional self-assessment starts
1993	RoSPA Gold Award for safety Employee profit sharing introduced Sun Alliance Team Award Carpet Supplier of the Year award Employee of the month scheme
1994	Business teams set up Carpet Supplier of the Year award Private health care for all introduced Company three year pay deal agreed Leadership 21st Century Programme
1995	Bridging the Gap programme Business team process reviews Investors in People launched Northern Ireland Exporter of the Year award Carpet Supplier of the Year award
1996	Investors in People Business team assessments

The process begins with a core brief of key messages which are developed immediately following the board meeting. The content is both a strategic look ahead and an operational review of current performance together with other important issues of the day. The messages are concise and presented in a clear way to minimise any misinterpretation.

The core brief is presented to the management team on a Tuesday following the board meeting. The management team members are then responsible for ensuring that the information is disseminated to employees on Friday of the same week. Timing is critical to minimise the "internal grapevine" effect and potential conflict arising between sections from a fragmented approach.

Understanding of the core brief throughout the organisation is essential and to facilitate this requirement, questions are encouraged from employees at the time of the briefing.

Figure 14.9 Communication process at Ulster Carpet Mills

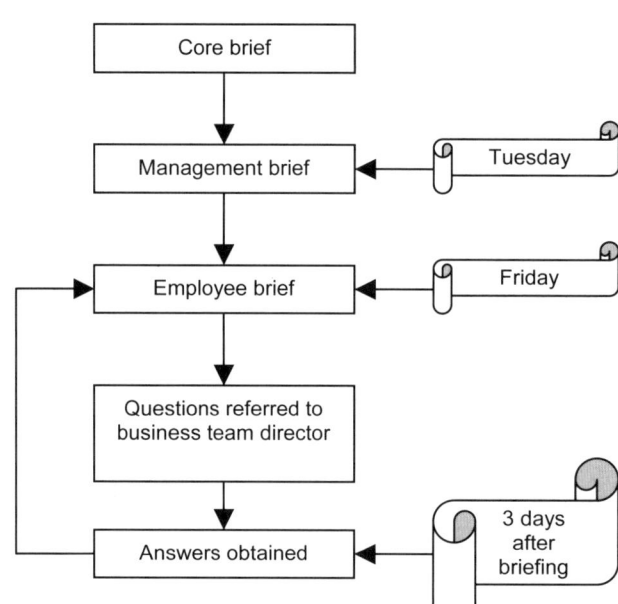

Questions are often resolved by the manager, but those remaining unresolved are referred to the business team director who is charged with the responsibility of obtaining answers within three days of the briefing.

To demonstrate a commitment to its people and emphasise the importance of fully understanding the key messages within the brief, questions raised at the briefing meetings are taken seriously:
- All questions, even those which are answered at the time of the brief, are noted together with the answers given, and circulated to the business team directors.
- All questions and answers are also typed and displayed on communication boards throughout the business.

The organisation also has a developed system to supplement the core briefing process whereby other important messages are given a rating of red or yellow alert. Red alerts are deemed very important and therefore require managers to cascade the information straight away. Yellow alerts are also important but can be communicated at some time within the same working day rather than straight away.

People satisfaction – managing outcomes from surveys
Following an employee survey, teams are set up to decide the action points which can be implemented and ensure congruence with company policy. These teams make a wide range of recommendations from which short and long-term actions are agreed. The long-term actions are accompanied by key milestones to measure their progress and, when reached, are communicated to employees to raise organisational awareness.

Royal Mail

Market and product range

Royal Mail provides a universal delivery service within the UK and is the largest business within the Post Office Group. Its turnover in 1993-1994 was £4.23 billion, which represented approximately 70 per cent of the group's turnover. There are approximately 160,000 employees at over 1,900 sites. They handle an average of 64 million letters per day which are collected from 120,000 points and delivered to 25 million UK addresses, six days per week.

Integrated market and product development is carried out through four of the Strategic Business Units: National for domestic UK, International for world-wide, Streamline for organisations posting large volumes of mail and Cashco for the cash security market.

Royal Mail's most widely used service is the nationwide collection and delivery for First and Second Class mail, but it also provides a wide range of other services for individuals and business:

- Priority services, such as special, recorded and registered delivery.
- Electronic services, such as electronic post, faxmail and electronic data interchange.
- Special collection and delivery services, such as collection direct from a business and the redirection of mail for delivery.
- Direct mail services specifically designed for businesses which post large numbers of letters or packages and are prepared to do additional preparation of the mail in return for discounts.
- Response services, such as Business Reply and Freepost, designed to make it easy for customers to respond to promotional campaigns.
- International services for posting letters, packets and other items overseas.

Launch of total quality initiatives

A decline in market share and increased dissatisfaction from customers and employees signalled the need for total quality management in 1988. The managing director and executive team concluded that a fundamental change to a new way of working for the whole organisation was required if the business was to halt its decline. This new way of working was branded "Customer First".

Clear statements of business focus were developed by the executive team including a mission statement, a set of values and a definition of quality – "the way of working which will enable the business to achieve its mission in a manner that is consistent with our values".

Mission and vision

Royal Mail's mission is to make the Post Office a world class benchmark of excellence: "to be recognised as the best organisation in the world distributing text and packages". This will be achieved by:

- Excelling in collection, processing, distribution and delivery arrangements.
- Establishing a partnership with customers to understand, agree and meet their changing needs.
- Operating profitably by efficient services which customers consider to be value for money.
- Creating a work environment which recognises and rewards the commitment of all employees to customer satisfaction.

- Recognising responsibilities as part of social, industrial and commercial life of the country.
- Being forward looking and innovative.

The values by which the business operates are an integral part of the total quality management approach within the business:

We each care about:
- our customers and their responsibilities for:
    - reliability;
    - value for money;
    - accessibility;
    - courtesy;
    - integrity;
    - security;
    - prompt and timely response;
- all our fellow employees and their needs for:
    - respect;
    - training and development;
    - involvement;
    - recognition and reward;
- the way we do our job and the way it affects our customers both inside and outside the business;
- our role in the life of the community.

Evolution of the process
- 1988-91. Employee opinion surveys and a customer satisfaction index were introduced together with a measurement system providing feedback on management behaviour.
- 1989-90. Recruited and trained 85 quality support managers who reported directly to key senior managers.
- 1990-91. Benchmarked the total quality process through visits to winners of the Malcolm Baldrige National Quality Award. This identified the need to simplify and realign the organisation to achieve the performance improvements required by customers.
- 1989-92. Team based Customer First workshops leading to quality improvement activities.
- 1992 onwards. The message of continuous improvement was first taken to front line staff. During this period the number of business units was reduced, the organisational structure was simplified and the European Foundation for Quality Management model was adopted for total quality at Royal Mail.

Continuous improvement

Creation of a continuous improvement culture at Royal Mail commenced in 1989 with senior and middle managers leading their teams through a five day workshop in a cascade format from the managing director downwards. This resulted in hundreds of quality improvement activities and an annual teamwork event, first held in 1992, at which they celebrate success.

The vision, direction and goals at Royal Mail are formally reviewed by the Royal Mail executive each year.

Policy deployment

Business policy and strategy begin with the strategic direction setting process which provides a framework within which the different parts of the organisation develop their own activities and action plans (see Table 14.2). Strategic direction provides a high level "steer" on where the organisation is heading and, therefore, is clearly linked to the vision. At this stage, the vision is reviewed for its appropriateness in a changing market by using external data and feedback from customers, staff and suppliers. Changes are normally more minor realignment than major significant change of direction to reflect the market conditions which have changed since the vision was originally developed.

Table 14.2 Deployment of business strategy

Process	Major activities undertaken	Main output
Strategic direction setting	Vision reviewed and communicated Directions defined, prioritised and communicated Goals specified, prioritised and communicated	Strategic direction provided
Planning	Targets related to goals are set Priority process determined and targets set for processes Process performance and target "gaps" understood through use of measurements Initiatives and plans developed to meet the targets Targets deployed into teams and individual objectives Prioritise, integrate, resource and commence initiatives	Direction translated into process targets and programmes of planned activities
Performance measurement and review	Review of measurements and goal achievement process performance and implementation of major initiatives	Performance reviewed against plan and feedback undertaken

The vision is underpinned by six direction statements to provide more details of what has to be collectively achieved in order to realise the vision. These direction statements are supported by defined goals so that staff are fully aware of what has to be achieved. They also serve as a framework for managers to develop local goals and targets within their defined area of responsibility. Communication is vital and so the strategic direction statements together with goals and priorities are cascaded throughout the organisation in a consistent and timely way.

The second phase of the process is planning, where the direction statements are translated into process targets and programmes of planned activities. This is the "what" phase of business policy and strategy as targets are set, process priority determined and current target gaps identified. At this stage the "numbers" are applied to the high level direction statements and understanding of what has to be achieved begins. The activities and initiatives necessary to achieve the targets are identified and prioritised as part of the planning process.

Having developed what has to be achieved, the targets are deployed into teams throughout the organisation as part of the teamwork culture. Teams own the targets and from them individual objectives are set for each staff member. The structure enables all staff to identify their key tasks and align them to the direction statements for the whole business.

Performance is reviewed and output used to feedback into the system as part of the closed loop process. Measurements are reviewed along with goals, achievements and the progress with major initiative implementations. The output from these reviews is evaluated and any significant variation "fed back" to the planning and/or strategic direction process to ensure the vision and strategy remain realistic and feasible.

Best practice implementation models
Royal Mail has a clearly defined quality improvement process (Figure 14.10), providing consistency of approach across the organisation. Each step is clearly defined and staff are trained in its application at a variety of in house training events.

Within Royal Mail there is a defined process and infrastructure which supports "good practice" throughout the business. All good practices begin at a local level, but to gain maximum benefit from their consistent application across the organisation requires an evaluation and collation with other "submissions".

Local practices deemed worthy of consideration as "good practice" are vetted against certain basic criteria as a method of pre-screening before proceeding through the business unit process groups (see Figure 14.11).

Good practices which have passed through the pre-screening are then subjected to more detailed evaluation, including whether such a practice is to be made mandatory for all business units or recommended for a decision at a local level. Having considered the good practice submitted, a review considers alternatives and evaluates the benefit to be gained from a modification to the original submission.

Each potential good practice requires documentation in a formalised and consistent form as detailed in the submission guidelines produced for all staff. The basic requirements of documentation include:
- Description – background and scope.
- Names and telephone numbers of any contacts listed.
- Dated submission.
- Process diagrams.
- Description of the main steps, who performs the steps and what is needed to do this work, implementation resources and risks/barriers.

Figure 14.10 Quality improvement process

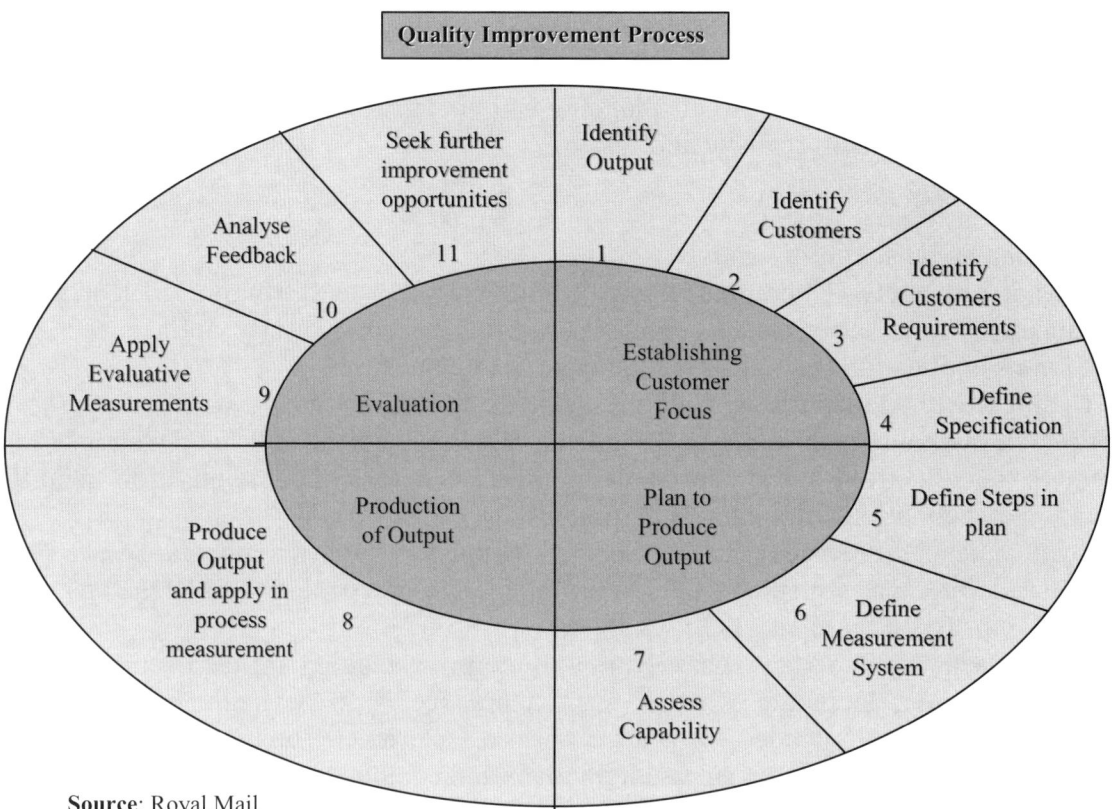

Source: Royal Mail

Best practices for best practice implementation
There are four main elements to the procedure which have to be considered: motivation to seek and implement good practice, making it visible, implementing good practice and building on success.
1. *Motivation* – sets best-in-class process performance targets and makes known the levels of performance achieved by high performing units. The process invites practices that help meet performance targets, promotes the idea of many practices rather than just one, recognises the contribution of everyone.
2. *Making it visible* – creates opportunities to communicate good practices through conferences, team meetings and news sheets. It encourages people to use the national and local database.
3. *Implementing good practice* – ensures that good practices are built into unit and business plans. Also the implementation is treated as a proper project.
4. *Building on success* – documentation of good practice is conducted in a user friendly way, preferably by the people who will do the work in future. Good practices are continually reviewed to try and improve them and extensive communication ensures access by a wide audience.

Figure 14.11 How business units feed into the national procedure

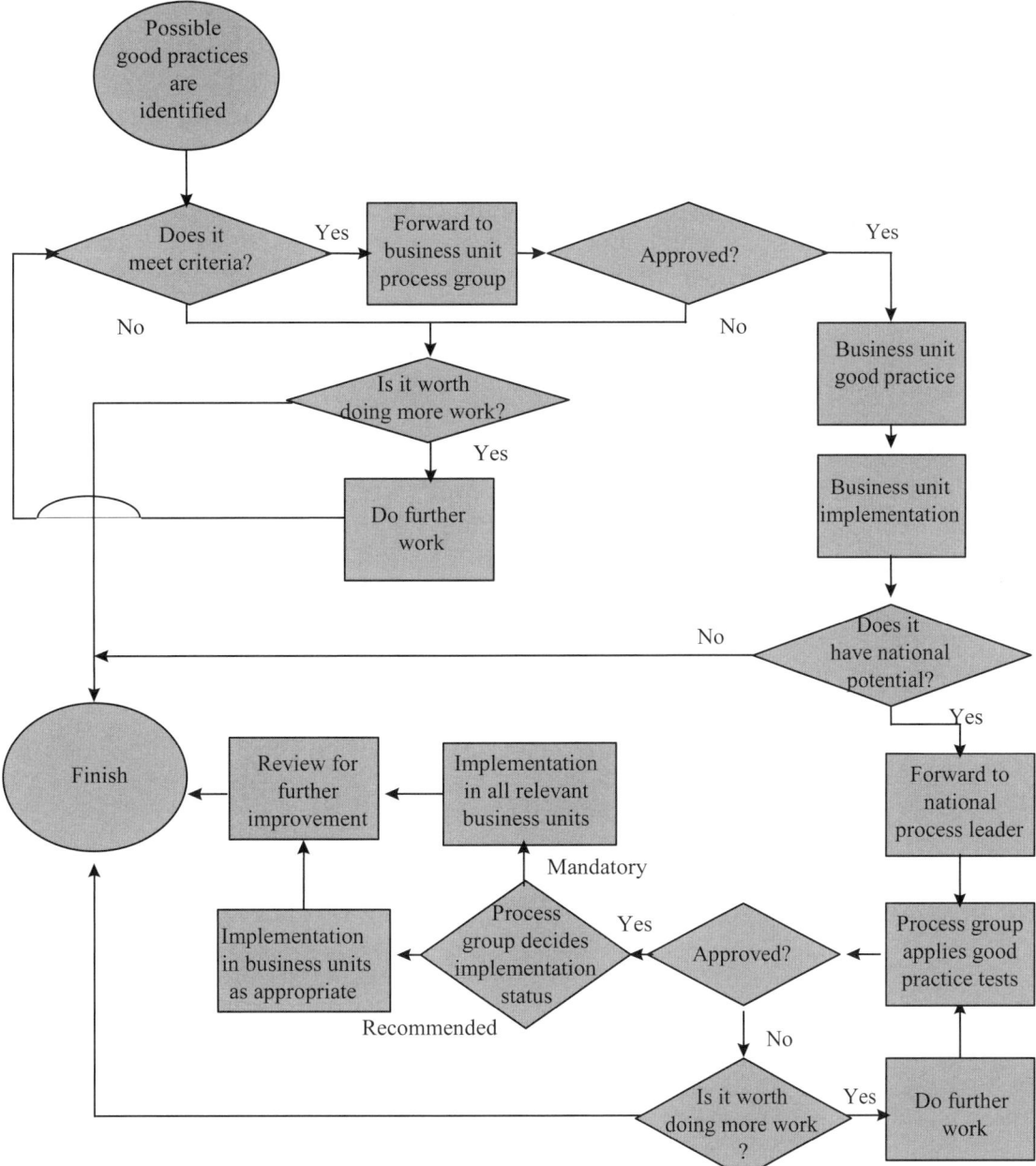

National process groups provide the vehicle for both communicating good practice and maintaining the good practice database. These groups plan the implementation using project management procedures and clearly identify time scales, capability and resourcing requirements. Clearly defined roles exist for process group leaders and members, line managers and other people involved, ensuring high levels of commitment and clarity of role.

The main sources of good practice are identified as work units recognised as: high performers, successful improvement projects, employees identifying potential good practices, business excellence reviews, unit excellence, national and local events, benchmarking with internal/external "best-in-class" and good practice database.

Conclusions of implementation review
Evidence is required of work undertaken to seek a more preferable solution. This evidence could include a list of locations where comparisons were sought and made, learning points taken from comparisons conducted and summary information of similar practices.

The cost of introducing the project is required with a fully documented business case report completed.

Impact on society – community care
Community involvement is a key focus of activity for Royal Mail due to its high profile within the community. Senior management commitment to this work is demonstrated by the appointment of nine full time community action managers. The activities undertaken centre around many areas of public concern, including crime, education, disabled people, charity and voluntary work.

The key role of the community action managers is to promote, co-ordinate and encourage community related activities within the organisation. Examples of community involvement activities include:

- Partnerships with local police forces.
- Children writing and posting a letter to Father Christmas receive a Christmas card.
- Mail containing support material for the blind is carried free of charge and company premises conform to disabilities guidelines.
- Aligning postal collections with rural bus times to improve the public perception of Royal Mail.
- Giving employees special leave for such work as the Territorial Army to promote goodwill.
- Supporting schools through posters, visits, worksheets etc. to improve the community perception of Royal Mail.
- Letter writing competitions to promote good writing skills.

Commitment to community activities was further demonstrated through sponsorship of the British Olympic and Paralympic teams for the 1996 games.

Texas Instruments: Defense Systems and Electronics Group

Market and product range
Texas Instruments: Defense Systems and Electronics Group (TI-DSEG) is a subsidiary of Texas Instruments Inc. It designs and manufactures precision-guided weapons, airborne radar systems, infra red vision equipment and other electro-optic systems and electronic warfare systems.

Launch of total quality initiatives
Quality at TI-DSEG started in 1982 with a concerted effort to educate managers and employees in the principles of TQM and to apply various concepts from gurus such as Deming, Crosby and Juran. A key feature of this effort was to focus on the end customer.

In 1989 the company decided to use the Malcolm Baldrige framework as a vehicle for managing the introduction and use of TQM within the business. Internal assessment was used.

Mission and vision
The vision of the company is to be the best defense electronics company in the world and to achieve this the fundamental objective for everyone is customer satisfaction through total quality. Underpinning the mission are the company values of ethics/integrity and respect for people.

Quality policy
TI's quality policy emphasises that quality begins before design by listening to the customers and making sure that their requirements are fully understood.

> For every product or service we offer we will understand the requirements that meet the customers' needs and we will conform to those requirements without exception. For every job which each tier performs the performance standard is do it right the first time (President and Chief Executive Officer).

Quality then continues through production transition and beyond to ensure continued customer satisfaction.

> Total quality encompasses everything we do, and is, in fact, the key factor in the success of the company. It drives us in the right direction with regard to our people, our customers and our technologies and innovations (President of the TI Group).

Total quality is achieved through three key elements: customer focus, continuous improvement and people involvement.

Evolution of the process
Since 1982 extensive training has been undertaken using material from Crosby, Juran and others to extend quality awareness throughout the business. SPC, teams, supplier partnerships and management by fact together with many other techniques have been added. Throughout the quality evolution the objective of customer satisfaction has remained.

In 1989, the Malcolm Baldrige National Quality Award criteria were selected as a framework for continuous improvement. Self-assessment was initiated and feedback used to focus improvement initiatives. In 1992, a new application for MBNQA provided a rallying point for revitalisation of the quality journey.

Total quality is now executed through an operational network of more than 1,900 quality teams. These include quality improvement teams who are chartered to steer the quality improvement process. The objective is to have everyone as an active member of one or more of these teams.

Continuous improvement
Providing services and systems that are on target requires designs and processes that are also on target. This can be achieved through continuous improvement by measuring and reducing variability, optimising design and process parameters for robustness, knowing and reducing the cost of quality and evaluating supplier performance. Five improvement thrusts which have been used are:
1. Customer satisfaction.
2. Stretch goals – six sigma implementation, cycle time reduction.
3. Benchmarking.
4. Teamwork and empowerment.
5. Integrated total quality.

Managing the strategic process
Within any large international organisation alignment of vision, mission and strategy across the business is critical to the future success of the company (see Figure 14.12). At Texas Instruments, the Europe vision is derived from the world mission by strategic leadership teams. The difference between the two visions is one of focus rather than any significant variation.

Having determined the Europe vision, the objectives for the organisation are established by the business managers, ensuring that the objectives set are both necessary and sufficient to attain the vision. The next stage is for the business support entities to develop the goals which, when collectively achieved, will meet the corporate objectives. The final stage in the strategic process is the results, which provide feedback on progress being made towards the corporate vision, provide evidence that processes and systems are under control and a focus for improvement activity.

The strategic development process is supported by an effective internal and external communication mechanism which, through two way feedback, provides consistency of message and confirmation of understanding throughout the business.

Underpinning the strategic development process is a quality culture across the business and this is demonstrated through a commitment to training and involvement in quality improvement. At the centre of the quality culture is the European Foundation for Quality Management framework which provides feedback on the current status of its quality journey. Each of the criteria on the model is assigned to a specific quality steering team to promote ownership and provide focus for improvement. The quality steering teams also formulate regional policies and strategies in accord with the world-wide objectives.

Strategy is formally reviewed on a quarterly basis with data from the EFQM model, internal and external communications, including customer and people satisfaction data, and quality improvement activity. The goals are reviewed to ensure alignment with the mission and objectives are reviewed for alignment with the world-wide vision.

Figure 14.12 Who is involved in the strategic process?

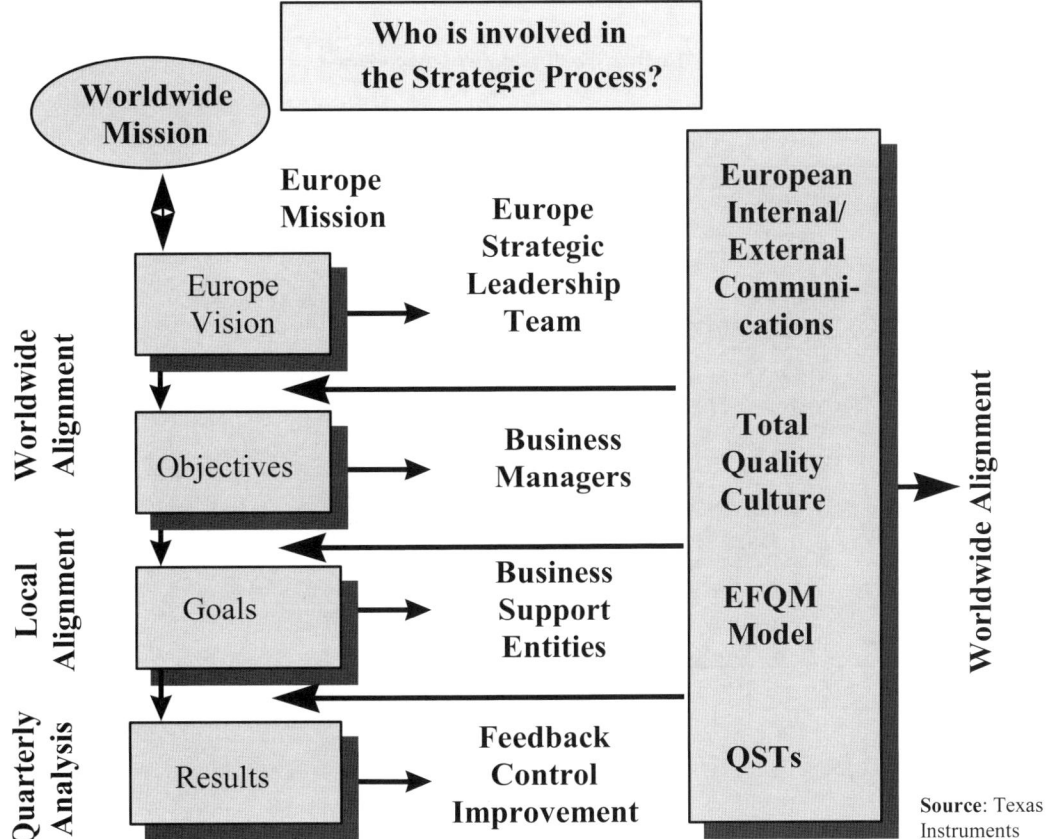

Aligning leadership competencies with business priorities

Aligning leadership competencies with business priorities is a key activity at Texas Instruments and the process begins with a review of the current business situation (see Figure 14.13). The review identifies the strategic business priorities necessary to move towards the organisation's mission in the short to medium term. These competencies underpinning the business priorities are identified as part of the strategic job analysis.

Having identified the business needs in terms of priorities and competencies to undertake the task, managers and high potential employees are assessed using a variety of different tests. The output from the assessments is reviewed and used to develop individual training and development plans for action over the months ahead.

Training and development plans are kept under review to indicate their importance to the employees and ensure progress is being made.

Impact on society – environmental, health and safety management

A global environmental, health and safety (EHS) leadership team was formed in 1994 at TI to develop a vision for the future and promote the EHS goals established for the corporation. The mission focused on organisational leadership in EHS and demonstrated that the goals are part of the company's core values and the dimensions are the key ingredients for sustained competitive advantage.

Individual champions are tasked to create teams at local or group level to develop and implement specific programmes to achieve these goals. Quarterly progress reports are delivered to the TI quality leadership team.

Figure 14.13 Aligning leadership competencies with business priorities

Source: Texas Instruments

Ritz-Carlton Hotel

Market and product range

Ritz-Carlton is part of the W.B. Johnson Properties development company and operates through 23 business and resort hotels in the USA and two in Australia. It set out as an American hotel group in 1983 with products and services designed to appeal to and suit the demands of both the prestigious travel consumer and the corporate traveller and meeting planner world-wide.

The fragmented and mostly limited independently operated hotels in the US luxury hotel industry offered an inconsistent level of service to their customers. Ritz-Carlton differentiated itself by offering a reliable service that catered for the inherent uncertainty of intangible hotel products and services.

Launch of total quality initiatives

Quality was introduced at the inception of Ritz-Carlton in 1983 when it pioneered its own service quality approach. Its "born at birth" approach to quality focuses on the principle concerns of their main customers. Through an analysis of the travel industry data and information it was able to identify the most important yet least consistent quality within hotels – highly personalised service, genuinely caring service delivery. A customer driven service delivery system was then built based largely on a commitment to a set of principles, designed to provide premium service. The system would understand the individual expectations of its 240,000 customers and prevent difficulties from ever reaching them.

Mission and vision

The company's mission is to serve to the delight of the customer, as expressed by the motto "We are ladies and gentlemen, serving ladies and gentlemen". The Ritz-Carlton mission is:

> The Ritz-Carlton Hotel is a place where the genuine care and comfort of our guests is our highest mission.
> We pledge to provide the finest personal service and facilities for our guests who will enjoy a warm, relaxed yet refined ambience.
> The Ritz-Carlton experience enlivens the senses, instils well being, and fulfils even the unexpressed wishes and needs of our guests.

Quality policy

To achieve its mission Ritz-Carlton relies on several key quality initiatives: training all its 1,500 employees to be quality engineers who can spot defects, correct them and then report to management; the company's top executives take active, dynamic roles in leading the quality initiatives; being meticulous gatherers of data on every aspect of the guests' stay to determine if the hotels are meeting customer expectations; recognition and reward for its employees who contribute to continuous improvement; asking its suppliers to join the chain in adopting the principles of TQM; and empowerment of its employees to "move heaven and earth" to satisfy customer needs.

Evolution of the process

The customer driven service delivery system is key to offering a personalised service and as the system has developed the employees have learned how to identify pattern problems and resolve them permanently. The Ritz-Carlton quality programme has evolved over time as shown in Figure 14.14.

Figure 14.14 Chronology of quality

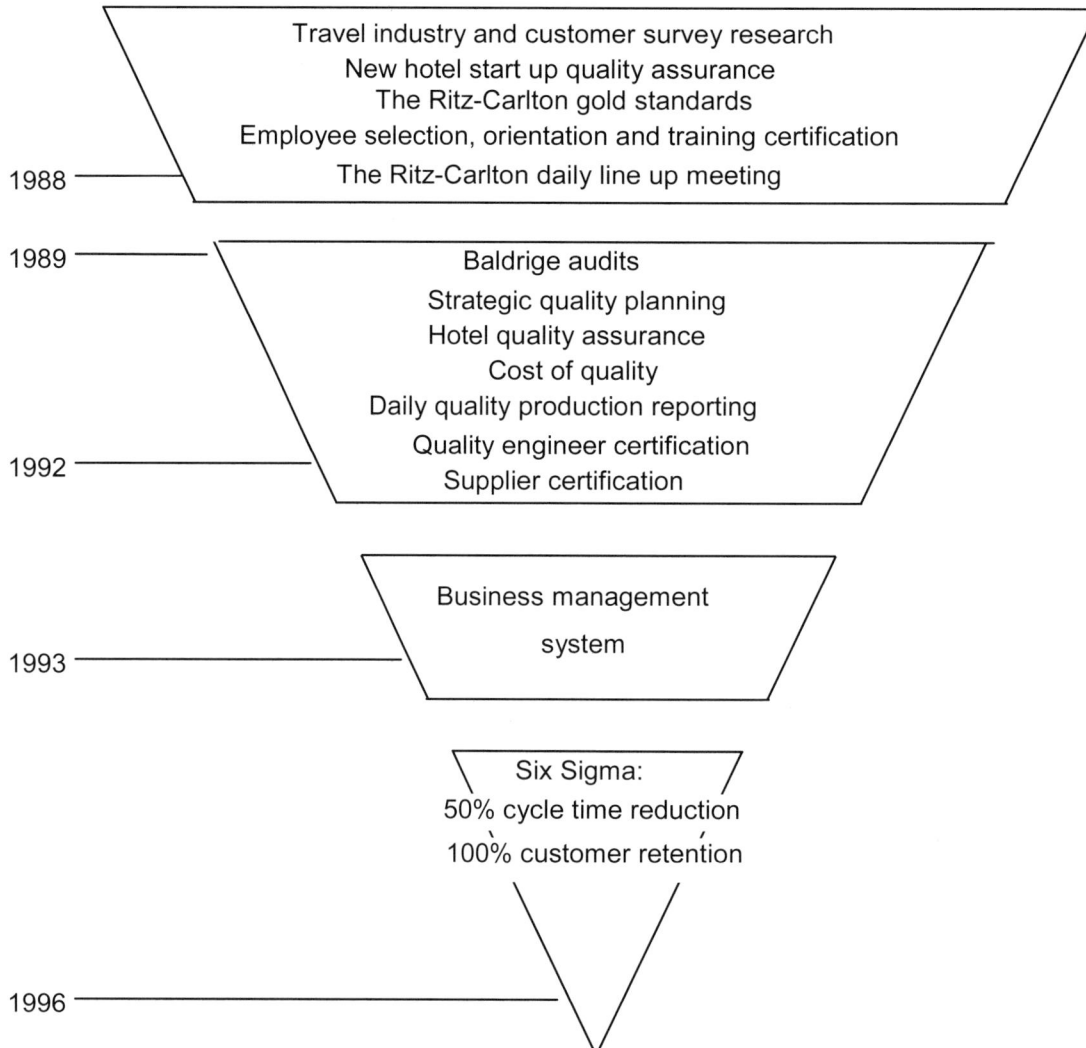

Design to Distribution (D2D) (now Celestica)

Market and product range

D2D is a UK based wholly owner subsidiary of ICL which procures and manufactures a range of high technology products from personal computers and UNIX workstations to mainframes, retail point of sale terminals and scanners. It operates in a world-wide market making and assembling printed circuit boards together with supporting after sales service through to repair and refurbishment.

In 1980, D2D had a revenue of £100 million which rose to £290 million by 1992 but a workforce reduction from 7,000 to 2,000. Later in 1992, D2D entered into a strategic partnership with Sun Microsystems to supply printed circuit boards and moved further into the contract electronics market by securing further customers who recognised its expertise to produce sub-components of its own brand of computer systems.

Launch of total quality initiatives

Total quality was first launched through a training programme in quality improvement according to Philip Crosby principles during the period from 1986 to 1988. Key areas for training included:
- The four absolutes of quality management.
- The 14 steps for quality improvement.
- Understanding corrective action.
- The process model.

This training gave D2D a common language of conformance to customer requirements and cost of non-conformance.

In 1986, nine quality improvement teams were set up each comprising six to 12 managers. Since that date all managers have been committed to a high level of quality awareness and committed to using self-assessment as a means of assessing awareness of quality within the business.

Mission and vision

The vision is to be European partner of choice for subcontract customers and this will be achieved through benchmarked best practice. To improve understanding of this vision and in particular what had to be done, the senior management team published "The Management Framework" in 1992. This document had three main objectives:
1. Explain how D2D will continue to strengthen its competitive position and achieve its mission.
2. Explain the organisation's values, philosophy and beliefs which give it competitive advantage.
3. Clarify what this philosophy means in practical terms for every D2D manager.

Quality policy

Quality is central to the vision, formulating policy and strategy and implementing the business plan at all levels within the business. Management commitment to quality includes:
- commitment to the business model;
- commitment to zero defects;
- continuous emphasis on total quality.

Evolution of the process

Quality has evolved through a series of developments at D2D which can be traced back to 1985. These developments are shown in Table 14.3.

Process reviews

Underpinning the process review process at D2D is the Deming cycle of plan, do, check, act (see Figure 14.15).

Table 14.3 Quality evolution

Date	Development
1985	60 quality circles in place Single status restaurant Use of first names Open plan offices
1986	Quality improvement process started All managers trained Measurement started Investing in People appraisal started Team briefing started
1987	Flow charting of processes Corrective action and recognition of cost of quality put in place
1988	All staff trained BSI ISO 9002 registration achieved Zero defect days at Ashton Harmonisation of working conditions Delivered quality audits started
1989	SPC started Best Factory of the Year Award Customer surveys started
1990	Zero defect days at Kidsgrove Failure mode effect analysis at Ashton Self-inspection of all processes British Quality Award Accredited vendor scheme
1991	Zero defect days at Bradley Wood Customer care training started Quality model system in place Design for manufacture toolset Michelin Award at Kidsgrove
1992	Customer care training completed Self-assessment started Sun Supplier Performance Award Michelin Award at Ashton
1993	dELTA launched Investing in People Business model introduced: leader element holder uses model for staff meetings Europe Quality Award Sun Supplier Outstanding Performance Award

Figure 14.15 Process review

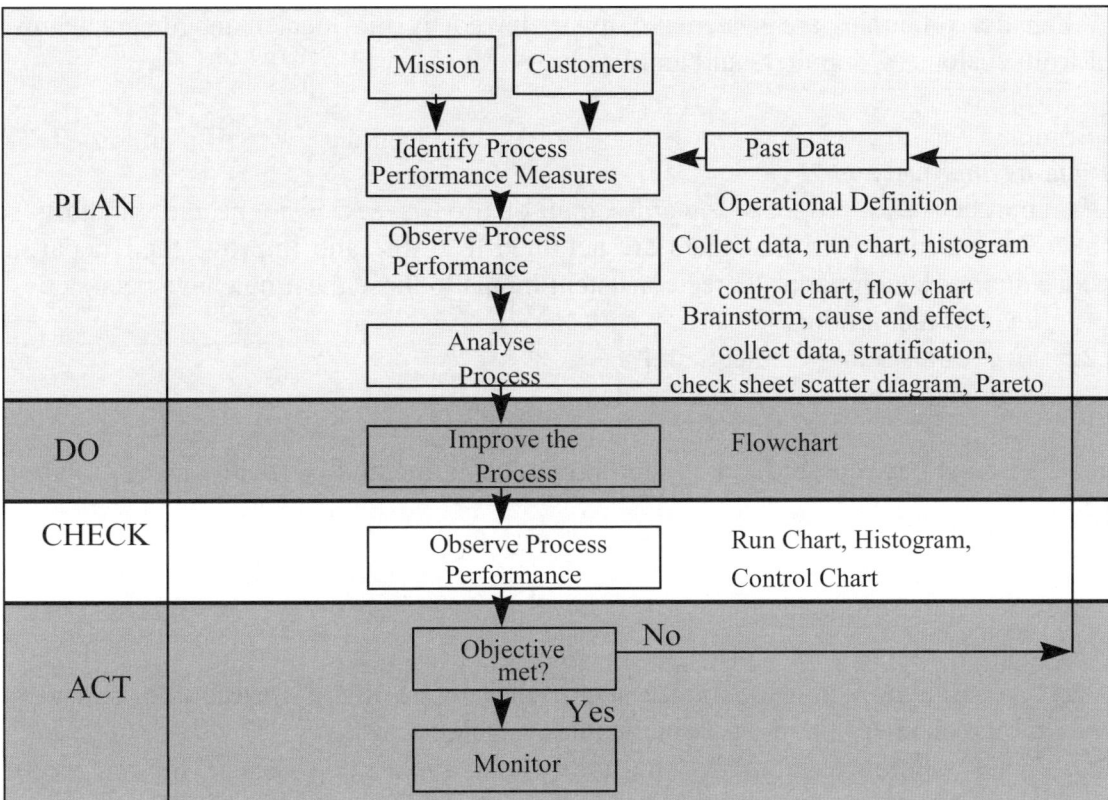

Plan. Using the mission and customer satisfaction as the main sources for the planning review, the key process performance measures are identified. Data is collected for these key performance measures using check sheets and analysed via a variety of tools and techniques such as run charts to identify graphically any trend in performance, histograms to group data within appropriate bands and locate the most frequently occurring items for Pareto analysis, control charts to check whether the process is in control using statistical process control charts and flow charts to locate bottlenecks in the process.

The process is then analysed as part of the "plan" to identify potential areas for improvement using the techniques of brainstorming to involve all levels of staff in open discussion, cause and effect analysis to identify all the possible causes associated with the one effect, collection and stratification of data to highlight potential areas for improvement.

Do. Process improvements are made following the data analysis and then flowcharting is used to implement a change and measure the effect which it has on the process performance.

Check. The techniques of run charts, histograms and control charts are used again to observe the performance of the process. The results are studied to learn what effect the change has made on performance of the process and it is important at this stage to evaluate whether the expected results were achieved. If not then corrective action is taken to "fine tune" the amendment.

Act. The first consideration is to assess whether the objectives of the process were fully met and, where this is found to be the case, the process change becomes permanent. The process will continue to be monitored as part of the on going review process, but where the objectives are not fully met the information will be fed back to the "planning" phase for reconsideration as part of the closed loop process.

All major processes are systematically reviewed by the local management teams with input from customers, suppliers and employees.

Continuous improvement

D2D's approach and progress towards total quality is reviewed at the monthly senior management meetings. All managers are actioned to refine and improve their department's approach against benchmarks. Three consistent inputs to these meetings have been:
1. level of recognition;
2. level of team involvement; and
3. error cause removal or dELTA ideas.

Since 1986 D2D has repeated the 14 step process as a method of reviewing the total quality process.

Success factors

Strategy is based on ten success factors, each one having a measurable objective and supported by a number of non-financial business results:
1. Total solution capability – the ability to complete the service for the electronics manufacturing customers. The objective is to be recognised as Europe's leading contract electronic manufacturer in IT. Measures include market share and new business generation.
2. The product quality objectives – customer delivered quality targets achieved for all products. Measures are directly related to customer satisfaction and identified through quality audits, feedback and scorecards.
3. The service quality objective – 100 per cent service levels achieved for all customers, identified through delivery time data as agreed with the customer.
4. The process quality objective – to become a customer friendly organisation, identified through self-assessment, quality improvement involvement, recognition awards, SPC implementation and the number of ideas submitted per person.
5. Organisation capability objective – to be acknowledged as the company that provides security of employability. This is measured through number of training days per person and satisfaction with training.
6. Time to market objective – capability to introduce any customer's product into manufacture in less than three months. This is measured through time to market benchmarking, programme change administration time and literature and software cycle time.
7. Procurement capability objective – to be recognised as a leader in material procurement. This is measured through number of vendors on electronic data interface, percentage of accredited vendors on EDI, electronic trading, buying price variance, ship to stock, reliability, data accuracy and cost reduction.
8. Lowest cost of ownership objective – no targeted business lost on grounds of total cost. This is measured in terms of the number of customers obtained compared to the number quoted together with annual cost reduction on repair boards.
9. Preferred partner objective – to be perceived as the best business partner. This is measured through growth in customer base and scorecard targets.

10. Technical capability objective – to have cost effective technology available to meet customers' current and future demands. This is measured through number of joint ventures to exploit R&D.

Best Practice Organisational Excellence

TNT

Market and product range

TNT started as a one man business in 1946 with just one truck in Australia. Ten years later it was incorporated as a public company and has since continued to expand on a world-wide basis to a current active customer base of over 35,000 active accounts together with *ad hoc* business orders of 2,000 firms per week.

One third of the market is still in the hands of the public sector operator Parcelforce and about 45 per cent of the market is divided up amongst half a dozen other major players including TNT.

Parcel carriage and, in particular, express carriage, which are TNT's core business, are extremely competitive. Leading players in the market such as Federal Express have withdrawn from the UK market due to sluggish demand but TNT has a prominent position with approximately 70 per cent of the 300,000 UK businesses which make use of a carrier.

TNT offers a unique range of guaranteed urgent parcel delivery services within the UK and its core business is nationwide door to door parcel delivery services within the UK. Other trading divisions provide more specialist transport services to support urgent parcel delivery systems.

Launch of total quality initiatives

Although quality had always been an integral part of the TNT culture since inception, after ten years of trading it decided to stand back and take a view of where the business was going and TNT's place in the market. This was delegated to TNT's senior managers and became known as Project 2000, the first specific total quality initiative. This resulted in a reduction of the number of trading divisions and:

- simplification of documentation to be more user friendly;
- launch of several competitive rate schedules; and
- review of operations to identify ways of enhancing customer satisfaction.

The outcomes formed the basis of the company's future strategy and in particular its Expressing Excellence Programme.

Mission and vision

TNT Express Limited is a market leader in logistics, providing a comprehensive range of transportation and supply chain management services. Its mission is:

> to be the best and most successful provider of logistics service on terms which allow us to well reward our employees and shareholders and to provide a sound base for continuing growth in the future.

Supporting this mission the company values and guiding principles are:

> People – we employ competent enthusiastic people and provide the highest standards of courtesy and customer care.
> Services – we provide a comprehensive range of reliable logistics services which are designed to match exactly the needs of our clients and prospective customers.
> Performance – we attain customer satisfaction by striving for excellence in all aspects of our service.

TNT guiding principles are:

> Teamwork – by setting high standards and working together we achieve the impossible for our customers.

Expertise – by taking care to recruit, train and develop the finest people we provide the best logistics service.

Technology – by employing the latest techniques we achieve cost effective solutions for our customers.

Leadership – through innovation and service excellence we aim to achieve leadership in all our markets.

Through the mission and values a TNT culture has developed:

Care – being sensitive and responsive to the needs of our customers.
Quality – producing consistent and reliable performance.
Accountability – taking full responsibility for the results of our actions.
Profit growth – always striving to beat our previous best performance.
Service is our only product

Quality policy

TNT philosophy is that quality is an integral part of the operation and not a bolt on accessory. Quality jargon is avoided throughout TNT to emphasise that it is regarded as "business as usual" and the message is reinforced by the quality supervisor, being the only person with sole quality duties.

The culture of the company is one of active involvement at all levels and, as quality is everyone's responsibility, each employee is responsible for quality. To support the quality drive each TNT location has a designated management representative with responsibility for all local quality related matters.

High profile management presence is seen as fundamental to demonstrating the commitment of management to quality.

Quality is defined by the customer and extensive research has shown that the express carrier customer is primarily concerned with on-time delivery and cost. This has therefore been the central focus of TNT's quality improvements and substantial progress has been made.

Evolution of the process

Senior management involvement in total quality was seen as essential if it was to gain corporate-wide support. Training all the general managers as facilitators to enable them to lead their groups effectively demonstrated managerial commitment to total quality principles. Embracing Excellence was the programme which emerged from the Beyond 2000 project. It combined all the main principles of total quality and customer commitment policies together with a visible link between the company's training and policy. This integrative approach was seen as a key success factor when developing the change culture.

The Expressing Excellence programme evolved from a comprehensive review of the company's customer care activities in 1992 and this major company-wide initiative was budgeted at £1.3 million. The key objectives were:
- to always exceed customers' expectations;
- to create a clear customer care policy soundly based on customer research;
- to communicate successfully and implement new customer care activities; and
- to measure and improve service quality and customer satisfaction.

Specific targets were agreed for each depot and translated into the following overall targets in:
1. new customers;

2. on-time deliveries;
3. telephone handling;
4. credit notes;
5. claims;
6. speed of invoicing; and
7. customer contact frequency.

This programme promoted the benefits of teamwork as the whole depot team were involved and performance towards the targets monitored on a weekly basis.

A best practice arising from the programme was the issue of a handbook to each employee for them to identify their own customers, internal and external, and define their job in relation to them. This then formed part of the appraisal process.

Training for the Customer Care Programme, which is a part of Expressing Excellence, is that latest example of management involvement in training. The most senior manager from each depot attends a centrally organised training course to equip him to become a facilitator at depot level. He then leads groups of up to 15 employees, made up of each depot function, until everyone receives the training.

Continuous improvement

TNT continues to improve its processes through regular meetings with both its suppliers and customers. A programme of customer and supplier visits is now part of managerial responsibilities throughout the business and opportunities are taken to fully establish future customer requirements and review current performance from which process improvements can be made.

Extensive use is made of staff meetings at all depots as they provide a forum for two way communication on strategic, operational and performance issues. They are also an opportunity to review suggestions for improvement and resolve quality issues.

Conferences are arranged throughout the year to review progress and refocus future activities. The sales teams, for example, attend a National Sales Conference each year where previous years' achievements are reviewed and targets established for the year ahead.

High standards are expected within TNT and its policy is not simply to achieve the standard but to be continuously looking for improvement. Managers and staff alike are judged according to their quality performance.

Quality training in 1993 amounted to £677,000, which demonstrated to the people the commitment which management has to quality. New employees are familiarised with the quality systems as part of their induction training and sign acknowledgement of their awareness.

Benchmarking is becoming increasingly used and benefits are being gained in terms of increasing competitive advantage.

Key benefits and achievements

Financial benefits from the adoption of a quality culture within the business are evident from increased profits, turnover, return on assets and asset growth. External recognition has been gained by being the first express carrier to gain ISO 9000 certification.

Non-financial benefits from quality include TNT's on-time deliveries, which have improved by over 3 per cent over the period 1990/91 to 1992/93. During that same time copy notes fell from over 70,000 to under 40,000 per annum. Misroutes also fell during that period from 21,000 to under 19,000 per annum.

Next steps and future challenges
Expressing Excellence is the major programme which TNT is using to equip its people with the skills, tools and techniques that build the continuous improvement and customer focused culture to meet the increasing competition which is ahead.

Custom Research Inc. (CRI)

Market and product range

Custom Research Inc. (CRI) is a privately owned marketing research company in the USA, founded in 1974 and now with approximately 100 full time employees. It has its headquarters in Minneapolis with client service offices in San Francisco and New York together with two telephone centres. Revenue growth has risen from $14 million in 1991 to $23 million in 1996.

CRI has a world-wide business in market research and customer satisfaction services with approximately 400 projects per year. Each project is stand alone and therefore has its own unique business objectives. The scope of its research activities include:

- product evaluations;
- package studies;
- product tests;
- new product volume simulations; and
- market structure studies.

Meeting and exceeding customer expectations every time is essential if they are to attract repeat business and thrive as a profitable company. The high level of customer retention is attributed to the soundness of their business system and quality of their people.

Mission and vision

The company has a distinct vision:
> to be seen as a STAR in the business world by:
> - clients – as a partner that always exceeds expectations;
> - employees – as the best place to work;
> - business world – as a model of success.

Evolution of total quality

1988 was the year when the true quest for quality began as the steering committee began to see their profitability plateau. The structure of the organisation changed to a company wide team based work environment, replacing functional departments with six to eight people in each cross-functional team.

The next significant step was to fire half its clients, cutting the number of clients from 138 to 67 as substantial effort had been going into clients who would always be just small clients instead of putting resources into the larger clients. This strategy proved successful as revenues started to climb.

CRI was able to devote more time to its clients and build a long-term relationship with them, which was particularly important where every project was virtually a "one off".

Continuous improvement

The steering committee informally reviews overall company performance daily with a formal review taking place each month and improvement areas being identified. A quarterly quality report is prepared which provides data and information on:

- client satisfaction by company, team and branch;
- quality index by company, team and branch;
- accuracy and timeliness measures of all team, branch offices and departments;
- internal client satisfaction for internal support groups;
- productivity measures by team;

- cycle time for the company;
- partner supplier ratings; and
- bidding summary for the company.

Process improvements are identified at two levels within the organisation; at an individual team account level, where technologies and feedback from clients are used to improve the process, and at a company level, where process improvements are first determined by a process task force and, second, a roll out task force, which includes a representative from every team and department.

Management of data and information

The steering committee, account teams and departments identify the data and information that is required to support the following:
- strategic plan and related goals;
- key business drivers;
- ongoing performance improvement.

The group then collects the information from a variety of sources within the business and uses the data as a basis for a number of key reports. Employees are involved in the data selection process by identifying their own performance measures to gain commitment and ownership to the review process. Key reports are prepared immediately from the data on:
- key clients;
- process;
- quality; and
- operational information.

This data is reported and analysed on a monthly, quarterly and annual basis to enable managers to take corrective action on any issues at an early stage. The effectiveness of the system can be judged from the company's approach, which requires all reports to lead to action being taken rather than being simply filed away. Therefore, where reports identify the need for improvement, action plans must be developed to resolve the problem and this approach is fully supported by the senior management team.

Action plans lead to implementation and review as part of the business culture within the company and measures are effectively used to prove that any change produces improved results.

The process of selection, collection, reporting, analysis, review and improvement is a continuous process within the organisation.

Corning Telecommunications Products Division
Market and product range
Corning TPD was formed in 1983 to manufacture hair thin optical fibres using pulses of light to carry large amounts of information over great distances. It is now the world's largest optical fibre manufacturer serving three distinct customer groups in more than 30 countries:
- cable manufacturers who incorporate optical fibres into finished products;
- end users who employ the cabled optical fibres to carry information; and
- joint venture fibre-making companies in Europe and Asia which TPD supplies with product and process technology.

Its sole manufacturing site is in Wilmington, North Carolina, where 1,200 of its 1,400 employees are located.

Launch of total quality initiatives
The chairman first announced his commitment to total quality in 1983 and by the year end the Quality Institute was established. During the early 1980s Corning developed the organisational infrastructure required to support total quality management and this included quality assurance, quality engineering, training and material control. The organisation was headed by a quality manager, who reported to the plan manager, and initially designed quality measures that included product returns and ship to promise date as the key service measures.

By the late 1980s a biennial employee climate survey was in place along with tracking and control procedures for measuring key product attributes. This constituted the first phase of Corning's journey towards organisational leadership through the implementation of total quality management.

Evolution of the process
Development of organisational leadership was an evolutionary process. Phase II (1986-1989) was the break out phase where the company began to focus on quality skills, training, work design and the development of sophisticated quality tools. Partnerships were established with customers and suppliers and quality leadership was disseminated more deeply into the business units. Phase III (1990-1992) was focused on world class quality and, most significantly, the introduction of self-assessment. Key result areas were established using benchmarking tools, process management strategies and customer satisfaction measurements. Total quality had become integral to the business. Phase IV (1993 onwards) is a quality integration phase, recognising the critical need to build on the strategies developed in the previous phases.

The common threads that have guided their quality journey have been:
- the need to build an infrastructure that ensured all business and manufacturing processes consistently perform at the required level;
- the need to train, develop and empower employees to maximise the capabilities of the process to create genuine customer satisfaction; and
- the need to integrate quality seamlessly throughout the business by embedding it in the fabric of everything they do. Quality had to be the responsibility of everyone.

Quality policy

It is the policy of Corning to achieve total quality performance by anticipating and meeting the requirements of its customers. Total quality performance means understanding who the customer is, what their requirements are and meeting those requirements better than anyone else, without error.

Quality is fully integrated into how the business is run. The quality plan is the plan to win, quality objectives are the business objectives and employees understand that when they are working to invest in values of people, process and technology and to deploy the strategic initiatives of customer satisfaction, markets of choice, affordable capacity and lowest cost producer, they are working on quality.

Mission and vision

The vision and mission provide stakeholders, such as the organisation's people, its customers and suppliers, with the medium to long-term direction in which it is travelling. The mission and vision are underpinned by Corning's total quality management system of four principles and ten actions. The four principles are:
1. Meet the requirements.
2. Produce error free work.
3. Manage by prevention.
4. Measure the cost of quality.

The ten actions are:
1. Make a commitment.
2. Work in teams.
3. Provide education.
4. Measure and display error rates.
5. Measure cost of quality.
6. Facilitate open communications.
7. Take corrective action.
8. Bestow recognition for quality performance.
9. Celebrate achievement with an event.
10. Establish goals.

Strategy is formulated from the organisation's mission and vision to address the question "What do we have to do in order to achieve our mission and vision?" Strategic indicators and critical success factors are a key part of the strategy formulation process and both are used to measure progress towards attainment of the vision/mission and enable early realignment where appropriate.

Short and medium-term plans are developed throughout the organisation. These plans support the medium to long-term strategic direction of the company and within these plans key result improvement measures (KPI) are developed to track progress. Plan deployment throughout the whole organisation is critical to attainment of the vision and mission within the organisation. A process is in place to ensure that all the employees are fully aware of the organisation vision and mission, the strategy to enable its attainment, the short-term plans to be actioned in the months ahead and how their actions align with the organisation's goals. Business plans and strategic direction statements are reviewed as part of the closed loop process, with any variance between actual and planned performance being carefully scrutinised and corrective action taken where appropriate.

Continuous improvement

Leadership is an integral process within Corning TPD and a key requirement to sustain this position is a commitment to continuous improvement. This is embedded in the business culture in two ways. First, through documentation of all the core business processes which require continuous improvement. Features of the documentation include:

- identifying a process owner for ensuring the effective performance of the process as well as continuously improving performance;
- establishing process metrics that measure the process performance level;
- conducting an annual evaluation of process performance using stakeholders as members of the review team and analysing process performance data against established performance criteria;
- formulating action plans that include objectives and responsibilities; and
- closing the loop by reviewing process performance improvement results regularly and by implementing corrective action steps as required.

Second, goal-sharing variable compensation programmes have been set up for all employees. These are based on continuous improvement in Corning's business key result indicators.

Index

7Ss model, 157
Accountability, 208-210, 212, 215
Accounting rate of return, 151
Accredited quality management systems, 3, 7
Accredited quality systems, 142, 156, 246
Action plans, 31, 33, 36, 45, 87, 115, 116, 118, 124, 162, 177-80, 200, 221, 260, 281, 284
Agility, 59
Aisin Aw Co. Ltd, 53, 55-58, 65
Alignment, 33, 95, 101, 157, 159, 185, 238, 239, 260, 266, 283
American Society for Quality Control, 58, 209
Ames Rubber Corp., 218, 225
Analysis, 8, 10, 11, 26, 47, 51-53, 60, 61, 84, 85, 89, 113, 117, 132, 133, 146, 147, 149, 157, 161, 165, 183-186, 197, 202, 206, 240, 241, 246, 252, 267, 269, 272, 273, 281
Analytical processes, 133
Appraisal, 36, 38, 45, 89, 104, 111-113, 115, 116, 121-125, 129, 138, 148, 149, 151, 173, 176, 179-182, 185, 186, 203, 205, 255, 272, 278
ASQC, 58
Assessment framework, 2, 50, 59, 62, 112
Assets, 90, 128, 139, 144, 145, 149, 218, 219, 235, 237, 238, 240, 243, 250, 278
AT&T, 11, 58, 68, 93, 217, 218, 225
Authority, 3, 7, 8, 83, 95, 165
Automation, 110
Balanced scorecard model, 9, 120, 145, 173-175, 179, 251, 274, 275
Baldrige Index, 216, 218
Benchmarking, 1, 3, 8, 9, 39, 62, 69, 86, 88, 91, 96, 99, 108, 111, 112, 113, 119, 123-125, 129, 132-134, 137, 142, 154, 155, 161, 162, 168, 170, 181, 182, 185, 186, 207, 216, 221, 222-224, 236, 238, 240, 264, 266, 274, 278, 282
Benefits and conditions, 203
Best practice, 1, 2, 5, 9, 11, 40, 59, 70, 72, 84, 86, 111-114, 118, 119, 123, 124, 129, 131-137, 143, 156, 160, 164, 168, 186, 195, 197, 200, 204, 206, 212, 221, 223, 248, 261, 262, 271, 278
Birds Eye Wall's Ltd, 113, 121
BP Chemicals, 157, 169
BPI, 165-168
Break-point performance assessment, 173, 176, 181, 182, 186
Breakthrough methodology, 45, 161, 165
British Gas, 33, 220
British Telecommunications Ltd, 137, 193
Business excellence certification model, 162
Business excellence model, 5, 9, 43-45, 118, 128, 221
Business improvement matrix, 33-40
Business planning process, 87
Business process management, 20, 43, 155, 159-162, 166-169
Business results, 2, 29, 39, 40, 43-45, 60, 71, 87, 93, 114, 128, 146, 172, 223, 229, 232, 274
Cadillac Motor Car Co., 58, 87
Career development, 112, 203-205
"Catchball", 104, 105
Celestica, 271
CERES Principles, 209, 211
Closed loop process, 202, 240-243, 254, 261, 274, 283
Coaching, 83
Communicating for quality, 2, 6
Communication process, 94, 118, 207, 254, 256
Community, 47, 50, 88, 91, 138, 208, 209, 210, 212, 213-215, 264
Company-wide quality control, 51, 127
Compensation, 111, 284
Competitive advantage, 7, 8, 38, 42, 47, 48, 96, 99, 101, 110, 111, 126, 128, 162, 216, 267, 271, 278
Competitive performance, 1, 82, 90, 176

285

Competitiveness, 1, 26, 50, 58, 82, 83, 90, 91, 95, 106, 110, 114, 134, 139, 145, 148, 156, 159, 173, 197
Complaints, 37, 39, 45, 57, 106, 146, 148, 154, 190, 191, 193-195, 197, 200
Compliments, 194
Computerisation, 110
Conditions of excellence, 37, 42
Conformance, 141, 142, 143, 148, 149, 226, 246, 271
Continuous learning, 19, 28, 29
Control charts, 10, 23, 25, 53, 273
Co-operation, 28, 45, 52, 81, 108, 125, 138, 139, 141, 210
Core values, 22, 24, 267
Corning Telecommunications, 204, 207, 217, 282-284
Corporate commitment, 90
Corporate culture, 116
Corporate goals, 157, 239, 240
Corporate responsibility, 210
Corporate targets, 87, 88
Cost of quality, 3, 10, 93, 145, 148, 182, 266, 272, 283
Creativity, 19, 38, 65, 66, 70, 83, 90, 110, 112, 122, 168, 173
Critical processes, 96, 98, 171
Critical success factors, 2, 96, 133, 176, 185, 206, 283
Cross-functional management, 7, 21, 67, 81
Cross-industry analysis, 113
CSFs, 2, 38, 39, 96, 98, 133, 176, 177, 185
Cultural change, 5, 114, 117
Custom Research Inc., 152, 280
Customer benefits, 137
Customer care, 203, 272, 276, 277, 278
Customer dissatisfaction, 145, 190, 192, 245, 248, 249
Customer expectations, 6, 87, 116, 165, 269, 280
Customer focus, 4, 8, 11, 27, 45, 84, 117, 158, 159, 207, 237, 245, 265, 279
Customer loyalty, 98, 196, 198, 199
Customer needs, 37, 66, 85, 103, 133, 165, 173, 191, 225, 242, 269
Customer orientation, 42, 47
Customer relationships, 37, 61, 66, 172
Customer retention, 11, 198, 280
Customer satisfaction, 7, 8, 10, 11, 27, 37, 39, 40, 44, 45, 57, 67, 69, 81, 87, 98, 106, 128, 134, 145-147, 158, 165, 166, 171, 172, 182, 187, 189, 190-192, 195-197, 200, 220, 223, 225, 226, 228, 231, 237, 238, 241, 242, 247, 248, 250, 251, 253, 255, 259, 265, 266, 273, 274, 276-278, 280, 282, 283
Customer value determinants, 199
Customer wants, 3, 10, 85, 241
Customer-driven excellence, 59
Customer-driven quality, 11
Customer-focus, 8, 61, 116, 189, 191-200
Customer-focused culture, 189, 191, 200
Customers' perception, 37, 172
Customer-supplier relationships, 139, 140, 179, 190
D2D, 4, 6, 7, 8, 69, 70, 147, 168, 171, 203, 219, 221, 271, 272, 274
Dana Commercial Credit, 207, 250, 251
Decision making, 85, 90, 108, 130, 132, 145, 151
Delight factor, 193
Delivery, 25, 37, 38, 43, 45, 47, 53, 57, 67, 69, 70, 77, 96, 99, 105, 106, 138, 139, 140, 143, 148, 152, 160, 171, 173, 192, 199, 218, 219, 220, 225, 244, 248, 253, 258, 269, 274, 276, 277
Deming Application Prize, 51, 53, 54, 56, 57, 58
Deming Prize criteria, 52
Deming, Edward, 20-22, 209
Design of experiments, 25
Design to Distribution, 69, 271
Documentation, 37, 48, 103, 129, 141, 179, 180, 246, 261, 262, 276, 284
Druker, Peter, 82
Eastman Chemical Co., 67, 131, 217, 225, 245

Education, 2, 4, 21, 24-26, 50-52, 59, 70, 73, 116, 157, 206, 207, 210, 214, 251, 264, 283
Efficiency, 28, 69, 93, 122, 139, 145, 154, 162, 168, 211, 241, 244, 246
Elida Faberge, 159, 160
Elida Gibbs, 113, 124
Employee attitude survey, 116
Employee development, 19, 90, 114, 115, 124
Employee relations, 110, 127
Employee satisfaction, 39, 120, 121, 173, 202-207, 225
Employment conditions, 207
Employment policy, 212
Empowering employees, 3
Empowerment, 1-4, 6, 83, 113, 115-118, 120-123, 125, 159, 165, 173, 195, 205, 220, 245, 266, 269
Enablers, 9, 34, 38, 39, 43, 45, 50, 62, 68, 71, 118
Enabling systems, 19
EQA assessment, 62
European Quality Award, 2, 5, 8, 9, 11, 50, 65, 70, 85, 89, 182, 221, 230
Evaluation of investments, 149
External customers, 8, 42, 85, 102, 166, 189, 190
External stakeholders, 209
Federal Express Corp., 58, 67, 156, 217, 218, 226, 276
Feedback, 22, 47, 95, 100, 103, 113, 115-119, 121, 123-125, 130, 138, 147, 173, 178, 180, 191, 193, 200, 202-206, 238, 240, 251, 253, 259, 260, 261, 265, 266, 274, 281
Financial management, 88, 145, 146, 147, 152
Financial resources, 144-146, 152, 240, 241
Financial results, 90, 112, 145
Financial strategy, 145
Fishbone diagrams, 25
Flexibility, 21, 37, 114, 135, 139, 187
Florida Power & Light, 56, 105, 106, 158
Flowcharting, 148, 161, 273
Focus on results, 59
Ford Motor Co., 10, 164, 165
GAO performance measurement model, 172, 174
Global responsibility, 210
Goal congruence, 84, 95, 97, 100, 101, 105
Goal deployment, 173, 175-177, 185
Goal translation, 100, 102, 103
GTE Directories, 68, 69, 217, 218
Hewlett-Packard, 9, 55, 103, 104, 134
Hierarchy of kaizen, 21
High Performance Technology, 144, 202-206
Histograms, 25, 252, 273
Hokushin Industries Inc., 57
Hoshin Kanri, 28, 99, 103
HR policies, 110
HR practices, 110-112
Human resource development, 84, 126
Human resources management, 43, 110
IBM, 6, 10, 11, 58, 69, 218, 226
ICL, 8, 69, 158, 220, 271
Impact on society, 39, 40, 172, 208, 223, 229, 232, 264, 267
Information and analysis, 84
Information processing, 130-134
Innovation, 19, 25, 32, 38, 48, 59, 65, 66, 70, 90, 110, 112, 114, 116, 121, 129, 135, 144, 145, 159, 160, 161, 167, 168, 173, 191, 209, 220, 245, 265, 277
Inspiration, 83, 103, 245
Internal customer, 47, 48, 84, 89, 163, 189, 237, 245, 255
Internal rate of return, 151
ISO 9000 certification, 7, 138, 155, 156, 278
Japanese Quality Control Medal, 51, 53, 57

Job security, 189, 190, 203-205
Kaizen, 5, 19, 21, 26, 53, 140
Kano model, 192, 193
Key drivers, 2, 200, 209
Key objectives, 19, 28, 277
Key performance indicators, 66, 111, 176, 177, 185
Key successes, 225
Kodak, 69, 131, 140-143, 152, 177, 245, 246
Komatsu Ltd, 53-55, 67, 102, 158
KPIs, 176-181, 185
Learning centre, 115, 124
Learning organisation, 115, 116, 124, 173
Lever Bros, 212
Lucas Automotive, 236
Malcolm Baldrige National Quality Award, 2, 4, 5, 7-9, 11, 37, 50, 57, 59, 60, 61, 69, 84, 182, 204, 216, 217, 221, 233, 251, 259, 265
Management by objective, 95
Management leadership, 26, 43, 100, 158
Management of process quality, 84
Management of processes, 8, 20, 168, 179
Management philosophy, 11, 26, 28, 112
Management style, 118, 203, 205, 206
Managing by fact, 59
Managing by process, 3, 8
Managing people satisfaction, 202
Market focus, 43, 60, 61
Market penetration, 11, 147
Marlow Industries, 58, 218, 226
Matrix chart approach, 33
MBNQA, 9, 33, 35, 37, 41, 45, 50, 57-60, 62, 64, 67-70, 84-88, 172, 216, 218, 221, 223, 225, 251, 265
MBO, 95
Measurement of customer satisfaction, 191
Mission statement, 1, 2, 39, 86, 88, 110, 113, 121, 176, 210, 237, 253, 254, 258
Mitel Telecom Ltd, 158
Mortgage Express, 128, 129, 203, 205, 206, 220
Motivation, 3, 5, 25, 42, 44, 45, 47, 61, 122, 128, 202, 237, 238, 262
Motorola, 9, 58, 217, 218, 226
Nachi-Fujikoshi Corp., 57
National Institute of Standards and Technology, 58, 216
National Roads & Motorists' Association, 88
Nationwide Building Society, 113, 118, 119, 200, 247
NatWest Bank, 119
NEC Kansai Co. Ltd, 57
Net present value, 149, 150, 151
Niigata Toppan Printing Co. Ltd, 57
Nissan, 4, 54, 58, 139, 140, 156
NIST, 58, 62, 224
Non-financial performance measurement, 186, 209
Open learning, 115
Operational excellence programme, 119
Operational processes, 133
Operational results, 84
Organisation capability, 101, 274
Organisational excellence, 1, 2, 40
Organisational learning, 59, 132
Organisational performance, 2, 6, 29, 59, 61, 177, 221
Organisational structure, 8, 88, 131, 135, 259
Organisational system, 19, 20, 131, 160
Original equipment manufacturers, 139
Output measures, 96, 176

Pacific Bell, 10
PAF model, 148
Pareto diagrams, 25
Participation, 3, 5, 42, 47, 90, 104, 113, 120, 121, 225
Partnership, 6, 7, 38, 66, 86, 90, 91, 116, 134-138, 141, 143, 144, 171, 204, 209, 225, 245, 254, 258, 264, 265, 271, 282
Pay, 109, 114, 119, 139, 147, 150, 182, 189, 190, 203, 204, 207, 255
Payback, 149, 150
PDCA cycle, 95, 98, 102-104, 182
PDSA cycle, 26
People creativity, 110
People management, 2, 3, 38, 40, 110-129, 207, 223, 228, 231
People satisfaction, 39, 40, 93, 113, 116-125, 145, 146, 171, 172, 202-207, 223, 229, 232, 251, 257, 266
Performance appraisal, 112, 173, 176, 179, 180-186
Performance assessment, 19, 140, 173, 176, 181, 182, 186, 207
Performance measurement system model, 176-187
Performance measurement, 2, 66, 94, 96-99, 129, 136, 142, 144, 168, 171-188, 195, 220, 260
Performance outcomes, 66, 172
Performance review, 88, 90, 122, 181, 238, 260
Performance standards, 62, 105, 216
Personal learning, 59, 122
Plan-Do-Check-Act cycle, 25, 95, 165
Policy management, 65, 99
Post Office Counters, 113, 116, 155, 165, 166
Problem solving cycle, 25
Problem solving process, 89, 136, 162, 163, 165
Problem solving, 21, 23, 25, 27, 83, 84, 87, 88, 89, 136, 140, 141, 156, 162, 163, 165, 168
Process capability, 8, 96, 142, 164, 168, 173, 178, 179, 186, 187, 192, 246
Process improvement, 9, 26, 28, 29, 94, 148, 161, 162, 165, 168, 171, 273, 278, 281
Process management methodology, 164
Process management, 8, 20, 43, 6061, 81, 96, 97, 155, 156, 158-173, 176, 178, 179, 185, 223, 228, 231, 282
Process measures, 71, 96, 176
Process orientation, 27, 29
Process-based approach, 8, 85, 87, 156, 158, 159
Procter and Gamble, 6, 99, 158
Productivity, 1, 4, 5, 7, 9, 19, 45, 70, 81, 83, 110, 112, 139, 140, 148, 159, 173, 175, 216, 218, 219, 226, 235, 237, 244, 281
Professionalism, 110, 138, 237
QIP, 118, 163, 165
QOS, 164, 165
QPD, 94-96, 101-106, 178
Quality assurance systems, 156
Quality awareness, 4, 70, 129, 220, 265, 271
Quality control techniques, 3, 10, 51
Quality control, 3, 10, 50-58, 65, 142, 246
Quality culture, 84, 129, 156, 253, 255, 266, 278
Quality deployment, 53, 94, 101, 102
Quality excellence, 3, 50
Quality factors, 2
Quality gurus, 3, 5, 6, 105, 157
Quality improvement process, 5, 47, 48, 86, 89, 162-167, 261, 262, 266, 272
Quality improvement projects, 48, 118, 138
Quality improvement teams, 84, 88, 118, 202, 206, 237, 265, 271
Quality management systems, 2
Quality manual, 140
Quality of design, 142, 246
Quality of information, 130
Quality of service, 142, 189
Quality operating systems, 164
Quality policy deployment, 94, 96, 98, 99, 101, 102, 104, 105, 158, 178

Quality results, 6, 145
Quality standards, 57, 65, 87, 138, 139, 144, 167, 168, 200, 244
Quality strategy, 8, 86, 89, 238
Quality structure, 156
RADAR logic, 62, 67
Radical change, 28, 159
Rank Xerox, 5-7, 43-45, 69, 70, 88, 89, 99, 103-105, 125, 152, 158, 159, 162, 163, 165, 195, 196, 200, 204-207, 236-238, 243
Rating system, 40
Recognition, 2, 5, 15, 36, 42, 47, 57, 7, 83, 84, 90, 93, 110-114, 117, 120-125, 128, 143, 148, 171, 173, 176, 180, 182, 184, 185, 186, 191, 202-210, 237, 259, 269, 272, 274, 278, 283
Re-engineering, 8, 28, 75, 135, 155, 157, 161, 186
Resource management, 130, 223
Responsiveness, 37, 135, 137, 139, 173, 247
Results-oriented approach, 85
Retention, 11, 111, 172, 190, 192, 196, 198, 199, 200, 280
Reward and recognition, 2, 84, 88, 90, 173, 176, 177, 179-182, 185, 186, 191, 205
Rewards, 5, 93, 114, 127, 176, 206, 259
Right first time, 156, 164, 189, 194
Ritz-Carlton Hotel, 58, 86, 87, 168, 189, 218, 225, 269
Rover, 140, 220
Royal Mail, 69, 129, 168, 203, 207, 212, 258, 259, 260, 261, 264
Run charts, 25, 273
Scatter diagrams, 25
Scoring, 6, 32, 35, 36, 40, 45, 46, 61-64, 68, 123
Self-assessment criteria, 41
Self-assessment, 2, 3, 9, 31-33, 37, 41, 50, 65, 67, 70, 71, 112, 115, 118, 119, 162, 171, 181, 182, 186, 221-223, 238, 255, 265, 271, 272, 274, 282
Service improvement programme, 120
Service level agreements, 117, 124, 166
Service quality, 51, 105, 106, 171, 195, 197, 200, 269, 274, 277
Shell Chemicals UK, 8, 158
Sin'ei Industries Co. Ltd, 57
SmithKline Beecham, 160
Social reporting, 208, 209
Social responsibility, 59, 61, 91, 208, 210, 212
Solectron Corp., 58, 217, 218, 225
Southern Pacific Airlines, 158
Statistical process control, 10, 142, 245, 273
Statistical quality control techniques, 51
Stewart, Walter, 23, 25
Strategic direction, 19, 44, 93, 152, 260, 261, 283
Strategic management, 7, 135, 185, 186
Strategic planning process, 5, 240, 251
Strategic quality planning, 84
Strategic thinking, 29, 59
Strategy development, 61, 99, 157, 173-177, 185
Superior performance, 1, 134, 176, 180, 181
Supplier benefits, 137
Supplier development process, 136, 138, 140
Supplier management, 2, 6, 134, 135, 143
Supplier partnerships, 134, 143, 265
Supportive processes, 233, 234
Sustainability of excellence, 1
Sustainability, 1, 2, 82, 95, 208, 209
Sustainable development, 1, 208, 210
Sustainable performance, 1
Systems perspective, 59
Teamwork, 2, 3, 5, 7, 27, 57, 66, 67, 83-88, 110, 113, 115, 118, 120, 123-125, 128, 154, 159, 173, 206, 210, 237, 250, 260, 261, 266, 276, 278

Telefonica Group, 6
Tennant, 10
Texas Instruments, 55, 58, 70, 87, 146, 218, 219, 225, 265-267
Thomas Cork SML, 157
TNT, 70, 204, 220, 221, 235, 276-279
Top management process, 133
Total quality fitness, 37, 40, 41, 43, 47
Total quality principles, 166, 277
TQM implementation, 1, 4, 5, 12, 15, 17, 18, 79, 85, 88, 89, 103, 112, 113, 124
TQM maturity, 1
TQM process, 3, 5, 7, 185
Training, 2, 4, 7-9, 15, 21, 24, 36-38, 47, 85, 86, 89, 90, 96, 111-120, 122-129, 154, 156, 159, 161, 169, 179, 203-207, 210, 212, 214, 221, 226, 237, 253, 254, 259, 261, 265-269, 271-274, 277, 278, 282
Two-way communication, 48, 117, 119
Ulster Carpet Mills, 207, 253-256
Value statements, 2, 128, 209, 250
Vision, 2, 3, 6, 9, 12, 19, 28, 29, 36, 37, 47, 66, 82-90, 99, 101, 110, 115, 119-121, 128, 129, 136, 158, 162, 173, 176, 185, 199, 204, 205, 209, 266-269, 271, 276, 280, 283
Visionary leadership, 59
Wainwright Industries, 69
Wallace Co. Inc., 58, 86, 218, 225
Waste elimination, 27, 86
Waste, 23, 27-29, 38, 144, 149, 160, 190, 211, 218, 226, 245, 246
Westinghouse Electric, 37, 41, 47, 58, 218, 226
Work objectives, 203
World class standards, 31, 40, 221, 223
Zytec, 58, 85, 86, 217, 218, 226